WAR IN ANCIEN

Ancient World at War

The books in this series are authoritative surveys of the relationship between warfare and the economy and culture of ancient Near Eastern and Mediterranean societies. The series explores the impact of military organization on social life and the place of war in the cultural and imaginative life of communities. It also considers the "face of battle," examining the experiences of combatants and civilians.

Published

War in the Hellenistic World
Angelos Chaniotis

War in Ancient Egypt
Anthony J. Spalinger

In Preparation

War in the Ancient World
Philip de Souza

War in the Assyrian Empire
Mario Fales

War in the Ancient Greek World
John Buckler

War in the Roman Republic
John Serrati

War in Late Antiquity
Doug Lee

War in the Byzantine World
Frank Trombley

WAR IN ANCIENT EGYPT

The New Kingdom

Anthony J. Spalinger

Blackwell
Publishing

BLACKWELL PUBLISHING
350 Main Street, Malden, MA 02148-5020, USA
108 Cowley Road, Oxford OX4 1JF, UK
550 Swanston Street, Carlton, Victoria 3053, Australia

First published 2005 by Blackwell Publishing Ltd

Library of Congress Cataloging-in-Publication Data

Spalinger, Anthony John.
War in ancient Egypt: The New Kingdom / Anthony J. Spalinger.
p. cm. — (Ancient world at war)
Includes bibliographical references and index.
ISBN 1-4051-1371-5 (hardcover: alk. paper) — ISBN 1-4051-1372-3 (alk. paper)
1. Military art and science—Egypt—History. 2. Egypt—History,
Military. 3. Egypt—History—New Kingdom, ca. 1550–ca. 1070 B.C.
I. Title. II. Series.
U31.S66 2004
932'.014—dc22
2004006269

A catalogue record for this title is available from the British Library.

Picture research by Thelma Gilbert
Set in 10/12pt Galliard
by Graphicraft Limited, Hong Kong
Printed and bound in the United Kingdom
by TJ International Ltd, Padstow, Cornwall

For further information on
Blackwell Publishing, visit our website:
www.blackwellpublishing.com

To Elizabeth
(7 July 1909 to 29 March 1999)

CONTENTS

FIGURES

MAPS

ACKNOWLEDGMENTS

The conception of this work has much to do with a preliminary study on Egyptian warfare written under the auspices of Prof. Daniel Snell. At that time I had envisaged a lengthy study covering the entire history of Pharaonic Egypt, a project that my editor, Al Bertrand, carefully revised in light of the wealth of information that would have to be included. To him, therefore, I render my thanks for allowing me to proceed at a more reasonable pace, one that has turned out to be as informative for me as I hope it will be for the reader. Equally, Angela Cohen and Annette Abel have proven to be worthy editors whose presence can be felt on every page.

The numerous specialized works concerning animal power, food intake (really fuel capacity), and war material have been assembled by me over a lengthy period of time. Through the kind offices of the University of Auckland's Research Library, I have been able to obtain many of these studies, either located in moribund governmental publications or else in recondite libraries. To a large extent, the study of ancient warfare entails the investigation of ancient technology, a field that has yet to become a subset of modern Egyptology, and for this reason published data are not easily obtainable from the expected quarters. Nonetheless, the careful researcher will discern that I have not hesitated in using unpublished research reports such as MA theses or PhD dissertations. It is hoped that such works will be available in final form at a later date.

Because the orientation of this study is as socially directed as it is political, I must alert the reader to Oleg Berlev's research, covered in Chapter 1 in particular. As it is too late to thank him personally, these remarks are intended for his memory. An additional indirect but by no means negligible influence upon this final product has been that of Dr. Andrea Gnirs, whose up-to-date work concerning the Pharaonic war machine is a mine for all scholars. In similar fashion I am dependent upon the extraordinary kind offices of Prof. Manfred Bietak of Vienna who, in a remarkable fashion, has regularly sent me a series of recent publications from his working group on New Kingdom military reliefs. Finally, I have to thank a host of postgraduate students at Auckland University whose presence in various seminars on Egyptian warfare, ideology and wall reliefs, and New Kingdom military inscriptions have enabled me to revise and hone my thoughts.

I would also like to thank Dr. Stephen Harvey for his kind assistance with regard to the figures of Ahmose's reliefs.

March 31, 2004

PREFACE

This study is an attempt to develop our understanding of the socio-political effects of the military system within the New Kingdom (ca. 1550 BC–1070 BC). Owing to the subject and the limitations of the framework, I have concentrated upon the basic logistics of the ancient Egyptian war machine within this limited time sphere. In addition, the ramifications of the expansion of one subsystem within Pharaonic society during the Empire Period has led me to balance the external imperialistic policies of these monarchs with the internal expansionistic attitudes of its practitioners. By and large the reader will find that the study concentrates upon the logistic side of New Kingdom warfare and avoids the commonplace historical surveys of the wars of the various Pharaohs.

The focus of the analysis aims at determining the military effectiveness of the Egyptian state. Hence, it places in a secondary position a description of the various weapons employed in battle, the defensive and offensive abilities of the Egyptians, and the resultant successes abroad. In a similar fashion I have avoided a blow-by-blow account of each Pharaonic campaign, preferring instead to concentrate upon the longer-range effects of the rise in Egypt of a new group of men, a social sector that hitherto played an important but by no means predominant factor in the nation.

Questions such as the probable level of population at this time in conjunction with the actual number of arm-bearing men form an important part of the discussion. I have placed emphasis upon the political and geographical situation outside of the Nile Valley, both in Asia (Palestine and Syria) as well as to the south (Nubia). There are various excurses placed at the end of each chapter which evaluate the issues of logistics, rate of march, food intake, population level, and the like. This approach, which I have borrowed from Hans Delbrück, has been employed in order to examine carefully the difficult issues that a study of the New Kingdom military system offers.[1] Mathematical points of view rarely have been taken into consideration outside of some pertinent comments concerned with the Battles of Kadesh (Dynasty XIX) by Kenneth A. Kitchen and of Megiddo (mid Dynasty XVIII) by Donald B. Redford.[2] Often the wars of the New Kingdom Pharaohs have been covered either with a purely geographical perspective or one concentrated upon elucidating the historical outlines.

The recent study of Andrea Gnirs concerning the hierarchical make-up of the Egyptian war machine and the crucial internal aspects of the social system of the day has proved to be extremely useful.[3] Therefore, detail has been given to the role of the military in Egyptian society. I have also followed Harry Holbert Turney-High who maintains that "the means of any implementing any motive or goal are secondary to the primary means of action."[4] Robert B. Partridge's *Fighting Pharaohs*, for example, expends a great amount of worthwhile energy in describing the various implements of military defense and offense without, however, analyzing either the logistics of Pharaonic warfare, the geographic and economic constraints, or the factors of population.[5] The reader is thus recommended to turn to his second chapter wherein the basic factors of armaments and weaponry are covered.

The limitations of the theme have meant that an in-depth perspective concentrated upon international relations has been circumscribed. My orientation is the warfare of the Egyptian New Kingdom, not the intense diplomacy, international correspondence, state marriages, and economic interconnections which pervade the entire era. On the other hand, I have spent some effort in estimating gross population sizes (Egypt and Palestine in particular), and that of the native army as well, in order to set some parameters upon the "military preparedness ratio." Portions of the various excurses have also been devoted to estimating the raw fuel that went into these armies, both for the soldiers as well as for the animals. By and large, the conclusions are rough, although such approximations may be self-evident to any Egyptologist owing to the limited extant data. This approach, however, is necessary for any scientifically advanced work on the New Kingdom army, and it is hoped that the discussions will provide a stepping-stone for scholars interested in such matters.[6]

While not purposely ignoring the numerous books and articles that have been written on this subject, and the related ones of chronology or international relations, I have thought it best to limit the number of sources given in the notes. The literature has been referred to in the most complete way possible in order to allow an ease of research, but as this volume is oriented to the interested public, the focus is directed more to the key primary and secondary sources than to the minutely oriented and often controversial studies that abound. I hope that this meets with the approval of the reader.

NOTES

1 For the importance of this historian, see Gordon A. Graig, "Delbrück: The Military Historian," in Peter Paret, ed., *Makers of Modern Strategy from Machiavelli to the Nuclear Age*, Princeton University Press, Princeton (1943), 326–53; and

Arden Bucholz, *Hans Delbrück and the German Military Establishment: War Images in Conflict*, University of Iowa Press, Iowa City (1985).

2 Donald B. Redford, *The Wars in Syria and Palestine of Thutmose III*, Brill, Leiden and Boston (2003); and Kenneth A. Kitchen, *Ramesside Inscriptions. Translated and Annotated, Notes and Comments*, II, Blackwell, Oxford and Malden (1999), 39–40. It is noteworthy that the size of an Egyptian division was set as early as 1904 by James Henry Breasted (5,000); see his later *Ancient Records of Egypt* III, University of Chicago, Chicago (1906), 153 note a. By and large, most military historians have followed his conclusions.

3 Andrea M. Gnirs, *Militär und Gesellschaft. Ein Beitrag zur Sozialgeschichte des Neuen Reiches*, Heidelberger Orientverlag, Heidelberg (1996).

4 Harry Holbert Turney-High, *The Military. The Theory of Land Warfare as Behavioral Science*, Christopher Publishing House, West Hanover (1981), 36.

5 Robert B. Partridge, *Fighting Pharaohs. Weapons and Warfare in Ancient Egypt*, Peartree Publishing, Manchester (2002). This study deals with the entire phase of Pharaonic history from Predynastic times to the fall of the New Kingdom (end of Dynasty XX).

6 A study on the logistics of the New Kingdom armies is in preparation by my student Brett Heagren.

CHRONOLOGY

OLD KINGDOM	2575–2150
FIRST INTERMEDIATE PERIOD	2125–1975
Dynasty XI	**2080–1975**
Nebhepetre	
Mentuhotep II	
MIDDLE KINGDOM	1975–1640
Dynasty XI	**1975–1940**
Nebhepetre	
Mentuhotep II	2010–1960
Dynasty XII	**1938–1755**
Dynasty XIII	**1755–1630**
Dynasty XIV	
SECOND INTERMEDIATE PERIOD	1630–1520
Dynasty XV	
Apophis	1630–1520
Dynasty XVI	
Dynasty XVII	**1630–1540**
Seqenenre II	
Kamose	1545–1539
NEW KINGDOM	1539–1075
Dynasty XVIII	**1539–1292**
Ahmose	1539–1514
Amunhotep I	1514–1493
Thutmose I	1493–?
Thutmose II	?–1479
Thutmose III	1479–1425
Hatshepsut	1473–1458
Amunhotep II	1426–1400
Thutmose IV	1400–1390
Amunhotep III	1390–1353
Amunhotep IV/Akhenaton	1353–1336
Smenkhkare	1335–1332
Tutankhamun	1332–1322

Ay	1322–1319
Horemheb	1319–1292
Dynasty XIX	**1292–1190**
Ramesses I	1292–1290
Seti I	1290–1279
Ramesses II	1279–1213
Merenptah	1213–1204
Seti II	1204–1198
Amenmesse	
Siptah	1198–1193
Twosret	1198–1190
Dynasty XX	**1190–1075**
Sethnakht	1190–1187
Ramesses III	1187–1156
Ramesses IV	1156–1150
Ramesses V	1150–1145
Ramesses VI	1145–1137
Ramesses VII	1137–1129
Ramesses VIII	1129–1126
Ramesses IX	1126–1108
Ramesses X	1108–1104
Ramesses XI	1104–1075
THIRD INTERMEDIATE PERIOD	1075–715
Dynasty XXI	**1075–945**
Dynasty XXII	945–715
Dynasty XXIII	830–715
Dynasty XXIV	730–715
LATE PERIOD	715–332
Dynasty XXV (Kushite)	715–657
Dynasty XXVI	664–525

After *Atlas of Ancient Egypt*, John Baines and Jaromir Málek, New York (2000). Reprinted with permission of the authors.

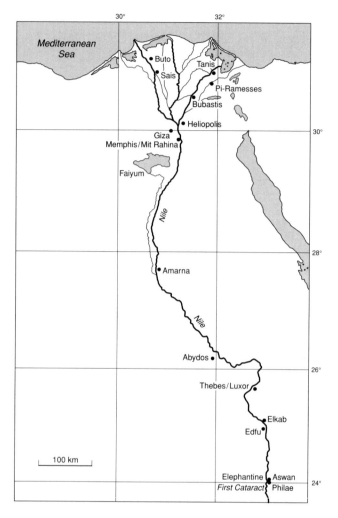

Map 1 Egypt

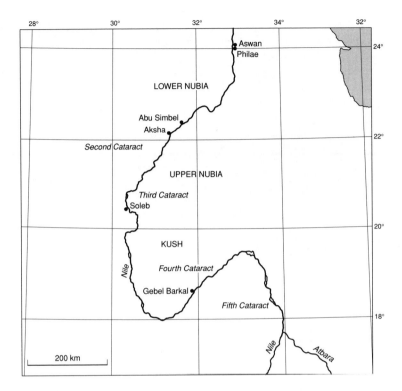

Map 2 Nubia

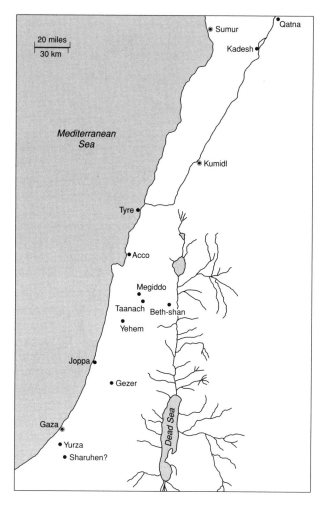

Map 3 Palestine and Syria during the New Kingdom

1

PRELUDE TO NEW KINGDOM WARFARE

The Egyptian Empire, founded at the beginning of the XVIIIth Dynasty ca. 1560 BC, experienced a lengthy period of economic growth and military success. The rapid expansion of the kingdom north into Asia and upriver into ancient Nubia began earlier when the native state was still divided into various realms and the Hyksos, Asiatic foreigners, controlled the north. The latter, of northern (Palestinian) origin, had been able to take over the Egyptian Delta, the age-old capital of Memphis, and a large portion of Middle Egypt upstream to Cusae. The result was that a native ruling house (Dynasty XVII) controlled only Upper Egypt, having its capital at Thebes and its southern boundary fixed at Aswan at the First Cataract. It was during this time, lasting approximately a century, that the Egyptians forged a far more effective means of centralized governmental control over their limited realm. At the same time the war machine of the Theban state had to deal with conflict to the south (Nubia) as well as with a cold war to the north. By and large, the XVIIth Dynasty managed to develop the use of the new military technology of the horse and chariot as well as other improvements in armament, most of which had come into Egypt from Asia at an earlier time. The Hyksos, in fact, had accelerated this trend owing to the weaknesses of the native Egyptian state of the Late Middle Kingdom (late Dynasty XII–Dynasty XIII) which had already lost control of the Eastern Delta. By the end of Dynasty XVII the Thebans felt themselves able to begin fighting in a regular fashion against their opponents on the Nile – both north and south – and it is at this point that significant transformations of the military commenced.

The best way to understand the military system of Pharaonic Egypt at the commencement of the New Kingdom is to analyze the famous war inscriptions of King Kamose, the last Pharaoh of the Dynasty XVII.[1] The narrative was written on two stone stelae and placed within the sacred precinct of the temple of Amun at Karnak. The king expressly commissioned this record to be set up by his treasurer, Neshi, an army commander and overseer of countries, whose figure and name were included at the bottom left of the inscription. The account lacks a high literary flavor, perhaps because his career was associated with the Egyptian war machine and foreign administration. On the other hand, Neshi's utilization of one important war record, an intercepted letter from the northern Hyksos foe, indicates that he was permitted access to an extremely important diplomatic document captured during the course of Kamose's northern campaign. The war record, although relatively straightforward in style and partly dependent upon a logical progression through time, nonetheless reveals a deep understanding of language and thought. This account presents a lively approach centered upon the key successes of the king, but without any reference to dates. Indeed, the original inscription lacked even a regnal year of the Pharaoh.[2]

Before delving into the actual sequence of events and how they reveal the military system of the day it is necessary to outline briefly the precise historical setting. At the end of Dynasty XVII Kamose had inherited the war against the Hyksos. He followed his father Seqenenre II to the throne of Egypt at a time when the Egyptians had begun to mass their forces against the northern enemy. In a later story centered on Seqenenre the latter are considered to be cowardly foreigners, Asiatics. Their non-Egyptian status is, in fact, one of the key elements in this patriotic record. The narrative of Kamose is as clear and organized in its physical aspects as in its nationalistic fervor. The author included royal speeches in order to heighten the dramatic aspect of the king's victories and to break up the separate events that Neshi preferred to write down. The beginning, however, throws one into a common literary setting of king in court, surrounded by his officials, both civilian and military, and his announcement of war.

Because the first stela was later retouched at the beginning of the opening line in order to date the text to Kamose's third regnal year, it is evident that the introductory backdrop serves more as a reflection of mood than of reality. At an unknown time Kamose had called his magnates into his palace for an official proclamation of war.[3] We may assume that high officials, including army leaders and naval men, were present. There is a simple sequence of policies. The king argues for war because Egypt is divided; the great men prefer the status quo. Not surprisingly, Kamose is displeased over their pacifistic approach and haughtily rejects their words. He concludes his rejection of the weaker policy with a prediction that after the campaign Egypt will recognize their ruler as a victorious king and a protector. Suddenly the narrative opens, and from then on the first person is employed. At this point the text presents an account as if spoken by Kamose himself. Henceforward, we gain in historical insight what the opening backdrop adumbrates through its stereotypical setting of king versus court.

The type of warfare is not as one might at first expect. It is oriented to the Nile.[4] The king's flotilla plays the key role in transport. Land battles are not described with any detail and chariot warfare does not play an overt role in the narrative. Kamose, for example, sails downstream and ends up at

2

Nefrusi, a settlement in Middle Egypt, while his army precedes him. The latter situation may imply that those men traveled by land. If so, they must have left days before the king's fleet. Necessary food supplies were probably brought along with the ship or else secured from the locals. An elite division of the army scoured the countryside for troublesome opponents. Then Nefrusi was besieged and sacked.

The specific type of warfare is barely presented in detail. On the contrary, we first hear of the siege at Nefrusi that seems to have taken place without any immediate opposition. The military encounter actually began the next day following the king's arrival, and from the tenor of the account it appears that the battlefield as well as the timing was prearranged: the Egyptians fought on land in the early morning and achieved success. Clearly, the siege was not as important as the land victory. Immediately afterwards, the Pharaoh traveled further north, frightening off any military opposition to his flotilla. Even though the system of fighting is not minutely described, its manner can be inferred. The Egyptians used their fleet to transport troops. They rapidly took over the enemy's territory owing to this method of transportation. Indeed, if a town or even a city resisted, all that Kamose would have to do is to bypass it and to attack one to the immediate north, thereby isolating the enemy in a pocket that could then be subdued afterwards. Only this can explain Kamose's sudden arrival in the East Delta at the capital of the Hyksos, Avaris, modern Tell ed-Dab'a. How else could he have achieved such a sudden dash north? Owing to the fragmentary condition of the first stela we do not learn of the fall of the key cities in the north. The account of the capture of Memphis at the apex of the Delta, for example, is lost. On the other hand, the isolation of Nefrusi and those regions immediately north of it lends support to the hypothesis that Kamose had sprung his army at a fortuitous time when the foe was unaware of his intentions.

At Avaris Kamose arranged his fleet to lay siege to the Hyksos capital. He places emphasis upon the timber used to construct his ships and taunts his royal opponent in two speeches that very well may reflect the actual situation. That is to say, the war is considered to be a duel, a personal conflict between the Egyptian king and the enemy leader Apophis. The Pharaoh commands his army on his golden flagship, allowing his elite troops to secure both sides of the river at Avaris. But he did not take the city, and, properly speaking, the military account ends the progressive narrative development at this point. The author ceases recounting these virile deeds with the last word of Kamose's second address of taunts to his enemy and instead turns to events preceding the arrival at Avaris.

A flashback is presented, serving as a lengthy coda to the Pharaoh's arrival at the Hyksos capital. In this portion of the second stela we learn that other towns had been burnt and that a messenger of the Hyksos king had been caught on the oasis route to the west of the Nile. That man had with him a crucial letter for the new ruler of Nubia (Kush). In it we learn that upon hearing of Kamose's move north, Apophis, the Hyksos king, quickly dispatched a messenger in order to effect an alliance with the new king of Kush. This attempt to circumvent Kamose failed. Nonetheless, it tells us that Apophis had learnt of his opponent's strike northward but had not been able to send his troops south. Granted that this is a modern interpretation, it nonetheless explains the apparent failure of Apophis to resist Kamose in Middle Egypt.

The strategy of Kamose is thereby presented by means of this short backdrop. In a separate section following upon the capture of Apophis's emissary, the Theban king indicates that he faced no resistance. This, of course, may be taken as mere boasting, but it reinforces the war account so well that we can suppose that his bragging is relatively free from exaggeration. In this light it is useful to note that Kamose originally sent his troops westward to secure his rear, for he was afraid that his opponent might have launched a preventative attack far away from the Nile in order to trap him as the Egyptian fleet moved north.

Lacking from the extant war narrative is any description of actual fighting. Granted, we have seen that the style of warfare tended to be locally arranged. The fleet moved the soldiers but the actual armed conflict was to take place upon flat ground. As a result, sieges were expected. No chariot encounters are described (as one might expect) nor is there any indication how the native Egyptian army was organized. We have to look elsewhere for these important details. True, Kamose stresses his capture of Apophis' chariots and fleet outside of Avaris, but little else is revealed concerning the make-up of either army.

Let us move a few years later into the reign of Ahmose, Kamose's Theban successor, and see from a private historical account how the Egyptian military operated at this time. The tomb biography of Ahmose son of Ebana, located at El Kab south of Thebes, is our major source for the wars subsequent to the death of Kamose.[5] Granted that we have to cover significantly more years of warfare, this personal account of valor is very instructive. Ahmose son of Ebana replaced his father in the royal fleet. He was originally a common soldier who, after marriage, officially entered the Egyptian war machine. (Subsequently, he became crew commander.) His narrative is laconic but nevertheless describes the art of war at this time. The king uses his chariot. Avaris is under siege more than once, and Ahmose is promoted to another and more important ship in the fleet. In the East Delta the fighting is hand-to-hand against the Hyksos. More than once in the melee Ahmose son of Ebana brings back either a hand from a dead enemy or a living opponent as proof of success. At the fall of Avaris the hero takes away one man and three women, the latter undoubtedly noncombatants. Yet we hear little of horses and chariots. In fact, there is no overt statement in the text that fast-moving chariots played the major role in warfare at this time; this we have to infer from the account and from the pictorial reliefs of

Pharaoh Ahmose. Even the subsequent capture of the city (
king Ahmose in southern Palestine indicates that the earlier m(
had to take place, proving that chariot-based attacks by thems(
always conclusive.

When Ahmose son of Ebana fought south of Egypt in Nubia t
fleet stood in good stead. Used again as a means of rapid transpo ⸺ ...ic
ships carried the Egyptian army until the disembarkation, at which point
the soldiers then fought on land. In this case we can assume that the better-
equipped and technologically superior Egyptian army was able to repel the
enemy with little difficulty. When further warfare was necessary it is not
surprising to read of the enemy's ship. This reference to naval affairs must
indicate a prepared foe whose orientation was sufficiently similar to the
Egyptians, possibly also indicating the presence of a yet remaining Nubian
state. Indeed, Ahmose son of Ebana specifically notes that this enemy, Aata
by name, moved against Egyptian territory.

The type of warfare within the Nile valley differed considerably from that
later encountered in Palestine and Syria.[6] There were no wide-open spaces
available for the deployment of chariots. Nor could such rapid maneuvering
and quick attack on land occur. The narrow and rugged Nile valley with its
umbilical cord of the great river reduced to a minimum the efficacy of
chariots. We can reasonably conclude that the latter sector had yet to receive
written emphasis in the war records of Kamose and his immediate successors, Ahmose and Amunhotep I.[7] Quite to the contrary, a different set-up
existed in the Egyptian army just before the creation of the Empire.

In fact, the terminology of the Middle Kingdom (Dynasties XII–XIII)
and the outgoing XVIIth was quite different from that employed later. The
two major terms employed by the Egyptians of this earlier age were "youths"
and "army"/"troops." The last two words are essentially identical. There
was a standing army, and it was considered to be a real profession for the
youth. The term for "warrior" is derived from the verb "to live," and it
designated a footsoldier dependent upon the king, a virile young man.
These youths were placed under a commander or a military leader. The
latter, considered to be "tutors," led the "youths," who often served in the
rowing teams. There is a generic designation for the "youths," a word that
literally means a collective group of people, but within a military context it
designated a "naval team" or a "detachment."

The ordinary warriors, the footsoldiers, were inferior to the sailors. The
naval men, perhaps sharpened by their more difficult service in the fleet,
were young officers. Soon thereafter, the Middle Kingdom word for
"naval team" replaced the more specific term, "rowing team." Evidently,
the two are the same. In the civil fleet the "commanders of the ships" stood
over the "tutors of the naval teams," but in the military flotilla the "captains"
of the ships directly obeyed the king. That is to say, the "captains" were
directly responsible to the Pharaoh. It is thus not surprising that later, at the

_eginning of Dynasty XVIII, Ahmose son of Ebana first stresses his naval service as well as his role in following his father in the same function. The flotilla, after all, was the basic military strength during the Middle Kingdom. It was at the direct command of the king and his closest officials, the highest being the vizier who communicated directly to the ship commanders.

The striking difference between Middle Kingdom warfare and that of the later Empire Period is thus self-evident. The army of the former was amphibious, and its foundation was the fleet. Being an officer in the royal navy was especially attractive to the nobility of the day. Especially at the beginning of the XIIIth Dynasty the officers were princes, members of the royal family and representatives of the highest nobility. During this time and later into Dynasty XVII we find the hereditary nomarchs of El Kab who were captains in the navy. Even though members of the military elite could be from the middle classes, the army ranks remained separate and lower than the naval ranks. The elite warriors were those in the royal navy.

But the New Kingdom army around the time of Kamose and Ahmose was undergoing a rapid transformation.[8] Consider, for example, the military activity in Asia during the Middle Kingdom and contrast it with the aftershocks of the capture of Sharuhen by Pharaoh Ahmose. Warfare in the earlier age lacked chariots and horses. As befitted the Nile it was water based. Hence, the Egyptians were able to make only sallies or razzias into Asia. They could not easily annex Palestine with their army, which had as its core the navy. Only the creation of a separate and strong division in the land-based army could render conquest permanent. At the time of king Ahmose Egypt was able to be unified but Asia, or at least parts of it, could not be so easily taken. Ahmose son of Ebana, who belonged to the elite of El Kab, finished his career as "commander of the rowing team." Under Thutmose I, the grandson of Pharaoh Ahmose, the navy was no longer called the royal army. By this time the land-based army was the main force with the chariots its core. The navy henceforth played only a supporting role in warfare.

The military society of the New Kingdom and of her neighbors operated within a system different than earlier.[9] The series of additional changes in both offensive and defensive weapons can be seen in the swords (in their various manifestations), spears, and body-armor. Previously, the main weapon was the bow and arrow, intended for long-range combat, in addition to a preponderance of weapons for hand-to-hand fighting. To the northeast in Palestine and Syria there were many fortified cities. The effects of this change would impact upon the Egyptian war machine when it decided to advance into southern Palestine. The soldiers themselves remained Egyptian, although Nubian "mercenaries" are also known as early as the Late Old Kingdom (Dynasty VI) and the First Intermediate Period. But the core of the native state of Thebes in Dynasty XVII was Egyptian, and through their strength the successful, albeit lengthy, wars against the Hyksos occurred.[10]

Before proceeding further it is necessary to examine more carefully the term "mercenaries."[11] Scholars normally employ this word when they deal with the non-Egyptians who were members of the army. But this designation is misleading. Mercenaries work for pay; so did the Egyptian troops of the Middle and New Kingdoms. These men, however, sell themselves, or rather their abilities, to whatever state or leader can afford them. They have no national loyalty. The situation with regard to New Kingdom Egypt therefore revolves around the case whether, for example, foreign troops soldiering with the Egyptians could leave at any time if their pay was in arrears or whether they could switch sides. There is no evidence that this occurred. Later, we also hear of captured elite Asiatic *maryannu* troops in Dynasty XVIII who were brought back to Egypt by the Pharaoh, presumably not as hostages but rather to serve in the army. Here, as well, I do not think that the term "mercenaries" fits them. These Asiatics were well versed with the art of war and so could form a useful permanent contingent within the native Egyptian war machine.

Later, in Dynasties XIX and XX (the Ramesside Period), the Sherden, originally sea raiders in the eastern Mediterranean, performed similar duty.[12] These foreigners appear both in texts as well as in battle reliefs serving the Pharaoh. They also owned plots of land in Egypt, small to be sure, but this must indicate that they had become settled within the Nile Valley. In other words, the Sherden were inhabitants of the land that they served. The males appear to have been organized into separate contingents within the Egyptian army. Indeed, they are connected with various "strongholds," presumably set up by the Ramesside kings in order to continue their separate way of life. The Sherden are also known to have been organized along different military lines than the Egyptians. But they did not remain loyal to their monarchs only for pay. They actually lived in Egypt and belonged to the economic structure of the land. Libyan troops fought in the Egyptian army in the same period, and they too became settled member of the society. I purposely have left aside the additional designation of "elite" Asiatic warriors, or in Canaanite, the "Na'arn." Whether or not these men who served in such divisions during Dynasties XIX–XX were Semites must remain open. But if they were, these soldiers further reveal the polyglot or polyethnic nature of the Egyptian military in the Late New Kingdom.

Owing to these factors, the commonplace term "mercenary" is inappropriate when referring to such troops. They were professionals, as all ancient and modern mercenaries were. But so were the Egyptians. Significantly, we hear of no mercenary takeover of Egypt. This point is crucial. Native rulers of the Nile Valley continued beyond the terminus of the end of Dynasty XX, notwithstanding the political vicissitudes of the day. As we shall see at the close of this work, there was a slow movement of Libyans upward, first into the middle levels of the state (administrative and military), and subsequently, at the end of Dynasty XXI, into the office of king. But even then this was no "takeover" by a strong band of hardy and well-prepared warriors. What occurred was the domination of a group of clans whose origins lay to the west. No Libyans rebelled against the government and took over the reins of power.

The social and political ramifications of foreign mercenaries cannot be seen in Egypt during the New Kingdom.[13] Normally, such troops end up being a major threat to the state that they served. Through blackmail, displacement, or supplantation they gain control of the state. In power, mercenaries prove themselves incapable of further development, normally retaining their system of warfare for many years, indeed centuries. The Mamlukes in Egypt provide an excellent example of heroes who never had the interest to alter either their tactics or their weapons.

But the foreigners in the Egyptian army were hired on a permanent basis. They became natives despite their outlandish clothing, social conventions, and, originally, language. To find, for example, Sherden in the middle of Dynasty XX owning parcels of land indicates that they had become cultivators, just as were the rank-and-file Egyptian soldiers. After all, land was the major commodity that provided sustenance and wealth. The real question that we must face is why did the Egyptians hire or use these foreigners. It is not enough to say that these men were able soldiers. Natives could be as well. Perhaps their military preparedness was on a level higher than the Egyptians. This supposition, however, remains moot. We simply do not know how the native soldier was regarded, militarily and socially speaking, in contrast to the foreign one. It may be the case that the population level of the Nile Valley was lower than many assume, and that correspondingly the number of Egyptian soldiers who could be trained to fight was not that large. This assumption will be tested later. Suffice it to say that the increased costs of military administration in Asia at the end of Dynasty XVIII and onward may have exhausted the ability of Egypt to provide larger and larger troop divisions which could set out on a major campaign.

Let us now turn to the military technology at the beginning of the New Kingdom. Chariots and horses were introduced from Western Asia into Egypt.[14] Warfare in Egypt thus came more and more to depend upon the acquisition of equids. True, horses at this time were small and their height up to the withers was on the average 1.40 to 1.50 m (between 13.7 and 14.6 hands). This is based upon data from archaeological data at Avaris dated to the beginning of Dynasty XVIII but also during the late Second Intermediate Period.[15] The famous "Buhen horse" in Nubia was 1.50 m in height at the withers. Recent analysis has revealed that Tell Brak in central Syria was the old center for the development of mules, bred from male donkeys and female horses.

Two types of horses are known from the New Kingdom.[16] The first group, which is called "long-lined," was relatively long with respect to girth. The thoracic cavity was narrow and weak whereas the scapula-ischial bones were strong. The voluminous head was also narrow and elongated. A second race, labeled "short-lined," was shorter in length and can be recognized by its short face and back, a large round croup that was raised, and an ample chest. Some scholars have remarked upon the resemblance of the first type to the famous Prezewalsky horse, in contrast to the second group. Pictorial representations indicate that these equids had been domesticated for a long time. Data conclusively reveal that this first group was the earlier one to be successfully utilized within the Nile Valley. Significantly, the second race appears from the beginning of the reign of Amunhotep II in middle of the XVIIIth Dynasty, a time when the chariot division of the army came into great importance. It would appear that during the first half of Dynasty XVIII one type of horse had been developed from those brought into Egypt by the Hyksos (if not somewhat earlier). The second, clearly more robust for a single rider although still small by our standards, later took over, and this took place when Egypt's Empire encompassed territories in Asia up to southern Syria. That is to say, the apparent switch – it is sudden within the pictorial art of the day – must have been dependent upon a new breed of horses that could only come from northern lands outside of Africa.

An Asiatic origin for the latter race is the only possibility, and we can hypothesize that the second more robust type of horse was a by-product of Egypt's imperialistic activity in the north. This conclusion is partly supported by the contemporary war records because they indicate that a large number of equids were captured from the enemy after battles. Moreover, we can suppose that others were exported to the Nile Valley during times of peace, a point that shall be covered later in this study. A recently excavated horse

Figure 1.1 Egyptian horses: (a) Long-lined and (b) short-lined. *Les Chevaux du Nouvel Empire Égyptien. Origines, races, harnachement* by Catherine Rommelaere, figures 4 and 5. © 1991 by Connaissance de l'Égypte Pharaonique. Reprinted by permission of Claude Vandersleyen, Connaissance de l'Égypte Ancienne.

from Tell Heboua in the Sinai shows that a medium-sized equid characterized by a heavy head and robust limbs belongs to the later "short-lined" race rather than to the earlier slender animals of the "long-lined" type.[17] The date of the skeleton was placed in the Hyksos Period. Hence, should we not regard the artistic representations in Egypt as conservative or at least indicating the presence of the later race somewhat after its importation in Egypt?

There is some evidence that the Egyptians practiced slitting the nostrils of their horses.[18] We can see it for the first time in the XVIIIth Dynasty on the chariot horses. Significantly, the excavators of the tomb of Thutmose IV found bridles with the reins attached to the nose-strap and the archaeologists tentatively concluded that the command of the animal was obtained through the nose-strap. No bits were found with the bridle equipment in the tomb of Tutankhamun. Later data from the Dynasty XIX capital of Tell ed-Dab'a/Avaris in the East Delta indicate that bits were standard. This recently published material, however, reflects an age when the Egyptians also manufactured shields of a foreign (Hittite) type and so cannot be used to interpret the evidence from an earlier time. The slit noses, of course, were instituted in an effort to compensate for the impairment in breathing caused by the nose-straps. More recently, in the 17th century AD, the noses were slit also to prevent the horse from whinnying, a problem that is all too frequent when scouts are sent out to reconnoiter the landscape. One might argue that the use of the bit was introduced in Egypt at a time after the mid point of Dynasty XVIII but the earlier war reliefs from the time of Ahmose and Thutmose II, however, indicate otherwise.

Nevertheless, from pictorial evidence of the Amarna Period we still see the practice of slitting horses' noses, and it might be argued that bits were introduced even later than we assume. Certainly, the large number of reliefs in the Ramesside Period that depict warfare may imply that bits were regularly employed by the reign of Seti I and later. But we are faced with the unfortunate situation of not having any chariot horses preserved in a tomb or on a site until the second half of the reign of Ramesses II (mid Dynasty XIX). In other words, we can only argue from the evidence of Tell ed-Dab'a/Avaris where foreign (Asiatic) military influences were great.

Stirrups were not in use at this early time, and from pictorial representations the forward position of the rider was not employed.[19] Instead, the horseman sat in a position similar to that which he used for a donkey; i.e., toward the rump. The lightness of the horses or, to be more accurate, their size and mass, combined with the technology of the day meant that no independent cavalry could be developed. Instead, all the civilized neighbors of Egypt in Mesopotamia, Anatolia, Syria, and Palestine used simple chariots. Horses and their vehicles were brought into Egypt during the XIIIth Dynasty by the Hyksos or other Asiatics. Although the exact date of introduction is a controversial problem, it remains true that the Hyksos rulers in the north of Egypt succeeded first in capturing the age-old capital of Memphis and

Figure 1.2   Egyptian chariot horses, Seti I, Karnak: Exterior of north wall
to Hypostyle Court. *Les Chevaux du Nouvel Empire Égyptien. Origines, races,
harnachement* by Catherine Rommelaere, figure 19. © 1991 by Connaissance
de L'Egypte Encienne. Reprinted by permission of Claude Vandersleyen,
Connaissance de l'Égypte Ancienne.

then repulsed the natives probably by means of this new system of warfare.
Unfortunately, the few Egyptian inscriptions that describe warfare at this
time (Dynasty XIII–XVII, excluding Kamose's account) avoid mention of
any chariots and horses. As we have seen, the navy remained the backbone
of the Theban military arm.

Stirrups were not yet invented, but their lack was not serious because the
horses were small. The large-barreled draught horses or the Medieval destriers
had yet to be developed. (Heavy horses are recognizable by their thick
fetlocks and wavy mane and tail.) Moreover, these animals were not used
for cavalry charges. The mounted rider, sitting to the rear, was in a position
effective for scouts and single riders but not useful for charging the enemy.
Because the decided factor in managing these animals is that of control, the
rear seated position placed a man at a disadvantage. We have to wait until

the period of the Neo-Assyrian Empire when the riders could sit in the forward position owing to the advances in selective breeding. The later heavy saddle with its pommel and cantle were absent. Indeed, there were no saddles. Men rode the horses bareback, although some type of cushion, such as a blanket, may be seen on the Pharaoh's horses. One leapt onto the horse; mounting was impossible owing to the lack of stirrups. In this case, however, it would not have been a great feat because of the small height of the equids.

The physical condition of the horses automatically implied that modern lances were never employed in war. Instead, we find javelins or spears sometimes held in the hand of the charioteer or his protector, the shield-bearer. Even then this man became unprotected as the shield had to be thrust aside. This action was further deleterious because he could not protect the driver. Therefore, it seems probable that the throw would take place when the chariot was slowing down or had ceased to move. The driver could take up his bow and shoot while the second man could throw the spear. Protection, nonetheless, was needed, and when the charioteer served as an archer he had to be protected by a shield.

The attitudes of the Egyptians regarding their horses are hard to determine. Earlier, the animals were buried in tombs at Avaris during the period of the Hyksos domination, but this was a foreign trait, and when the Egyptian reconquered the East Delta this practice ceased.[20] Only the foreign Hyksos observed this practice, one that strikingly indicates their warrior ethos. Oddly enough, this situation can be seen in Early Medieval Europe.[21] When the Lombards had been converted to Christianity they ceased to include horses in the burials of their warriors, although from time to time they included bridles and even saddles in their graves. But since the gates of heaven prohibited imports, the official religious ideology banned horse-burials. In the case of Egypt the native age-old habits of burial persisted.

Later we shall note the repeated accounts of Dynasty XVIII in which horses and chariots were delivered to Egypt. This was a standard practice in peacetime but also prominent after a successful battle. One papyrus dated to Dynasty XIX mentions the presence of horse-teams and "fine young steeds" from Sangar in North Syria as well as top stallions from the Hittites (P. Anastasi IV; partly paralleled by P. Koller).[22] Their masters underneath the king's "Window of Appearances" led the animals. This small portion of the composition refers to the preparations for the arrival of the king, and among the requirements are resplendent chariots of superior quality.

John Keegan has observed that we should not be surprised over the rapid dispersion of the chariot.[23] Indeed, he adds, they may have been a chariot industry and chariot market. Certainly, the numbers recorded in the annual impost from Asia sent to Egypt are not that large, and this requirement ought not to have exhausted the economic foundations of the Asiatic city-states. The technology is relatively simple, and the transportation of the vehicle not that arduous. Keegan specifically notes an Egyptian relief that shows a man carrying a chariot on his shoulders, and the assumption is that the vehicles were not heavy.

As an aside, let us keep in mind that horses were not employed as draft animals. This has less to do with the absence of horseshoes, which were not important in these climes at any rate, but a result of the absence of the horse-collar. Because yoke-collars had been in use for a long time it might be supposed that the equids theoretically could have been used in agriculture. But with a yoke-harness the neck-strap pressed on the jugular vein and windpipe tended to lead to suffocation and the cutting of blood flow to the animal's head. Moreover, as Lynn White Jr. remarked, the point of traction came at the withers, too high for good mechanical effect.[24] The ratio is 5:1 for horse-collar versus yoke-collar. We have to wait for about two millennia until horses replaced oxen.

From later representations of chariots in Dynasty XVIII, and even from Ahmose's few broken reliefs, the chariots appear light and small.[25] Four spokes to the wheel betoken a simple war machine, one that was not suitable for anything but two horses, and very small ones at that. The wheels on the first chariots known to us from Western Asia were light and strong, and extremely useful for warfare in arid regions. This should alert us to their origins outside of the so-called "Fertile Crescent." The floor was generally shaped in the form of a D and was made of meshed rawhide. The superstructure was also light, and generally curved in the back. The sides were closed by the end of Dynasty XVIII, but pictorial representations from Ahmose, Thutmose II, and Amunhotep II indicate the opposite. In other words, the earliest scenes of Egyptian chariots show a simpler and lighter vehicle than the later ones. The latter, mainly dating from Dynasty XIX and XX, reveal a more substantial body. In fact, by the end of the XVIIIth Dynasty the number of spokes had been fixed at six, and it is highly probable that this occurred owing to the newer types of horses introduced into Egypt from the late reign of Thutmose III and onward.

Both the Asiatic and Egyptian chariots of this time were virtually identical, further indicating their northeastern origin. Their width was around one meter and the length of the cab one half of that figure. The diameter of the wheels also came to one meter. We can also note the extension of the axle system that afforded more velocity to these vehicles. Among the woods employed, the evidence indicates that elm and birch, non-native to Egypt, as well as tamarisk were employed. Because elm grows in Northern Palestine, it is reasonable to conclude that the Egyptians scoured this region and felled the trees after they had controlled it. Birch, however, is native to Anatolia, and therefore would have been imported, probably by ship, from the Hittites who lived there.

From the specific parts of a chariot (chassis, wheels, yoke pole), some of which have been found in Egypt, we can reconstruct their effect in battle.

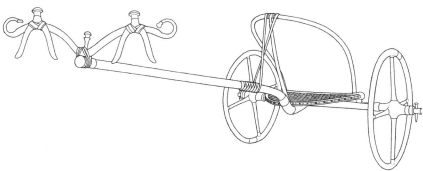

Figure 1.3 Egyptian chariot from Thebes. Florence, Museo Archeologico. Photo AKG-Images, Nimatallah. Drawing after J. Morel in *Wheeled Vehicles and Ridden Animals in the Ancient Near East* by M. A. Littauer and J. H. Crouwel. E. J. Brill, 1979, figure 42.

In Egyptian scenes of warfare dating from Dynasty XVIII the Asiatics use four-spoked vehicles. At that time, only the Pharaoh might be depicted in an eight-spoked one. It seems probable, however, that four spokes remained the rule in Egypt until late in this period. The top of the sides approximated the flared upward-turning croup of the horses. In order to enter the vehicle all that a man had to do was to make one simple upward

14

step. No jumping was necessary. The charioteer was therefore able to see over the heads of the two horses with no difficulty because the animals were not tall enough to obstruct his vision.

Although the Egyptian army began to employ this new war machine in the Second Intermediate Period, its effect can be seen only at a later date. In contrast, the rapid introduction and development of the Asiatic composite bow meant that both the developing chariotry as well as the footsoldier-archers began to play a greater and greater role in military affairs. In this case the combination of chariot and bow was essential. Because the horse was not yet specialized for cavalry attack, archers remained very important. In this case the driver or charioteer switched from directing his vehicle into an archer. Therefore, both the Egyptians and their opponents used the chariots in a specific way, one quite different from that usually assumed by laypersons. Finally, it has been doubted whether the Hittites of Anatolia used the composite bow, at least as a weapon employed from one of their chariots. John Keegan stresses their virtual absence in the Egyptian reliefs of the XIXth Dynasty because the Hittite chariot crews are usually represented as spearmen.[26]

Because the Nile Valley lent itself to naval warfare, the necessity of expending time and expense upon chariot warfare was not that urgent. Both the native Egyptians of Thebes (Dynasty XVII) and their Hyksos opponents relied upon fleets. Have we not seen Kamose boasting of his seizure of Apophis' ships? But if the archer was so important, having now a more effective weapon in his hands, how could he be used? Here, as well, we can see that the period of Kamose and Ahmose was a transitional one during which techniques of chariot warfare began to grow in importance, but when fleets still played a key role.

With his arrows, the archer could now penetrate simple armor. Hence, the need for a thicker bodily protection, which was now made of leather and metal. This soldier could also cover a greater distance in a chariot. Hence, it was not necessary for him to be very close to a battle line. All of this meant that a second division of footsoldier-archers remained in the infantry, while others could be placed on chariots.

As noted earlier, the composite bow was an additional weapon introduced to Egypt during the Hyksos Period.[27] Middle Kingdom reliefs show the Egyptian employing double-complex bows that were made from one strong piece of pliable wood. The older type, the single-arc ones, has been found in tombs dated to the same time. There remains the problem whether the Egyptians in Dynasty XII had the quiver. Although it would appear likely, and such an item could have been developed independently by many cultures, it is noteworthy that the New Kingdom word for the quiver was Semitic. But whether this indicates that quivers were borrowed from Asia (via Palestine) or not, scenes dated to the Middle Kingdom show that the Egyptian bowmen carried their arrows in bundles. This situation can be better explained by assuming that the Egyptian archers used to prepare their forces outside of a city by carrying along a number of arrows, too many for a single quiver. In fact, because an actual quiver was found from Upper Egypt dated to Dynasty XII, it is clear that for ordinary combat between two divisions of footsoldiers, such a policy would be counter-productive.[28] The contemporary pictorial representations of siege indicate a type of warfare separate from the clash of two infantry-based armies.

It is useful to concentrate upon these earlier weapons because they indicate a type of warfare quite different from the reign of Kamose and later. For example, the archers, lacking any chariots, stood behind the protective shields of their compatriots. In earlier siege depictions these men formed a contingent separate from the footsoldiers. None of these soldiers have body-armor. They also lacked helmets. Their shields were of moderate to large size, composed of hide stretched between thin wooden sides. From this information we can reconstruct the earlier type of warfare practiced in the Nile Valley.

The army was organized through the state, and the naval contingents were the elite class. The footsoldiers were transported by the ships to the battlefield. By and large, the combat would have taken place on a field or flat surface, and we might assume that the time was announced. Movement of troops on land is slow. The lack of horses and chariots was the obvious reason even though combat at this earlier time was not simple and lacking in carnage. The lack of protective armor is explained by the short distance of arrow flight, the relative simplicity of the tension in the bowstrings, and the presence of large though cumbrous shields. A flat cutting axe was held into the haft by three tangs. By and large, this type was not employed outside of Egypt during the Middle Kingdom. In Syro-Palestine (and also further east) the axes were set within sockets. It is evident that such weapons depended upon their sharp blades to cut into unarmored flesh. Later in Western Asia we see the rise of the eye axe, which, when developed, served more as a piercing weapon than a cutting one. Hence, the rapid need for protective armor first developed outside of Egypt and then later was introduced, once more indicating the importance of foreign technology. With the expansion of leather helmets and corselets, the axes switched to a weapon geared even more to piercing and penetration. This forced, as a logical counter-reaction, small shields and more armor.

Egypt, which lagged behind the military technology of Western Asia, was not resistant to such changes. The cause for its conservatism in weaponry has to be looked for elsewhere. By and large, in the Nile Valley the necessity of wars was limited. Except for expansion southward into Nubia, the Middle Kingdom feared no invasion. To put it another way, once the state was unified in late Dynasty XI and internal difficulties pacified, the Pharaohs ruled a stable land. Continual warfare of an internecine nature ceased, and except for a desire to take control over portions of Nubia the army was not that important within the Nile Valley. Unlike the situation to the northeast in Asia where city-states vied for control over small patches of land, Egypt was at peace. Therefore, the nature of warfare in Egypt tended to be conservative, and the demand for new technology limited, especially as her southern Nubian foes were even less developed, at least in the military arts, than herself.

We are faced with a common economic and social situation, one where a contrast can be made between Asiatic warring cities and small states whose needs for independence and self-sufficiency were more marked than Egypt's. The virtual monopoly of the Nile waterway, a perfect conduit for trade and political control, effected a stasis in Egypt with respect to the art of war. Those lands that frequently fought, on the other hand, were not blessed with such a peaceful condition. Hence, the tug of war between defense (armor) and attack (axes, swords) did not take place in the Nile Valley. When, however, the Hyksos took over the north during the weakened period of Dynasty XIII, the situation altered.

The move to sickle swords in Western Asia provides a good example of this dichotomy.[29] The blades were relatively short, and in many ways this implement can be considered to be similar in purpose to an axe. Later, the blades were extended, a result of the growing use of defensive armor. At the same time the Egyptian axes were converted to piercing types, and two well-known examples, dated to Kamose and his successor Ahmose, indicate how the Egyptians had to adapt their weapons to new developments. Both axes are short and have a wide edge. Their mode of use depended upon a swift and steady blow that caused a thick cut because the blade had a wide edge. Instead of cutting, these new weapons depended upon piercing.

In similar fashion, the introduction of the composite bow further hastened the need for armor protection. Reed arrows with bronze tips were placed upon the bowstring, which, because of the strengthened wood, was far more taught than the strings of earlier bows. The later Egyptian archers could inflict considerably more damage than their Middle Kingdom predecessors. Unfortunately, we do not know exactly when the composite bow came to Egypt. That it was used by the Egyptians in Dynasty XVIII is clear. The regular use of bronze in Egypt (middle to the end of Dynasty XII) provides a terminus of a sort. The written records of Kamose and Ahmose son of Ebana, however, do not tell us anything about these weapons.

The reason why archers were more effective on chariots than on foot is easy to see. First, it was necessary to speed up the transportation of these men to the battlefield. Insofar as the use of the composite bow made the archers more effective than previously, the need for them became all the more important. These warriors also required some protection as it was impossible to hold a shield and shoot arrows at the same time. So two men in a chariot were necessary, and both would have to work with each other. Therefore, the wheeled vehicles served a double purpose: to move the

17

archer to the melee as soon as possible and to provide protection to that man by a shield-bearer. Furthermore, the quivers could be set against the side of a chariot, generally on the right, thereby allowing the two men to work as a team before the archer actually shot his arrows. (The chariot warriors also could carry quivers on their backs.) One can immediately see why the Hyksos Period was so important in Egypt. The new warfare that so upset the traditional way of fighting now focused more attention upon the archer. The reliefs on the sides of the chariot of Thutmose IV (mid Dynasty XVIII) indicate this. In fact, this royal vehicle possessed at least two quivers, both set on the right and left.

A brief look at the Egyptian chariot teams with two men per vehicle needs explication. They would have hastened to the battlefield. The ground had to be moderately level, otherwise the riders would have been unable to operate effectively. Traditionally, the navy had sped the troops to the encounter. Now chariots could do the same, especially if there was no river. In Egypt, on the other hand, the royal fleet would have still transported the infantry with the charioteers and their vehicles, but after disembarking the army would have formed into two major sectors and then quickly advanced upon their opponents. The latter still took place under Kamose and Ahmose, and was probably commonplace during the southern expansion into Nubia and the later conquest of that region.

The charioteer was supported by his man at arms, the shield-bearer, who held his shield in front of the driver with his right hand. The first man held the reins, and stood to the right in the vehicle. Next to him was the quiver, although it is also possible that a second quiver would be placed on the left. Representations in Dynasty XVIII and later indicate that there was a bow case also attached on the right side of the cab, and it was normally set over the quiver. The charioteer stopped pushing his horses forward at a point in time. He then took up his bow with his right hand, set it in his left and placed arrow after arrow on the bowstring, shooting his missiles into the advancing army. The shield-bearer remained as a protective unit, perhaps using a spear or javelin if need be.

Some have hypothesized that the charioteer tied together the reins behind his back while shooting in battle.[30] Evidence for this is circumstantial with one exception, but I still feel that it would have been foolhardy to attempt such an action unless the actual combat was relatively well organized. Scenes of the Pharaoh in chariot charging the enemy alone with the reins tied in such a manner are common. However, they must be viewed carefully, with the appreciation of the intent of the artist and the imposed structure of representation with which he worked. We can readily dismiss the solitary nature of the royal warlord. If he acted thus, he would be suicidal. The presence of the tied reins, however, can be seen in a war scene of the late XVIIIth Dynasty.[31] In depictions of royal hunting the king in his chariot pursues lions or bulls with the reins tied behind his back. But here there was no worry of physical attack. Could such have occurred during a melee? This question is crucial, as it forces us back upon the nature and logic of war. Protection for the archer was needed. Hence, there always were two men in a chariot, including the one of Pharaoh. But when the charioteers became archers, how could this use of the reins be accomplished in an efficient and quick manner when the warrior had already reached the enemy? Consider the enemy chariots advancing, behind which came the infantry. Add the flying arrows, the need for a shield-bearer, and perhaps more importantly, the presence of spears or javelins. In other words, we have to treat the official pictorial representations of king in battle with a degree of caution, although some evidence indicates that this use of the reins was in practice.

Now let us analyze the arrows and javelins/spears. Later Egyptian kings have a javelin holder attached to their chariot and it is usually placed on the left side.[32] That is, it was meant to be thrown by the second man, the shield-bearer. But if he did this, how could he protect the charioteer? The spear or javelin, therefore, was probably hurled before the charioteer stopped his vehicle. Furthermore, both arrows and javelins are most effective against large objects, not small ones. That is to say, they would most probably have been employed to bring down horses. It is easier to strike a horse with a spear than a man, especially if, as we know, the downward position of the hand is employed with the spear. Equally, arrows are more effective against horses than men, especially if the latter are protected by shield-bearers. All in all, I consider the dual role of charioteer and shield-bearer to be complementary, notwithstanding the more important – and the more elitist – role of the former.

Taking into consideration this new method of warfare, it would appear that the Egyptians used the new technology to defeat the Hyksos. Yet, as we have seen, up through the reign of Kamose the naval contingent remained in the key position of the Egyptian army. By and large, it is assumed that the chariot arm of Kamose was the means by which he defeated the Hyksos, notwithstanding virtual silence by the extant sources on this matter. On the other hand, the need for a fleet was as important as the newly developed chariot division. Both sectors, therefore, played equal roles in the reconquest of northern Egypt without one taking prominence. Fortunately, recent support for this modified interpretation can be given owing to the discovery of a number of fragments of Ahmose's war reliefs from his temple at Abydos.[33]

This pictorial evidence meshes perfectly with the analysis presented above. The archers use the convex bow; the royal ship is present; and oars and sails may be seen on additional fragments. The presence of horses and their vehicles is significant. One solitary scene shows four spoked wheels on a chariot, whether of the enemy or not cannot be determined with accuracy. Two additional depictions shows bridled horse pairs, and from their precision we can determine that the Egyptians employed the bit in the corner of

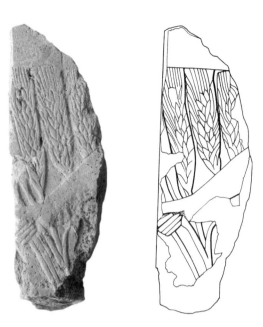

Figure 1.4   Limestone relief depicting the harvesting of grain from the pyramid temple of King Ahmose at Abydos. Photo by Laura Foos. Drawing by William Schenck. Courtesy of Stephen P. Harvey.

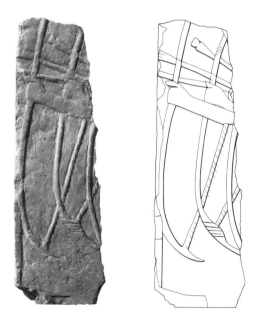

Figure 1.5   Limestone relief showing Nubian archers with longbows firing into the air, from the pyramid temple of King Ahmose at Abydos. Photo by Laura Foos. Drawing by William Schenck. Courtesy of Stephen P. Harvey.

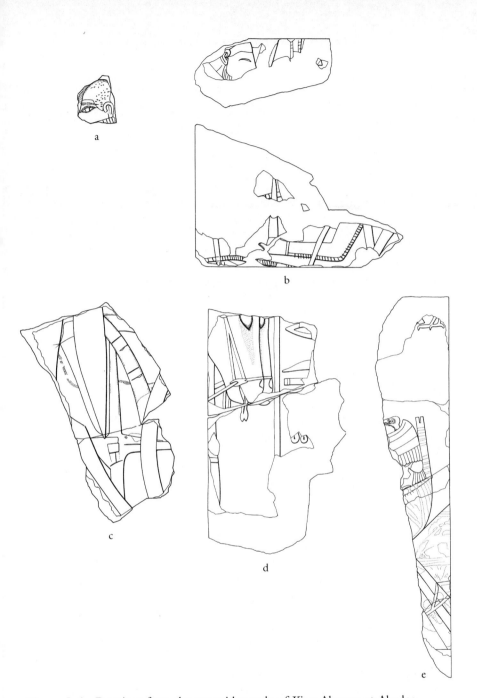

Figure 1.6 Drawings from the pyramid temple of King Ahmose at Abydos.
(a) Head of an Asiatic enemy (?), perhaps with shaved head. (b) Head of a
bearded Asiatic enemy, and arm of an Asiatic with long fringed garment holding
a sword. (c) Limestone relief showing overlapping horse teams and chariots.
(d) Bridled chariot team at rest. (e) Painted limestone fragment depicting the
stern of a royal ship with an aftercastle in the form of a vulture. Drawings by
William Schenck. Courtesy of Stephen P. Harvey.

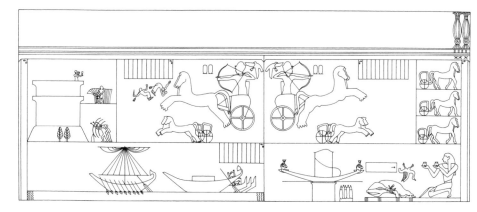

Figure 1.7 Tentative reconstruction of the battle reliefs of King Ahmose from his pyramid temple at Abydos. Drawing by Tamara Bower, after Stephen P. Harvey. Courtesy of Stephen P. Harvey.

the horse's mouth, an important point because, as previously observed, this system of control has been queried. All in all, these recently discovered scenes indicate the interweaving of chariotry and ships. The attack depicted must be at the Hyksos capital of Avaris, and I cannot but conclude that the final conquest of the East Delta was at the heart of the action. Whether or not one can reconstruct the original scene of Ahmose with an advance on water, carved below (Nile channel; flotilla) with land above (king in chariot), is another matter. It is sufficient to lay emphasis upon the key elements of the army: navy and chariotry with the foot archers taking a secondary role. As in the Middle Kingdom, the latter stand on the ground aiming their bows upward, undoubtedly at the Hyksos citadel.

The war scenes of Ahmose thus reflect the older system of Egyptian tactics with the use of the new mobility caused by chariots. Yet the physical location of Avaris must be taken into consideration. It was a city located close to a water channel or river. One could lay siege to it with the help of the royal flotilla, and this was accomplished by the Pharaoh. Chariot battles would have been of secondary importance. There was no large expanse of dry land in the environs sufficiently broad enough to allow for a great clash of two presumed horse-driven armies. True, the heroic figure of Ahmose in chariot can be assumed to have been an integral part of the depiction. But unless his opponent chose to meet him in battle on the field, the actual encounter would have been different. Indeed, the final capitulation of Avaris would have come about through a lengthy siege, which is, in fact, what the biography of Ahmose son of Ebana indicates.

Thus the traditional interpretation of Hyksos, horses, and chariotry has to be revised in light of these facts. Just as earlier at the end of the Middle Kingdom there was no lightening descent of a hoard of semi-nomadic horse warriors upon the inhabitants of the Nile Valley, so too were there no later counter-attacks by enraged natives wheeling their fast-moving vehicles on wide plains and penetrating the footsoldier divisions of a hated enemy. Quite to the contrary, the outgoing XVIIth Dynasty and the beginning XVIIIth witnessed a perpetuation of the older form of local warfare, buttressed, of course, by the chariot. Let us not forget that the wars against the Hyksos were a series of campaigns led by three successive kings of Egypt that became more and more successful. The eventual success of the Thebans took a long time, with eighteen or so years a reasonable estimation. This does not indicate a quick victory, indeed it may hide a few setbacks, none of which would be allowed, either in print or in picture, to stain the escutcheon of the royal house.

If we examine this last phase of internecine warfare in Egypt solely from the geographical perspective, I believe that the tactics of Ahmose can be ascertained. The biography of Ahmose son of Ebana, laconic though it may be, indicates that a siege of Avaris took place. The Hyksos capital was isolated. The remnants of the enemy could not secure aid from outside; nor could they use their own ships as a counter-measure against the Egyptians. Thereafter, the Pharaoh marched upon Sharuhen in Southern Palestine and laid siege to that city.[34] This time the enemy withstood the Egyptian army for three years.

A second soldier, Ahmose Pen-Nechbet, tells us that he fought in Djahy, a vague term for what has to be southern and central Palestine.[35] More useful is a later insertion written on the center of the verso of the famous Rhind Mathematical Papyrus.[36] Dated to the eleventh regnal year of an unknown Pharaoh, a series of brief diary entries inform us that Heliopolis (north of Memphis) was taken, and then Sile on the extreme eastern border of Egypt.[37] The last Hyksos king must have originally controlled both areas. In this case it is relatively easy to ascertain that: (1) the Egyptian fleet was involved; and (2) that around ninety days had occurred between the fall of Heliopolis and the capture of Sile. No mention is made of Avaris.

Can we assume that Avaris fell in the interim or, more likely, that this account was written in the north by a follower of the Hyksos, and that the enemy capital still remained in enemy hands? The second interpretation has the advantage of the record. (The importance of this city was so paramount that surely the insert should have referred to that fact.) Nowhere in this tiny report is there any evidence of the capture of Avaris. In fact, the account states that "One heard that Sile was entered," thereby implying that the writer received message of the capture. I feel that these words refer to the effective isolation of the Hyksos capital. In addition, Heliopolis had to be seized before the assault upon Avaris, especially because Kamose did not seize the Hyksos capital during his earlier march north.

Tactically, then, Kamose was able to cut the Hyksos capital off from any of its territories. But he could not force the issue to a successful conclusion.

Ahmose, on the other hand, first mopped up the surrounding Hyksos strongholds and then took Avaris. The report in the Rhind Mathematical Papyrus indicates that the land northeast of the Hyksos capital as well as that in the southwest was seized. After this, the final blow took place. Yet if the end of Avaris was the final result of a protracted war, and the chronology of Pharaoh Ahmose supports this contention, the advance to Sharuhen was a logical outcome. But in this case the Egyptian fleet could not be of much use. The only means of insuring its collapse had to be by investing it.

EXCURSUS

1. The social effects of the Egyptian military upon the state are frequently overlooked. This is in part due to prevailing research that has concentrated on the armaments, the historical texts as literature, or the prosopography of a specific time period. Owing to this, the social ramifications of the war machine have been overlooked, and key studies in the general field of warfare have been neglected. Stanislav Andreski's work, *Military Organization and Society*[2], Routledge and Kegan Paul, London (1968), is useful to employ when covering the rise of the new chariot division of the New Kingdom and its connection with social stratification. This work should be read with the volume of Andrea Maria Gnirs, *Militär und Gesellschaft. Ein Beitrag zur Sozialgeschichte des Neuen Reiches*, Heidelberger Orientverlag, Heidelberg (1996), a study that I will refer to frequently.

Andreski emphasizes the warriors as a privileged stratum during the Ramesside Period (Dynasties XIX–XX), and he correctly notes that this elite was balanced by other corporate elements as well – for example, the priestly class and the bureaucrats (whom he labels "literati"). In other words, even when the new social elite of the army had become significant, it was unable to secure control over the state. At first, this might appear surprising insofar as the history of New Kingdom Egypt appears to lead inexorably to a military domination of the society. This was the thesis of Wolfgang Helck in his epoch-making volume, *Der Einfluss der Militärführer in der 18. ägyptischen Dynastie*, J. C. Hinrichs, Leipzig (1939). Yet the role of Pharaoh as military commander did not predicate that he was solely, or even primarily, a warrior. Various other factors of kingship, such as the connection to the main god, Amun of Thebes, were crucial. At the same time, religious leaders as well as the scribal bureaucrats remained in the key positions in the Nile Valley, a conclusion that is easily seen from the numerous tombs of the officials. I feel that a too rigid separation of the military's role and function had led to this misunderstanding, one that, in fact, Andrea Gnirs refutes in her publication.

2. Various detailed studies concerning the New Kingdom military can be listed at this point. Alan Richard Schulman's *Military Rank, Title and Organization in the Egyptian New Kingdom*, Bruno Hassling, Berlin (1968),

was a useful attempt to grasp the data of Dynasties XVIII–XX in relation to the actual military protocols and arrangements of battalions, divisions, and the like. It was, however, subjected to a critical review by Jean Yoyotte and Jesús López in "L'organisation de l'armée et les titulaires de soldats au nouvel empire égyptien," *Bibliotheca Orientalis* 26 (1969), 3–19. The earlier work of Vsevolod Igorevitch Avdiev, *Military History of Ancient Egypt* II, Sovetskaya Nauka, Moscow (1959), is rarely consulted.

Subsequently, Ahmed Kadry, *Officers and Officials in the New Kingdom*, Kédült az ELTE skoszorosítóüzemében, Budapest (1982), retraced the procedures of Schulman, although he still remained within the older methodological bounds of Helck. For a helpful list of New Kingdom military men, see now P.-M. Chevereau, *Prosopographie des cadres militaires égyptiens du Nouvel Empire*, Antony (1994).

A general overview of the Egyptian army, particularly during the New Kingdom, can be found in "Sheik 'Ibada al-Nubi, "Soldiers," in Sergio Donadoni, ed., *The Egyptians*, trs. Robert Bianchi et al., University of Chicago Press, Chicago–London (1997), 151–84. Three additional general surveys worth noting are: Ian Shaw, *Egyptian Warfare and Weapons*, Shire Publications, Haverfordwest (1991), with his later work "Battle in Ancient Egypt: The Triumph of Horus or the Cutting Edge of the Temple Economy?," in Alan B. Lloyd, ed., *Battle in Antiquity*, Duckworth, London (1996), 239–69; and Andrea Gnirs, *Ancient Egypt*, in Kurt Raaflaub and Nathan Rosenstein, eds., *War and Society in the Ancient and Medieval Worlds*, Harvard University Press, Cambridge, MA–London (1999), 71–104.

For a more detailed exposition, I can refer to Robert B. Partridge, *Fighting Pharaohs. Weapons and Warfare in Ancient Egypt*, Peartree Publishing, Manchester (2002). This is a valuable survey of the art of war from the Predynastic Period up to the end of the New Kingdom. Unfortunately, while useful with regard to the technical aspects of weapons and other physical attributes of soldiers, the problems of tactics, strategy, logistics, and history needed to be expanded.

3. Much of the background to this chapter relies upon the work of Oleg Berlev, "The Egyptian Navy in the Middle Kingdom," *Palestinskij Sbornik* 80 (1967), 6–20 (in Russian). This article, referred to in note 4, was the first to come to grips with the often-expressed position among scholars that Egypt in the Middle Kingdom had no standing army. His conclusions regarding the importance of the navy in Dynasties XI–beginning XVIII cannot be ignored. Moreover, Berlev specifically oriented himself to the hierarchy of the army at this time and so was able to reconstruct the social set-up of the early war machine of Pharaonic Egypt. His conclusions, with those of Gnirs' major work cited in this excursus, allow one to reconstruct the various social and political transformations of the Egyptian military in the New Kingdom. It remains unfortunate that the research of Berlev has been ignored by later scholars, especially as he was able to understand the ramifications of the military elite within Pharaonic Egypt. The organization of the army during the Middle Kingdom, and its exact subdivisions (companies or divisions),

undoubtedly was the basis for the New Kingdom (or even the late Second Intermediate Period) system. The exact number of men per division at this earlier time, however, remains unknown.

Hitherto overdependence upon major inscriptions at the time of the outgoing XVIIth Dynasty and the newly established XVIIIth (e.g., the Kamose Stelae and the biography of Ahmose son of Ebana) often have led to a false emphasis being placed upon texts and inscriptions of a purely military nature. Berlev's detailed work has laid the basis for a new synthesis of the rich material of the Second Intermediate Period, a work that is now complemented by K. S. B. Ryholt, *The Political Situation in Egypt during the Second Intermediate Period, c. 1800–1550 BC*, Museum Tusculanum Press, Copenhagen (1997). Thanks to these two scholars we are now able to perceive more clearly the military aspects of the native rulers and the key social groupings of Dynasties XIII and XVII.

For a general analysis of the role, function, and social status of certain high military men, during the Second Intermediate Period, see Bettina Schmitz, *Untersuchungen zum Titel S3-njśwt "Königssohn"*, Rudolf Halbert, Bonn (1976).

NOTES

1 H. S. Smith and Alexandrina Smith, "A Reconsideration of the Kamose Texts," *Zeitschrift für ägyptische Sprache und Altertumskunde* 103 (1976), 48–76. This article is the best study of the inscriptions. The authors connect the two stelae of the king with the military and political situation at Buhen, the key fort located at the Second Cataract. The work of K. S. B. Ryholt, *The Political Situation in Egypt during the Second Intermediate Period, c. 1800–1550 BC*, Museum Tusculanum Press, Copenhagen (1997), 171–4, has added much to their analysis. His detailed survey of the military organization of Dynasty XVII – garrisons in key cities, warriors, the martial outlook of the kings and their sons – is extremely important. The earlier series of essays in Eliezer D. Oren, ed., *The Hyksos: New Historical and Archaeological Perspectives*, University Museum, Philadelphia (1997), provide an important background to the military situation at this time, but Ryholt's discussion of the Hyksos and Dynasty XVII remains crucial.

2 This fact was first pointed out by Alan Gardiner, "The Defeat of the Hyksos by Kamose: The Carnarvon Tablet No. I.," *Journal of Egyptian Archaeology* 3 (1916), 95–110. Later, "year three" was added: Donald B. Redford, *History and Chronology of the Eighteenth Dynasty of Egypt: Seven Studies*, University of Toronto Press, Toronto (1967), 40 and note 60.

3 This setting is often assumed to reflect the literary topos of the "King's Novel" (*Königsnovelle*), and in this case the emphasis is upon the deeds of the Pharaoh. According to Antonio Loprieno, such narratives focus upon the human characteristics of the monarch because he was the pivot between the political-social reality of Pharaonic Egypt and the mythical-literary one: "The 'King's Novel',"

in Antonio Loprieno, ed., *Ancient Egyptian Literature. History and Forms*, Brill, Leiden, New York and Cologne (1996), 277–95.

Earlier, Aadrian de Buck discussed the military setting of Thutmose III at the Battle of Megiddo in *Het typische en het individuelle bij de Egyptenaren*, Boek- en Steendrukkerji Eduardo Ijdo, Leiden (1929), and the orientation of his work was expanded considerably by Alfred Hermann, *Die ägyptische Königsnovelle*, J. J. Augustin, Glückstadt, Hamburg and New York (1938). It is sufficient to note the two parameters of military setting and war conference. With Kamose, and earlier under his father Seqenenre II, the decisions were in the court. (See Hans Goedicke, *The Quarrel of Apophis and Seqenenre'*, Van Siclen Books, San Antonio [1986], for a reevaluation of the latter account. I follow the analysis of Edward F. Wente, in William K. Simpson, ed., *Ancient Egyptian Literature*², Yale University Press, New Haven and London [1973], 77–80.) A study of this literary account and its relation to the more sober historical data is presented by Donald B. Redford in "The Hyksos Invasion in History and Tradition," *Orientalia* 39 (1979), 1–51.

De Buck covered the aspect of Egyptian art in connection with these literary settings. His position was that the Egyptians consistently depicted types or ideas rather than personalities or events, a conclusion with which we cannot entirely agree. Note the remarks of the Dutch historian Johan Huizinga, who followed De Buck: "Renaissance and Realism," in his *Men and Ideas. History, the Middle Ages, the Renaissance*, Eyre and Spottiswoode, London (1960), 290.

From Dynasty XVIII onward the Egyptians developed various narratives of their Pharaohs' wars. These accounts were often of a high literary form. See chapter XI of my *The Transformation of an Ancient Egyptian Narrative: P. Sallier III and the Battle of Kadesh*, Otto Harrassowitz, Wiesbaden (2002).

4   I am dependent upon the seminal article of Oleg Berlev, "The Egyptian Navy in the Middle Kingdom," *Palestinskij Sbornik* 80 (1967), 6–20 (in Russian). His later study, "Les prétendus 'citadins' au Moyen Empire," *Revue d'Égyptologie* 23 (1971), 23–47, is not a translation of the earlier Russian one.

P.-M. Chevereau in "Contribution à la prosopographie des cadres militaires du Moyen Empire," *Revue d'Égyptologie* 42 (1991), 43–88, and in "Contribution à la prosopographie des cadres militaires du Moyen Empire B. Titres Nautiques," *Revue d'Égyptologie* 43 (1992), 11–24, presents an extremely useful outline of the military men from Dynasties XI–XVII.

See as well, Peter Lacovara's study "Egypt and Nubia during the Second Intermediate Period," in Oren, ed., *The Hyksos: New Historical and Archaeological Perspectives*, 69–83.

5   An excellent translation of the text is by Miriam Lichtheim, *Ancient Egyptian Literature* II, University of California Press, Berkeley, Los Angeles and London (1976), 12–15.

6   See Berlev's two studies cited earlier in note 4. Schulman, *Military Rank, Title and Organization in the Egyptian New Kingdom*, Bruno Hassling, Berlin (1964), 19–20, covers the ship contingents during Dynasties XVIII–XX. The example of P. Butler 534 (P. British Museum 10333) used by him (pp. 27–8 and no. 120; see now Kitchen, *Ramesside Inscriptions* VII, Oxford, Blackwell [1989], 13–15) is important. In this account the first column enumerates the religious

contributes of at least one military company (*sa*) associated with a ship; see as well Jean-Yoyotte and Jésus López, *Bibliotheca Orientalis* 26 (1969), 6.

7   This will be indicated in more detail later when we consider that no Asiatic wars are known to have taken place under Amunhotep I. Berlev argued very strongly for this interpretation.

Donald B. Redford, "A Gate Inscription from Karnak and Egyptian Involvement in Western Asia during the Early 18th Dynasty," *Journal of the American Oriental Society* 99 (1979), 270–87, published some key early Dynasty XVIII fragments that refer to Asia. They can be dated better to Thutmose I than to Amunhotep I.

8   In general, see the overview of Robert B. Partridge, *Fighting Pharaohs. Weapons and Warfare in Ancient Egypt*, Peartree Publishing, Manchester (2002), chapter 2. This book replaces the compendium of Yigael Yadin, *The Art of Warfare in Biblical Lands* I, McGraw-Hill, New York, Toronto and London (1963).

For the social changes that were occurring in the New Kingdom up to the middle of Dynasty XVIII we now have at our disposal the volume of Andrea Maria Gnirs, *Militär und Gesellschaft. Ein Beitrag zur Sozialgeschichte des Neuen Reiches*, Heidelberger Orientverlag, Heidelberg (1996).

9   Gnirs, *Militär und Gesellschaft*, chapter 1.

10 This is not to deny that there were Nubians (the Medjay in particular) in the pay of the Dynasty XVII (and earlier). See most recently, Stephen Quirke, *The Administration of Egypt in the Late Middle Kingdom*, Sia Publishing, New Malden (1990), 21–2 (referring to a contingent of these men under Kamose, the predecessor of Ahmose, the founder of Dynasty XVIII). Quirke also discusses the Late Middle Kingdom titles and duties on the Egyptian military on pages 81–4 of the same work. He points out that "all officials in the lower sector of the lists [of the court at Thebes during early Dynasty XIII] belonged to the military sector" (p. 81).

11 The key theoretical works concerning these men are: S. E. Finer, *The Man on Horseback*, Frederick A. Praeger, New York (1962), especially chapters 2, 7, and 9; Stanislav Andreski, *Military Organization and Society*[2], Routledge and Kegan Paul, London (1968), 34–7, 42, 84–6, with chapter XI; and John Keegan, *The Mask of Command. A Study in Generalship*, Pimlico, London (1999), 5, 125, and 312–14.

12 For these peoples and others covered in this paragraph see our later discussion in chapters 13–16.

13 Finer's remarks in his *The Man on Horseback* are pertinent here.

14 In general, see M. A. Littauer and J. H. Crouwel, *Wheeled Vehicles and Ridden Animals in the Ancient Near East*, E. J. Brill, Leiden and Cologne (1979); Anja Herold, *Streitwagentechnologie in der Ramses-Stadt. Bronze an Pferd und Wagen*, Philipp von Zabern, Mainz (1999); and Joachim Boessneck and Angela von den Driesch, *Tell el-Dab'a VII*, Österreichische Akademie der Wissenschaften, Vienna (1992). Concerning the physical condition of chariots, see J. Spruytte, *Early Harness Systems. Experimental Studies*, J. A. Allen, London (1983); and Littauer and Crouwel, *Chariots and Related Equipment from the Tomb of Tut'ankhamun*, Griffith Institute, Oxford (1985).

15 To the sources listed in the last note add Louis Chaix, "An Hyksos Horse from Tell Heboua (Sinai, Egypt)," in M. Mashkour et al., *Archaeology of the Near*

East IV B. Proceedings of the fourth international symposium on the archaeozoology of southwestern Asia and adjacent areas, ARC-Publicatie 32, Groningen (2000), 177–86; Angela von den Driesch and Joris Peters, "Frühe Pferde- und Maultierskelette aus Avaris (Tell el-Dabʻa), östlisches Nildelta," *Ägypten und Levante* 11 (2001), 301–11; and Louis Chaix and Brigette Gratien, "Un cheval du Nouvel Empire à Saï (Soudan)," *Archéologie du Nile Moyen* 9 (2002), 53–64.

  The Buhen Horse was anatomically described by Juliet Clutton-Brock, "The Buhen Horse," *Journal of Archaeological Science* 1 (1974), 89–100.

16 I am following the research of Catherine Rommelaere, *Les chevaux du Nouvel Empire égyptien. Origines, races, harnachement,* Connaissance de l'Égypte ancienne, Brussels (1991), and "La morphologie des chevaux dans l'iconographie égyptienne," in L. Bodson, ed., *Le cheval et les autres équidés: aspects de l'historie de leur insertion dans les activités humaines, Colloques d'histoire des connaissances zoologiques* 6 (1995), 47–79.

17 See the article of Louix Chaix referred to in note 15 above.

18 Mary Aiken Littauer, "Slit nostrils of equids," *Zeitschrift für Säugetiere* 34 (1969), 183–6. Subsequently, Littauer and Crouwel, "The Earliest Evidence for Metal Bridal Bits," *Oxford Journal of Archaeology* 20 (2001), 333, noted the first depiction of metal bits in the reliefs of Ahmose from Abydos: see Harvey's studies referred in note 25 below.

19 The classical treatment of the horse's use as a mount is ably summarized by John Keegan, *A History of Warfare,* Vintage Books, New York (1993), 177–8.

20 See the key references in notes 14–15 above.

21 Lynn White, Jr., *Medieval Technology and Social Change,* Clarendon Press, Oxford (1962), 23–4, 27.

22 Ricardo A. Caminos, *Late-Egyptian Miscellanies,* Oxford University Press, London (1954), 201, 446. One tantalizing passage in that text refers to the provisioning of the ports for Pharaoh; see our comments in the following chapters.

23 *A History of Warfare,* 156–69. David W. Anthony has elaborated on these matters in a series of important articles, among which we may cite: "The 'Kurgan Culture,' Indo-European Origins and the Domestication of the Horse: A Reconsideration," *Current Anthropology* 27 (1986), 291–313, (with Dorcas R. Brown), "The origins of horseback riding," *Antiquity* 65 (1991), 22–38, (with Nikolai B. Vinogradov), "Birth of the Chariot," *Archaeology* 48.2 (1995), 36–41, and "The Earliest Horseback Riders and Indo-European Origins: New Evidence From the Steppes," in Bernhard Hänsel and Satefan Zimmer, eds., *Das Indogermanen und das Pferd,* Archaeolingua, Budapest (1994), 185–95.

24 *Medieval Technology and Social Change,* 59–60.

25 To the studies of Littauer-Crouwel and Herold referred to in note 14, add the significant work of Stephen P. Harvey, *The Cults of King Ahmose at Abydos,* University of Pennsylvania Dissertation, Philadelphia (1998), 303–72. Note as well W. Raymond Johnson, *An Asiatic Battle Scene of Tutankhamun from Thebes: A Late Amarna Antecedent of the Ramesside Battle-Narrative Tradition,* University of Chicago Dissertation, Chicago (1992).

  The last study of Harvey may be read with the tentative remarks from him: "Monuments of Ahmose," *Egyptian Archaeology* 4 (1994), 3–5, with "New

Evidence at Abydos for Ahmose's Funerary Cult," *Egyptian Archaeology* 24 (2004), 3–6; and Janine Bourriau, "The Second Intermediate Period (c 1650–1550 BC)," in Ian Shaw, ed., *The Oxford History of Egypt*, Oxford University Press, Oxford (2000), 213, figure on p. 213. The center top fragment has been inverted, as Stephen Harvey has gratefully indicated to me.

26   *A History of Warfare*, 176. See now Richard Beal, *The Organisation of the Hittite Military*, C. Winter, Heidelberg (1992), 148–52. There is now a more detailed study of mine, "The Battle of Kadesh: The Chariot Frieze at Abydos," *Ägypten und Levante* 13 (2003), 163–99.

27   In general, see Yadin, *The Art of Warfare* I, 7–8 and Partridge, *Fighting Pharaohs*, 42–4.

28   Yadin, *The Art of Warfare* I, 9, 164–5; and Partridge, *Fighting Pharaohs*, 45.

29   Yadin, *The Art of Warfare* I, 10–11 (with a stress upon its lack as a decisive weapon), 172–3; and Partridge, *Fighting Pharaohs*, 50–1.

30   This is the main argument of Littauer-Crouwel, 91–2. I have responded to this in the study referred to in note 26.

31   Johnson, *An Asiatic Battle Scene of Tutankhamun from Thebes*, 59, referring to Schulman, "The Egyptian Chariotry: a Reexamination," *Journal of the American Research Center in Egypt* 2 (1963), 88–9.

I still feel that the use of reins tied behind the back by the chariot driver would have led to major problems. Instead, can we propose that chariot attacks, outside of surprises such as happened under Ramesses II at Kadesh in Dynasty XIX (see chapter 13), were more of a "set piece" in which the two opposing chariot divisions were permitted to attack each other? If so, each would have avoided the almost suicidal results of such a measure. This speculation is not too far-fetched insofar as other epochs of human history have allowed their elite warriors a high degree of formal, or "ludic," behavior in war.

32   The problem that faces us when interpreting Egyptian pictorial evidence is a simple one. Namely, how far can we trust the evidence? People and objects (chariots in particular) can be represented moving to the left or to the right. It is well known that the direction to the right is the key one. For this problem, see Gay Robins, *Proportion and Style in Ancient Egyptian Art*, University of Texas Press, Austin (1994), 16–21.

The following two studies present detailed commentaries concerned with the New Kingdom war reliefs: Susanna Constanze Heinz, *Die Feldzugsdarstellungen des Neuen Reiches*, Österreichische Akademie der Wissenschaften, Vienna (2001); and Marcus Müller, *Der König als Feldherr. Schlachtenreliefs, Kriegsberichte und Kriegsführung im Mittleren und Neuen Reich*. Tübingen Dissertation, Tübingen (2001).

By and large, we can trust those war scenes in which the Egyptians are advancing to the right. For example, some depictions reveals two quivers, one on the left and one on the right, as well as a third, placed on the back of the Pharaoh. Others have only one located on the side of the cab. Although we should not over interpret this pictorial evidence, it is equally unwise to discount the differences automatically.

Johnson, *An Asiatic Battle Scene of Tutankhamun from Thebes*, 59, discusses the archer or spearbearer "who often has the reigns of the chariot horses tied around his waist and is the driver as well."

33 I refer the reader to the dissertation of Stephen Harvey cited in note 25.

34 I follow the interpretation of Nadav Na'aman, "The Shihor of Egypt and Shur that is Before Egypt," *Tel Aviv* 7 (1980), 95–109, but see his earlier remarks in "The Brook of Egypt and Assyrian Policy on the Border of Egypt," *Tel Aviv* 6 (1979), 68–90. Anson F. Rainey, "Sharhân/Sharuhen – The Problem of Identification," *Eretz-Israel* 24 (1993), 178*–87*, now proposes Tell Abû Hureirah.

That latest detailed analysis is that of Eliezer D. Oren, "The 'Kingdom of Sharuhen' and the Hyksos Kingdom," in Oren, ed., *The Hyksos: New Historical and Archaeological Perspectives*, 253–83. The study is important, but I question whether there was a "state" (of Sharuhen) in this area.

It appears probable that Sharuhen cannot be equated with modern Tell el-'Ajjul, directly south of Gaza. Whether Sharuhen is to be identified with Tel Gamma or Tel Haror in Southern Palestine is another matter. See also Patrick E. McGovern, *The Foreign Relations of the "Hyksos,"* Archaeopress, Oxford (2000), 73.

35 A translation of this biography will be found in James Henry Breasted, *Ancient Records of Egypt II*, University of Chicago Press, Chicago (1906), 10.

36 Ryholt, *The Political Situation in Egypt during the Second Intermediate Period*, 186–8. I assume that the "year eleven" refers to the last Hyksos ruler.

37 For the site of Sile, see most recently Mohamed Abd el-Maksoud, "Tjarou, porte de l'Orient," in Dominique Valbelle and Charles Bonnet, *Le Sinaï durant l'antiquité et le Moyen Âge. 4000 ans d'histoire pour un désert*, Editions Errance, Paris (1998), 61–5.

31

2

THE SYSTEM OF EARLY
DYNASTY XVIII:
TECHNOLOGICAL AND
PHYSICAL CONSTRAINTS

A new means of tactics had now come into being, one dependent upon the lack of any major river, and the effectiveness of the chariots would become increasingly important against Egypt's Asiatic opponents. But one cannot attack fortresses by chariots alone. They are actually quite useless for siege warfare or even protracted resistance by an enemy city lasting over a few weeks. Starvation, of course, is the key element, but this could only take place when the Egyptians had control of the surrounding territory, when they feared no external support sent by a neighboring city or kingdom, and when they could quarter their troops for a lengthy period of time. The latter required the requisitioning of food, tents, and other war material, and an open road for communication to a supply base. This could be attempted with Sharuhen as the Egyptians were not far from the Delta. Then too, there were no major states, kingdoms, or large territories in Palestine. Quite to the contrary, that land was peppered with small city-states, the well-fortified capital of each located on a hill or mound.

Distance, as well, began to play a key role with regard to the speed of the Egyptian armies. As a comparison, let us examine first the situation within the Nile Valley.[1] When Herodotus visited Egypt it took four days to travel from Thebes to Elephantine. The distance is 220.6 km. Therefore a ship at that time (ca. 450 BC) would travel approximately 55 km/day. In contrast, it took 26.6 km/day to march rapidly on foot. The difference is about 50 percent, a very high figure, but we must take into consideration that this information derives from the Greek historian's account of travel south into Napata (modern-day Sudan), a very inhospitable region that demanded ample water supplies.

With armies, all depends upon how large is the number of troops, how many divisions are they divided into, how good is the leadership, and how many supplies are brought in the trains that followed the soldiers. As a case in point, it took Alexander the Great seven days to traverse the distance between Pelusium in the northeast Delta and Gaza, whereas only five were necessary for Ptolemy IV who left Pelusium and arrived in the vicinity of Raphia, not too far from Gaza.[2] The emperor Vespasian spent merely five days traveling from Pelusium to Gaza. The later *Itinerarium Antonini* states that the Gaza to Pelusium distance was 134 *milia passuum* or ca. 201 km. This comes out to around 20 km traveled per day, and 10 days elapsed at a normal rate.

Pharaonic data help us to refine these figures.[3] From Qantir in the West Delta (adjacent to Avaris) to Thebes a messenger could travel by ship in 24 days, although 21 days is also reported. In early Dynasty XXVI the more leisurely Nile voyage of Nitocris, the Pharaoh's daughter, lasted 17 days from the north to Thebes, and we can assume that Memphis was the embarkation point. The result is 55 km/day. For the Assyrians under Assurbanipal the voyage lasted one (lunar) month, although in this case it is unclear if they went by Nile or by land. The following situation presents more useful information. From Heliopolis to Thebes one record gives 9 days or 80 km/day. In summation, and taking into consideration the effect of the regular north wind and night stops, as well as the condition of the ships, it is reasonable to conclude that an unhindered Nile voyage between Avaris and Thebes would last about 21 days. Let us keep in mind that some of these accounts imply stops of a day here and there. And, as a late account dated to 475 BC records, from the end of December to the middle of February no ships docked at Elephantine.[4] The lengthy sailing season thus encompassed about ten Egyptian months. Nonetheless, the situation is clear. Travel by ship on the Nile in Egypt was rapid.

On land such was not the case. Already we have seen from Herodotus' account that the voyage south of Elephantine lasted more than twice as long as that on the river. What was the time it took for the Egyptians to march in Palestine and Syria? One source (time of Thutmose III) allows us to calculate an unimpeded advance of the Egyptian army at about 20 km/day.[5] Interestingly, Machiavelli points out that an army ordinarily marched 32 km/day, but when advance scouts, ditch-diggers, and pioneers precede the soldiers, then the pace is halved.[6] Here we must take into account the difficulties of moving a large number of men and supply trains and the necessity of relaxation and sleep. Evidence from the army of Alexander the Great provides some helpful facts as it allows us to estimate a maximum of 31.4 km/day, with around 21 km/day as the norm.[7] At first sight the latter figure seems to be identical to that of Thutmose III's account. But the armies were quite different. The expected carrying weight of the soldier had increased by the time of Alexander, the physical capabilities of the men were different (the height of a man had increased, as did his legs), far more horses were present, and the baggage trains were better run and the horses stronger. Considering all of these imponderables, we would not be far off the mark by concluding that an ordinary march by the Egyptian army in Dynasties XVIII–XX would take about 16 to 24 km/day maximum. The roads, after all, were not paved, being pebble-based in parts at best.

The contrast between Nile travel and land travel was therefore the major inhibiting factor for the Egyptian army. Chariots played no role unless isolated cases of messengers or a few squads were involved. Armies marched by foot. But the situation of supplies was of paramount importance. How could an army march to a destination, if not a battlefield, without its war equipment and food? These encumbrances delayed the advance, unless there were supply depots in friendly cities available for the trip. Such were not the case at the beginning of Dynasty XVIII. For this reason alone, we can see why a deep strike into Palestine did not occur immediately after the fall of Sharuhen. In fact, it was not until the reign of Thutmose I that the Egyptians moved forward in a large and successful manner. Their eyes were instead cast southwards.

The situation of provisioning likewise arises. With some degree of accuracy we can provide statistical data of value to the lengthy campaigns of the Pharaohs with respect to these costs.[8] First and foremost, the Egyptians brought their horses. These animals had to travel with a good average pace, and their walk is about 6.4 km/hour. The actual mileage varies with the unit load carried, of course, and mounted infantry would cover 8–9.7 km/hour including halts. These facts must be altered somewhat owing to the type of horse that the Egyptians had, and we would not be far off in concluding that a normal pace lasted somewhat longer. (Remember that if chariots were brought along, the horses or even accompanying oxen would drag them unless the vehicles were dismantled and placed on the animals.) Halts are always necessary to refresh the horses, and the early twentieth-century practice was to rest these animals for a few minutes every hour or so. We do not know if the Egyptians placed them in small units so as to avoid problems with dust on the roads. In order to avoid horses from fatiguing, especially those located either in the middle of a long column or especially at the end, short distances between squadrons is the policy. This is a common problem on hot days. But watering and feeding are crucial. Every two or three hours are necessary. I assume that the Egyptians gave water to the equids by means of shallow vessels so long as their bridles were removed, or that they would depend upon wells (as in the Sinai) or streams.[9]

With regard to the provisioning of soldiers, it may not be out of place to indicate that the ancient Romans avoided wine and used vinegar. Nor did they provide baked bread. Instead, they supplied the soldiers with flour and let each man use his lard or fat for whatever purpose. Barley, naturally, was reserved for the horses. Machiavelli also points out that the Romans ordinarily had herds of animals that followed the army, but in the Egyptian case we can assume that the locals supplied the meat, milk, and cheese, or that foods were taken from the fields near to a town or city.

Creating delays or at least slowing up the advance were the transport animals. Here again, the Egyptian sources are completely laconic. From the war scenes of the Battle of Kadesh under Ramesses II (Dynasty XIX) we see that the enemy Hittites used special wagons to transport their supplies and war material, and that they were very heavy.[10] In later times, mules and ponies were employed as pack animals and the weight was distributed evenly on both sides of the animal.[11] The loads were set over the tops of the ribs and never touched the animal's body. Mules, however, have very peculiar attitudes concerning water, being very particular in choosing the right type. They may drink as much as a horse of similar size, but normally they are not greedy and endure thirst well. The pace of these animals is between 4.8 and 6.4 km/hour, but those facts derive from modern sources. American mules are said to be able to "amble" or "jog" when required, and are known in the early twentieth century to have covered up to 161 km/day when carrying quite a heavy load (550 kilos). Donkeys, which are excellent pack animals, have a slow pace compared with the mule, and the load that they can bear is around 220 kilos. It is significant that ox carts, which we shall see were employed by the Hittites and other foreigners, can only achieve a distance of 3.2 km/hour, even though their bearing load is far greater than donkeys, mules, and horses. One additional disadvantage with these animals is that they can only work for a very short period of time, 5 instead of 8 hours/day. Therefore, we can conclude with a high degree of certainty that the Egyptians rarely employed oxen when the Pharaoh went out on a long campaign. Yet horses and donkeys may be seen in the Egyptian camp of Ramesses II at Kadesh, as well as oxen. (This is also true with regard to the camp of the enemy.)

The minimum food necessary per day works out as follows:[12]

Men:	6.6 kilos of grain or its equivalent.
	1.9 liters of water.
Horses/mules:	22 kilos of forage.
	30 liters of water.

For horses smaller than ours the amount would be somewhat less.

These figures provide the minimum amount needed on hot days, with grain as the major staple. But we must take into consideration the size of both men and animals. That both were small is an accepted fact. Moreover, it is necessary to consider the geographic setting. Palestine and Syria are considerably warmer than Europe and water supplies inland were not that plentiful.

Finally, there is the problem of diminishing supplies. Unless re-fed, the amount of food would logically decrease and the pack animals would inexorably end up carrying a considerably lighter weight, especially after 5 days or so. All depends upon the number of troops, horses, and supply animals, not including the men who were noncombatants. Indeed, it has been calculated that in actual practice, an ancient army of the Hellenistic Period could carry with it enough food rations for about 10 days.[13] This limiting factor allows us to see the necessity for the Egyptians to have supply posts within a reasonable number of days between the start of a journey and its end. No wonder that the royal inscriptions consistently refer to arrivals and departures from specific towns when recording in detail the northern campaigns. These localities gave the necessary sustenance to the troops and animals. And, I suspect, the Pharaonic army remained outside of the specific city in tents, simply because there was no room for the entire army and its support inside. Indeed, the horses and other animals could forage within sight of the city walls.

We do not know the number of troops that the Egyptian kings met on major campaigns. In the Battle of Kadesh under Ramesses II (Dynasty XIX) it is claimed that the enemy Hittites, already ensconced around the city, had at least 3,500 chariots.[14] Two divisions of elite *teher* warriors are listed as 18,000 and 19,000 men, thereby making 37,000 warriors. These conveniently round numbers are simply too high, and in fact there was no way that the Egyptians could have counted so many opponents. In the earlier battle of Megiddo under Thutmose III (mid Dynasty XVIII) the figures are more trustworthy. This is due to the fact that the account is based upon the official war records that were written up after the battle.[15] The booty included 340 captured enemy, 83 hands, 2,041 horses and 191 young ones, 6 stallions, an unknown number of colts, and 924 chariots. The last figure is the most useful to employ and we can assume that there were at least 1,848 enemy soldiers.

The discrepancy between the figures of chariots and horses is simple to resolve. Many of the animals had died, probably being shot by the Egyptians, and some may have escaped. The defeat was total, even though some of the chiefs managed to reach the security of Megiddo before being caught by the Pharaoh's army. Nonetheless, I feel that we can assume that Thutmose faced at least 2,000 opponents.[16] This figure may be augmented somewhat, but the totals of captured horses nearly fit the number of chariots, when we remember that there were two horses for the vehicle. Thutmose's own army was probably not too much greater, and even though this point will be reviewed in detail later, I do not think that we can assume that he arrived at Megiddo with more than 5,000 active troops.

This analysis is useful as a preliminary foray into the logistics of Egyptian warfare. But more can be said. Thutmose's trip from Sile on the extreme east of the Delta and Gaza took 10 days to cover 201 km.[17] This is why I assume an average march at about 20 km/day to be reasonable. The trip covered a most inhospitable region, one virtually devoid of forage. Water may be found, especially at the Qatia Oasis, and it is abundant enough to supply armies traveling up and down the road. For a man subsisting upon those minimal rations listed above, we must conclude that the army had to supply around 2,500 soldiers. Perhaps this figure can be reduced, but only if we assume that the Egyptians could depend upon additional troops stationed at Gaza and other towns on the way to Megiddo. For example, the king reached Yehem after 12 days' journey from Gaza. It too was friendly. For one day's travel we arrive at a figure of 16,500 kilos.[18] The carrying capacity of the support animals for the same time comes to 528 kilos. (The figure is derived from 550 minus 22 kilos.) This means about 31 pack animals were needed. Perhaps we should augment this last figure somewhat, but for the moment, I prefer to use the barest minimum of integers. For 2 days, however, the situation is more complex. The calculation results in 65 animals. For 10 days we end up with 500. Note that I am purposely excluding water for the animals.

The famous "Brook of Egypt," often referred to in later cuneiform texts, was the actual boundary of southeast Palestine.[19] It is located at Nahal Besor, and the Megiddo report of Thutmose III as well as the later Amarna Letters at the close of Dynasty XVIII indicate this was the beginning of "Asia," properly speaking. One commenced the journey at Sile at the end of the East Delta and passed through Raphia on the way to Gaza, which lay close by. The first city of Asia was therefore Gaza. The site of Yurza (Tel Gamma), mentioned by Thutmose III when he describes the revolt of the Asiatics, is probably to be equated with Arza, well known from later Neo-Assyrian accounts.[20]

From sources dated to Dynasty XIX one can ascertain the numerous places that were situated between Sile and Raphia, the latter just preceding Gaza in southern Palestine. Strongholds and Migdols (fortified "castles") are mentioned in the war reliefs of Seti I.[21] Mentioned as well are various wells, of primary importance, in addition to some newly built towns. A few of these localities are also covered in the satirical tract of P. Anastasi I, dated to Ramesses II.[22] From both of these later sources it would appear that the road leading from the northeast of the Delta and ending at Raphia–Gaza was well provided with stops and resting places in order to enable any advancing army the possibility of refreshing its men and animals. Moreover, this crucial artery was fully organized so that all and sundry could pass along it with the least amount of trouble. I cannot believe that it was very different in the time of Thutmose III because this route was of such importance that it had to be well regulated and provided with fully equipped stations. Considering the numerous campaigns of this Pharaoh and those preceding him, we may very well conclude that the Sile–Gaza road was very early reorganized to allow the transport of necessary war material and people to the north.

We can now add the water situation. Some was needed if there were a large number of soldiers. Let us use English measures. For one day there is 2,500 (men) × 2 quarts imperial × 10 pounds or 12,500 pounds.[23] This integer is to be divided by 240 pounds. The result is 52. For 10 days we arrive at 833 animals. Again, keep in mind that I have not brought into the calculations the water supply for the animals. The result of these tentative calculations indicates that the Egyptian army would need 1,333 support animals. If by chance they marched in single file, given 4.6 meters per animal, the result is 6.1 km. But this figure of Donald Engels is actually dependent upon camels marching single file.[24] For New Kingdom horses we can reduce the number to around 2.76 meters or so. The army's train would have been still large: 3.7 km. If the animals traveled ten abreast the result is .37 km, although this seems too excessive. The road in the Sinai was not very broad. I assume that, at best, the animals did not march Indian style.

Each of the working animals needs about 8 imperial gallons per day. Because 1 gallon = 22 kilos, this means that the pack train required 176 kilos/animal as well. Adding this figure to the equations we arrive at 2,500 men or 32 animals for one day. For 10 days we have 3,000 support animals. By now we have reached the end of the arithmetic. It is self-evident that an Egyptian army crossing the northernmost portion of the Sinai would either have to have located water sources, and there were enough, or else it was not assembled in full force when Thutmose III left Sile. Fortunately, we know that there were oases on this route. But even if we wish to reduce the number of Egyptian troops present at the Battle of Megiddo, it appears reasonable to dismiss the possibility that all of Thutmose III's army was ready and prepared for war solely within Egypt.

Of course, the men could carry their own food supplies as well as water skins. But the latter are not useful for even a day's journey through the Sinai where game is virtually nonexistent. At the minimum, I feel that some food provisions had to be brought in a baggage train at the end of the column or columns. In Palestine and Syria, however, so long as the troops could march from one locality to another in a single day, these problems did not exist. Indeed, the animals, especially the horses, could eat the grass in the valleys or in the vicinity of a city. Delays would have resulted if the army stopped for a couple of hours between cities or towns, and it was always necessary to halt near a water supply. Thutmose III, for example, moved from the exit of the Aruna Pass in central Palestine to the Qina Brook partly because of the need to provision his animals but also to insure that both man and beast had fresh water. But if the army needed to reach a strategic point within a certain time, any delay would have been costly. The march through the Aruna Pass would have been very difficult if all and sundry were not refreshed. That is why I believe it reasonable to conclude that Thutmose's army must have carried some supplies.

This provisioning was hazardous. If the Egyptian army entered hostile territory, it could not necessarily expect to obtain fresh water and fodder unless the region was devoid of enemy troops. If a city opposed the Egyptian advance, it would have to be besieged. In other cases the fields surrounding it would have to be confiscated, at least temporarily, so that the army would not become exhausted. Noteworthy are the frequent remarks concerning the exploitation of these food-bearing areas, especially in Syria where the king met stiff resistance. And if the enemy decided to contest the field, then a battle resulted. With control of these cities and towns the Pharaohs were able to diminish the food and water situation to a great extent.

Later on I will discuss the same situation but with more detailed arithmetical analyses. For the moment, however, these tentative calculations should put us on our guard, and enable us to become aware of the complex nature of the problem. The first approach is the most reasonable one: do not trust the numbers of dead enemy, captured soldiers, and booty (chariots and horses in particular) unless the account appears logically reasonable. By this I mean that the figures given in a text should neither be too large nor assumed to be automatically valid. We have to consider the society during this era and the terrain, as well as the length of the journey undertaken. Furthermore, it will be necessary to insure that the report has some claim to veracity. Thutmose III's Megiddo campaign has come down to us from one reliable source, although there are subsidiary ones that enable us to reconstruct the events with some additional details. Fortunately, the king's official report to Amun is partly based upon the war diaries of the army, and the final booty list can also claim first-hand knowledge of the events. Owing to this, the time intervals of his northern advance as well as the number of chariots taken at Megiddo may be trusted. The total of enemy dead, on the other hand, is not reported, and as I have stated earlier, we can only estimate the size of the Egyptian army.

From this tentative groping in the dark some useful aspects of Egyptian military policy are revealed. Pharaohs embarking on a major campaign must have been well prepared. The monarch would have arranged his supply points, the towns and cities in Palestine, and Syria if necessary. He also would have set up these resting points so that they could supply his troops and animals with fodder and water. Horses and other quadrupeds were able to graze off the land, but soldiers could not. Men need different sustenance, and it was required that the cities insure this support. A supply train as well as the troops need not have been assembled as a unit at Sile or elsewhere in the Delta. Each city in Palestine had some Egyptian troops as well as the necessary supplies if not war material (horses and chariots). Gaza, for example, was a crucial staging-point for the Pharaoh's northern ventures, but there remains the strong possibility that a great marching army would have been slowly assembled. That is to say, the troops would have been sent north, and only after some time would the soldiers come together to form a massive unit. The other possibility is that the Egyptian army was not large by later standards in the ancient world, an interpretation that needs careful examination when we turn to the actual key battles.

EXCURSUS

1. The work of Donald W. Engels, *Alexander the Great and the Logistics of the Macedonian Army*, University of California Press, Berkeley, Los Angeles and London (1978), has the distinct advantage in that the author provides detailed references to the primary sources that concern the basic parameters of armies. He supplied the necessary references to sizes of animals, their food and water intake, the minimum calories needed per day, the lengths of columns, and similar parameters concerning soldiers. Comparative data for Egypt ca. 1910 may be found in Ministry of Education, Egypt, Department of Agriculture and Technical Education, *Text-Book of Egyptian Agriculture II*, National Printing Department, Cairo (1910).

The position that ca. 3,000 calories/day are necessary per human male is supported by A. Keene, "Nutrition and Economy," in Robert I. Gilbert, Jr., and James H. Mielke, eds., *The Analysis of Prehistoric Diets*, Academic Press, Orlando (1985), 171, 180-1, and 184. This study can be supplemented by Department of the Army, *Nutrition*, (= Technical Manual TM 8-501), Government Printing Office, Washington DC (1961), 21 (Table IV). Basing the age group of males at 25 years of age, this manual arrived at 3,000 calories/day for a weight of 69 kilos.

The height of such men would be, on the average, 180 cm (table XV, p. 65 in the same volume). The result corresponds to a desirable weight for a man living today who has medium frame (table V, p. 21). Naturally, the data are derived from recent United States standards, but it is useful to compare these figures with the only statistical worthwhile facts concerning the size and robustness of soldiers in ancient Egypt.

H. E. Winlock, in *The Slain Soldiers of Neb-Hepet-Re' Mentu-hotpe*, Metropolitan Museum of Art, New York (1945), published his discovery of about 60 soldiers found at the west of Thebes that were dated by him to the latter half of Dynasty XI. The heights of the men average to 169 cm, and they died at the approximate age interval of 30–40. According to the present situation, these facts suggest desirable weights ranging from 56.4 kilos (small frame) to 71 kilos (large frame). Yet the investigations of Winlock and his anatomical assistant Douglas Derry led to a remarkable conclusion. The men, undoubtedly slain in battle, showed a series of characteristics that were not present in the south of Egypt. This quandary was resolved by hypothesizing that the soldiers were possibly from the northern border territories of the southern Theban state. Subsequently, Hans Wolfgang Müller felt that they may have been Asiatics: *Der "Armreif" des Königs Ahmose und der Handgelenkschutz des Bogenschützen im alten Ägypten und Vorderasien*, Phillip Von Zabern, Mainz am Rhein (1989), 16–17. Were they an elite group of mercenaries or, as Müller felt, captives? The Egyptian names on the wrappings, however, fit perfectly into the known facts of this time.

Owing to the uncertainties it cannot be claimed with a high degree of certainty how large and how tall was the average male in the Egyptian army. These facts, therefore, are presented as a basis for future research.

40

2. Sizes of humans/columns have been discussed by many military officials and scholars. F. Maurice, "The Size of the Army of Xerxes," *Journal of Hellenic Studies* 50 (1930), 229 n. 42, deserves to be quoted: "A pre-war brigade of British Infantry 4000 strong occupied a distance of a little more than two miles of road space. The principal armament of the Persian army was spears. Men with spears would require a greater interval between sections of fours than men with rifles"; two miles = 3.2 km. He also states that "British experience on active service is that a horse requires an average of 8 gallons a day" (p. 221 n. 35); 8 (imperial gallons) = 36.368 liters.

3. Hans Delbrück has also supplied useful facts concerning the logistics of warfare throughout history. In his *Warfare in Antiquity* (*History of the Art of War*, vol. I), Walter J. Renfroe, Jr., trs., University of Nebraska Press, Lincoln–London (1990), 35, he notes that in marching order a pre World War I German army corps of 30,000 men covered "some 14 miles, without its supply train"; 14 miles = 22.4 km. On p. 90 he provides the useful facts that the German running pace was 1 m long whereas the French was 80 cm. Pages 84–5 further deal with the marching pace of an army on the road: the Prussian double-time rate was 165 to 175 m/minute and consequently 6 minutes/km. A further helpful point mentioned by him is that the interval between Roman legionaries, as between Greek hoplites, was greater than today, "in order to allow the free use of weapons" (p. 293). The breadth of a file was ca. 3 feet, whereas the width of a man at the shoulders is ca. 1.5 feet; 3 feet = .9144 m; 1.5 feet = .4572 m.

These parameters will be used in the subsequent discussion of the length of New Kingdom armies.

4. A useful inscription dated to the sixth regnal year of Seti I (early Dynasty XIX) describes an expedition of 1,000 men ("soldiers") being sent out to acquire sandstone for one of the king's building projects. See Kitchen, *Ramesside Inscriptions* I, Blackwell, Oxford (1975), 59–61, with *Ramesside Inscriptions, Translated and Annotated. Translated*, I, Blackwell, Oxford (1993), 51–2, and *Ramesside Inscriptions, Translated and Annotated. Notes and Comments* I, Blackwell, Oxford and Cambridge MA (1993), 56–7.

The account provides some useful details concerning the rations: 20 deben (1.82 kg) of bread; vegetables (in bundles); 1 piece of roast meat; and 2 sacks (the reading is somewhat unsure) of grain per month. Additional food items were included. The bulk of the daily ration was therefore composed of breads, and the caloric intake would have been about 4,175, as my student Mr. Brett Heagren informs me. The percentages work out to 73.3 bread, 4.2 fresh vegetables, and 22.5 meat. But these figures may have been set up with regard to an increased ration.

Moreover, the two sacks of grain/month have to be taken into consideration. In modern terminology we have 153.76 liters/30 or .1563 liters per day. By dividing by 1,000 we can see that this amount was rather small if we consider each man. Are we dealing with wages at this point rather than work rations? In addition, these calculations assume an equal distribution of foods; i.e., the officers' and supervisors' amounts are not differentiated from the ordinary workmen.

Dieter Mueller, "Some Remarks on Wage Rates in the Middle Kingdom," *Journal of Near Eastern Studies* 34 (1975), 249–63, covered this situation at an earlier time. Add Barry Kemp, "Large Middle Kingdom Granary Buildings (and the archaeology of administration)," *Zeitschrift für ägyptische Sprache* 113 (1986), 123–36. Mueller considered the connected problem of food-wages and rations. Kemp, as well, observed that working out bread rations is a tricky affair. He concluded that the daily rations based on evidence uncovered from the Middle Kingdom fortress of Uronarti at the Second Cataract (one hekat of wheat and two-thirds hekat of barley per every ten days) led to a surprising result. The caloric intake per man came to ca. 1,448/day, a figure considerably short of the expected 3,000 or so.

Kemp followed a 1917 report concerning modern Egyptian prison diets: 1,800 calories were necessary for subsistence, 2,200 for no work, 2,800 for light labor, and 3,200 for hard labor. This is one reason why I prefer to place a cap of calories/day for a marching soldier around 3,250. See note 12 to this chapter.

A further inscription of Ramesses II, the Manshiyet es-Sadr Stela, is somewhat helpful as well. Kitchen provides the text and commentary in his *Ramesside Inscriptions. Historical and Biographical* II, Blackwell, Oxford (1979), 360–2, with *Ramesside Inscriptions, Translated and Annotated. Notes and Comments* II, Blackwell, Oxford and Malden (1999), 216–8. See also Helck, *Wirtschaftsgeschichte des alten Ägypten im. 3. und 2. Jahrstausend vor Chr.*, Leiden and Cologne (1975), 231.

The reader will find Helck's volume, a summary of the scholar's abiding interest in economic matters, extremely helpful with regard to military provisioning. This work must be consulted with that of Jac. J. Janssen, *Commodity Prices from the Ramessid Period*, E. J. Brill, Leiden (1975), Part III.

Additional remarks will be found in excursus 2 to chapter 5.

5. A final note is necessary regarding fodder. As will be shown, a typical Egyptian campaign led by the Pharaoh was dependent upon free access to various cities and towns that the army encountered. Those loyal to him must have supplied food. For the animals in the army their feeding was of prime importance. There are essentially three different kinds of fodder: hard (a grain product such as barley and oats); green (crops grown on farms especially for animals – hay and straw are often further specified as dry fodder but other crops could also be used – clover, vetch, broad beans); and pasturage (grasses and vegetation consumed by the animal directly from the field).

Horses, donkeys, mules, and oxen ideally need a combination of hard and dry (or green) fodder. These animals can also subsist on pasturage, but they then have to consume double the regular amount. In addition, a pasturage diet usually must be supplemented by a small quantity of hard fodder. The camp scenes of Ramesses II at the Battle of Kadesh (Dynasty XIX) reveal donkeys being fed by what appears to be hard fodder, but the bulk of their intake was probably derived from pasturage.

The best figures for daily consumption (and a discussion of the animals' requirements) are those of J. Roth, *The Logistics of the Roman Army at War (264 BC–AD 235*, E. J. Brill, Boston and Leiden (1999), 62–7; see as well Engels, *Alexander the Great and the Logistics of the Macedonian Army*, 126–30 and 145.

NOTES

1 The study of travel during Pharaonic Egypt is still in its infancy. Nonetheless, there is an excellent brief analysis by William J. Murnane, *The Road to Kadesh. A Historical Interpretation of the Battle Reliefs of King Sety I at Karnak*, University of Chicago, Chicago (1985), 145–50. The following additional works may be cited: Frank J. Yurco, "Sennacherib's Third Campaign and the Coregency of Shabaka and Shebitku," *Serapis* 6 (1980), 227 (on Nile travel in Nubia); Ricardo A. Caminos, "The Nitocris Adoption Stela," *JEA* 50 (1964) 74 (travel from the north, probably from Memphis, to Thebes at the beginning of Dynasty XXVI); Irmagard Hein, *Die Ramessidische Bautätigkeit in Nubien*, Otto Harrassowitz (1991), 134 (reasonable travel times in Nubia); Louise Bradbury, "Reflections on Traveling to 'God's Land' and Punt in the Middle Kingdom," *Journal of the American Research Center in Egypt* 25 (1988), 127–31 (Red Sea travel); K. A. Kitchen, "Punt and How to Get There," *Orientalia* 40 (1971), 188–99 (more detailed information concerning the Red Sea voyages; add Pliny, *Natural History* VI xxvi, 101 for later information); Wolfgang Helck, *Wirtschaftsgeschichte des alten Ägypten im 3. und 2. Jahrtausend vor Chr.*, E. J. Brill, Leiden and Cologne (1975), 9; and the helpful overview of Rolf Krauss, "Reisegeschwingigkeit," in Eberhard Otto and Wolfgang Helck, eds., *Lexikon der Ägyptologie* V, Wiesbaden (1984), 222–3.

  Donald B. Redford, *The Wars in Syria and Palestine of Thutmose III*, Brill, Leiden-Boston (2003), 203–5, provides the most recent analysis of the Egyptian armies' rates of march at this time (Dynasty XVIII).

2 Jakob Seibert, *Untersuchungen zur Geschichte Ptolemaios' I.*, C. H. Beck, Munich (1969), 208–9. Eugene N. Borza, *Travel and Communications in Classical Times. A Guide to the Evidence*, Pennsylvania State University, University Park (1969), presents a basic list of the Classical data.

  Donald W. Engels, *Alexander the Great and the Logistics of the Macedonian Army*, University of California Press, Berkeley–Los Angeles–London (1978), chapter 1 and appendix 5, provides the reader with a wealth of primary sources concerning rate of travel, distance, food requirements for men and animals, and the like. To a large extent I will be using his data. See as well his mathematical study in appendix 1.

  Supplementary information may also be found in Eugene N. Borza, "Alexander's Communications," in *Archaic Macedonia II: Proceedings of the Second International Symposium on Ancient Macedonia at Thessalonica*, Thessalonica (1973), 295–303.

3 The data in this paragraph are taken from the sources cited in note 1.

4 Ada Yardeni, "Maritime Trade and Royal Accountancy in an Erased Customs Account from 475 BCE. on the Ahiqar Scroll from Elephantine," *Bulletin of the American Schools of Oriental Research* 293 (1994), 67–78 and pp. 69–70 in particular.

  For the expenses incurred in Nile travel, see Jac. J. Janssen, "The Cost of Nile Transport," *Bulletin de la Société Égyptologique de Genève* 18 (1994), 41–7. The wages for the sailors came, on the average, to 1/10 of the cargo.

5 R. O. Faulkner, "The Battle of Megiddo," *Journal of Egyptian Archaeology* 28 (1942), 2.

6 Niccolò Machiavelli, *The Art of War*, Christopher Lynch, trs., University of Chicago Press, Chicago and London (2003), 104 (Book V 42). It is interesting to read that scouts in the old American West preferred a good mule to a horse: General G. A. Custer, *My Life on the Plains or Personal Experiences with the Indians*, Folio Society, London (1968), 119. This was due to the ecology of the Plains where forage was virtually impossible. Hence, a good parallel can be drawn between that observation and parts of ancient Western Asia.

7 Engels' work cited in note 2 provides the necessary data. Some of the detailed studies on horses and other quadrupeds include: F. Smith, "The Maximum Muscular Effort of the Horse," *The Journal of Physiology* 19 (1896–6), 224–6, with his "Relation between the Weight of a Horse and its Weight-Carrying Power," *The Journal of Comparative Pathology and Therapeutics* 11 (1898), 287–90; General Staff, War Office, *Animal Management 1908*, London (1908), 89, 118–29, 136–7, 197–9, 272–5, 285–9, and 302–3; W. B. Tegetmeier, *Horses, Asses, Zebras, Mules and Mule-Breeding*, H. Cox, Washington, DC (1897), 129; Harvey Riley, *The Mule. A Treatise on the Breeding, Training, and Uses to Which he May be Put*, Dick and Fitzgerald, New York (1867), 49; H. W. Daly, *Manual of Pack Transportation*, Government Printing Office, Washington, DC (1917); and Anthony Dent, *Donkey. The Story of the Ass from East to West*, George G. Harrap, London, Toronto, Wellington and Sydney (1972), 165–6.

8 Here, I follow the primary material ably analyzed by Engels in his work *Alexander the Great*.

9 For the situation in the Sinai, see the two studies of D. G. Hogarth, "Geography of the War Theatre in the Near East," *The Geographical Journal* 45 (1915), 457–71, and "The Land of Sinai," *The Geographical Journal* 119 (1953), 141–54.
    From the Egyptological side, the classical study is Alan H. Gardiner, "The Ancient Military Road between Egypt and Palestine," *Journal of Egyptian Archaeology* 6 (1920), 99–116. The Seti I pictorial data are now available in The Epigraphic Survey, *The Battle Reliefs of King Sety I*, Oriental Institute, University of Chicago, Chicago (1986); and Murnane's *The Road to Kadesh*, appendix 1.

10 Elmar Edel, "Kleinastische und semitische Namen und Wörter aus den Texten der Qasesschlacht in hieroglypischer Umschrift," in Manfred Görg, ed., *Fontes atque Pontes. Eine Festgabe für Helmut Brunner*, Otto Harrassowitz, Wiesbaden (1983), 99–105.

11 For mules, donkeys and the like, see the studies referred to in note 7 above. James K. Hoffmeier, "Tents in Egypt," *Journal of the Society for the Study of Egyptian Antiquities* 7.3 (1977), 13–28, discusses temporary bivouacs of the Egyptian army during the New Kingdom.

12 In addition to Engels' *Alexander the Great* (chapter I and appendix 5), I follow the caloric intakes for barley and wheat (for men) as determined by Klaus Baer, "The Low Prince of Land in Ancient Egypt," *Journal of the American Research Center in Egypt* 1 (1962), 25–45; add Colin Clark and Margaret Haswell, *The Economics of Subsistence Agriculture*, Macmillan, London (1964), 12–19, 57–67.

Engels assumed a daily caloric intake of 3,600/day (*Alexander the Great*, 123). I feel that this is too large and prefer ca. 3,250 based on modern army handbooks that deal with a reasonable *minimum* necessity per soldier (excluding equipment); some even argue for 3,000, a figure that I find too low. Haswell–Clark have now provided more standard data. See excursus 4 to this chapter.

13 Once more I am relying upon Engels, *Alexander the Great*, chapter I.

14 Sir Alan Gardiner, *The Kadesh Inscriptions of Ramesses II*, University Press, Oxford (1960), 9 (p. 84 for 2,500 Hittite chariots), 10 (p. 153 for 1,000 more enemy chariots), 41–2 (R 43–4 for 18,000 + 19,000 *teher* warriors). Could we reduce the latter two integers by tenfold?

15 Miriam Lichtheim, *Ancient Egyptian Literature* II, 29–35 provides a very useful translation of the war account of Thutmose III.

16 I will return to this situation later on in chapter 5.

17 Lichtheim, *Ancient Egyptian Literature* II, 30, provides the two key chronological marks.

18 The arithmetical formulae for this computation are derived from appendix 1 in Engels, *Alexander the Great*.

19 The classic study on this rivulet is Nadav Na'aman, "The Brook of Egypt and Assyrian Policy on the Border of Egypt," *Tel Aviv* 6 (1979), 68–90.

20 In addition to the preceding study, see Donald B. Redford, "The Historical Retrospective at the Beginning of Thutmose III's Annals," in *Festschrift Elmar Edel*, Bamberg (1979), 338–41; add Hans Goedicke, "The Background of Thutmosis III's Foreign Policy," *Journal of the Society for the Study of Egyptian Antiquities* 10 (1980), 201–13. Redford's *The Wars in Syria and Palestine of Thutmose III* provides an excellent study of the main hieroglyphic account of the Pharaoh.

21 See the references in note 9 above.

22 Hans-Werner Fischer-Elfert, *Die satirische Streitschrift des Papyrus Anastasi I.*, Otto Harrassowitz, Wiesbaden (1986), 230–5.

23 Engels, *Alexander the Great*, 22 n. 35 and appendices 1 and 5. Two imperial quarts are .5 imperial gallons; one imperial gallon weighs 10 pounds (4.55 kilos).

24 This and the following data are taken from Engels, *Alexander the Great*, 14–22, 57–60. As he states (p. 61 n. 39), "We must also remember that marching rapidly to conserve provisions is a standard practice."

Personal investigation had led to the following useful parameters concerning the situation of a train of horses at the present time. Naturally, we must reduce these figures somewhat in order to analyze those equids of New Kingdom times.

The closeness of horses depends upon how tired the animals are, their speed, how familiar they are with each other, the type of terrain, and probably their load. Notice how the gap between cars changes as they start after the lights go green, and as they pick up speed. People vary in how closely they follow on the motorway; horses vary similarly. Finally, a tired horse (and rider) tends to allow more room in front so that they have more time to respond to slowdowns in front.

Horse length varies between 2.15 and 2.25 m; the distance between two is from .4 to 1.1 m. Therefore, one horse + gap is between 2.55 and 3.35 m.

3

SOUTHERN AND NORTHERN EXPANSION

Nubia was a different theater of war than Asia, and the first push into this region took place under Kamose. His famous victory stelae indicate that a previous attack upon the king of Kush had occurred before the decision to face the Hyksos. From this time on, the Egyptian kings moved southward in a concerted and well-planned manner. The first key point reached was the site of the Middle Kingdom fortress of Buhen, located on the Nile at about the Second Cataract. Kamose and Ahmose justified their attacks at this site by considering the territory between Elephantine and the Second Cataract to be theirs. This was not mere boasting. In the Middle Kingdom all the lands upstream from Aswan at the First Cataract and reaching a point not too far south of the Second Cataract had belonged to the Egyptian kings. This area was retaken at the death of Kamose and secured by his successor Ahmose. Once again, the usefulness of the royal flotilla meant that troops could be hastened to any site as rapid as possibly. The men were easy to supply because the fleet would have included the necessary war material, food, and the like. At this time Buhen was set up as a stronghold and a commandant placed over it. The Egyptians, however, decided to go further south.

The Middle Kingdom system of expansion had stopped at the Second Cataract, and a series of large fortresses were constructed around this vicinity.[1] They were predominantly located on the west of the river or on islands within it. Utilizing the rocky terrain as well as the natural course of the Nile, these citadels served as a final expression of Egyptian might. Although filled with troops, silos, and weapons, their purpose remained defensive in nature, being mainly geared for control rather than attack. We hear of Dynasty XII Pharaohs proceeding further upstream, and the kingdom of Kush was reached more than once during this time. But it is fair to state that the level of military technology limited the ability of the Egyptians to secure domination of Nubia beyond Buhen and the other fortresses.

The major change in military technology that had occurred between the Middle Kingdom and early Dynasty XVIII was that of chariot warfare. How did this alter the situation in Nubia when Amunhotep I, the son of Ahmose, came to the throne? All that we read from the biography of Ahmose son of Ebana are a few sentences dealing with the slaughter in the south. Amunhotep I went south "to widen the boundaries of Egypt," a phrase that first occurs in his reign.[2] But from the private war accounts little is revealed. To take an example, the booty included living prisoners or hands (for counting the enemy dead), as is reported under the reign of Amunhotep's immediate predecessor, Ahmose. No war equipment was taken nor are any cities or towns reported to have been invested, much less burnt. The reasons for this are simple. Nubia, whether Lower (Wawat) or Upper (Kush), was not an urban region. Indeed, the territory south of the Second Cataract, though somewhat lush and able to support a large number of cattle, was not one organized into cities. From the account of Ahmose son of Ebana we gain some insight into the need of the Egyptians to station themselves on the Nile. Finally, the manner of fighting in this region was similar to that of the Middle Kingdom, although, it must be stated, there is little doubt that the chariots and horses came along with the fleet and troops.

One question to be asked is: why was Nubia so important to Egypt. A second logically follows: why were there no forays into Palestine at this time? But of overriding importance is yet another. Namely, why should Egypt have embarked upon an empire-building policy? I believe that all three can be answered so long as we keep our attention focused upon the social aspects of the military in early Dynasty XVIII. The wars against the Hyksos had produced an outlet for the military cast. The kings' campaigns had heightened the nationalistic fervor of certain sectors of the state, in particular the elite centered in Thebes and the immediate zones north and south of that nome. (A nome was the basic geographical and administrative region of Egypt, and it may be roughly equated with our "states," "departments," or "counties.")

Internally, the Theban kingdom of late Dynasty XVII resembled a militarily politicized nation.[3] From contemporary documents we can see the importance of garrison leaders who held their positions side by side with their civilian compatriots. Edfu is a key example. That nome, located not too far south of Thebes, had a long-serving line of military men whose ancestry could be traced back to the XIIIth Dynasty. In addition, the local records of the Second Intermediate Period indicate that quite a number of important men who were born into elite families bore the title of "king's son."[4] By no means does this term indicate a direct blood relationship with the living ruler. On the contrary, it reveals the military aspect of that age, one in which the chief soldiers were dependent upon Pharaoh for their living, and which distinguished the warriors from their civilian equivalents. These "king's sons" belonged to the higher echelons of the army, and expected the natural rewards due to their military service.

Such warriors formed the rank and file of the Theban state of Dynasty XVII and the opening XVIIIth.[5] From the private war records of these men we can see that all soldiers expected benefits from their years of military service. Booty gained from battlefield encounters, such as slaves, was normal. But Ahmose son of Ebana, to take a case in point, received plots of land from his Pharaoh. Evidently, additional financial or economic rewards were part and parcel of being a successful warrior.

Consider the situation at the end of the wars with the Hyksos. A standing army, flush with victory and heaped with financial rewards, stood at the gateways to Asia and Nubia. Unless the state – i.e., the Pharaoh – sent these men home permanently to cultivate their fields or to oversee their plots of land, what could they do? Coupled with the presence of an already active and successful military army was a desire by the kings to expand beyond their boundaries. Hence, what could have been more alluring than to obtain the lush cattle-raising territories to the south, lands which happened to possess goldmines? With that precious metal, Egypt could buy wood and other necessary items from abroad, particularly from those foreign countries that had been in contact with her for many years. The Aegean, to name one area, had been in mercantile and political contact with the Hyksos for many years. In the hinterland of Western Asia were regions with large amounts of wood for export: the Hittites in Anatolia, for example, not to mention the Lebanon. Granted that Egypt's sea-borne commercial fleet was probably rather small at this time, nonetheless her ability to trade by means of these ships was in place.

It is thus not surprising to read of a massive move southward under Amunhotep I.[6] The first series of major temple building can be traced to his name, and the site of Sai, approximately halfway between the Second and Third Cataracts, indicates that this ruler expanded his control southward from the older boundary. The difficulties of terrain, land communication, and physical distance limited the Egyptians from automatically moving far north. In many ways it is as if we were seeing the sudden alteration of the military arm of Spain far later in AD 1492. In that year the last remnant of Moorish control ended in the Iberian Peninsula. With the conquest of Granada, what could the two Catholic rulers of Spain do? Originally, they planned to attack and subdue Morocco. Suddenly, a grand vista of gold and land opened their eyes to the possibility of a new direction, the west. At the beginning of Dynasty XVIII it was the south.

Equally, what could the Pharaoh accomplish with his resilient and belli-cose army after the fall of Avaris? A foray into southern Palestine would prove arduous and most probably costly. Why not move southward against easier foes, or at least seize territories not so well organized and militarily equipped as the city-states to the northeast? This is exactly what occurred under Amunhotep I. Yet after the arms of Egypt had moved to the Third Cataract, at his death there still remained the independent patchwork-quilt system of Canaan.

At this time Palestine and part of Syria were composed of numerous city-states, none able to control a sizeable portion of territory.[7] Some, such as

48

Megiddo, owed their importance to their location on the key highways within Palestine. Others, Taanach for example, served as trade entrepots between the highly urbanized sector of Palestine and the more remote and less dense regions of the Trans-Jordan to the east. Few ports could be found in Palestine. Indeed, this area was devoid of much sea-borne commercial trade. Canaan also lacked political unity. Each of the small states was jealous of its own rights and power, and each was equally defensive regarding its independence. Last, there was no major northern power contiguous to them except in the hinterland in central Syria, far away from Palestine.

This was the strategic situation that faced Thutmose I upon his accession after the death of his father Amunhotep I.[8] No great kingdom stood in the immediate way of a possible march northward. The states of Palestine were small and could not, at least individually, mount any great resistance to Egyptian arms. For example, if the king were to proceed northward with a combined infantry–chariotry army, who could provide effective opposition? If a city resisted, from where could it receive aid? Perhaps support could come from a neighboring locality, but by what means and how great could it be? Such imponderables meant that the Egyptians could simply "show the flag," and then receive the homage of one ruler without having to engage in combat. Indeed, the Egyptian army could bypass a city, after having laid siege to it, allowing the main portion of the army to advance northward. Subsequently, the recalcitrant enemy would be forced to capitulate.

Naturally, the local potentates knew the military and political situation.[9] Those in the south and on the coast (e.g., Gaza and Gezer) were hamstrung by their vulnerable geographic position. The Egyptians were able to move north at any time and take them without much difficulty. Some resistance seems to have occurred early, because an oblique reference referring to Gaza in Thutmose III's official "Annals" indicates that the city had previously been captured. But as no large state or kingdom stood by, the locals could do nothing but submit to the Pharaohs. On the other hand, they lost little while gaining much: relative calm. It is for these reasons that the so-called Egyptian Empire spread itself northward in a remarkable fashion, bringing with it the first signs of foreign occupation. The army, of course, was the key.

Egypt's northern expansion commenced with Thutmose I.[10] His predecessor, Amunhotep I, avoided entangling himself in the affairs of Asia. Now, however, the foreign policy to the north changed. Once more we can observe the tactical plans of the king: first Nubia, second Asia. This two-pronged expansion reveals the motives of Thutmose. Nubia was still the major area of warfare, or at least at the beginning of his reign. At that time the focus initially remained aimed at Kush or Upper Nubia. Remarkably, the Egyptians reached the rock of Haga el-Merwa, located between the Fourth and Fifth Cataracts. But this was a raid and led to no permanent occupation of those distant Nubian lands. Quite to the contrary, the center of opposition was in the area south of the Third Cataract but before the Nile turns upward (north) for a lengthy distance. Thutmose I's poetical hymn of praise over these southerners, more akin to a hero's "Leid," was written in year two at Tombos (located at the Third Cataract).[11] From additional royal and private inscriptions we can ascertain that virtually upon his accession warfare took place in Upper Nubia. The Egyptian monarch and his flotilla, with himself at the front, went south, defeated the Kushites, and established his real boundary at Tombos. The expansion to Hagar el-Merwa indicates that the flotilla was able to sail upstream unimpeded, although no permanent annexation was accomplished in that area. After all, Thutmose was miles into unknown and remote territory. But in his topographical list of southern captured countries the Pharaoh includes at least two localities that are considerably south of the later boundary of Gebel Barkal at the Fourth Cataract.

There is a historical background in an inscription of Thutmose II, the next Pharaoh, which describes the new political set-up of Nubia.[12] The specific area is called Kush, and various fortresses built by his father, Thutmose I, are mentioned. At those citadels the Nubians were accused of intending to steal cattle to the north of them. According to the war account of Thutmose II, Kush was divided into five small sectors, each probably run by a Nubian chief who was allied to Egypt. This must have been a result of the earlier monarch's successful annexation of Upper Nubia, an ill-defined area that surrounded the Third Cataract both to the north and south, and which extended even further upstream. The poetical Tombos account may, in fact, indicate the final boundary settlement at the time, whereas other inscriptions at Tanger and Sai in Nubia indicate the final mopping-up operations of the Pharaoh.

This detailed information serves more to elucidate the focus of Egyptian imperialism under the third ruler of Dynasty XVIII than to provide us with direct evidence concerning the military. Yet we can see some key policies now put into place by the Pharaohs. Fortresses were built and manned. Local potentates were allowed to exercise some type of internal policing over their areas, but only in the newly won territories of Kush or Upper Nubia. This was relatively simple to institute because of the availability of naval transport. The Nile still formed the conduit for military support. At about this time the king instituted a more direct administrative control over the area by instituting the policy of appointing his commandant of Buhen to the rank and title of "king's son," conveniently translated as Viceroy. Thus the Egyptian forces were now placed in a different position, more of control rather than expansion. There was no longer a major external threat to the southern client states even though internal difficulties would remain for some time. We can also see how effective the Egyptian fleet was. It passed way beyond the Third Cataract and, in fact, moved onward to Kurgus, south of which lay El-Kenisa where the king may have built a mud-brick fort. This rapid expansion upstream depended upon the conduit of the Nile as well as the relatively inferior technological development of the Nubians. After all, the Egyptians could transport their horses and chariots by ship with ease.

In Asia, however, the situation remains unclear to us. Thutmose I's remarkable northern campaign (or campaigns) has always been a stumbling block to scholars.[13] It is therefore necessary to link his success in Palestine and Syria with the developing chariot-based army. The Pharaoh's Asiatic warfare relied heavily upon his ability to travel far north and to coordinate his supply trains and depots with his army, and upon the seemingly lack of resistance in Palestine. From royal and private sources we know that he reached the Euphrates in Syria. In that region hunting took place and the king set up a rock inscription denoting his presumed northern boundary. There, he met a major enemy, the ruler of Naharain (or Mitanni). From two biographical texts we learn that horses and chariots were taken. The war situation was therefore quite different than in the south. Additional information, derived from a gate inscription at Karnak, indicates that the cities of Tunip and Qedem ("East") submitted to the king.

The advance into hostile territory in the far north has to be explained. The account of Ahmose son of Ebana laconically describes the campaign as directed to Retjenu, Syro-Palestine.[14] But this soldier later adds that Thutmose I reached Naharain, that is, Mitanni east of the Euphrates. Such success could not have been achieved without the pacification of lands to the immediate south and west. The official rationale given for the war by the soldier was not "to widen the boundaries" but rather to "take pleasure." In other words, Thutmose's Asiatic foray was not intended to effect permanent control over Syria. We do not know why conflict arose between Thutmose I and the king of Mitanni. Perhaps the Pharaoh was caught off guard when he was busy hunting elephants in Niy, which was located very close to Mitanni if not belonging to it. I do not believe that the Pharaoh originally intended to move against the enemy monarch. In fact, Ahmose son of Ebana expressly states that Thutmose attacked the king because the latter was marshaling all of his troops. If we take the evidence on face value, this would imply that the armed encounter may have been accidental.

To march so far north was a remarkable undertaking. We must assume that Palestine was pacified at this time. From the brief references in the private biographies it is also evident that the Egyptian army had to have had chariots with them. Armies do not march simply for pleasure, and normally not even on a whim of their commander. Thutmose I must have had no fears about striking so far north, but whether his policy depended upon a weakened condition of the Palestinian city-states cannot be argued with certainty. On the other hand, their inability to show a military counterpoise to the Egyptians indicates the ease of his success.

We see immediately how the Asiatic policy of Thutmose I differed from his Nubian one. To the south, the king had to arrange a more permanent system of control, one that involved direct annexation and a military presence through key fortresses. Such was not the case in the north. Even the largest of the Palestinian cities could not oppose the Egyptians. Hence, they simply accepted the inevitable: a tentative or fragile domination by a superior foe. There was also no need to set up a series of Egyptian-run forts in Asia. As there was no immediate threat from a major enemy, it was sufficient to place some troops within these cities and control the major staging points. I will elaborate upon this system of indirect control later. For the moment let us keep in mind the relative low level of military preparedness on the part of the Egyptians concerning Palestine and contrast it with Upper Nubia.

But it was not merely on land in Asia that the New Kingdom Pharaohs marched. From data in the war reports of Thutmose III we learn of the importance of the coastal shipping that was also necessary for the Egyptians to maintain their empire.[15] The key port in the Levant was Byblos, located about 42 km north of modern-day Beirut. If we follow the coastline, which the Egyptian ships regularly did, then this city was approximately 649 km from the easternmost Nile branch in the Delta. Given that the coast of Palestine provides little in the way of port facilities for large ships, it is not remarkable that from a very early time coasters sped north from Egypt to this important trading center. Byblos in Phoenicia was always closely associated with Egypt and its rulers often allies of the Pharaohs. By the time of the XVIIIth Dynasty a regular sea trade was in place, with the Egyptians obtaining a superabundance of pines for their needs. Therefore, the necessity of providing the Egyptian army with supplies came to the fore at a time when the Pharaohs marched into Syria. Byblos, as well as other ports, also served as disembarkation points for needed war material. There was no possibility of such support being hindered because there were no major kingdoms located on the coast of Palestine or Syria. In fact, the major city-state north of Byblos was Ugarit, which to all purposes remained a mercantile trading center having some control in the hinterland. But to all purposes it was limited in size.

Contemporary Red Sea vessels have been estimated at 21 to 30.5 m long, 5.5 m wide, and between 1.2 and 1.5 m deep.[16] (The volume was 170 cubic m.) With oars employed they could clear not less than 18 m. In the palace accounts of Seti I dated to his second and third regnal years there are official reports concerning shipbuilding.[17] As the papyrus on which these records were written came from the Memphis region, we may presume that the ships were connected to the New Kingdom royal dockyards at Perunefer ("Bon Voyage") in that city. The entries refer to an inspection of houses in various wards of the city from which inspectors obtained various timbers; the owners were of middle status. Most of the woods in the accounts were in the form of ships' parts or else suitable for such vessels. The basic type was pine, ultimately coming from Lebanon. Masts of 6 to 17 m are recorded.

Perhaps we can assume that the taller ones were suitable for seagoing ships that followed the eastern coastline of Palestine and Syria. Their maximum size has been estimated at 17 cubits deep or wide and up to 50 cubits long. That is, the vessels were 9 m wide and 30 m long. These figures equate rather well with the rough estimates for the Red Sea vessels, and I believe can be used for the New Kingdom Levantine trade and war.

For the Red Sea an average velocity of 5.6 to 6.4 km/hour is taken as reasonable. If the total sailing time is in the order of 8 to 9 hours per day, then a minimum of 45 km/day results. Now there are many reefs in the Red Sea and the wind conditions are very different than in the eastern Mediterranean. But for the necessities of war the Egyptians would have known when, exactly, to set sail so that their flotilla was not becalmed or forced to row for a long time.

The time it would take for ships to leave Egypt and reach Byblos without stopping is unclear. If we take as our starting point the rough estimates for Nile travel (north to south) to be 55 km/day, we arrive at approximately 12 days. If we operate with the figure of 13.6 km/day for the Red Sea traffic, then the result is 13.4 days. I have not taken into consideration the rougher conditions in the eastern Mediterranean and the vagaries of wind, which were not regular as in the Nile Valley. Because these Egyptian figures are derived from one of the more leisurely voyages, that of Nitocris in Dynasty XXVI, our approximations must be taken with some degree of caution.

Additional evidence indicates that direct sailing from the Nile Delta to the Phoenician coast, Cyprus, and even Cilicia in Asia Minor took about a week or two, with consistent side winds in both directions (west and north-west) rarely exceeding 25 knots.[18] A route close to the shore took longer, but allowed overnight shelter as well as fresh supplies of food and water. Significantly, the duration of travel from Crete to Egypt was five to ten times shorter than from Egypt to Crete. Comparing the rate on foot, the 649 km come out to about 29–34 days. The time difference between land and sea therefore approached a magnitude of three times. Even though it is necessary to consider stops at certain ports, I believe that the actual ratio was greater, if only because we are following land travel rates in Asia. In sum, the Egyptians were able to send war supplies and troops northward by sea considerably faster than overland.

But there were inherent constraints imposed upon the use of the sea for war in Asia. The ships were not large by our standards. Not that many soldiers, food, and material could be transported on a single coaster. The sizes of these boats are unfortunately unknown. Indeed, there are difficulties in interpreting why they were called "Byblos ships" or "Keftiu ships." (Keftiu was the Egyptian name for modern Crete.) Some have maintained that these terms indicate that they were adaptations of Nilotic vessels. This interpretation assumes that the two geographic terms Byblos and Keftiu merely refer to the destination or origin of travel. It is better to view such seagoing vessels as having originally been constructed at these localities or else associated with these maritime regions. Early in their history the Egyptians would have utilized the foreign know-how to transport goods on their own ships, which were made on the specifications of the foreigners. In the Old Kingdom, at the latest, "Byblos ships" were made very different than Egyptian ones.

Nile vessels were very impractical for long seagoing voyages in the Mediterranean.[19] An alternate means of construction employing different woods was used for those ships, and even the masts had to be built along lines far different than those of the easy-going Nile types. For the Egyptians at an earlier time, the ship-making facilities and know-how of the Levant, in particular Byblos, served as the model. Let it not be forgotten that artisans as well as artists circulated through the communication channels of sea, river, and land at a rate that is often overlooked, and their expertise would be of prime necessity for the Egyptian merchant flotilla in the Mediterranean. Indeed, the naval archaeologist George Bass emphatically argued that with respect to maritime trade in the eastern Mediterranean, the overwhelming number of Egyptian tomb paintings in Dynasty XVIII reveal commercial ships manned by Syrians, or at least having Syrian merchants.[20] It would appear that Egypt's dependence upon the maritime ports of Phoenicia for her Syrian forays was connected to her reliance upon Levantine ships and traders.

The seagoing ships of the New Kingdom had a more streamlined hull than the Nilotic ones. It was deeper, as may be expected, and the sails wide by contrast, being more strongly supported to the masts. The bow was sharp and the stern designed to offset the possibility of being swept on the broadside. There was no true keel and large oars accomplished the steering. Egyptian ships that traversed the Red Sea to the fabulous land of Punt, for example, show that there were two types.[21] From contemporary models of boats and from various pictorial representations it is clear that the hull was far better supported than in earlier epochs. Cargo boats exhibited all of these factors except that they were beamier than ships designed for large numbers of men.

We can supplement this information with respect to warships owing to useful data from the reign of Ramesses III in Dynasty XX.[22] These war reliefs show that his vessels were long and low, although there remains the possibility that the pictorial representations actually reveal vessels solely designed for the protection of the harbors in the Delta. Nevertheless, the central mast remained in place, as with the nonmilitary ships, although it had a top in which fighters kept watch. The sails in Ramesses III's scenes are narrower than earlier and they could be secured in order not to interfere with fighting. It must remain a moot point whether loose-fitted sails were introduced late in the New Kingdom, but a change in design seems to have taken place at the end of Dynasty XVIII. Under the reign of Ramesses II we read for the first time of *menesh*-ships, seagoing vessels that become more common in the later Ramesside Period (Dynasties XIX–XX).

It is unfortunate that the size of the ships' complements is unknown. In fact, the number of troops that one of Ramesses III's warships could hold is also impossible to determine with any accuracy, although a reasonable hypothesis sets the figure at about twenty-five men for a Nile ship. Those designed for the ocean, however, surely held more. The only useful figure of troops that a warship could contain is embedded in an early Dynasty XII story, "The Shipwrecked Sailor," and in this case the vessel operated in the Red Sea. One hundred and twenty sailors are recorded, including any soldiers.[23] Hence, we cannot ascertain how many troops could be transported from Egypt to Byblos, but a figure of around 200 appears a reasonable maximal limit. In a famous text of Amunhotep II referring to the king's sporting activities, one ship contained 200 rowers, but again the vessel was suited for the Nile and was a royal one.[24] Since the term employed for a company of an army, *sa*, contained 200 men, perhaps the entire naval contingent was organized along similar lines. However, we must not forget that the example of Amunhotep II refers solely to oarsmen. Sails play the main role on the sea, even with regard to hugging the coast, and those ships would naturally contain considerably fewer rowers. Finally, it is perhaps well to recall that large fleets, like large armies, are difficult to control, and even if Thutmose III sent his ships north to Byblos laden with soldiers, they probably were divided into small groups and so better able to arrive safely.

The military organization of the royal fleet is likewise difficult to ascertain.[25] In the reign of Thutmose III a certain Nebamun was the chief of the king's navy, and he was not of royal blood. Under him would have been the various ships' captains. Nebamun was a typical bureaucrat of the day, unlike his successor Suemniut who lived under Amunhotep II. The latter man came from the chariot division of the army and moved up from the position of a stablemaster to commander-in-chief of the Egyptian navy. Yet like his predecessor, Suemniut finally became a royal butler. It is important to note that this final grade is identical to the last step in the career of the officer Minmose (time of Thutmose III–Amunhotep II), a man who also ended up being a royal butler.

Hence, we can visualize the naval commanders in early–mid Dynasty XVIII as originally having been office holders. At a later date, men moved over from high ranks of the army into the navy. The switch in backgrounds parallels that of the army officers, a point to which we shall return later. For the moment, it is sufficient to note that in the reign of Thutmose IV, a navy man, also called Nebamun, originally had been a standard-bearer and chief of police. In other words, these naval officials, like the army marshals, came from nonmilitary families. Only gradually did professionalization take place, with a connection between army and navy more frequent. Later a crossover appears to have been a norm. The commandant of the border post of Sile,

Nebi, was a high military officer who reached the position of a marshal. He eventually controlled the route from Egyptian into Asia but also supervised the Nile mouths. In this case, although his activities were land based, there was a strong connection between him and the fleet commanders.

The lack of prosopographical data concerning Egypt's seagoing fleet in the New Kingdom remains troubling. In contrast, the wealth of information concerned with the army – footsoldiers, officers, and charioteers – is large, and such a difference cannot be laid solely on the basis of the haphazard nature of our primary sources. From the amount of data in Dynasty XVIII it would appear that the more important branch of Egypt's military was the army. The same may be said for Dynasties XIX and XX even though the control of the eastern Mediterranean became more crucial at that later date. By and large, it is fair to conclude that advancement in the army and leadership of the chariot divisions, coupled with a rise to the position of marshal, was the road of importance. The state placed great emphasis on one's ability to fight on land; the sea remained secondary. Thutmose III's development of the Lebanese ports was concentrated upon securing bases for the transportation of supplies and men. Sea battles were unknown at this time, and there is no evidence that the Egyptians developed squadrons for naval warfare. The navy, therefore, remained in a subsidiary position, one oriented to provisioning and communication but not armed combat.

Likewise in Nubia, once effective control was secured in the reigns of Thutmose I onward, the navy was relegated to the position of a transport arm. Here, the increasing number of garrisons and even Egyptian towns (e.g., at Gebel Barkal) served to control the foreigners. Ships were employed to bring back goods to the state, gold in particular. Temples in Egypt also benefited because some of them owned tracts of land in the far south, and merchant ships voyaging in the upper regions of the Nile could easily transport agricultural produce and other raw materials.

Evidence of close mercantile contact by sea in Dynasty XVIII is clear, but even earlier the Hyksos rulers had strong contacts with Crete. The native Egyptians simply replaced them as the determinant factor. In fact, the naval flotilla on the Nile provided a paradigm for the later warlike sea transport. It is unfortunate that we lack any data concerning the Pharaohs' investment in the maritime arm until the reign of Thutmose III. In his fifth campaign of victory (regnal year 29) the king's official account mentions the transport of booty from Syria (the city of Tunip is indicated) by what apparently was a surprise because two ships were seized from an unknown enemy.[26] But in this case the chance occurrence of taking over foreign seagoing vessels cannot be taken as a norm. These vessels were laden with copper ingots, lead (presumably in bars), and emery. Male and female slaves were also found. All were brought back to Egypt. By means of this brief mention we can reasonably hypothesize that the Pharaoh was not only in the hinterland of Syria, but that some of his troops likewise operated on the coast of Lebanon.

By regnal year 30 Thutmose III embarked upon a more concerted effort to wrest control over central Syria.[27] In order to do this he needed an army larger than before, one that could lay siege to the capital of Amurru, Kadesh, located on the river Orontes. Kadesh, however, was allied to the great kingdom of Naharain or Mitanni. Owing to this, Thutmose III required many more troops than were necessary for a small and localized war. Furthermore, his enemy was aligned by treaty with the powerful kingdom of Mitanni. The king had to set up a permanent supply base for his army and, after his envisaged control over central Syria had taken place, to have an outlet for his booty and tribute.

In the account of Thutmose during his sixth campaign (year 30) two additional harbor-towns were taken. This military activity also occurred after the main focus of the war was completed. By contrast, in the preceding year the king had seized Tunip where he found the famous *teher* warriors, later associated with the Hittite king.[28] On this occasion, Thutmose III first seized Kadesh and then moved to the coast. The strategy in both cases was identical. First, a land-based army moved into central Syria, and only after its aim was completed did the soldiers go westward to the Mediterranean coast. Yet both campaigns reveal the necessity of dominating the coast.

It is the following campaign of the king that allows us to see his maritime policy in full action. Ullaza, also a port in the Levant, was overcome in a short period of time. The crucial section of the account presents a statement concerning the Levantine ports. Every harbor at which the king arrived was already provided with food provisions, oils, incense, wine, and fruit from the country. The submissive locals had stored these items up in order to refresh the royal troops.

I will leave off the question whether the king proceeded by sea on this and other campaigns and turn to the record of year 33.[29] At that time the harbor provisioning is given in a somewhat different fashion:

> Now the harbors were supplied with every thing according to their levy of their yearly requirement, together with the labor of Lebanon as their yearly requirement, together with the princes of Lebanon . . .

The ports were now under the full control of the king and forced to supply the necessary items to the state or, as it might be, to the army. In year 34 a further remark on the same situation may be found:

> Now all of the harbors of his majesty were provided with every good thing that his majesty received in Djahy, consisting of pine, Keftiu ships, Byblos ships and *seket* ships,[30] laden with wooden posts, beams, and large trees . . .

In this case semi-processed woods were sent to the harbors in order to build ships for the Pharaoh. First, Thutmose III required the security of his coast. This was accomplished with little difficulty owing to the weak military nature of the harbor cities. Second, there was already a merchant fleet in place, indeed one that could easily transport supplies and troops to the Levant. Both factors were of key importance when the Egyptians moved north into Syria. Previously, when Egyptian control was solidified over Palestine, this was not necessary. But when Thutmose III decided upon the strategic move into the hinterland of Syria, Lebanon suddenly became crucial for his endeavors. Third, the establishment of this control meant that the king could arrange his ships to take produce out of Asia. This meant that the ports also served as embarkation points for precious goods and various native woods. Last, the two previous quotes reveal the Pharaoh's efficacy in controlling the harbors. A yearly requirement of items came into place in the king's 33rd regnal year and various raw woods, undoubtedly seasoned on the shores of the sea, are also listed.

The harbors also became staging points for additional divisions of the army that could be sent north in a very rapid fashion. These troops would be supplied with their necessities while at the same time the Egyptians could employ the locals to handle their exports. Thutmose thereby secured his left flank, allowing himself free action to the east. No enemy was expected to attack these harbors en masse, and the king could operate on foot in Syria without fearing any interruption to his supplies. This was further necessary because the king and his troops were quite distant from any inland strategic base. In other words, the whole coastline of the southern Lebanon became a major base for supply and reinforcements. By the end of the XVIIIth Dynasty, however, after the loss of Byblos, the Pharaohs had to establish a different strategic location.

Owing to the evidence from Thutmose III's war reports, it appears that his sea policy was a new one. This fact, reflected in the report of his campaigns for years 30 onward, indicates that his predecessors, in particular Thutmose I and Hatshepsut, had not arrived at the same decision. We can thereby conclude that the former's attack into Niy and his Euphrates campaign indicate an overextension of the Egyptian military power. Mere chariots and horses were not enough to offset the presence of a major foe, that of Mitanni. True, Thutmose I was able to defeat his royal opponent and to set up a stela of victory at the Euphrates. He was nonetheless unable to make these Syrian conquests permanent. Tactically, he needed more support, and it had to be on a permanent basis. Remember that the initial campaigning of this Pharaoh owed its success to the patchwork-quilt political arrangement of Palestine. No doubt owing to his rapid success in Asia, Thutmose I found it relatively easy to accept the submission of many local princes in their city-states. But the farther he traveled north, the more difficult it became for him to supply his troops. There were no prepared supply bases, nor even settled Egyptian troops to enable him to maintain a firm control over any erstwhile ally. It was one thing to accept homage, another to have it regularized as permanent. In addition, the military arm of Egypt was still engaged in wars in the south, and the resources of the Egyptian state were expended there on garrison building and the establishment of a permanent army of occupation.

Upon the accession of Thutmose II, further difficulties took place in Nubia and, although he ruled for only a few years, the conundrum of Asia still remained to be solved. In fact, preceding the wars of Thutmose III we have only one major account of battle after the reign of Thutmose I. True, there are brief references to campaigns of Hatshepsut in Nubia.[31] Notwithstanding their importance for the development of Egyptian imperialism, the significant account remains that of Thutmose II.[32] The king had ordered a report to be written on the road from Aswan to Philae, thereby indicating the southern orientation of the campaign. It was directed against Nubia and began in the first regnal year of the Pharaoh. It is useful to summarize the inscription because it reveals the common attitude of the Egyptians concerning their desire to smash the rebels to the south. The introductory details are concerned with the domination of the ruler. A report sent to the court indicated that the military and political set-up of Thutmose I was threatened. But the facts indicate that the revolt, though serious, was not dangerous enough to entail the presence of the monarch. The Nubians had taken the cattle "behind" one of the fortresses in Upper Nubia built by Thutmose I. The area is Upper Nubia, the territory around the Third Cataract and further south. One chief to the north in this region had conspired against Egypt. Two others among the children of the chief of "vile Kush" were also involved with the rebellion. As I have stated earlier, apparently this territory was administratively divided into five parts, and I presume that each had its own local ruler as administrator, who naturally was subservient to the Pharaoh.

The army reached Kush and put down the revolt. One of the male children of the Kushite foe was brought back alive to the king and all of the main instigators "were placed under the feet" of the king, later to be ceremoniously killed. (The account does not indicate the latter point but this is a most reasonable interpretation.) The tenor of the composition indicates the might of both Pharaoh and his father, god Amun. Both are linked, an aspect that we have seen already present decades earlier.

Subsequent to the reign of Thutmose II, Nubia was not a major area of the advancing Egyptian war machine after the army's final victory. At first, this conclusion goes against the grain of many modern scholars who have resuscitated the grandiose role that Nubia played within the Egyptian New Kingdom. But even if we allow a great degree of hyperbole and rhetoric on the part of the Egyptians, there remains little doubt that the armies of the Nubians were second rate compared to those of Egypt or Asia. This salient fact is based upon the ease with which Egypt's army traveled upstream and met little resistance, if any, on the Nile. The flotilla of the Pharaoh traversed

Figure 3.1a and b Thutmose II battle scenes from his mortuary temple. *Deir el Médineh.* Année 1926, Bernard Bruyère. L'Institut Français d'Archéologie Orientale du Caire. Published by Le Caire: Imprint Fouilles de l'Institut Français d'Archéologie Orientale du Caire, 1952, pls. III and IV. Reprinted by permission of Archives Scientifiques IFAO.

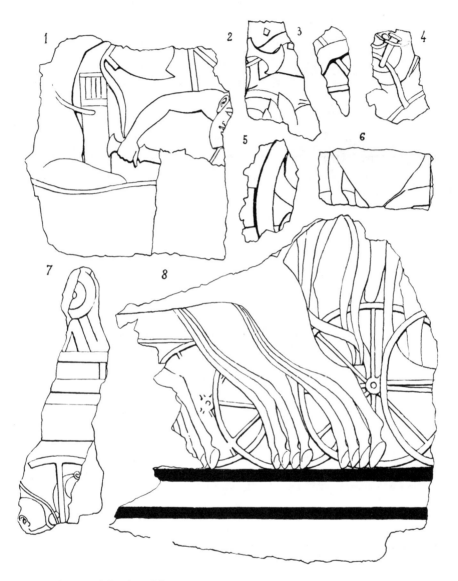

Figure 3.1a and b (*cont'd*)

the upper regions of the Nile and expected little resistance. Never, in fact, did the Nubians oppose this fleet, undoubtedly because they lacked naval preparedness.[33] Therefore, troops, war material, and supplies to beleaguered towns and numerous functionaries could be rapidly sent to any quarter in Upper Nubia.

Figure 3.2 Suggested reconstruction of the left side of Asiatic battle scene from the temple of Thutmose II at Thebes. Drawing by Tamara Bower, after Stephen P. Harvey. Courtesy of Stephen P. Harvey.

On land, the Nubians did not possess a war machine comparable to what Egypt developed by the reign of Thutmose I. How could they obtain copper and tin? Smelted together, these two metals make bronze. Yet tin was imported from the north into Egypt. Therefore, the Nubians lacked the requisite armor to defend themselves against the Pharaohs. They could, of course, threaten and even overrun some citadels. The Egyptians, on the other hand, possessed bronze weapons, and a sizeable number of horses and chariots. These factors were the deciding points of Nubia's failure to repel the might of Egypt. Chariots, after all, are easier to transport by ship than on land. Horses, of course, are more rambunctious, but they as well could be moved with little difficulty. The boundary of Egyptian control was eventually fixed at Gebel Barkal, not too far from the Fourth Cataract. Evidently, even though the arms of Pharaoh could extend further, this location was suitable as a defining boundary. But we must be careful not to over-interpret the successive campaigns. The monarch ceased advancing south in person by the reign of Thutmose I. Thereafter, the king's legs traversed Asia on a regular basis, as the wars of Thutmose III indicate. But the Pharaoh never set foot in Nubia except on an official mission of a peaceful nature.

The Egyptian administration in the south is reflected by the wealth of prosopographical and archaeological data. As noted earlier, the original system of control was to "appoint" or confirm local rulers. Lower Nubia was divided into three portions and Upper Nubia probably into six. The original three key regions of Kush were Sai (halfway between the Second and the Third Cataracts), Kerma (south of the Third Cataract), and Bugdumbush (at the Wadi Hawar, virtually at the beginning of the Letti Basin). The viceroy and his subaltern officials resided in these provinces until late in their careers. Many of the officers in the Egyptian army would return to their native land and be rewarded with yet a higher military position. The system of administrative and economic control will be touched upon later, but for the moment it is sufficient to add that only the expenses of control burdened the Egyptian state.

Asia was clearly the more difficult to administer. By the reign of Hatshepsut some type of indirect control had been established in Palestine. But as the events surrounding the death of the aged queen indicate, an enemy coalition was able to come into being, one that had at its fingertips the necessary war material and combat soldiers. We must not forget that even the Asiatic princes had soldiers and chariots as well as corselets of bronze and leather in addition to archers, helmets, and sufficient horses. All that was needed was support from outside, and this happened owing to the machinations of the ruler of Kadesh in Syria, who, together with his ally at Megiddo, prepared to resist Egyptian control.

EXCURSUS

1. The time of land travel was first used extensively in Egyptological literature by William Murnane, *The Road to Kadesh*, when he had to determine the logistics of the opening two campaigns of Seti I. The seagoing voyages, however, have never been covered from a military viewpoint.

The article of Lambrou-Phillipson cited in note 18 ("Seafaring in the Bronze Age Mediterranean") provides the necessary data concerning the velocity of the prevailing winds, and a useful chart gives the predominant directions of the Mediterranean currents (nautical miles/day) in July. I believe she has proved her case that sea travel from Crete to Egypt was relatively common, but that voyages from Egypt to Crete probably did not take place.

For a helpful overview of the Egyptian marine at a later date, see Alan B. Lloyd, "Saite Navy," in G. J. Oliver et al., *The Sea in Antiquity*, British Archaeological Reports, Oxford (2000), 81–91.

2. In the light of the parameters of travel discussed here, it is useful to know how crucial such basic data are. For example, Frank Burr Marsh, in his *The Reign of Tiberius*, W. Heffer and Sons, Cambridge (1959), 93 n. 3, worked out that it took a messenger 17–18 days to travel by boat between Rome and Judea, but the voyage could only have been accomplished under favorable conditions. The normal time was ca. 40 days when navigation was closed (November 11 to March 15), owing to the prevailing winds.

In similar fashion, despite the "coastal-hugging" nature of Pharaonic ships, and the shorter distances, the wind direction was the most important factor for the Egyptian navy. Certain times of the year were highly unfavorable for sea voyages. According to Avner Raban, "Land voyage from the Nile Valley to Phoenicia might have taken two to three months in ancient times": "Minoan and Canaanite Harbours," *Aegaeum 7* (1991), 144.

3. Lambrou-Phillipson in her article observes that "ancient mariners traveled mainly during the summer, particularly when it came to long voyages, in order to avoid the harsh conditions and dangerous storms of the winter months." Hence, commencing in late spring, the expeditions of the Pharaohs coincided well with the sea currents, winds, and lack of dangerous storms.

Note as well the remarks of Vegetius 39 on ideal times for sailing in the Mediterranean (*Vegetius: Epitome of Military Science*, N. P. Millar, trs. and ed., Liverpool University Press, Liverpool [1993], 137). He states that one ought to commence sea travel on May 15 at the earliest, with the best time between May 27 and September 14, and he adds "greater caution should be shown when an army sails by warships than in a hasty venture of private commerce."

4. The influence of the shipbuilding industry and expertise of the Levantine ports is not described here. The reader will find the matters ably covered by Lucian Basch in his series of articles cited in notes 16 and 22. Steven Vinson and Dilwyn Jones, whose works are referred to in note 16, present general surveys concerning this vexing problem.

NOTES

1 On the economic foundations of the Middle Kingdom fortress system, see Barry J. Kemp, "Late Middle Kingdom Granary Buildings (and the archaeology of administration)," *Zeitschrift für ägyptische Sprache* 113 (1986), 123–36, and *Ancient Egypt. Anatomy of a Civilization*, Routledge, London and New York (1989), 166–78. See excursus 4 to the previous chapter.

2 Franz-Jürgen Schmitz, *Amenophis I.*, Gerstenberg Verlag, Hildesheim (1978), chapter VIII, presents a study of this Pharaoh's foreign policy. As I indicated earlier in chapter 1 n. 7, the evidence presented by Redford "A Gate

Inscription from Karnak and Egyptian Involvement in Western Asia during the Early 18th Dynasty," *JAOS* 99 (1979), 270–87, is better placed to Thutmose I than to Amunhotep I.

3 Ryholt, *The Political Situation of Egypt during the Second Intermediate Period*, 167–83, 265–81, 309–12.

4 Schmitz, *Untersuchungen zum Titel S3-njśwt "Königssohn"*; with Ryholt, *The Political Situation of Egypt during the Second Intermediate Period*.

5 Compare the background data provided by Gnirs, *Militär und Gesellschaft*, 1–5, 17–21 (on generals).

6 In this context see the work of Schmitz, *Amenophis I*.

7 A recent study of the first phase of Egyptian imperialism in Palestine (pre Thutmose III) is presented by Nadav Na'aman, "The Hurrians and the End of the Middle Bronze Age in Palestine," *Levant* 26 (1994), 175–87. He counters some of the scholarly interpretations concerning Egyptian influence (through war) upon the destruction and abandonment of the Middle Bronze II urban society in Canaan. Indeed, it is hard to determine whether Ahmose himself had the wherewithal to annex much of southern and central Palestine. We have to wait for Thutmose I, and then after him Thutmose III, for the effects of Egyptian chariot warfare in Asia.

William G. Dever, on the other hand, strongly rejected Na'aman's thesis, preferring to avoid an exclusively "text-based" orientation: "Hurrian Incursions and the End of the Middle-Bronze Age in Syria-Palestine: A Rejoinder to Nadav Na'aman," in Leonard H. Lesko, ed., *Ancient Egyptian and Mediterranean Studies in Memory of William A. Ward*, Brown University, Providence (1998), 91–110. Although I find it hard to follow the author when he subscribes to a "revenge theory" on the part of the Egyptians (p. 101) in order to account for the later destruction of key urban centers in Palestine and the transition from the Middle to the Late Bronze Age, many of his points are worth considering. My feeling is that Canaan was "up for grabs," but that inland Syria was too close to Mitanni and too distant from home for the Egyptians to effect permanent domination.

Dever's arguments are mainly based on his understanding of the archaeology of this region, but whether Egypt systematically ruined the urban civilization of Palestine at the beginning of Dynasty XVIII is difficult to prove. He believes that "these coordinated destructions over a period of some 60 years or more were the *result of deliberate Egyptian policy and military action*" (p. 101; his emphasis). The difference between him and Na'aman is inexorably connected to the decrease in population from the Late Middle Bronze Age to the Early Late Bronze Age in Palestine. Were the Egyptians solely responsible for this diminution? If so, is their policy of deportation partly to explain for this? Neither two questions can be resolved by present archaeological evidence. See excursus 3 in chapter 5.

Donald B. Redford, *Egypt, Canaan, and Israel in Ancient Times*, Princeton University Press, Princeton (1992) Part Two, deals with Egyptian imperialism in the New Kingdom. Of equal importance is his earlier study, *Egypt and Canaan in the New Kingdom*, Ben-Gurion University of the Negev Press, Beer-Sheva (1990), in Shmuel Ahituv, ed., *Beer-Sheva* IV, Ben-Gurion University of the Negev, Beer-Sheva (1990). To some extent Redford's studies have replaced the compendium of Wolfgang Helck, *Die Beziehungen Ägyptens zu Vorderasien im 3. und 2. Jahrtausend v. Chr.²*, Otto Harrassowitz, Wiesbaden (1971). Barry Kemp's "Imperialism and Empire in New Kingdom Egypt (c. 1575–1987 BC)," in P. D. A. Garnsey and C. R. Whittaker, eds., *Imperialism in the Ancient World*, Cambridge University Press, New York (1978) 7–57, presents a more theoretical archaeological perspective to the imperialism of the New Kingdom. To his work we can add the modern perspective of Mario Liverani, *Prestige and Interest. International Relations in the Near East ca. 1600–1100 BC*, Sargon srl, Padova (1990).

8 For the reign of Thutmose I there is no standard monograph. However, see the unpublished MA Essay of John C. Darnell, *Studies on the Reign of Thutmosis I*, Johns Hopkins University, Baltimore (1985), chapter V. With respect to the southern extension of the Egyptians under Thutmose I to Thutmose III, see now W. Vivian Davies, "La frontière méridionale de l'Empire: Les Égyptiens à Kurgus," *Bulletin de la Sociéte Française de l'Égyptologie* 157 (2003), 23–37.

9 This factor is often overlooked. Owing to the lengthy time it took for an Egyptian king to prepare for war and then to march out of Egypt, it ought to be clear that the locals in Palestine and Syria would have known his war plans. Indeed, the causes for this military intervention were probably of no surprise. If diplomacy and/or threats did not suffice, then war was imminent. I feel that the situation of an inevitable war in Asia surrounds the seriousness of the perceived threat to Egyptian control and extent of mobilization on the part of the Pharaoh.

10 Here I depend upon Darnell's work cited above in note 8.

11 An old translation may be found in Breasted, *Ancient Records of Egypt* II, 27–3; see Kurt Sethe, *Urkunden der 18. Dynastie*, J. C. Hinrichs, Leipzig (1927–30), 82–6, for the Egyptian text; add Anthony Spalinger, "The Calendrical Importance of the Tombos Stela," *SAK* 22 (1995), 271–81; add Goedicke, "The Thutmosis I Inscription near Tomâs," *JNES* 55 (1996), 161–76.

12 This key inscription may be found in a dated English translation in Breasted, *Ancient Records of Egypt* II, 48–50. The standard Egyptian text remains that of Sethe, *Urkunden der 18. Dynastie*, 137–41.

13 Redford has seen that both Hatshepsut and Thutmose III considered Thutmose I to be the "real founder of Egypt's empire in the Levant," *History and Chronology of the Eighteenth Dynasty of Egypt*, 79 and n. 119.

14 The difficulties in ascertaining the exact geographical significance of "Retjenu" are covered in chapter 8 n. 2.

15 I will discuss the maritime policy of Egypt later. The following studies cover the actual factors of time, distance, and wind: Connie Lambrou-Phillipson, "Seafaring in the Bronze Age Mediterranean: The Parameters Involved in Maritime Travel," *Aegaeum* 7 (1991), 11–19; and Avner Raban, "Minoan and Canaanite Harbours," *Aegaeum* 7 (1991), 129–46, with "Near Eastern Harbors: Thirteenth–Seventh centuries BCE," in Seymour Gitin, Amihai Mazar, and Ephraim Stern, eds., *Mediterranean Peoples in Transition*, Israel Exploration Society, Jerusalem (1998), 428–38.

16 For the data contained in this paragraph and the following ones: Dilwyn Jones, *Boats*, British Museum Press (1995); Steve Vinson, *Egyptian Boats and Ships*, Shire Publications, Haverfordwest (1994); K. A. Kitchen, "Punt and How to

Get There," *Orientalia* 40 (1977), 184–207; Louise Bradbury, "Reflections on Traveling to 'God's Land' and Punt in the Middle Kingdom," *Journal of the American Research Center in Egypt* 25 (1988), 127–31; Lucien Basch, "Le navire *mnš* et autres notes de voyage en Égypte," *The Mariner's Mirror* 64 (1978), 99–123, with "Phoenician Oared Ships," *The Mariner's Mirror* 55 (1969), 139–62 and 227–45; and George F. Bass, "Sailing between the Aegean and the Orient in the Second Millennium BC," *Aegaeum* 18 (1998), 183–91.

Torgny Säve-Söderbergh, *The Navy of the Eighteenth Egyptian Dynasty*, Almquist and Wiksells, Uppsala (1946) is still highly useful. We can also add the modern edition of Lionel Casson, *The Periplus Maris Erythraei. Text with Introduction, Translation, and Commentary*, Princeton University Press, Princeton (1989).

17 There is a detailed study of these accounts in K. A. Kitchen, *Ramesside Inscriptions, Translated and Annotated* I, 219–22, and *Ramesside Inscriptions, Translated and Annotated. Notes and Comments* I, 176–79, 181–85.

18 Connie Lambrou-Phillipson, "Seafaring in the Bronze Age Mediterranean: The Parameters Involved in Maritime Travel," *Aegaeum* 7 (1991), 11–19. The best overall study of sailing times remains that of Lionel Casson, *Ships and Seamanship in the Ancient World*, Princeton University Press, Princeton (1971), chapter twelve ("Seasons and Winds, Sailing, Rowing, Speed"). He reminds us that in the eastern Mediterranean, "the sailing season par excellence is from 27 May to 14 September" (p. 270). This indicates that when a Pharaoh set out on land to Asia in mid April–early May, he would have had to secure his ports in the previous year. In the Classical world the average sailing time (with reasonable favorable winds) was 4–6 knots (4.6–6.9 nautical miles/hour). But with unfavorable winds, the voyage was reduced to 2–2.5 knots (2.3–2.875 nautical miles/hour).

Casson also provides a helpful study of sailing in the Classical world in his "Speed Under Sail of Ancient Ships," *Transactions and Proceedings of the American Philological Association* 82 (1951), 136–48. He observes that it took about 11–14 days to travel from Alexandria to Crete yet only 3–4 days in the reverse direction (p. 145).

19 Basch, "Les bateaux-corbeilles des Haou Nebout," *CRIPEL* 4 (1976), 13–51, for the old data.

20 George F. Bass, "Sailing between the Aegean and the Orient in the Second Millennium BC," *Aegaeum* 18 (1998), 183–91.

21 Dimitri Meeks, "Locating Punt," in David O'Connor and Stephen Quirke, eds., *Mysterious Lands*, UCL Press, London (2003), 53–80, provides a new analysis of the location of this fabulous country. He argues, contrary to most Egyptologists, that Punt lay on the southern western perimeter of the Arabian peninsula rather inland from the Somali Coast.

22 Basch, "Le navire *mnš* et autres notes de voyage en Égypte," *The Mariner's Mirror* 64 (1978), 99–123.

23 Miriam Lichtheim, *Ancient Egyptian Literature* I, University of California Press, Berkeley–Los Angeles, London (1973), 212–13. For a useful discussion of the Old Kingdom data, see Manfred Bietak, "Zur Marine des Alten Reiches," in John Baines et al., eds., *Pyramid Studies and other Essays Presented to I. E. S. Edwards*, Egypt Exploration Society, London (1988), 35–40.

24 Lichtheim, *Ancient Egyptian Literature* II, 41. I disagree with Schulman, *Military Rank, Title and Organization in the Egyptian New Kingdom*, 26, regarding the Egyptian *sa* or "company." Instead, I follow Helck and Faulkner and set the total number of men in this segment at 200.

25 Säve-Söderbergh, *The Navy of the Eighteenth Egyptian Dynasty*, 71–91, presents a detailed analysis of the ships' crews.

26 Breasted, *Ancient Records of Egypt* II, 195–7; and Sethe, *Urkunden der 18. Dynastie*, 685–8. Säve-Söderbergh, *The Navy of the Eighteenth Egyptian Dynasty*, 39–57, covers the Egyptian naval activity during mid Dynasty XVIII.

27 Breasted, *Ancient Records of Egypt* II, 198–201; and Sethe, *Urkunden der 18. Dynastie*, 689–90.

28 On the *teher* warriors: Gnirs, *Militär und Gesellschaft*, 57–8.

29 The standard article on this campaign is that of Faulkner, "The Euphrates Campaign of Thutmosis III," *Journal of Egyptian Archaeology* 32 (1946), 39–42, but see the new work of Redford, *The Wars in Syrian and Palestine of Thutmose III*. Note as well Breasted, *Ancient Records of Egypt* II, 202–5; and Sethe, *Urkunden der 18. Dynastie*, 696–703.

30 In addition to the basic studies on Egyptian ships by Jones and Vinson cited above in note 16, see Säve-Söderbergh, *The Navy of the Eighteenth Egyptian Dynasty*, 50–1. For the problems in identifying the extent of Djahy, see chapter 8 n. 2.

31 Redford, *History and Chronology of the Egyptian Eighteenth Dynasty*, chapter 4, was the first scholar to cover the warfare of Hatshepsut in detail. Subsequently, an additional important source was published by Walter-Friedrich Reineke, "Ein Nubienfeldzug unter Königin Hatshepsut," in *Ägypten und Kusch*, Erika Endesfelder et al., eds., Akademie Verlag, Berlin (1977), 369–76. Additional data gathered from the Berlin Academy's work in Lower Nubia will be found in Fritz Hintze and Walter F. Reineke, *Felsinschriften aus dem sudanesischen Nubien*, Akademie Verlag, Berlin (1989). A recent overview of Egyptian imperialism to the south is that of David O'Connor, *Ancient Nubia. Egypt's Rival in Africa*, University Museum of Archaeology and Anthropology, Philadelphia (1993), chapter 5. This study provides a welcome new perspective on Egyptian–Nubian relations.

For the local Nubian princes of The-Khet who were part of the early-middle Dynasty XVIII control in the south, see T. Säve-Söderbergh, "The Tomb of Amenemhet and the Princes of The-Khet," in Torgny Säve-Söderbergh and Lana Troy, eds., *New Kingdom Pharaonic Sites. The Finds and the Sites*, Almqvist and Wiksell Tryckeri, Uppsala (1991), 182–211. He also provides a recent summary of the imperialistic and colonial policy of Egypt in Nubia on pp. 1–13.

We can also cite the standard works of Bruce Trigger, *Nubia under the Pharaohs*, Westview Press, Boulder (1976), 103–14; and William Y. Adams, *Nubia. Corridor to Africa*, Princeton University Press, Princeton (1977), chapter 9.

32 Breasted, *Ancient Records of Egypt* II, 48–50; and Sethe, *Urkunden der 18. Dynastie*, 137–41 for the Egyptian text.

33 The limit to which Egyptian control could justify itself (politically and economically) appears to have depended upon geographic factors such as distance

and the difficulty of controlling territories to the east and west of the upper reaches of the Nile.

Two important studies concerning Upper Nubia (and beyond) by David O'Connor can be mentioned in this context: "The Location of Yam and Kush and their Historical Implications," *Journal of the American Research Center in Egypt* 23 (1986), 27–50, and "The Location of Irem," *Journal of Egyptian Archaeology* 73 (1987), 99–136. See as well the more recent discussion of Kitchen presented later in note 24 to chapter 12.

Note also Robert Morkot, "Egypt and Nubia," in Susan E. Alcock et al., eds., *Empires. Perspectives from Archaeology and History*, Cambridge University Press, Cambridge et al. (2000), 227–51.

4

SOCIAL AND RELIGIOUS IMPLICATIONS OF THE NEW MILITARY SYSTEM

In the early years of Dynasty XVIII the Egyptian army, at least up to Thutmose I, was consolidated into a two-tiered system, but the chariot arm had yet to become the one and only elite sector.[1] The careers and backgrounds of the warriors reveal another aspect of this era of transition. In this case the earlier civilian-oriented role of the high-ranking soldiers was growing into an independent self-standing profession. Although the following analysis covers a somewhat later time frame than the opening era of Dynasty XVIII, it serves well to elucidate the main developmental vectors within the Egyptian state. The generals, for example, were extremely close to the king. Their titles came to include such attributive phrases as "of the king" or "of the Lord of the two Lands." In similar fashion, the chief (or first) charioteer was referred to as one "of his majesty," thereby announcing in an explicit fashion the intimate connection of ruler with the high officers of war. True, many charioteers with this expanded title occur at the close on Dynasty XVIII. Yet the increasingly lengthy epithets attached to the highest-ranking military men indicate that the army, unlike the treasury, for example, was closely associated with the Pharaoh. The king, after all, was a war leader. He led the army into battle. He was the first on the battlefield, or at least in the official dogma the king had a function identical to the original role of the chess piece bearing the same name.

Older functions as well as titles quickly faded under the first kings of Dynasty XVIII. Previously, the generals' activities included paramilitary functions. They were laid aside, or to be more specific, the highest military officers performed a role purely military. A few older titles connected to the marshaling of able-bodied men disappeared, if only because they were connected with activities of a nonmilitary nature such as quarrying expeditions or work projects. But representative of the new military organization were men who held the positions of marshal, field marshal, master of the stalls (an administrative functionary), first officer of the chariotry, and the charioteer. In late Dynasty XVIII we hear of a field marshal and the chief charioteer.[2] The rank of a stallmaster appears in the written evidence under Thutmose III; i.e., in the middle of Dynasty XVIII. The non-infantry positions develop until the end of the reign of Amunhotep III when the system that is normally described for the New Kingdom appears in full bloom. This interpretation may reflect the paucity of onomastic evidence for the first half of Dynasty XVIII, although most soldiers still entered into the state bureaucracy at the end of their career, a situation that subsequently was to change.

The army was also the outlet for the virile young princes. Evidence throughout the New Kingdom allows us to conclude that these royal sons worked themselves up through the chariotry rather than in the infantry. From the reign of Thutmose I we know of one king's son, a certain Wadjmose, who was a generalissimo of his father and who had prowess in horsemanship, that is to say, with chariots. Tutors of king's sons may have once held the rank of marshal. But the civil–military division within the state remained in force during the early century or so of Dynasty XVIII. Minmose, who lived under Thutmose III and Amunhotep II, moved from a purely military role to a civilian one. His career ended with him being a supervisor of building projects. Indeed, in his biography he stresses his bureaucratic role over that of his earlier warrior one.

We see a growing specialization of the military ranks during the expansion of the Egyptian Empire. The first switch, which is hard to pinpoint, was that of the alteration from a naval-based military force to a land-based one. The latter included the chariotry as the faster and more elite arm. Horsemanship, meaning ability to use chariots, inevitably came to the fore. It is easy to note the growing importance of this sector and its rise to elite status within the army. By the reign of Thutmose IV, the career of a general had its basis within the chariot division: marshals became generals if they were successful. These men also controlled the northeast zone of Egypt, from the border post of Sile right through Syria (Upa or Damascus). Such men led their troops in the field, or else field marshals, also associated with the chariotry, performed this function.

It is incorrect to view the earlier phase of Dynasty XVIII as representing a lopsided or incomplete system. True, the second half of Dynasty XVIII witnessed a more regular military organization in which the chariotry became paramount. During the reigns of Thutmose I to Thutmose III, however, the army was a corporation whose units were still in flux.[3] The connection of military careers with civilian ones is one example. In addition, the personal association of high-ranking officials with their lord, the Pharaoh, is another. Even at the end of the XVIIIth Dynasty important military men ended up in high state functions. Officers serving in the south often became overseers of Nubia or the provinces of Egypt. But late in life they could also perform other roles in the state of a nonmilitary nature. This is even to be observed in the reign of Ramesses II. Therefore, it is incorrect to view the duality between civilian versus military in a narrow fashion.

We must remember, theoretically and in practice as well, that all officials were servants of Pharaoh.[4] Treasurers, secretaries, and other state functionaries were dependents of their monarch. What singled out the military men of high rank was their primary purpose of war. But it must not be forgotten that armies do most of their jobs outside of the battlefield. They administer, regulate, and control. In the case of New Kingdom Egypt most of the lower ranks went home to organize their fields for cultivation. Middle-level soldiers as well as the highest ones owned plots of land that, if they were relatively well-off, were supervised through overseers. Although dependent upon the state (i.e., the king) for their career, they were nonetheless landowners. The concept of a standing army run by the state must not be viewed from a modern perspective. We should actually consider the officer class as men who had bases of economic freedom independent of their profession.

A comparison can be brought into the discussion so long as it is not considered to be an equivalent situation. In pre-Revolutionary France the high positions of the state bureaucracy were paid, but those men allowed to perform these functions belonged to the upper middle class. They received a salary yet at the same time they had some wealth of their own. State officials such as the kings' finance ministers, judges, lawyers, and the like were royal dependents. These *noblesse de robe* could have lived without performing their state roles, although on a very diminished level. Since the reign of Louis XIV the aristocracy, the *noblesse d'épée*, had been officially prevented from serving in these capacities, although often they were high-ranking officers in the military.

But there was no true nobility in Egypt at this time. Since late Dynasty XII bureaucrats, officials of the state, ran the kingdom.[5] All were dependent upon the Pharaoh for their salaries. Yet the highest men in the officialdom came from important land-based families, and they belonged to powerful and wealthy families. Yet none of them were holders of extensive acreage. At best, they were possessors of latifundia which were not grandiose. Hence, when the army became an important sector in the Late Middle Kingdom, it was state run. The developments in the Second Intermediate Period altered the organization of the military to some degree, but it remained geared to the earlier system of naval warfare. When the chariot arm began to be important in late Dynasty XVII, one elite sector (charioteers) began to replace another (naval commanders). The common footsoldier, on the other hand, belonged both economically and socially to a very different level than the chariot warrior. Only the latter might expect to be given a bureaucratic job after retiring from active service.

Changed, however, was the ethos of warfare, its success, and the rise of a more complex system. From the outgoing XVIIth Dynasty to the middle of Dynasty XVIII Egypt continued an aggressive foreign policy. As we have seen, this was first directed to subduing Upper Nubia south of the Second

Cataract. At a certain point, undoubtedly during the reign of Thutmose I, a more fixed organization was developed with regard to the south. There, military men moved up the ladder of promotion solely within this region. Other army officials experienced their rise through a graduated series of steps in a system that was more regularized by the reign of Thutmose IV. Marshals could become generals; troop commandants or officers of the standing army were able to climb up to the position of marshals. The scribes of the king who were associated with the army, however, were previously connected to the state bureaucracy, and so have to be considered separately.

I do not think that it is correct to regard any of these promotions as based upon firm and fixed rules of promotion.[6] Excluding battlefield prowess and extraordinary deeds in the field, the officers were not subjected to standardized tests as today. The system of advancement did not follow a predetermined code. It was personal as, indeed, were all high positions. Let us remember that the economic and social system of New Kingdom Egypt was not on the level of even Early Modern Europe. Importance was fixed by one's economic status at birth. Choices of a profession could be made by at least the relatively well-off, and if an army career was desired, then training was necessary. Coupled with this was the link of a family to the court or to other high officials. Having a connection to power mattered. Possibilities of advancement often depended upon the social rank of an individual, taking into consideration parameters that we cannot evaluate owing to the paucity of information. For example, we do not know whether the eldest son in a family, or even a junior son, had to choose a military career for himself. We are equally ignorant of the family background of most of the men who became the high officials of the army. There are no data extant that can elucidate the question of military preparedness except for some cases where a military man had a father who also served in the army. From the limited corpus of XVIIIth Dynasty army officials we are better able to trace the military careers of these men than to comment upon their reasons for choosing the profession of warrior.

It is readily agreed that the aggressive policy of royal imperialism fostered by a strong nationalistic feeling owing to the wars against the Hyksos was an important propellant in the rise of the military. Yet the military men did not yet form themselves into a "cast."[7] As we have seen, there still was a strong interconnection between civilian jobs and military ones. But certainly for the high-ranking army commanders this arrangement had been in place for over a century before the successful campaign of Kamose. We have already touched upon the term "king's son" and its relevance to the warrior case of the Late Middle Kingdom. Throughout Dynasties XIII to XVII the army was part and parcel of the entire bureaucratic state. Under the pressure of the Hyksos, commencing in Dynasty XIII, the native Egyptians faced an inordinate amount of pressure from the north. The loss of the eastern Delta, followed by the fast takeover of this entire region following upon the fall of Memphis, indicates that the technological level of the Late Middle Kingdom was as limited as it was unprepared. A more rigid military system had taken over in Dynasty XVII, one in which garrisons at key cities were the norm, and a dual civilian-administration ran such localities. By the reign of Kamose the standing army had become partly focused upon military camps. Yet in no way were the warriors a separate and exclusive corporate body within the Nile Valley. Sons might follow fathers in the profession, but the low- and middle-ranking men did not spend a complete year in service.

The distinction of performing war deeds coupled with a nonmilitary setting is crucial. By and large, the Egyptian soldiers of Dynasties XVII and XVIII did not form a professional entity separate and isolated from the civilians. That is why I have not used the term "cast" when describing their role within society. Except for some hardy "mercenaries" from the south, the army was basically Egyptian in nationality. "Strongholds" for soldiers had yet to be a regular part of the military system; there were neither permanent settlements of troops nor military colonies. The confusion that many have concerning the New Kingdom military system is centered upon the premise of a free-standing army owing its allegiance to the Pharaoh. Not only was such an institution in place earlier, but, more importantly, it also remained encapsulated within the nation. In other words, the early New Kingdom army was not a corporate body comparable to the priesthood. The growing need for specialization in ranks and organization only made itself necessary after many years, and this came to the fore around the reign of Thutmose IV if not a bit earlier. But even then, its greater social importance was due to the rise in significance of the chariot arm.

Nationalism, as might be expected, played a major importance in the lives of the soldiers. We can witness this fervor for the first time in Pharaonic Egypt during the wars against the Hyksos. The self-conscious image of Egypt versus the enemy and the phrase "our land" aptly reveal this new direction in the social ethos of the country. These attitudes are as commonplace in extant biographical texts of the warriors of early Dynasty XVIII as is the strong contemporary anti-foreign bias within the royal inscriptions of the Pharaohs, Kamose and Ahmose in particular. But whereas chauvinistic rhetoric is one thing, the actual organization of a war machine remains a quite different matter. It must be granted that the successful campaigns of the Pharaohs within Egypt and later in Nubia and Asia fostered to some degree the feeling of superiority on the part of the warriors. Striking, nonetheless, is the lack of any hostility shown to this group by the other sectors of Egyptian society. This will come later in Dynasty XIX when a different military set-up was in place and when the wars in the north were more threatening. Earlier, the soldiers were still well integrated within Egyptian society.

It is relatively straightforward to hypothesize the development of the warrior ethos among the males in the royal family. Prince Wadjmose, to take a case in point, but also Ahmose, Kamose, and even his predecessor Seqenenre II, had to lead the army. By the inculcation of a new attitude of personal valor on the field of battle an expanded concept of kingship came into being. Here, as well, we can trace the early Dynasty XVIII hero-kings back into the murky past of the Second Intermediate Period. During that time, Thebes was threatened from the north owing to the successful campaigns of the Hyksos. Indeed, the city itself was on the defensive for a lengthy period of time, and during this era the even older concept of "Victorious Thebes" came once more to the fore, thereby signifying the constricted nature of the only native kingdom in the Nile Valley.[8] Thereafter, with the inexorable march north coupled with a second front to the south in Lower Nubia, the kings became the physical incarnation of bellicosity.

All of this is made self-evident in the conclusion of the second Kamose stela. After returning from Avaris, Kamose docked at Thebes, precisely at the quay in front of the temple of the god Amun, the chief deity of the city. By this time both Thebes and Amun were intertwined. State, king, and godhead were intimately connected. To fight for the land meant to follow the banner of the hero-king as well as the chief god, Amun. No wonder that Kamose first entered the holy precinct of Karnak in order to render homage to his father Amun. From this short section at the very end of the war account Kamose reveals what later would become one of the major facets of the Egyptian nation: Amun coupled with Pharaoh. The god received some of the benefits from the successful campaign, be it booty or prisoners. And following an age-old practice, the captive foe, prince or king, would be ritually sacrificed. There was thus a growing symbiotic relationship between king and deity, which naturally was broadcast through the official theological dogma of the day.

The term for this apparent combination of theology and politics is labeled Political Theology, and it played a crucial factor in the development of a new royal ethos connected to warfare.[9] The rhetoric of legitimization of kingship was expanded to include an ever-increasing emphasis played upon the role of the king as the son of Amun. In the Middle Kingdom we meet for the first time the idea of the Pharaoh as a "good shepherd." Later this is extended to the god Amun and other key deities. The earlier double-sided concept of Pharaoh remained. The king is beneficial when connected to the cat goddess Bastet, or violently aggressive against his enemies when he puts on the position of the lion goddess Sekhmet. This duality, also known in Dynasty XII, is repeated in scenes and texts of the New Kingdom relating to the king in battle. The anger of Pharaoh is expressed through the fire of his uraeus, *nesert*, blazing against the enemy. This virulent disposition, both political and military, was repeated again and again in early Dynasty XVIII. God (Amun usually) reveals himself in the king who, with his power and anger – the Egyptian word *bau* – moves against the enemy. At the same time this new direction in Political Theology manifested itself in an opposite direction. To those foreign lands and peoples who remained friendly, so too was the king. The word used here was *hetepu*, connected to "peace," "contentment," or even "submission."[10]

In the New Kingdom this development extended far beyond the political sphere of Egypt's imperium. Yet the difference between love, connected to Bastet, and fear, linked to Sekhmet, remained a basic part of the worldview of the Egyptians. If the foreign potentates of Palestine and Syria recognized the Pharaoh, then according to this schema they rendered "peace," *hetepu*. In order to insure their loyalty, the New Kingdom Pharaohs instituted a practice of invoking an oath, but to achieve further subservience, they required that his sons or brothers come to Egypt. This policy of captivity is first recorded in the reign of Thutmose III and explicitly associated with the northern city-states. Thus an additional difference between Egyptian imperialism in Asia and that in Nubia can be noticed. To the south, Thutmose I first established an intermediary between him and the locals, the viceroy or "King's Son of the Southern Foreign Lands."[11] (The title was later to change to "King's Son of Kush.") The Egyptian ruler further let the local potentates handle their own affairs within the bounds of Egyptian domination. Later, however, and this can be seen under the reigns of Thutmose II and III, a more exacting and centralized control was established. But in all cases, whether the rebel was Nubian or Asiatic, it was the king's *bau*, his ferocious and powerful anger, that came into play whenever there was rebellion. By the reign of Thutmose I destruction of the enemy as well as "widening the boundaries" became two joint themes.

Associated with the rapidly expanding political-theological viewpoint was publication in text and pictures of the divine birth of Pharaoh through god Amun.[12] At the same time the military aspect of both king and deity was altered. Even though this aspect is barely visible in Dynasty XVII, it is most notable in the early XVIIIth Dynasty. For the first time the "king in battle" became a theme for the artists and writers alike.[13] The pictorial record of Ahmose, fragmentary though it may be, is a prime case in point. Hitherto, the monarchs presented themselves smiting the enemy (always one man, the enemy chief) with the archaic mace in age-old stereotypical representations. Now, however, things changed. The record of Ahmose's flotilla points to this fact as does his scene of chariot fighting. Subsequently, Thutmose II emphasized his land battles with the enemy – note the chariots – and subsequent kings enlarged upon this theme. By the reign of Amunhotep II, there was developed a regular program for such visual narration. The king fights in the field; he returns with his prisoners. In fact, the Pharaohs could provide a whole series of interrelated pictorial themes of a campaign. Commencing with the departure and including the arrival at the battlefield, we can see the slaughter, the reception of the booty, and the final presentation to Amun. How many of these subscenes could be portrayed was left up to the artists and carvers, all of whom were dependent upon the amount of space at hand.

Later narrative war records were developed in a parallel systematic fashion. The style of Kamose war record was not followed.[14] His first-person account was abandoned for two different types of written presentation. For small campaigns or battles in which the king often did not fight, a free-standing stela or a moderate-sized rock inscription was carved. The major wars, on the other hand, tended to be carved on the temple walls (especially those of Karnak) or on lengthy stelae set up within a religious edifice. A certain approach in the language and grammar was preferred, often called a "court style."[15] This reflected the serious nature of the conflict but likewise indicated the preference for a certain elevated tone. Yet within the background of either presentation was the role of Amun as the helper father.

The major theme of these two forms of historical narration was that of the suppression of chaos. Anarchy was the attribute of the enemy. Egypt (Amun, king) represented Truth (*Maat*) and permanence.[16] No wonder that the pictorial aspects of war concentrated upon the confused and unorganized nature of the foe. The enemies fall over, flee, are scattered around in small groups, or individually show cowardice and lack of strength. Unlike the regular system of Egyptian artistic portrayal, the opponents with their horses and chariots are completely unorganized. The incoherence of the battle melee in opposition to the superhuman figure of a solitary king in chariot shooting his bow provides the best example of this new artistic representation. Frequently omitted are the lines separating one register from another. True, often the lowermost portions of the battle scenes show a more regular pattern of marching soldiers and chariots, or rows of guards. Nonetheless, the key elements of representation had changed. Because the focus of victory was always personalized, the Pharaoh's superhuman size could be juxtaposed with another large figure, that of the chief enemy. The foe naturally was not as large as the king, but his presence indicated a personal "duel" between Pharaoh and foe.

This visual personalization of war goes hand in hand with the New Kingdom concept of warfare. The Egyptian king, as deputy and son of Amun, wars against the recalcitrant foes. Always in a chariot, Pharaoh shoots his arrows and fells the major opponent. When there was no enemy king on the field and a citadel had to be conquered, Egyptian Pharaohs are depicted boldly attacking the fortress city while their troops are ready to smash open the gates. The local prince pleads on the top of the battlement for peace as he cannot resist the might of Pharaoh. Some regularity of organization is apparent, although all remains in a state of mass confusion outside of the invested city as the Egyptian footsoldiers advance, with the chariots remaining somewhat distant from the action. Even here the battle is personalized into a duel. Instead of a superhuman Pharaoh piercing the chief enemy he fights a large citadel with his arrows.

It should not surprise us that all of these concepts lack political dimensions that are commonplace today. The actions of foe and king alike are presented in a rigid political-theological framework, one that views war as a personal contest of the Pharaoh against chaos. The enemy, be he king, prince, or even city, has taken the role of the one who upsets Truth (*Maat*). The conflict, in fact, remained intimately linked with the godhead of Egypt, Amun. Much of the booty secured from a successful campaign ended up being delivered to that deity, a situation that meant in practice that Amun's temple of Karnak benefited to no small degree. Prisoners were placed as work slaves within this massive complex, one that owned numerous parcels of land throughout Egypt. Those who led the rebellion were ritually killed. Amunhotep II, for example, recounts on his Amada Stela that he brought back seven dead princes.[17] Six he hung on the walls of Thebes and a seventh on the walls of Gebel Barkal at the Fourth Cataract. Significantly, both places were major centers of Amun. In other words, once more the godhead is directly associated with the victory.

Pictorially, the same theological aspect was represented. One portion of the war scenes included the presentation of prisoners to Amun; an early example may be found on a block of Amunhotep II.[18] There, the Pharaoh is shown in front of fourteen Asiatics, and the king stretches his right hand to Amun as a sign of the final action of the entire war. On another block the same number of defeated chieftains is arrayed on the back of Pharaoh's horse as well as in the cab, on the yoke pole, and walking behind him. These scenes indicate the drastic result of the king's campaigns by means of the captured leaders who will later be given up to Amun.

EXCURSUS

1. Because this chapter deals with the interrelationship of the internal social set-up of the early New Kingdom and the military expansion of the Egyptian state, the situation arises concerning the predominance of one or the other aspect. That is to say, should one place emphasis upon the domestic or foreign policy of the Pharaohs? This is not a simple matter to overlook. Indeed, it is one that has vexed modern historians for over two centuries.

In the nineteenth century it was commonplace to argue that the power of the state depended upon its external relations, or at least that *Außenpolitik* rather than *Innenpolitik* had preference in the diplomatic and political spheres of the nation state. This received its Classical statements in the works of Droysen, Treitschke, and Meinecke, even though Jacob Burckhardt weighed heavily upon the Berlin School of political historians. (See now Lionel Gossman, *Basel in the Age of Burckhardt. A Study in Unseasonable Ideas*, University of Chicago Press, Chicago and London [2000].)

The complexity of both sides of any nation, state, kingdom, or even an archaic state such as Pharaonic Egypt, which was basically a primitive realm, is a crucial one. The growing military corporation in Dynasty XVIII was spurred on by the bellicose actions of the kings upstream to Nubia and later northward into Palestine. The warrior tradition of the XVIIth Dynasty, which was a result of the divided nature of the Nile Valley at that time, had its origins within Egypt rather than without.

Yet the rather limited nature of social development throughout the period under consideration meant that the military arm, directly connected to the Pharaoh as war leader, took long to fuse and, in fact, never really became a totally independent body. With the arrival of new peoples (Libyans) and different social arrangements at the close of Dynasty XX this was to alter to a degree greater than at the beginning of Dynasty XVIII. Hence, it is not surprising to see that the warriors of the Ramesside Period decorated their tombs in basically the same manner as nonmilitary men. There was no division between civilians and military men in the conception of the afterworld and its demands upon the living.

2. It is my contention that the external demands placed upon the Pharaohs owing to their aggressive policy of warfare must be seen in the light of the internal situation of the Nile Valley. I do not feel that a sharp differentiation between internal and external affairs, at least during the New Kingdom, took place. As a healthy antidote to a purely "outside orientation," I can refer to the seminal study of Eckart Kehr, *Economic Interest, Militarism, and Foreign Policy. Essays on German History*, Grete Heinz, trs., University of California Press, Berkeley (1977).

Concerning the issues of this chapter, a similar dichotomy between two Egyptological outlooks concerning the Egyptian military may be seen in Helck's *Der Einfluss der Militärführer* and Alexander Scharff's thought-provoking review of that work in *Orientalia* 9 (1940), 144–8. Both scholars focused their attention upon the affects of the military within Egypt.

On the other hand, the links between politics and the military seem self-evident today. Helck, in his pioneering study, argued that the effects of the expanding Egyptian war machine inevitably led to a takeover by the army after the close of the Amarna Period (late Dynasty XVIII). This was too extreme a position, and one of the salutary conclusions of Gnirs' work is that the "primitiveness" of the New Kingdom war corporation is readily ascertained. For example, if generals were involved in building projects, this merely reveals the somewhat fluid characteristics of the various subsystems in Pharaonic Egypt. The same may, in fact, be said with regard to the clergy and the bureaucracy. No sharp divide between these two units can be made even for the Old and Middle Kingdoms much less than in Dynasty XVIII.

We have to thank Hans Delbrück for his lifetime's work as this scholar always concerned himself with the links between politics and warfare. See in particular the useful studies of Arden Buchholz, *Hans Delbrück and the Germans Military Establishment. War Images in Conflict*, University of Iowa Press, Iowa City (1985); and Gordon A. Graig, "Delbrück: The Military Historian," in Peter Paret, ed., *Makers of Modern Strategy from Machiavelli to the Nuclear Age*, Princeton University Press, Princeton (1943), 326–53.

3. The concept of the military as a corporation parallels that of the officialdom (bureaucracy) and clergy (priesthood). For the most part I have borrowed extensively from the works of Elias and Luhmann, a few of which are cited in note 3 to this chapter. Kehr's work considers the ideal case when an internal social movement (including the military, but not totally run by warriors) forces its outlook upon the state. His example was the famous *Flottenpolitik* of pre World War I Germany.

Helck, equally, would have placed the internal outlook of Horemheb (end of Dynasty XVIII) and his supporters in the same category. This scholar felt that general Horemheb's attempt to stabilize the dynastic situation within Egypt (as well as his personal interests) cannot be seen independently from his (presumed) anti-Hittite policy as revealed by the Zannanza affair, which involved the Hittites of Anatolia at the close of Dynasty XVIII. (See note 12 to chapter 10). A useful summary of his ideas on the interconnection of the military and politics may be read in his volume *Politische Gegensätze im alten Ägypten*, Gerstenberg Verlag, Hildesheim (1984), 47–52, 63–6, 74–5. The reader should keep in mind that he labeled this work as "Ein Versuch," although he did not subscribe to the views of such historians as Freidrich Meinecke concerning the unified national state (e.g., in *Cosmopolitanism and the National State*, Robert B. Kimber, trs., Princeton University Press, Princeton [1970].) Recognizing instead the level of social development within New Kingdom Egypt, Helck tended to emphasize a dichotomy between "conservatives" and "progressives," and he acutely saw the great importance of personal relations in influencing royal policy. New Kingdom society, although containing a sophisticated and well-organized bureaucracy, clergy, and now a military, nonetheless was at a rudimentary level in which social relations still depended upon close personal contacts as well as family relations. Berlev would have agreed with this position.

NOTES

1 Gnirs, *Militär und Gesellschaft*, 1–39, covers the structural developments within the social system of the Early New Kingdom military system. The recent volume of Partridge, *Fighting Pharaohs*, avoids this important work. As noted earlier in excursus 2 to chapter 1, Schulman did not cover the internal ramifications of the new chariot-based army; Kadry presented an outline.

2 Gnirs, *Militär und Gesellschaft*, 28–34.

3 The socio-historical conception of corporations operating within a given social system has been explored by two major German scholars: Norbert Elias, *The Court Society*, Edmund Jephcott, trs., Pantheon, New York (1983), with *The Germans. Power Struggles and the Development of Habitus in the Nineteenth and Twentieth Centuries*, Eric Dunning and Stephen Mennell, trs., Columbia University Press, New York (1996); and Niklas Luhmann, *Social Systems*, John Bednarz, Jr. and Dirk Baecker, trs., Stanford University Press, Stanford (1995).

For a modern Egyptological viewpoint see Jan Assmann, *The Mind of Egypt. History and Meaning in the Time of the Pharaohs*, Andrew Jenkins, trs., Metropolitan Books, New York (2002), Part Four, and "State and Religion in the New Kingdom," in William Kelly Simpson, ed., *Religion and Philosophy in Ancient Egypt*, Yale Egyptological Seminar, New Haven (1989), 55–88. Add my "Sovereignty and Theology in New Kingdom Egypt: Some Cases of Tradition," *Saeculum* 47 (1996), 217–38.

4 Oleg Berlev, who was the first to systematize the military during the Middle Kingdom and the Second Intermediate Period (excursus 3 to chapter 1), repeatedly stressed this point. Among his publications we may single out his summary "Bureaucrats," in Donadoni, ed., *The Egyptians*, 87–119.

5 Stephen Quirke, *The Administration of Egypt in the Late Middle Kingdom. The Hieratic Documents*, Sia Publishing, New Malden (1990), provides a detailed analysis of the social and administrative set-up from the reign of Sesostris III through Dynasty XIII.

6 This point needs to be emphasized. In her study on the New Kingdom army, *Militär und Gesellschaft*, Gnirs cautions us against assuming that any of the high military men had careers that could be placed within a narrowly defined *cursus honorum*. Paramilitary functions were often performed in conjunction with warlike ones, and at best a connection can be drawn between men who were first marshals and then later generals.

7 By "cast" I mean a specific social subsystem within an entity (in this case Dynasty XVIII Egypt) that has developed to such a degree that it views itself as separate from other subsystems. Even the later New Kingdom military arm was never completely or nearly endogamous. The term "corporation" is more applicable.

8 Classically, see the study of Detlef Franke, "Erste und Zweite Zwischenzeit. Ein Vergleich," *Zeitschrift für ägyptische Sprache* 117 (1990), 119–29 and pp. 124–6 in particular.

9 The two studies of Assmann referred to above in note 3 cover the conception of Political Theology as applied to Pharaonic Egypt. His later work, *Politische Theologie zwischen Ägypten und Israel*, Carl Friedrich von Siemens Stiftung, Munich (1991), is more explicit. See as well *Herrschaft und Heil. Politische Theologie in Altägypten, Israel und Europa*, C. Hanser, Munich (2000).

10 The best analysis of this term and the attitude of the Pharaohs toward the cities of Syria and Palestine will be found in Liverani, *Prestige and Interest*, Part Two ("War and Alliance"). One must avoid a too strict legal analysis of these relations.

11 See now Gnirs, *Militär und Gesellschaft*, 35–6, and her prosopographical data assembled on pp. 134–41.

12 G. A. Gaballa, *Narrative in Egyptian Art*, Phillip von Zabern, Mainz am Rhein (1976) 53–60, presents a summary.

13 For the XVIIIth Dynasty the work of Harvey, *The Cults of King Ahmose at Abydos*, 303–72, is crucial. See as well Johnson, *An Asiatic Battle Scene of Tutankhamun from Thebes*.

The Amunhotep II evidence was published by Abdel Hamid Zayed, "Une représentation inédite des campagnes d'Aménophis II," in Paule Posener-Kriéger, ed., *Mélanges Gamal Eddin Mokhtar* I, Institut Français d'Archéologie Orientale, Cairo (1985), 5–17.

See now the studies of Heinz, *Die Feldzugsdarstellungen des Neuen Reiches,* and Müller, *Der König als Feldherr. Schlachtenreliefs, Kriegsberichte und Kriegsführung im Mittleren und Neuen Reich.* An earlier work of the second scholar is *Die Thematik der Schlachtenreliefs,* MA Thesis, Tübingen (1995). Finally, there is the older compendium of Gaballa, *Narrative in Egyptian Art,* 99–129 (Ramesside Period; Dynasties XIX–XX).

14 For this data, see my *Aspects of the Military Documents of the Ancient Egyptians,* Yale University Press, New Haven and London (1982).

15 Thomas Ritter, *Das Verbalsystem der königlichen und privaten Inschriften. XVIII Dynastie bis einschließlich Amenophis III.,* Otto Harrassowitz, Wiesbaden (1995). Unfortunately, this work does not address the socio-historical nature of the material. The reader should keep in mind that the hieroglyphic texts of the later Ramesside Period were written in a style and linguistic level that is best described as a "language of tradition," following the term coined by the Egyptologist Pascal Vernus.

16 In general, see now Assmann, *Ma'at. Gerechtigkeit und Unsterblichkeit im Alten Ägypten,* C. H. Beck (2001); and *The Search for God in Ancient Egypt,* David Lorton, trs., Cornell University Press, Ithaca and London (2001), chapter 9.

17 Peter Der Manuelian covers the wars of this king in his *Studies in the Reign of Amenophis II,* Gerstenberg Verlag, Hildesheim (1987), chapter II and pp. 47–56 in particular.

18 Der Manuelian, *Amenophis II,* 78–83; and Zayed's study referred to in note 13 above.

5

THE BATTLE OF MEGIDDO
AND ITS RESULT

The Megiddo campaign of Thutmose III was so crucial to the reconsolidation of the Egyptian Empire that modern scholars still continue to fight with one another regarding its importance. To us moderns as well as to the king himself the significance of Thutmose's victory paved the way to a more permanent occupation of Palestine. At Karnak, the Pharaoh ordered a lengthy account to be drawn up, one that, to no small degree, depended upon the official war diary of the army.[1] As a result, the narrative presents a sober and straight-forward tenor, in which specific days and even the hour on one occasion are marked. By using these ephemerides the author stressed certain events, which owing to their significance formed the skeleton of the account. This was the monarch's first war in Asia after he had become the sole Pharaoh of Egypt, his stepmother Hatshepsut having died around six months before the departure from Egypt. Indeed, the campaign is officially listed as Thutmose's first, thereby indicating that he had begun to rule as an independent Pharaoh.

The backdrop to the narrative is presented in a very short introduction.[2] The rationale was a simple one and we can restore the key opening phrases that indicate an expansion of the boundaries of Egypt. In this preamble the anarchistic state of Asia is presented. Mentioned is the garrison town of Sharuhen, and the political situation is called a rebellion, specifically from Yurza (the border river site leading into southern Palestine) to the extreme north. In a nutshell, the *cassus belli* was that of a revolt against Egyptian domination. But the attempt of the Asiatics was more complex than this introduction supposes, and from additional data presented further on in the inscription it is clear that with the support of the key Syrian city of Kadesh, whose prince was at Megiddo, the local city-states in Palestine had broken away from Egypt.

Behind this campaign, therefore, lay some time in which the revolt gained strength. Although this is obliquely alluded to in the official Egyptian record, it is nonetheless clear than many months of preparation had taken place. Megiddo lay in the Esdraelon Plain and was the most important centrally located city in Palestine.[3] It controlled the trade routes to the east

83

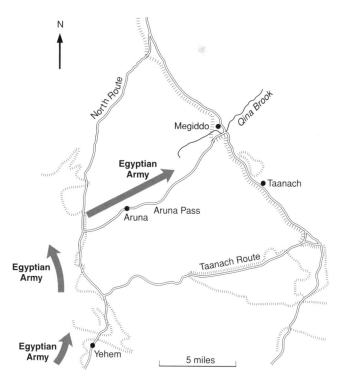

Map 4   The battle of Megiddo

to Trans-Jordan as well as to the north, in fact directly to Kadesh. The King's Highway, the major arterial route running north–south, passed by this locality; Egyptian control of Megiddo was necessary for that of Palestine, and city could only be reached through this interior route. Otherwise, it was necessary to traverse the hill region located immediately to the west, and the passes there were narrow. The other major northern artery, the Via Maris or Sea Road, was located near the coast and separate from the inland King's Highway. Practically speaking, both routes were independent of each other. We are not totally certain if Mitanni was behind the revolt, but if we keep in mind that Kadesh was allied to that inland Syrian power, then some indirect support was probably behind the rebellion.[4]

Tactically the march of Thutmose would have been organized for some time. Indeed, there is little doubt that the protagonists knew beforehand that an Egyptian campaign to Megiddo was necessary. The preparations for war were first set in place by the withdrawal of Megiddo from Egyptian control concomitant upon military aid shown to it by the king of Kadesh who resided in Syria. Likewise, all of the locals in Palestine were aware of the oncoming conflict. Those that remained loyal to Egypt, such as the key

84

city of Gaza and the small one of Yehem, may have remained pro-Egyptian owing to the presence of an Egyptian military garrison. Other kinglets, and I would add those in southern Syria as well, were far enough away from the center of resistance not to be immediately affected by any Egyptian counter-attack. Hence, they undoubtedly supported the rebellion, whereas those situated near to Megiddo or Kadesh attempted to free themselves from Egyptian domination.

From the account it is certain that the king amassed a large army. He went north in person as his grandfather Thutmose I did earlier, and it would have taken some time to assemble the troops and material and reinforce the local cities that remained faithful to the Pharaoh. Solely from the account of Thutmose, the need to subdue the rebellion was considered to be of prime importance. With outside help, most of central Palestine had broken with Egypt. Both sides knew this and both maneuvered themselves into two hostile parties. Nothing was secret.

The latter point is worth stressing if only because of the contemporary awareness of the inevitability of war. The goals of the two antagonists were as blatant and public as was their military consolidation. Everyone had recognized that the Egyptians would act, and that they would employ much strength in attempting to subdue the rebels. Then too, the direction of the king's march would have been self-evident to the Asiatics. Thutmose had to leave Egypt from Sile in the Eastern Delta to reach Megiddo. Gaza, already in his hands, was the first place he would pass through.[5] All must have understood that the focus of the king's march would be this city. Thutmose's aim was no surprise. His method of warfare – the tactics that he would employ – was also clear. Hence, the Pharaoh would have to be opposed on a battlefield, not by simple town or city defenses.

The date for departure was at the beginning of the month of April, a time when the harvest of the crops had already begun and was proceeding apace.[6] Wheat is presently first harvested in Egypt at the beginning of April, one month later than barley. Roughly between AD 1000 and AD 1800 the agri-cultural schedule for wheat began at the beginning of October and ran up to the end of March; land on which barley was grown lay fallow after the beginning of February. Even so, these two crops and their agricultural cycle were different in Pharaonic times, owing to the rudimentary system of basin agriculture coupled with only the shaduf or water basket. I feel that Thutmose's date of departure was set when the main grain crops had ceased their annual cycle and the foot soldiers could be mustered.

Such a war may appear ludicrous to us moderns.[7] After all, when is the goal so well defined and known to friend and foe alike? Today, the plan of attack is rarely perceived in so exact a manner. The enemy recognized the direction and staging points of Thutmose as well as his bases for supplies and reinforcements. Therefore, we must view this war with an attitude far different from modern ones. Granted that, tactically, Thutmose caught the enemy outside of the city of Megiddo, but this was not a strategic event. By experience as well, peoples of the Late Bronze Age knew that a marching soldier cannot carry his own supplies for more than 10 or 11 days. How much of his food was imperishable is hard to say, but we can be assured that the Thutmose's army needed regular provisioning.

We do not know the size of the Egyptian forces. It could not have been greater than 10,000.[8] Indeed, I feel that this number is an exaggeration. But did he leave Sile with all of his soldiers?[9] Support troops could have been added to his army at Gaza even though the narrative leaves our suppositions in the cold. But the ease in which the royal army halted and set up tents for the night coupled with the relative simplicity of departure tends to indicate a rather well-coordinated military force with a good leader at its head. It also implies that the number of troops, horses, chariots, and supply wagons were not that numerous. Proceeding at an average daily march of 20 km/day, the Egyptian army reached Yehem, a small city located just before a chain of hills west of Megiddo. This took place about the eleventh day of the first month of the harvest season (*shemu*).[10]

The Egyptian army on this campaign still retained a large number of Palestinian allies. The enemy controlled the key central sector of the Esdraelon Plain but not the lands to the west or the south. Thutmose III knew that in such a war, with people dispersed in a wide area that had many settlements, an army need have no permanent base at all. All that it required to operate was the ability to draw military supplies (in particular food) either behind it by river or by land on clearly defined and well-worn roads. The troops could feed on the produce of the friendly districts through which they marched. All that the Egyptians required to win was discipline, drill, and a belief in themselves. The Pharaoh could supply all three.

Nowhere is it stated whether the army rested at a town between Gaza and Yehem. Because the king was traveling in friendly territory we can suppose that he took advantage of any possibility of a halt, especially when his troops could be supplied. Here we see one of the historical imponderables that occurs owing to the limited nature of the information. In fact, it is identical to the situation of pictorial representation. The king can be shown leaving Egypt at Sile as, for example, we see in the battle reliefs of Seti I.[11] But the next phase of his war concentrates upon the actual battles or deeds that were significant enough to be carved; the rest was ignored.

In an identical fashion the military narratives leave off any occurrence that was ancillary to the focus of attention. In the Kadesh Bulletin of Ramesses II the conflict between the Egyptians and the Hittites opens when the king is in Asia. The first major occurrence is his arrival at Shabtuna, an important site, because it was there the Egyptians received news from two Shasu Bedouin who claimed to have defected from the Hittites. The more detailed Poem reports that Ramesses II left the border post of Sile. The following halt at a royal fortress in the Lebanon Valley bypasses a great amount of time. The same may be said for shorter military accounts such as those of Amunhotep II. By and large, the departure from Sile appears to have been the required narrative beginning for lengthy war records, and even Seti I, in pictorial style, follows this practice. But thereafter, the precise stages of the Egyptian advance are left aside until a memorable event occurred. The reason why Yehem, an insignificant town, was mentioned in Thutmose's account is revealed by the narrative. It was there that the war council took place and conflicting plans were brought forward concerning the way to move upon Megiddo.[12]

Let us now return to some presuppositions already mentioned in this study. Did the king leave Egypt with his entire army or were preparations already in place allowing him to argument his troops further? Most certainly, the Pharaoh would have had to arrange his progress northward. The requisite procuring and rationing of supplies must have been enacted at an earlier time. I also feel that some war material must have been demanded or else already in place through previous deliveries. After all, so long as the Egyptians were in lands loyal to them they could depend upon a series of bases (the towns) at which to stop, refresh, and garner more equipment. The greater the size of the royal army, the more likely it would have been that massive war plans had been put in place. We cannot rely upon the overtly personalized accounts in which the Pharaoh, all by himself, accomplished the work of war. For this reason I feel that Gaza was more important as a rest halt and procurement center at this time than as a city of tactical importance. After all, the king stayed there for one mere day, enough time to reinvigorate his troops.

One useful point for a more exacting calculation occurs near the end of the narrative. Before the battle took place the Egyptian army came out of the narrow Aruna Pass, thereby performing a feat that the enemy did not expect.[13] The inscription states: "Now when the leading detachments came forth upon this road, then the shadow turned." Parker was correct to see the use of a shadow clock to determine the time of day.[14] If we follow him, then the king reached the south of Megiddo on the bank of the Qina Brook when the seventh hour of the day had turned. This was an important position because Thutmose could water his horses at this site and refresh his tired soldiers, who also had need of water. The time would have been in the very early afternoon. This means that somewhat over one hour had passed for the soldiers to reach their fixed position. The army was led through the pass by the king who then waited for the final portion of his rearguard to debouch before he went to the front to command his forces. The pass of Aruna is about 13.4 km long.[15] It is about .8 km from the exit of that pass to the Qina Brook. The distance from Yehem to Aruna is 21 km, about one day's journey, and from Aruna to the end of the pass about 15.3 km.

How big would have been the camp? We know that for a Roman legion of 6,000 men an area of 60 acres would be occupied.[16] This is approximately .24 km². On a campaign the camps were probably smaller, but it has been noted that this dimension is still found in armies at the end of the nineteenth century: 10 acres were used to bivouac 1,000 men. This large figure is impossible given the topography of the region around Megiddo. For 6,000 men the area would have had a side of approximately one half of a kilometer. The topographic nature of the locality indicates that this also would have been too great, indeed more than the area of the mound upon which the ancient city of Megiddo lay. The physical layout permits the possibility of the smaller number. Once more, the result indicates a moderate-sized Egyptian force instead of a very great one.

The army assembled in the plain at the mouth of the Aruna Pass and then moved on. Parker is right to conclude that it reached its desired position in about 80 minutes or so. We can therefore conclude that at about noon the rearguard finally left the pass. At this time the army was not operating in the near single-file system that it had to endure when it traversed the pass. There, it is said that the first troops in the fore were leaving the pass when the last were entering it.

Four facts, therefore, are of prime importance:

1   It took 80 minutes or so for a partially or completely assembled army to march for .8 km. I assume that after the rearguard left the pass, Thutmose then went to the front and soon thereafter ordered the advance to Qina. In other words, the troops at the end would have had enough time to assemble for the march.

2   The same army, traveling Indian style, would cover 15.3 km from front to rear. In this case we have to include soldiers, pack animals, and the horses. All of this would have to have been arranged before departing from Yehem. Because the Egyptians remained at that town for three days, there was more than enough time to prepare for the arduous journey.

3   The account indicates that the horses followed each other in Indian style, but nothing specific is revealed concerning the march of the soldiers.

4   Two men in a chariot drawn by two horses occupy the same road space as 12 infantrymen. We can increase this figure by two owing to the small chariots of the day.[17] As the horses were also smaller, the ratio may be retained. Moreover, the chariots were probably dismantled and carried by the horses if not also by other pack animals.

Before we enter into the calculations we must take into consideration the width of a marching column. How many were there before Qina? The breadth of a file of two or more men is approximately 3 paces or .91 m and the width of a man at the shoulders is only .46 m.[18] The depth varies somewhat, dependent upon the type of march (close order or relaxed).

We might assume .91 m per man for the march through the Aruna Pass. Now the file breadth is an estimate based upon the intervals of Roman legionaries as well as that between lines of Greek hoplites. Actually, this is an overestimate by today's standards because those ancient peoples allowed a greater distance between files in order to allow the free use of weapons. When marching, of course, the files would be closed up. (I prefer .84 m per man in an army at this time.) This might seem too large for the arduous task to filing one by one through the pass, but two useful data can be brought into the discussion. A pre World War I brigade of British infantry occupied a space with .806 m per man plus interval; men with spears would require a greater distance. The contemporary German marching order required only .76 m. Considering the expertise of drill and military preparedness in this earlier epoch, we can set upon .84 m as the maximal unit per man.

Finally, I assume that this march would have had the foot soldiers proceed four abreast *at most*. If they advanced in a single file, then the number of troops must be significantly decreased. (The account only states that the horses followed one another and did not advance side by side.) Ancient roads were narrow, passes even more so, and always it was necessary to keep section of a path, on the left or right, open for communication and rearrangement. The Egyptians usually knew the types of roads that they would encounter. For example, the Kadesh Poem of Ramesses II claims that "His majesty's army traveled on the narrow paths as if on the roads of Egypt," thereby indicating that, once off the main arterial routes, the army was faced with less traveled paths that were not as easy on which to march and were small in width.[19]

The army awoke around sunrise on day nineteen of the first month of the harvest season (*shemu*). The rearguard of the army came out into the valley at noon. We can assume that Thutmose III with the vanguard entered the Aruna Pass at approximately 6.00 a.m. or slightly later. Sunrise actually represented the beginning of the second hour of the day, a fact proved by the ancient shadow clocks in employ at this time. The whole army therefore took about 6 hours to traverse the pass, not a very long time, especially when we consider that it was strung along with one man following another and one horse following its companion. Perhaps we might assume as well that some men sat on the horses; this, however, is unclear. For the sake of argument, let us suppose that only pack animals and horses made the journey. We arrive at a maximal number of 16,720.[20] This figure excludes any soldiers as I have allowed only the king. It there were only soldiers, the maximal limit of troops comes to about 18,240. These gross integers provide the upper limits for the forces.

Now taking into consideration a ratio of 1:3 for troop followers:combatants, we can reduce the combat troops to around 13,680 without any animals.[21] But if we allow for at least 2,500 active warriors, they would have covered

2.1 km, leaving the remainder of the distance to be traversed by 4,811 animals. But the total number of men would have been about 3,333, leaving 4,554 horses and pack animals. Finally, we have to deal with the animals that were not engaged in the actual battle; i.e., donkeys, possibly oxen (which the Hittites brought to the Battle of Kadesh in Dynasty XIX), and the like. In this case, I feel that an approximate figure of 4,000 horses can be argued, with the maximum being not too much greater than 4,200. This means around 2,000 chariots. One additional point has to be mentioned here. Climbing up and around difficult terrain such as that in a pass extends the battle line. This is why I have taken the most conservative estimates for the length of a man plus the space behind him and the length of an animal in the same fashion.[22]

As we shall see, the Asiatic coalition was able to muster at least 924 chariots. This implies that if all were used for chariot warfare then the enemy would have had around 2,000 or so horses. A little over that number were captured (2,041 to be precise), and hence we can regard the enemy's chariot force as having been the sum of those abandoned vehicles. It should be pointed out that all of these war vehicles were left on the battlefield after the victory of the Egyptians because the narrative explicitly states that the enemy had abandoned their horses and chariots. The men had to be hauled up on the ramparts of Megiddo. But owing to the number of enemy chariots, I feel it most probable that the Egyptians had more than that number in order to win. The tentative figures given in the last paragraph fit reasonably. In fact, from this rough analysis we can see that the army of Thutmose III was by no means grand by our standards, much less those of ancient Rome or even Assyria. Redford's assumption of 10,000 (or so) warriors ought to be reduced by some factor.

Final points concerning the size of the Egyptian army may now be approximated. Thutmose's account expressly indicates that he arrived with his vanguard at Qina. Then a camp was prepared, probably being set into place during the arrival of the lagging troops. Rations and provisions were only handed out when the entire army had reached its destination, but we do not know when, exactly, this occurred. Parker's calculations for nightfall in 1468 BC may be followed.[23] Thus the maximal time for the arrival of the king and the dispositions for the night runs from ca. 1.20 p.m. to ca. 6.30 p.m. (sunset), only a bit over 5 hours. Taking into account the camp preparations, food distribution, and preparedness, we should not go far wrong and conclude that all was ready at 4 p.m. at the latest. More importantly, it took 1 hour and 20 minutes for the king to arrive at Qina.

There are now problems concerning the date of the battle. Modern scholarship has returned to the earlier position that two days elapsed between the departure from the pass and the actual combat in the morning of the twenty-first.[24] What occurred in between? If there is no error, then day twenty would have seen the tactical dispositions of the army's wings: one was stationed northwest of Megiddo and a second at a hill south of the Qina Brook. But the narrative specifically indicates that in the late afternoon of day nineteen the king told his troops to expect battle in the morning of the following day. Moreover, the account reads as if Thutmose III only just had divided his army into three parts, with the major force placed logically in the center. Yet there was no surprise attack. The enemy later established its position outside of Megiddo as well. Evidently, not only the place of battle but also the timing was prearranged. The two enemies were in sight of one another, and modern topographical analysis indicates that the Egyptian troops were originally at most one mile (1.6 km) from Megiddo. Subsequently, we can assume that the melee occurred close to the city owing to the rapidity by which the fleeing enemy, on foot, was able to reach the walls.

It has been argued that the enemy force was caught while still deploying.[25] There is no evidence for this. They were simply overwhelmed by the Egyptian success. I prefer to view the battle as one in which the arrangements for defense and offense could have be seen by either protagonist. In many ways the Battle of Megiddo resembles a set piece, a chess game in which both participants could view their foe and rely upon their own strength. One further point can be argued. We do not know who attacked first. The account, as all Egyptian reports, views the success from one side, and is a very nationalistic one. Yet it remains impossible to ascertain the reasons for the Egyptian success except to emphasize the qualities of leadership, the numerical superiority of men and weapons, and the morale of the Egyptian army. The subsequent delay among the Egyptian troops owing to their plundering of the enemy camp is another thing, although it reveals that the enemy had set up their equipment and tents outside of Megiddo before the battle ensued. Thutmose and his army could have observed this as well.

Thus either the Egyptian allowed their foe to prepare for battle some time before the day of combat (the twenty-first) or else the enemy was already encamped outside of Megiddo when the king reached the Qina Brook. Do we opt for the second for these reasons: (1) a battle took place outside of the city; and (2) the enemy expected to win there? These two points are very simple to explain. The first implies that Thutmose hoped to avoid a lengthy siege. Indeed, he later railed against his soldiers for allowing the plundering before they reached the citadel. His men had wasted time and energy in the foe's camp. The second point indicates that the battle was fought where his opponents wished, and not too far from the resisting city.

Thutmose surprised the enemy coalition by choosing the Aruna Pass. No major defense was prepared against him at the all-important exit. The enemy, in fact, was not around. Nor were they on day nineteen at the Qina

Brook some .81 km distant. Did Thutmose allow his opponent the privilege of preparing his troops on the battlefield for combat on the subsequent day? However we interpret the text, it is clear that philological analysis cannot explain all of what happened. The topography, on the other hand, provides some useful evidence. None of the distances in this region were large. The Pharaoh wisely divided his troops, sending some of his chariot divisions north and south. (Foot soldiers would have marched too slowly.) By doing this he hemmed in the enemy's divisions between three points, all of which were located at key locations, and one of which was at a hill. (His chariots would, of course, have been at the base and not at the top.) From the ground plans we can see that the northern wing had to have been placed within a narrow vale surrounded by the city to the east and the chain of steep hills to the left. Perhaps it is useful to point out that none of the two other sections of the Egyptian army are said to have come into play on the battlefield. Nevertheless, owing to the limited nature of the Egyptian written presentation, this interpretation can be countered.

But the problem of day twenty still remains. In the text the singular mention of the feast of the Egyptian first lunar day coinciding with day twenty-one may, in fact, provide additional support to follow the wise principle of non-emendation. At dawn the king's messengers reported that his two wings had already been in their places. This, as well, had to have taken place on day nineteen. But some type of conflict had already taken place. Not in the pass, for the account is explicit. In that area the Egyptian army faced no "single enemy." And when the king arrived safely at the exit, it is reported that the southern wing of the enemy was at Taanach and the other one at the north side of the Qina Valley. This makes perfect sense. The coalition of Asiatics had expected the Pharaoh either to take the southern route to Taanach or else the northern one, the road of Djefti. Therefore, they had prepared for a possible conflict in either of these two cases, but they did not expect the Pharaoh to choose the middle way, the pass of Aruna. Yet a fragmentary portion of the narrative indicates that Thutmose met some resistance, although it was feeble. I follow most scholars and interpret this passage as indicating that a skirmish took place when Thutmose left the pass.[26] To leave unprotected any entrance to the land of Megiddo would have been rank foolhardiness, even though the enemy did not expect the Egyptians to take the most difficult road.

One later account on a stela from Armant indicates that "all countries were mustered, standing ready at its mouth." That is to say, the enemy troops were already prepared to resist the king outside of the city when he left the pass. In so far as this inscription presents a vaguer and more generalized account of the battle than the official narrative at Karnak, we may consider its report to be highly condensed. What is crucial, however, is the timing. From the Megiddo report only two possibilities are left open: (1) either the battle took place on day twenty and an emendation is necessary; or (2) it occurred on the twenty-first with the intervening day left for final preparations for combat during which the protagonists allowed themselves time to set up the place of combat. The second hypothesis implies a situation in which military encounters are announced publicly, such as is assumed during the Late Medieval phase of warfare between nobles or knights.[27]

Moving beyond the problems of chronology for the moment, a look at the booty captured in the enemy camp is rewarding. Horses and chariots were taken, including those of the princes in the coalition. Even the tent of the prince of Megiddo was ransacked. It is as if we were at the battle of Grandson between Charles the Bold of Burgundy and the Swiss coalition. But it is clear that the costly war booty was taken from the enemy who fled from the field. The plundering occurred soon after the flight of the defeated troops who hastened back to the city walls of Megiddo on foot, only to be hauled up by the inhabitants. In this case we cannot presuppose that the Egyptian infantry remained on the battlefield (and then plundered the enemy's camp) while their chariotry pursued their opponents. Otherwise, many of the foes would not have reached Megiddo.

On the other hand, we do not read of any confusion within the Egyptian army despite the sacking of the camp.[28] Had order to be restored when the soldiers felt that the booty belonged to he who took it? We do not know. Yet the rebuke given by Thutmose to his army may, in fact, hide the true situation. As I have indicated, if the chariots had sped after the fleeing Asiatics, many of the enemy would not have managed to reach the city. Looting on a large scale occurred, and this prevented the fall of Megiddo, exactly as the Pharaoh states. The fault, however, was one of discipline, and this must be charged to Thutmose and no one else.

The booty list includes the following items: 340 live enemy, 83 hands (from counting the dead after the victory), 2,041 horses, 191 foals, 6 stallions, and an unknown number of colts. In addition, we read of 1 chariot of the prince of Megiddo, 30 of his allied chiefs, and 892 of the charioteers. The total was 924. Coats of mail were thrown aside by the fleeing enemy, and they include one belonging to the prince of Kadesh and another to the ruler of Megiddo. Finally, an additional 200 leather corselets were found discarded by the troops. The captured cattle included goats, sheep, and cows, all of which were still outside of Megiddo when the battle took place.

This summary list presents interesting data. Because the opponents of Thutmose fled after defeat, they left all of their heavy armaments and war material on the field. Some of the horses must have been killed while others had run away. Still, the total number of military items is not high. The 924 chariots indicate 1,848 men, and they belonged to the local princes as well as the two chiefs of Megiddo and Kadesh. The 2,041 horses indicate about half that number in chariots. Thus the figure of 924 coincides rather well with that of 2,041. Because these vehicles were eventually abandoned, there apparently were 193 horses not tethered to their chariots. The 340 living prisoners plus 83 hands come to 423. Does this mean that 1,525 men are missing (1,848 minus 423)? I believe so, but where were they? Could all of them have fled to the walls of Megiddo and have been pulled up? That is too large a number to have been rescued in a small amount of time, unless we regard the camp plundering far more seriously than at first supposed, and also assume that a lengthy period of time had passed. Furthermore, it would have been a remarkable feat for the inhabitants of Megiddo to let down enough ropes to drag up such a large body of men.

Another restrictive limit must be placed, but only with respect to the horses and chariots of the coalition. Foals most surely were not employed, and colts are not useful for chariots. I assume that a portion of the equids was not assigned to any of the war vehicles. Some of them could have been employed for scouts and messengers, of course. The total number of prisoners plus hands indicates a small force. Eighty-three is not at all an impressive figure, but neither is 340 or 423. If many of the enemy ran away on foot, surely they would have been captured later, although one might hypothesize that the booty list reflects only the people and items actually acquired from the battle and not any later picked up by Thutmose's soldiers. Our calculations cannot allow for a very large Egyptian army, although I suspect that the victory was due to the extra chariots that Thutmose had with him. His army must have been at least twice the size of the enemy.

But why did this victory occur? Simple numerical superiority in manpower is not enough. In fact, the Pharaoh had already split up his forces before the melee outside of Megiddo. The account supplies the answer, albeit with some ambiguities owing to the fragmentary nature of the text at this point. The southern wing of the enemy was at Taanach, and the northern at an unknown locality. Lichtheim has proposed that it lay on the northern side of the Qina Valley, and I believe that this interpretation better explains the tactical dispositions of the enemy coalition.[29] To locate a central reserve somewhere along the northwest–southeast road leading south from Megiddo (and hence south of the Qina Brook) makes little sense. Of the two routes that Thutmose was expected to choose, one lay to about 13.4 km to the north of Megiddo and the other 16 km distant. It would take somewhat over one day's normal march for the Egyptian army to reach the desired locality, whichever of these two roads was chosen.

The report further indicates that the core of the enemy was caught between two wings. The opposing Asiatic force was stationed outside of Megiddo with its right wing to the north and its left to the south. How many troops were sent away from the center is unknown. Can we hypothesize that they were a large number? Both roads leading from the north and south to Megiddo cut through hills. If the Egyptians went from Yehem in either direction they could have been trapped by a relatively small number of

enemy forces. Thutmose countered this expectation. He chose the more difficult route because he thought, correctly as it turned out, that the enemy
would not expect such a risky venture. After all, the Egyptians had to march
single-file through the Aruna Pass, but if the army had gone on either of the
other two, this dangerous undertaking would have been spared.

One result of this success was the reordering of Egyptian control over
Palestine. Possibly during the siege, but more probably subsequently,
Thutmose III placed economic demands upon three peripheral cities that
were dependent upon Megiddo: Yeno'am (at the border of Palestine with
Trans-Jordan); Harenkal (an unknown town); and possibly Neges (a still
problematic area).[30] After the fall of Megiddo, the elite Asiatic *maryannu*
warriors were taken as well as the children of the princes who were allied
to the local ruler. A relative large number of slaves, males and females,
including their children, were brought back as well; 1,096 are recorded.
Non-combatants are also mentioned, and they numbered 1,003. (The total
came to 2,503.)

The harvest of Megiddo was assigned henceforth to the administrators of
the king's house in order to control the reaping.[31] The text reckons the
importance of that undertaking as 207,300 Egyptian *oipes* of wheat; i.e.,
3,984,306 liters (dry measure). To transport the grain would have required
about 22,613 animals to transport the wheat on land. This appears impossible.

We know that the workmen at the royal tombs of Thebes received a
monthly wage of 4 *khar* of emmer wheat.[32] This amount, 300 liters, served
for the man's whole family of about 10 members. Given the previous figures,
we end up with a monthly amount that could take care of 13,281 Egyptian
Theban families, or 132,810 people/month. Is this number roughly equivalent to the entire population of that region? Considering the size of Late
Bronze Age cities of Palestine, and taking into consideration the size and
importance of Megiddo, I doubt the result.[33] Yet the grain could be considered to be the total amount necessary to feed the inhabitants of the
region plus a surplus. If the population was around 50,000 then there
would have been a surplus of two-thirds of the total produce. Although this
might appear reasonable, there remains the problem of transport.

I am very reluctant to take these figures on face value. If the figures are
reckoned in simple *hekats* (1/4 of an *oipe*), then the results are 517,341 kg,
5,653 animals, and 3,320 families fed/month or 33,320 people/month.
This is more reasonable, and the result may not contradict the reading of
the grain measure. Nonetheless, the number of animals in the supply train
is still large. Perhaps a portion of the corn was sent to the local cities or
even the Egyptian garrisons in Asia. However we wish to interpret these
numbers, there remains the strong possibility that the original contains
a fault. At any rate, the account of Thutmose III nonetheless reveals the
immense economic reorganization that took place after the victorious
Megiddo campaign.

EXCURSUS

1. Because the so-called "Annals" of Thutmose III provide our major contemporary source for the Megiddo campaign, it is necessary to list three studies concerned with their historiographic content and organization. The two early ones are Martin North, "Die Annalen Thutmosis III. als Geschichtsquelle," *Zeitschrift des deutschen Palästina-Vereins* 66 (1943), 156–74; and Hermann Grapow, *Studien zu den Annalen Thutmosis des Dritten und zu ihnen verwandten historischen Berichten des Neuen Reiches*, Akademie Verlag, Berlin (1947). I later returned to their work in *Aspects of the Military Documents of the Ancient Egyptians*, 134–42. By and large, the "Annals" tend to follow the official daybook (ephemerides) account when the editor (author) refers to a specific location, especially a city or town.

There is a key problem in the account concerning the events of day twenty, one that I have discussed in this chapter. The study of Goedicke referred to in note 1 does not solve the chronological quandary whereas Redford's work, *The Wars in Syria and Palestine of Thutmose III*, is far more exacting and accurate.

2. In order to estimate food intake in calories, especially of grain (wheat and barley), it is necessary to know the exact volumes. Fortunately, the capacities of the various Egyptian grain measures are relatively secure. For a helpful summary, see Janssen, *Commodity Prices from the Ramessid Period*, 109–11. Part of this material has already been discussed in the excursus to chapter 2.

For soldiers in other pre-modern societies, Janssen (ibid., 463 n. 51) refers to the daily intake of 680 g of wheat bread/day in addition to 1.5 liters of beer, 225 g of butter, as well as cheese and beef or mutton. Clearly, the caloric intake was far greater than in Pharaonic Egypt. On the other hand, the research of Richard Duncan-Jones, "An Epigraphic Survey of Costs in Roman Italy," *Papers of the British School at Rome* 33 (1965), 223, emphasizes that the average adult male ration of corn from the end of the Republic and onwards was 5 modii/month (43.76 liters/month). As Duncan-Jones remarks, the 5 modii/month approximate 3,000–4,000 calories/day, a very reasonable figure. (NB, this author places the theoretical idea of 3,300 calories/day for male adults.)

Additional data will be found in the study of K. J. Carpenter, "Man's Dietary Needs," in Sir Joseph Hutschinson, *Population and Food Supply*, University Press, Cambridge (1969), 61–74. As we have seen, Engels, *Alexander the Great*, 18, places a minimum ration for each adult soldier on the expedition to be 1.36 kg of grain per day "or its nutritional equivalent" and at least 2.2 liters of water per day.

3. The population situation in Palestine is of paramount consideration when one reflects upon the ability of the Egyptians to wage war in this area as well as to administer it. The following studies (in chronological order), kindly brought to my attention by Alexander H. Joffee, are the most recent significant articles.

Ram Gophna, "The Settlement of Landscape of Palestine in the Early Bronze Age II–III and Middle Bronze Age II," *Israel Exploration Journal* 34 (1984),

24–31. Although the orientation of the author is upon an earlier period of time, this analysis, partly superseded by the following studies, is quite useful.

Rikva Gonen, "Urban Canaan in the Late Bronze Period," *Bulletin of the American Schools of Oriental Research* 253 (1984), 61–73.

Magen Broshi and Ram Gophna, "The Settlements and Population of Palestine During the Early Bronze Age," *Bulletin of the American Schools of Oriental Research* 253 (1984), 41–53. The methodological considerations discussed by the two scholars are important.

Broshi and Gophna, "Middle Bronze Age II Palestine: Its Settlements and Population," *Bulletin of the American Schools of Oriental Research* 261 (1986), 73–90.

Ram Gophna and Juval Portugali, "Settlement and Demographic Processes in Israel's Coastal Plain from the Chalcolithic to the Middle Bronze Age," *Bulletin of the American Schools of Oriental Research* 269 (1988), 11–28. This study is useful for comparative purposes.

Magen Broshi and Israel Finkelstein, "The Population of Palestine in Iron Age II," *Bulletin of the American Schools of Oriental Research* 287 (1992), 47–60. The authors discuss the later population of Palestine in the eighth century BC.

Gloria Anne London, "Tells: City Center or Home?," *Eretz-Israel* 23 (1992), 71*–9*. Her conclusion is that in "ancient Israel" the "vast majority of people lived in rural towns and villages close to where they worked the land" (p. 77*). She also places emphasis upon the "small size of ancient sites in Israel," leading to the conclusion "that large tells were home to the rulers, their extended family, servants, and some military personnel" (p. 77*). The population is reduced from the figures presented in the aforementioned articles.

A reasonable estimate is to set the population of Canaan (Palestine) ca. 60,000–70,000 ca. 1200 BC, a decline from ca. 160,000 at 1600 BC, following Broshi and Finkelstein.

Liverani (*Prestige and Interest*, 147) briefly discusses assumed population of 89,600 of the eastern territories (re-)conquered by Amunhotep II. We shall turn to this problem in chapter 9.

Last, the estimates given above directly affect the scholarly dispute between Dever and Na'aman concerning the "devastation" of Palestine in the transition between the Middle to the Late Bronze Age. See note 7 to chapter 3.

NOTES

1   The text, which is often referred to as the "Annals," is available in the excellent English translation of Miriam Lichtheim, *Ancient Egyptian Literature* II, 29–35; the text will be found in Sethe, *Urkunden der 18. Dynastie*, 647–67.

The study of Harold Hayden Nelson, *The Battle of Megiddo*, University of Chicago Libraries, Chicago (1913), is still of great use, especially because his detailed topographic maps are inestimable for logistic analysis. Faulkner's "The Battle of Megiddo," *Journal of Egyptian Archaeology* 28 (1942), 2–15, covers the events from the time of the war council to the actual clash of arms outside the city of Megiddo. Hans Goedicke's volume, *The Battle of Megiddo*, Halgo, Baltimore (2000), can be cited in this context. However, the recent study of Redford, *The Wars in Syria and Palestine of Thutmose III*, is presently the most valuable and up-to-date analysis.

Anson F. Rainey, "The Military Camp Ground at Taanach by the Waters of Megiddo," *Eretz-Israel* 15 (1981), 61*–6*, presents too many assumptions concerning the tactical positioning of the enemies.

2 Donald B. Redford, "The Historical Retrospective at the Beginning of Thutmose III's Annals," in *Festschrift Elmar Edel*, 338–41.

3 For a useful geographic background to the historical-geographical nature of Palestine at this time, see Yohanan Aharoni, *The Land of the Bible*[2], A. F. Rainey, ed. and trs., Westminster Press, Philadelphia (1979).

4 See Nadav Na'aman, "The Hurrians and the End of the Middle Bronze Age in Palestine," *Levant* 26 (1994), 183, for an important discussion of the Hurrian influence in Palestine at this time. He states that "Mitanni gained supremacy in northern Syria and apparently operated in the Canaanite areas through the center of Kadesh." This study has to be read in the context of the Dever–Na'aman dispute discussed in note 7 to chapter 3.

5 On Gaza at this time: Redford, *History and Chronology of the Eighteenth Dynasty of Egypt*, 60 n. 27.

6 Karl Butzer has presented an extremely important analysis of the Pharaonic agricultural schedule in the Nile floodplain in *Early Hydraulic Civilization in Egypt*, University of Chicago Press, Chicago and London (1976), 48–51.

7 On pp. 17–19 of his *The Battle of Megiddo*, Nelson attempts to explain the military backdrop of the campaign. Once more Redford has provided pertinent historical reasons connected to the lengthy preparations of war by Thutmose III during the last months of the life of Hatshepsut: *History and Chronology of the Eighteenth Dynasty of Egypt*, 86–7; see as well Helck, *Geschichte des alten Ägypten*, E. J. Brill, Leiden and Cologne (1981), 157.

8 See note 22 below.

9 In the account of the "Annals," Thutmose III is first placed at Sile: Sethe, *Urkunden der 18. Dynastie*, 647.12.

10 For the time frame, see Murnane, *The Road to Kadesh*, appendix 1. See as well the other sources referred to in note 1 to chapter 2.

11 See Murnane's comments cited in the previous note.

12 This portion of the narrative has been used as a key example of the *Königsnovelle* or King's Novel: see our comments in note 3 to chapter 1.

13 For the difficulties associated with mountain passes, see Delbrück, *Warfare in Antiquity*, 93. He points out the key situation: "the tactical theory requires you to take a position with your concentrated forces opposite the defile, or on one of the defiles, from which the enemy is about to debouch." This was not done by the Pharaoh's opponents. Because they had expected him elsewhere (south or north of the Aruna pass), they sent their troops to those two areas.

However, there was a skirmish at the mouth of the pass: Faulkner, "The Battle of Megiddo," *Journal of Egyptian Archaeology* 28 (1942), 7–8.

Redford, *The Wars in Syria and Palestine of Thutmose III*, 27–9, attempts to explain the problems with the missing "day twenty" in the official account. He concludes (objecting to Parker's analysis in the following note concerning the phrase "when seven hours had turned in the day"), that a calendric notation for day twenty is missing in the account.

14 Richard A. Parker, "Some reflections on the lunar dates of Thutmose III and Ramesses II," in William Kelly Simpson and Whitney M. Davis., eds., *Studies in Ancient Egypt, the Aegean, and the Sudan. Essays in honor of Dows Dunham on the occasion of his 90th birthday, June 1, 1980*, Museum of Fine Arts, Boston (1981), 146–7. He follows the accession date of Thutmose III as 1290 BC. A change to 1279 BC, as presently argued by Egyptologists, does not alter the timing present here to any appreciable degree.

15 The distances used here are taken from the maps in Nelson, *The Battle of Megiddo.*

16 J. F. Verbruggen, *The Art of Warfare in Western Europe during the Middle Ages: From the Eighth Century to 1340*, Sumner Willard and S. C. M. Southern, trs., North-Holland Publishing Company, Amsterdam, New York and Oxford (1977), 10, for this fact and the following one.

17 On the size of Egyptian chariots, see Littauer-Crouwel, *Wheeled Vehicles and Ridden Animals in the Ancient Near East*, 75–7, and their later study, *Chariots and Related Equipment from the Reign of Tut'ankhamun*, Griffith Institute, Oxford (1985), 96–104.

18 For the data concerning these calculations, see excursus 3 to chapter 2.

19 The account is in P 33: Gardiner, *The Kadesh Inscriptions of Ramesses II*, 8.

20 For these calculations, see note 24 to chapter 2. I follow 2.8–3.2 m/animal as the common interval in marching order in difficult terrain. On flat ground I would opt for about 2.77 m.

21 This is the average figure that is assumed by most military historians, including Delbrück. Engels, *Alexander the Great*, 12, indicates that there was an overall rate of one servant per every four combatants in the armies of Philip of Macedon. With Alexander the Great until the battle of Gaugemala the ratio of 1:3 is maintained (p. 13).

22 Redford, *The Wars in Syria and Palestine of Thutmose III*, 197, feels that around 10,000 men were with Thutmose. My calculations indicate that this figure is too high if we consider only the able-bodied military men. I would reduce it by four to five thousand.

23 See his study and my comments cited in note 14 above.

24 A summary of this position will be found in Rolf Krauss, *Sothis- und Monddaten. Studien zur astronomischen und technischen Chronologie Altägyptens*, Gerstenberg Verlag, Hildesheim (1985), 121–3. See the most recent analysis of Redford discussed in the following note.

25 Faulkner, "The Battle of Megiddo," *Journal of Egyptian Archaeology* 38 (1942), 13, assumes such a maneuver. His analysis also depends upon the enemy's counter-moves, which are seen to have been incomplete at the time that Thutmose attacked. His argumentation at this point appears to me to be a reasonable explanation for the subsequent panic of the coalition forces, although it is open to criticism.

Redford, *The Wars in Syria and Palestine of Thutmose III*, 27–9, on the other hand, feels that the account of Thutmose lacks an entry for day twenty. Hence, he argues, "the king and an advance guard must, against all logic, have returned to camp or remained in the pass overnight" (p. 28). This fresh interpretation, however, remains open to dispute. A further possibility is envisaged on p. 29. Namely, "the report issued to the king on the morning of that day [= the 20th] indicated the field was clear: the enemy had not yet redeployed." But this hypothesis requires a conclusion that passes beyond the official account.

26 See note 13 above.

27 Redford's series of possibilities avoids this somewhat precarious interpretation.

28 The problems with unexpected war booty are neatly covered by Machiavelli in his *The Art of War*, Christopher Lynch, trs., 109 (Book V 97–8).

29 *Ancient Egyptian Literature* II, 36 n. 6 (to the text on p. 31).

30 Na'aman, "Yeno'am," *Tel Aviv* 4 (1977), 168–77. For the siege of Megiddo, one must keep in mind that if an attack on the battlefield can set up a blockade, and at the same time prevent needed supplies from entering the locality, then starvation and disease will decimate the local population, thereby reducing the number of opposing troops: Harry Holbert Turney-High, *The Military. The Theory of Land Warfare as Behavioral Science*, Christopher Publishing House, West Hanover (1981), 186–7. In addition, the defense's ammunition will slowly be reduced.

31 See the commentary of Breasted, *Ancient Records of Egypt* II, 189 with note a; the text is in Sethe, *Urkunden der 18. Dynastie*, 667.14. I am assuming that the amount is recorded in *oipes* rather than the Egyptian bushel, the *khar*, owing to its smaller capacity. There remains the possibility that the measure is the Egyptian *hekat* (1/4 of an *oipe*). Although the reading does not support this contention, a fourfold reduction is very reasonable. The number of Egyptian bushels, or *khar*, come to 51,825. The number of modern bushels is 113,065. (A bushel of wheat weighs about 18 kg.) Finally, we can assume a 90 kg load per pack animal.

32 Jac. J. Janssen, *Commodity Prices from the Ramessid Period*, 455–71. Four *khar* = 16 *oipe*.

33 The population of Late Bronze Age Palestine is discussed in the excursus to this chapter. The importance of this data for analyzing the New Kingdom Egyptian military in this region will be covered later.

6

THE PHARAOH ON CAMPAIGN: IDEAL AND REAL

The role of the Thutmose III during his march to Megiddo highlights the developed character of the royal figure as military leader. At this time, over two centuries had passed during which a new scope to the functions of Pharaoh had become firmly entrenched. His role is best subsumed under the rubric King as Hero.[1] When the Theban state of Dynasty XVII had begun to contest the Nile Valley with the Hyksos, the monarch was the supreme war leader or the *Feldherr*, to use the German term.[2] This hallmark of the New Kingdom rulers meant that, as a prince, the prospective monarch had to learn quite a lot concerning the art of war. Around him was the increasingly important corporate entity of the army. This was a male society *in extremis*. Continual warfare in Nubia and a growing sense of combat preparedness with regard to Asia expanded this new concept of kingship, one in which the Pharaoh would be away from home, often for an extended period of time. The local administration now had to cope with absences by its ruler, and the state often would have to be run by the royal deputy, the vizier. On the march and in battle, Pharaoh was depicted as victorious, and all the expected traits of a war chief can be found in the inscriptions as well as in the pictorial representations. Determination and fairness characterized his "mask of command." For example, we have remarked on the commencement to the Kamose stelae in which the two plans of the native Egyptians are set side by side. This setting is paralleled to some degree by the various hieroglyphic records of the so-called "King's Novel" in which a similar presentation is given.[3] But now, instead of a building project or a long sea voyage to the fabulous and remote southern land of Punt – both organized by the Pharaoh – we have the decisions of war thrust upon the stage. As a result, it was necessary to provide a viewpoint that contrasted with that of the high officials, be they courtiers, civilian officials, or army officers.

In the Megiddo account, with which we have been so much occupied, the image of Thutmose III is a fair and even-handed one. The king does not falter. He neither shows cowardice nor acts as a martinet. It is assumed from the onset that Thutmose is an effective warrior. Does he not choose the more difficult pass through which to advance upon Megiddo? Pharaoh is ever ready, resolute, and strong. He listens to advice and avoids digressing from his aim. True, he pushes on his troops, but he always follows sound military practice. The camps are left soon after dawn; there is no delay. The center of his army remains the strongest, even when two wings are set up around the enemy.

Note the difference between the role of Thutmose III and two earlier Pharaohs. In the first of Kamose's two stelae the monarch called together his "great men," meaning the nobles who were in the suite of their monarch. The ensuing report is therefore not concerned with an actual battle but instead with the opening salvos in a possible war. The king recommended an aggressive policy and the courtiers responded by offering a passive one. Kamose, though displeased, persevered with his nationalistic war plans. Whereas we may contrast this account with that of Thutmose purely on the basis of the discussion and the retort of Kamose, it must be kept in mind that the second was not yet on the march. In the later case we witness the actual strategy to be taken in a war. The conference in the Megiddo report avoided the strategic objective but instead concentrated upon the tactics of marching and the road to take. Years earlier, the story of Apophis and Seqenenre (the father of Kamose) highlights a similar situation.[4] In this case the ruler of Thebes of late Dynasty XVII had to respond to a threatened message sent to him by Apophis, the Hyksos overlord of Avaris and the north. Seqenenre summoned the chief officials (civilians) but also "every high ranking soldiers of his." These men were simply astounded and could not provide an answer. What is crucial is the combination of men at court: juxtaposed are the civilian and military leadership of the Theban state. But once more the account is set at home and in the capital, not during a march to battle.

As John Keegan remarks, mystification is the necessary cement that is employed by great generals in order to bond the twin-opposed factors of love and fear in his warriors.[5] Fear through harsh sanctions, including death, is effective, but only for a short period of time. Soon the soldiers become unruly and quarrelsome if not deserters. Love, the reciprocal vector between two people, is as crucial, yet too much of it weakens the supreme head of an army. Hence, there arises the necessity of allegiance cultivated by means of a social bond separate from punishment and fraternization. Henry V in the Shakespeare play may walk around the camp at night. Nonetheless, he also checks on the morale of his troops before the oncoming combat. Clarence may have a dream at night in one of his ships, but this topos is employed by the playwright of Richard III to enhance the oncoming battle.

Thutmose spoke to his troops. He performed the same act at Yehem that other war leaders regularly did and still do before the battle. This is an ancient stereotypical form, but one that reflects an event that actually took place. Not surprisingly, the Germans have coined a word for it: *Feldherrnrede*.

The general's speech before battle is a standard portion of the Classical authors, and in fact must have been part of the ancient German leader's rhetoric when he rallied his clan against the foe.[6]

Remarkably, we find this procedure stressed by the Imperial general Montecuccoli during the Thirty Years' War.[7] Among the prescriptions of this man we can single out the necessity to incite soldiers to fight through the deprecation of the enemy, the right of one's cause, the superiority of one's arms, the quality of the army, and the like. In addition, the seventeenth-century general recommends the speaking qualities of war leaders, especially the commander-in-chief. Even the way the general acts is crucial. One must "put on a brave face," be lighthearted, full of hope, and even banter with the men. Confidence is raised by means of these dissimulations, but especially through oratory. Machiavelli, in Book Four of his *The Art of War*, points out that, whereas it is easy to persuade or dissuade a few owing to the power position of the general, when it comes to a large number of men – the soldiers – oratorical expertise is necessary.[8] "Speaking takes away fears, inflames spirits, increases obstinacy, uncovers deceptions, promises rewards, shows dangers and the way to flee them." Hence, he concludes, it is necessary to accustom generals to speak skillfully.

Let us see how Thutmose III performed during his Megiddo campaign. At Yehem he discussed the tactical situation with his army. Can we assume that only the highest-ranking soldiers were present at this conference, or simply the officers, or perhaps did it take place with all the men present? At the beginning of the conference Thutmose first ordered a consultation "with his victorious army." This must imply more than a few highly regarded men. At that time he outlined the situation at Megiddo and then asked for advice. Note the implicit sense of equality, at least in offering a war plan. The army replied that they wished to avoid the difficult pass. Subsequently, additional information was relayed through dispatches and then the king made up his mind. The consultation was therefore a fair one and not oriented to hectoring the troops or urging them to take a dangerous road. With the new facts at hand, the king resolved to set out through the Aruna Pass. He also provided negative incitement. If any man were to follow either of the two lesser dangerous paths, he would not be angry. This is pure rhetoric, but effective exhortation. Thutmose indicated that he, as Amun's hero, would pass through the unexpected defile. Then a proclamation to "the entire army" was communicated. It is thus clear that these events began with a small consultation, possibly between the king and select army commanders, but we are not informed who were present outside of Thutmose.

After the king led the way through the Aruna Pass he debouched at the head of his army. The war leader must always be first. The "army," presumably the soldiers who were with the Pharaoh, then spoke their mind and demanded that their monarch "hearken unto us this once." (An implied personal characteristic of the troops is thereby revealed.) They requested that Thutmose guard "for us the rear of his army and his people." Perhaps the latter word indicates the noncombatants may have been at the back of the military train. The point of this declaration, however, is clear. Pharaoh should remain at the exit of the pass until the entire army has come out. This was done.

A third address of the king is given at the time that the Egyptians reached the Brook of Qina. Thutmose rallied his troops by urging them to be ready and prepared for battle. This time I think it valid to assume that he personally called out to all of his troops. He dictated the next day as the one for combat.

Even though the account of the battle of Megiddo is not lengthy by Classical standards, much less in comparison to modern ones, it nonetheless reveals some of the expected "real" actions and scenes in actual combat. This record is thus not a mere soldier-scribe's bland official report of the campaign but instead one that interweaves drama with facts.[9] Above all, it is the role of Pharaoh that is paramount, and Thutmose III's image is thereby heightened in heroic stature as it is in wisdom. This account can serve as a paradigm of what the Egyptians in mid Dynasty XVIII conceived their war commander to be: wise, determined, strong, effective, and heedful of advice. The first discussion is presented to indicate the choices left open to the king. The second shows his reasoned decision on the basis of new information whereas the third indicates the king's willingness to follow the advice of his army. The final exhortation is to be expected from a general, but it had to be recounted. Does not the war leader provide the necessary words of support before battle?

In light of the detailed account of Thutmose III face to face with the enemy at Megiddo it is useful to analyze how the Egyptians set up their war camps when they were upon a campaign.[10] The war report of Thutmose III indicates what booty could be found in the enemy camp. It does not give us much more. The enemy chief had his own war tent, and chariots and horses, later part of the booty, were ready for combat. Thutmose had his camp erected at the Qina Brook, and here the account mentions some useful particulars. The king spoke to the "whole army" and exhorted them to be ready for combat on the next day. Provisions were subsequently given to the officers and rations to the attendants. (Note the duality.) The sentries were posted and they were given words of encouragement: "Steadfast, steadfast! Vigilant, vigilant!"[11] It has been argued that these were the passwords of the watch, an interpretation that may be correct, but in light of no additional information this conclusion may be regarded with some skepticism. On the other hand, the main events are connected with the king. Here, and in many other Egyptian war accounts, there is a common refrain of "resting in the tent" of the king, "awakening in the royal tent," and so forth. The timing of the army was set by the activities of Pharaoh.

But it is only the battle reliefs of Ramesses II at Kadesh that reveal evidence of these military bivouacs. Even though this scene is dated to a later time, it is reasonable to use these depictions as a model for reconstructing the actual set-up of the royal army. Fortunately, there are many reliefs in the various major temples of Egypt recounting this war.[12] The king's tent was in the middle of an enclosure. It appears rectangular rather than square in shape. The shields of the soldiers formed the barriers on the four sides, a very useful means of protecting the troops from a sudden unexpected onslaught of an enemy. Guards may be seen at the two entries to the camp that were located in the middle of the protective barrier. They were divided into two groups, both of which stood at the left and at the right, with one man on each side facing inward while the others face outward. They appear to carry sticks and not swords, but this is somewhat questionable. The entrances led directly to the royal tent. No soldiers were outside.

Everything was enclosed within the four sides of the camp: men, horses, chariots, supplies, pack animals, and weapons. This follows common military practice of later times, and it must imply a lengthy period of military preparedness that set a rule for proper bivouacs. The horses were first disengaged from their chariots if, in fact, they had been in use. Otherwise, these animals were simply brought together in rows, apparently standing behind their chariots. The latter situation is specifically shown in the Kadesh battle reliefs at Abu Simbel. Donkeys seem to predominate over oxen, and some of the latter are attached to their heavy vehicles in the same scene. We may note as well the repair of weapons in addition to other equipment. The food supplies of grain brought along with the army are heaped up in regular piles. Soldiers are depicted in various poses of ordinary professional life. Some are drinking wine while one at least (Abu Simbel provides the evidence) is drinking from a water sack. The troops reveal their tired condition: one man is asleep and another drunk. Some mock fighting can be observed. Furthermore, we can point out the presence of boys in the army, an oft forgotten fact that indicates the various levels of support that existed within an army on the march. We must not forget the pet lion that Ramesses II brought along with him. The animal is not merely a representation of the victorious king. There is even a brief hieroglyphic legend next to his figure. Can we not assume that this was common practice?

The above remarks depend upon the battle reliefs at Abu Simbel. The scenes are not overly detailed owing to the limitations of space in that grotto. Additional evidence can be presented by examining the other representations. At Luxor (the L1 version), for example, a somewhat more detailed depiction is presented.[13] Here the royal tent has three food supplies, exactly as at Abu Simbel. Some of the horses are arranged in groups without any chariots in front of them. But many of the other themes at Luxor are exact duplicates of those found in the other temple: one tired man, the transportation of foods, the pet lion, and a donkey eating. In the king's mortuary temple, the Ramesseum, two additional versions of the battle are presented. One of them (R1) shows two rows of guards at one of the two entrances and the path leading to Ramesses' tent.[14] No man looks backward. The lion has his own chariot or cart to transport him, surely a minor point, but one that is omitted at Abu Simbel. One boy helps a soldier to take grain out from a container.

This pictorial evidence is welcome as it allows us to visualize the actual encampments that the Pharaohs set up during their intermittent campaigns. Whether or not there were four entrances must remain unclear. The difficulty in ascertaining this is due to the camp scenes themselves. All the depictions record the quiet and settled condition of the bivouac yet at the same time reveal the attack of the Hittite enemy. The latter had, in fact, reached the camp and apparently entered it, or at least cut through parts of the stockade of shields. Therefore, the remaining two sides are not completely drawn to indicate whether all of them were provided with entrances. This is likely, however, if only because the army needed the four main directions covered.

It is a different matter regarding the number of guards and their disposition. All the extant reliefs depict the men in different arrangements. I presume that Abu Simbel is the least reliable, if only because it is somewhat constricted in space. A problem remains with the placement of the horses. Surely, one would expect them to be depicted resting in front of their vehicles. This is not the case, however. In fact, in some cases they appear to be separate from the war vehicles (the L1 version). But the lack of barracks is disconcerting. Was it the case that the ordinary soldiers slept on the ground protected only by a coverlet and some type of cushion underneath them? There is also no explicit differentiation between ordinary soldier and officer, or any recognition made between the chariot warriors and the foot-soldiers. But the expressed purpose of this key scene was not to delineate all the details of the camp. Rather, it was drawn to indicate the successful end of the lengthy journey and the sudden attack of the Hittites.

EXCURSUS

1. Heinz's detailed and exemplary study, *Die Feldzugdarstellungen des Neuen Reiches*, which I have cited frequently in this work, provides the reader with a wealth of details concerning the pictorial nature of the New Kingdom battle reliefs. It is supplemented by the earlier unpublished work of Marcus Müller, *Die Thematik der Schlachtenreliefs*, MA Dissertation, Tübingen (1985). Owing to their detailed studies, both of these works have partly replaced the analysis of Gaballa's *Narrative in Egyptian Art*, cited above in note 12 to chapter 4.

Heinz does not, however, deal with the art historical development of these reliefs. To a degree this lacuna has been replaced by the pertinent comments of Stephen Harvey in his *The Cults of King Ahmose at Abydos*, 303–72, a study that I briefly covered in my review of Heinz, *Journal of the American Oriental Society* 122 (2002), 125–7. We can now see the XVIIIth data with far better clarity than earlier. The data include the war reliefs of Ahmose (fragmentary scene from Abydos), Thutmose II (Karnak; mortuary temple), Amunhotep II (Zayed, "Une représentation inédite des campagnes d'Aménophis II," in Paule Posener-Kriéger, ed., *Mélanges Gamal Eddin Mokhtar* I, Institut Français d'Archéologie Orientale, Cairo (1985), 5–17; Karnak), Thutmose IV (Thebes, royal tomb; chariot sides); Tutankhamun (Thebes, royal tomb; wooden chest); and either Tutankhamun or possibly Ay (mortuary temple scenes, probably from the west bank: Johnson, *An Asiatic Battle Scene of Tutankhamun from Thebes*, who covers the battle scenes and connects those depictions with the later Ramesside war reliefs). Johnson assembles other Dynasty XVIII examples on pp. 92–106 of his work.

In contrast, Müller concentrates upon the set scenes that a Pharaoh would use for his pictorial narrative, and he correctly observes that it was not obligatory to include a "full set" of such depictions. The amount of space available on a temple wall, for example, would often determine what specific events in a campaign would be recorded.

2. For the Kadesh scenes, see my study "Notes on the Reliefs of the Battle of Kadesh," in Hans Goedicke, ed., *Perspectives on the Battle of Kadesh*, Halgo, Baltimore (1985), chapter I. This is now supplemented by Heinz's compendium volume in which she presents a "vector-oriented" analysis. That is to say, her study focuses upon the directions and movements of the protagonists (Pharaoh, soldiers, and chariots). The positions of individual components (men and horses, for example) are likewise described. Kemp, in *Ancient Egypt. Anatomy of a Civilization*, 226–9, contains pertinent comments with regard to the Egyptian fear of the outside world as well as the danger of invasion caused by unsettled populations.

3. For the inherent limitations of these pictorial representations, the following works may be consulted: Heinrich Schäfer, *Principles of Egyptian Art*, John Baines, trs., Clarendon Press, Oxford (1974), 186–9, 301–2; Meyer Schapiro, "On Some Problems in the Semiotics of Visual Art. Field and Vehicle in Image-Signs," *Semiotica* 1 (1969), 232; Heinrich von Recklinghausen, "Rechtsprofil und Linksprofil in der Zeichenkunst der alten Ägypter," *Zeitschrift für ägyptische Sprache* 63 (1928), 14–36; and Henry Fischer, *L'écriture et l'art de l'Égypte ancienne. Quatres leçons sur la paléographie et l'épigraphie pharaoniques*, Presses universitaires de France, Paris (1986) 55 and 82–3. These authors discuss the basic constraints of ancient Egyptian artistic representation and avoid the problems of anachronism, misleading or false depictions, and overt "plagiarism."

The introductory remarks of Gay Robins, *Proportion and Style in Ancient Egyptian Art*, University of Texas Press, Austin (1994), 16–21, cover the right- and left-facing actors in Egyptian wall reliefs.

107

4. The kings' sportive activities, hunting, archery, oarsmanship, and racing in chariots, became part and parcel of the image that New Kingdom Pharaohs publicized. These strenuous physical performances must be seen to belong to the warrior ethos of this age. Let us not forget that Xenophon and Machiavelli emphasized the value of hunting in military education: Neal Wood, "Introduction," in Machiavelli, *The Art of War*, Da Capo, New York (1965), xlix with n. 96. This image was a real one in Egyptian military society because the virile young princes of Egypt learned at an early age the arts of horsemanship, archery, and chariotry, among other war-oriented activities. For this background, Wolfgang Decker, *Die physische Leistung des Pharaos. Untersuchungen zu Heldentum, Jagd und Leibsübungen der ägyptischen Könige*, Deutsche Sporthochschule, Cologne (1971), provides a complete analysis.

NOTES

1   This theme has been frequently discussed in the scholarly literature. *Inter alia*, see Assmann, "Die Zeit Hatscheputs und Thutmosis' III. in religionsgeschichtlicher Sicht," in Arne Eggebrecht, ed., *Ägyptens Aufstieg zur* Weltmacht, Phillip von Zabern, Mainz am Rhein (1977), 47–55; Redford, *Egypt, Canaan, and Israel in Ancient Times*, chapters 6–7, and *History and Chronology of the Eighteenth Dynasty of Egypt*, 64–5; Partridge, *Fighting Pharaohs*, 190–277; and Spalinger, *Aspects of the Military Documents of the Ancient Egyptians*, chapters 5–6.

In a similar context we can cite the well-known scene of Pharaoh who smites his enemies: Schulman, *Ceremonial Execution and Public Rewards*, Vandenhoeck and Ruprecht, Göttingen (1988), with pp. 45–7 in particular; Emma Swan Hall, *The Pharaoh Smites his Enemies. A Comparative Study*, Munich, Deutscher Kunstverlag; Berlin (1986); and the detailed review of the preceding work by Charles Van Siclen III, *Varia Aegyptiaca* 3 (1987), 171–6. Although this victorious ceremony was age-old, the act must have become extremely important owing to the Pharaohs' successes abroad. See now W. Raymond Johnson, *An Asiatic Battle Scene of Tutankhamun from Thebes*, 93–4.

2   I do not deny that such an attitude existed earlier, but it became commonplace during Dynasty XVIII with the expansion outside of Egypt. Naturally, the development of the army with its chariots aided this trend. In other words, the frequency of external war coupled with the necessity of maintaining a relatively large and more mobile army differentiates the New Kingdom phase of Egyptian kingship from earlier times.

For an earlier inscription that reflects a powerful military ethos of the king as war leader, see Henry George Fischer, *Inscriptions from the Coptite Nome*, Dynasties VI–XI, Pontificium Institutum Biblicum, Rome (1964), 112–18. In this case the Pharaoh (Montuhotep II of Dynasty XI) was involved in wars. I consider the text to be an early example of the "King's Novel."

3   See our remarks in note 3 to chapter 1.

4 Ibid.

5 *The Mask of Command*, 315–18.

6 Delbrück, *The Barbarian Invasions* (*History of the Art of War* II), Walter J. Renfroe, Jr., trs., University of Nebraska Press, Lincoln and London (1990), chapters I–II.

7 Raimondo Montecuccoli, "Concerning Battle," in Thomas M. Barker, *The Military Intellectual and Battle. Raimondo Montecuccoli and the Thirty Years War*, State University of New York Press, Albany (1975), 134; Keegan, *The Mask of Command*, 320–1; see as well Delbrück, *The Dawn of Modern Warfare*, Walter J. Renfroe, trs., (*History of the Art of War* IV), University of Nebraska Press, Lincoln and London (1990), who briefly discusses this important military figure.

8 As is well known, Machiavelli's basic concepts were dependent upon the contemporary state of war as well as upon his knowledge of Classical, especially Roman, antiquity (Vegetius, Frontinus, Polybius, and Livy are his major sources.) The following quote is taken from his *The Art of War*, Christopher Lynch, trs., 98 (Book IV 139).

9 This is why the report of the Megiddo campaign must be viewed from a literary viewpoint as well as from a historical one. See the references in chapter 5 n. 1.

10 Military writers have not hesitated to discuss the necessity of proper camps and how to construct them: Machiavelli, *The Art of War*, VI; and Vegetius 24–5 are two well-known examples.

11 Goedicke, *The Battle of Megiddo*, 66, argues that this indicates the use of passwords. I believe this interpretation is too speculative.

12 Heinz, *Die Feldzugsdarstellungen des Neuen Reiches*. For the Abu Simbel reliefs of Ramesses II's Kadesh war, see Ch. Deschoches Nobelcourt et al., *Grand temple d'Abou Simbel. La bataille de Qadech*, Centre de Documentation et d'Études sur l'Ancienne Égypte, Cairo (1971), and Plates IV–V in particular. Scenes from the other temples (Luxor, Karnak, and Abydos) may be found in Walter Wreskinski, *Atlas zur altägyptischen Kulturgeschichte* II, J. C. Hinrichs, Leipzig (1935).

13 Wreszinski *Atlas* II, pls. 82–3.

14 Ibid., pls. 92–92a.

7

THE LATER MILITARY
SITUATION IN ASIA AND
AT HOME

The war records of Thutmose do not stop with the Megiddo battle, and
it is therefore necessary to examine them in relation to the role of the
Egyptian military system during the subsequent years of this Pharaoh.
Because it would overburden this discussion to examine each particular
campaign, I have preferred to highlight the strategy, tactics, and results of
the main Asiatic conflicts of Thutmose III subsequent to the Megiddo
campaign.[1] In regnal year twenty-nine of Thutmose, during his fifth campaign, we have already seen the Pharaoh busy in Asia concentrating upon
the coastline as well as inland Syria. Ships were employed to transport the
booty back to Egypt. Whether or not the king accompanied the produce
and captives is impossible to say. This hypothesis, however, would allow us
to understand better the focus of the following wars. Because Thutmose
later marched into the kingdom of Mitanni and reached the Euphrates, it
was necessary for him to secure his supply routes. The local cities and towns
in Palestine, but more importantly in Syria, had to be friendly, but this was
more problematical owing to the proximity to Mitanni. Fighting remained
land based, but now dependent upon the sea routes of the coastline of
Lebanon with Byblos and other ports serving as major staging points and
supply depots.

The Egyptian army also ransacked the port city of Arvad during this
war. Therefore, the necessity of supplying or even paying the troops was
easily resolved. The seizure of additional elite soldiers from the hinterland
of Asia was equally important. Once more Thutmose reckoned the specific
number of *maryannu* troops captured and transported back to Egypt.
Because these men were able warriors, they must have been inducted into
the Egyptian army. Indeed, they are not listed with the noncombatants, the
slaves, the relatives of the local princes, or the kinglets themselves. Considered separately, the *maryannu* provided worthwhile soldiers for the
Egyptian army, a point that I will return to later when discussing the foreign

component of the Egyptian war machine. Noteworthy is the additional report of the capture of two ships laden with copper, lead, and emery in addition to the slaves that were brought back to Karnak for god Amun. Evidently, the Egyptians were now intent upon controlling much of the Levantine coast. The produce obtained, undoubtedly by means of the Egyptian fleet, is presented in a final subsection. From it we can conclude that the king raided territories inland from coast of Lebanon and that many cattle were transported back to the Nile Valley.

During the sixth and seventh campaigns the strategic focus of the king remained the same. He was able to capture Kadesh on the river Orontes in year thirty. Here, as earlier with Megiddo, the grain was harvested. This implies a period of time during which the luckless inhabitants were forced to reap their produce for the Egyptians. It must have been sent back in ships after being loaded upon pack animals. Once more horses and chariots (188 and 40 respectively) were also obtained. These two components were added to the Egyptian army, but for the moment let me stress the presence of a list separate from the individual military undertakings. For the first time we read an official account of the "plunder" taken from Asia. It included male and female slaves, chariots, and horses.

The word "plunder" is hard to analyze. Often translated as "tribute," the Egyptian noun, *inu*, is ambiguous.[2] Within a native context, it generally referred to extraordinary deliveries of goods. A clear-cut distinction between *inu* and a second word, *baku*, can been seen with regard to the Egyptian administration over Nubia. Wawat, or Lower Nubia, sent to Egypt *baku*, a word that originally designated "worked" products, whereas Upper Nubia, Kush, sent *inu*. Because the accounts of Thutmose III include sections that are derived from official administrative records, it seems most reasonable to conclude that this differentiation reflects the actual economic policy of Egypt toward its southern territories. Note that a third term, *biat*, was employed for goods sent to Egypt in extraordinary circumstances and from faraway lands that did not belong to the empire. All in all, it is *inu* that is the most difficult to understand.

In the case of Thutmose's sixth campaign, this word is employed with respect to the imperious demands of Pharaoh. But the mention of the children of local potentates or their brothers being sent to Egypt and serving as "hostages" implies that a regular system of coercion was also applied. From the bare-bones account it seems that after a city had submitted or, equally, when it had sworn allegiance to Egypt, these important men would be taken away. During this year we find 36 men sent back to Egypt. *Inu*, then, does not refer to a regularly imposed set demand. Rather, the designation suits the indirect type of physical control that Egypt set up in Asia. With regard to this region, *inu* is always connected to the local princes. Can we thus assume that Upper Nubia, which also sent *inu*, was still divided into several small chiefdoms, but nonetheless dependent upon the

Pharaoh? Or, by the middle years of Thutmose III's life, did the final reorganization occur in which only two provinces, Wawat and Kush, were recognized?

An account dated to Dynasty XIX presents a letter sent by a military man to his underling describing the requirement for the royal *inu* from Kush (P. Koller).[3] Although there remains the possibility that the writing is fictive, and was intended for advanced scribal training, the details are useful. The "overseer of the foreign land of Kush" points out that various quadrupeds, barges, gold, and other rare items are to be delivered to Egypt. Numerous precious stones, other exotic animals such as cats, monkeys, and baboons, must belong to the "tribute." The purpose of the composition is oriented to memorizing these outlandish things. Even the southerners are expected to arrive with their exotic wares, and all of them would eventually march below the king's Window of Appearances at the palace. It is sufficient to note that the term *inu* is not specified with regard to number or amount. The "tribute," nonetheless, is specifically applied to Upper Nubia, Kush.

The seventh campaign of Thutmose III is recounted by an account of booty and plunder. The port of Ullaza submitted to him and one commander of the son of the prince of Tunip (a key city located to the east in Syria) was captured in addition to a second military officer. Horses, chariots, and weapons of war were also obtained. Again a list of the *inu* is recorded, but no specific historical details are given. Of equal if not greater importance is the first mention of harbor provisioning. This must imply that Thutmose III was now able to act with a free hand in the Levant, and so prepare for a major onslaught through inland Syria and Mitanni without having to march north through Palestine. The supplies included the necessities for an army: breads, oil, incense, wine, honey, and fruit. If a modern restoration in the official record is correct, these items were provided by the port cities themselves. In other words, Thutmose III no longer had to worry about some of the basic foods for his army. Beer, however, is not mentioned, and because water was plentiful enough, it too is ignored.

The harvest of Asia then follows, and it was required to be sent back to Egypt. Since the grain produce is not included under the *inu* of the year, it must have been required impost and hence most akin to our word "tribute." Besides barley, wheat, and emmer wheat, we find incense, oil, wine, and fruit. The royal treasury kept an official account of these items. This harvest was reported to Egyptian officials, and it remains open whether all of this was dispatched homeward. Nevertheless, I assume that it all went south because a further comment indicates that the total could be checked at the royal treasury. (The *baku* of Nubia was likewise recorded there.) Of course, some of the items could have been assigned to the local Egyptian garrisons abroad.

As an aside we ought to keep in mind that any Egyptian garrison needed to have a large capacity for the storage of grain. From the Middle Kingdom the archaeological evidence is clear. At various fortresses around the Second Cataract the capacity of the granaries has been approximated so that we can roughly determine the upper and lower limits of the actual population fed.[4] The numbers vary from around 779 to 3,264, thereby indicating well-established garrisons whose troops were not too small in number. But a further analysis of the same material shows that these Nubian forts could serve not only as a means of static defense but also as staging points for a campaign. Undoubtedly, the same situation existed in the New Kingdom. In Nubia from the reign of Ahmose, if not Kamose, Buhen served as a defensive line and also as a take-off point for war. The developments at Sai and other more southerly fortresses in Lower and Upper Nubia would have served the Pharaohs well when they decided to travel by ship further upstream.

Naturally, the same can be said with regard to Asia. But there the necessity of building new fortresses was less urgent. There already were cities and towns, some of which were located at key junctures on the various highways. Moreover, the ports could also serve as depots for the kings' army. And we must not forget that the numerous cities in Palestine and Syria could provide supplies for an advancing Egyptian army as well as for a local garrison. In fact, the Pharaohs had at their fingertips the harvests of various princedoms, so long as the citadel in each locality remained loyal to him. If it resisted, his overwhelming force easily prevented the locals from blocking food. No wonder that we frequently read of the army felling trees, scavenging in the vineyards, cutting the grain, and in a wholesale fashion looting the area in the vicinity of an opposing city.

At the end of the year's report for the seventh campaign is the list of goods sent to Egypt from Wawat and Kush in Nubia. Nowhere in these war records of the king do we read of any Nubian revolt. Apparently, the final campaigns of Hatshepsut and Thutmose III in that region ended all major resistance. The standard order is Kush before Wawat. From the former territory, gold and slaves were brought back, but also ten male Nubians to be "followers," possibly for military officers although this is unclear. Note the importance of the precious metal gold. It is regularly listed at the beginning of each record. With this metal, Egypt could export it to the other kingdoms in Western Asia, Babylon in particular. Gold, as might be expected, was a very important commodity in the world market of that time. In return, Egypt could receive other precious and necessary items. One thinks of imported tin to make bronze, but also woods from lands not under direct Egyptian administration. In addition, rare and costly fashioned objects as well were sent to Egypt from the Asiatic potentates in exchange for gold. Other goods brought north from Nubia included oxen, short-horned cattle, bulls, from Kush ebony and from Wawat, grain. A summary list will be given later.

The famous Euphrates campaign of Thutmose III took place in year thirty-three of Thutmose.[5] He went north to the port of Qatna, probably arriving by ship. Then he reached Aleppo, crossed the Euphrates, set up a stela of victory next to his grandfather's, and subsequently plundered the settlements (not towns or cities) of the king of Mitanni. To the west of Aleppo the king also fought a battle. Therefore, we can reconstruct the strategic focus. It was in north Syria, to the west of the Euphrates. The Lebanese ports of Byblos, Sumur, and Arvad were the bases for supplies and troops. Qatna apparently was the first major city seized, and the king must have traveled inland north of Kadesh. From this metropolis he chose the western of two roads to Aleppo. The army then moved on to Carchemish, the most important city in the region, which was located in the heartland of the western portions of Mitanni, but it does not appear to have fallen. The soldier Amunemheb who accompanied his king during this campaign reports only that he "captured" in this region.[6] No indication is given that Carchemish was taken, and its absence from the official war record is telling. The historical account then describes the river trip of the Pharaoh and the attacks upon local settlements. At Aleppo, Amunemheb received more war booty than he had obtained near Carchemish.

The other route that Thutmose III might have taken led from Damascus through Homs and then turned eastward to reach Hamath. From Hamath going northward, Aleppo would have been reached, and across eastward one meets the Euphrates. This journey, however, was not taken. Moreover, the area around Kadesh and that city itself were hostile to the Egyptians. We cannot but assume a more northern west–east focus at the beginning of this campaign. Egyptian domination was weaker in the far north of the Lebanese coast. Ugarit, for example, remained under Egyptian control for some years, but eventually regained its independence. At any rate, the king was unable to march eastward unopposed through Alalakh to Aleppo. Yet in regnal year thirty-eight Alalakh sent an *inu* delivery to Egypt and Nukhashshe in central Syria was plundered. No horses or chariots were given to the Egyptian monarch by the second locality, and it is reasonable to conclude that Thutmose did not wage war against it. This second route had the advantage as it led more quickly to Carchemish. The terrain in this corner of Syria is not overly difficult, although the steep and rugged Beylan Pass exists in the far north. In many ways, Thutmose was in an advantageous position as he avoided the region around Antioch and so avoided Alalakh.

From yet a third source, a stela set up by the king at Gebel Barkal in Nubia many years later, we learn that he had built boats near Byblos and had them dragged overland by oxen.[7] This feat must indicate that Thutmose had already planned to reach the Euphrates. Therefore, the northern advance to Carchemish was no mere accident. We must also surmise that the Egyptians were reasonably conversant with the local geography, a fact supported by the earlier campaign of Thutmose I. With these ships Thutmose III was able to defeat another group of foes. The Gebel Barkal stela implies that he desired to meet the king of Mitanni in battle. The official report at Karnak, however, does not refer to this. Instead, we receive notice of the booty brought to the king after he fought in the territory of Mitanni, previously having left his ships in order to move his army across the land.

The return journey of Thutmose saw him attack the foreign land of Niy, and he set up that stela of victory there. Amunhemheb, on the other hand, is more specific. He notes war in the region of Sendjar, modern Qala'at Sejar, south of Niy. Kadesh was now reached and taken. This focus of attention is worthy of mention. As this city sided with the enemy, the king of Mitanni, we can now see why the plan of operation was so far north. The Pharaoh had control of the ports of Lebanon and he could bypass Kadesh, now in enemy hands, by marching directly north to Aleppo. The aim of the campaign was geared to reaching the Euphrates and sailing downstream (southward) on it. The importance of that river was paramount in the mind of the Pharaoh. Thutmose knew that it formed an effective boundary between the heartland of Syria and the eastern lands of Mitanni. Thus the aim of this campaign was to seize control over all regions to the west of the Euphrates and north of Kadesh, with the latter city being forced to submit at the end of the trip. Indeed, in Syria, only the city and territory of Alalakh remained outside of Egyptian control. Takhsy, closely associated with Kadesh, also fell to the Egyptians during the Pharaoh's southerly rollercoaster march. The second city, interestingly, is the only one at which Amunemheb captured any *maryannu*, two to be precise.

From the narrative direction of Amunemheb's biography we see that the homeward incidents of war included the following (in order): Sendjar, Kadesh, Takhsy, and Kadesh. The army first went south to Kadesh, won a victory there, operated in the regions east of the Orontes River, and finally resumed the march back to that locality. The famous elephant hunt of Thutmose took place at Niy. Apparently, Thutmose III considered the fighting to be at an end. Why else would he have turned back and indulged himself in sportive activities? Otherwise, as has been surmised, this private account encases more than one campaign.

One major difficulty with reconciling the three major sources presented here is that no dates are given except in the official annalistic report of the king.[8] But in the Amunemheb's biography account Niy is also recorded as well. Notwithstanding some difficulty in interpreting this narrative, I believe that the general geographic order presented here fits. More important, however, was the political effect. In the "Annals" at Karnak the results are made clear. The major superpowers of the day recognized the might of Egypt. The Hittite kingdom, Babylon, and possibly Assyria (or Mitanni?) are listed one by one after the subsection dealing with the provisioning of the Lebanese harbors. Hence, this campaign was as important politically as it was strategically.

Above all, we should recognize the difference between Thutmose III's Euphrates campaign and the earlier ones. The sea was the key. For at least four years Thutmose III had prepared for his overland thrust. The task was arduous, and it required the transport of ships inland, a remarkable feat.[9] This region of Syria – mainly north of Kadesh, located on the river Orontes – was deemed separate from those countries to the south. That city was first bypassed but later taken. When we take into account the total northern aspect of the campaign it becomes clear that the king regarded central Syria very differently than the city-states in Palestine and southern Syria. There, if need be, he could trek on foot. Even from central Palestine up to Kadesh the campaign could be land based because the Beqa Valley allowed an easy entrance to that citadel. Further north, however, with Kadesh always being in the border zone, the Pharaoh followed a different strategy. He marched laterally, first west–east, and then north. He returned south partly by means of the Euphrates, and eventually reached central Syria. In some ways this area resembled Upper Nubia in contrast to Lower Nubia.

By this time the Egyptians considered their possessions in Asia to be very different from those in Nubia. But in both regions there was a sub-division. An official bifurcation similar to that of Kush–Wawat can be noted. Palestine was placed under more efficient control after year twenty-three of Thutmose III. Excluding the situation of impost in grain, the following political and military controls occurred. In southern Basan Yeno'am, east of the Jordan River and probably located at modern Tel esh-Shihab, was one of three cities that were taxed with annual dues for Amun of Karnak.[10] The other two cities were Neges and Khukkuri which had been previously under the control of Megiddo. Now, however, they passed to the Egyptians. It would seem that the Pharaoh, after besieging Megiddo, sent some of his troops to the north in order to subdue the Lebanon as well as the Bashan. The eastern Palestinian city of Beth Shan soon became one of the Egyptian garrison points, thereby effecting control of the east–west highway leading off Megiddo. Thutmose III was the first Pharaoh who established an Egyptian center in this city. Egyptian supremacy in Palestine was thus cemented, with Beth Shan and Megiddo serving as the two most important points. Yeno'am's position controlled the area west of Edrei on the Yarmuk River. Hence, it, too, was of crucial importance to the Egyptians. It is useful to note that earlier Mitanni was recognized as having sovereignty over the region, and Megiddo as well. Now Egypt was in control.

In Syria, on the other hand, Kadesh was the major thorn in the side of the Egyptians.[11] As a result of Thutmose's eighth campaign in year thirty-three, lands north of Kadesh came under the suzerainty of the Pharaoh. Perhaps at this time Kumidi, in southern Syria, was transformed into a garrison city. In the latter case a local prince ruled, although the presence of Egyptian troops prevented him from claiming independence. But in regnal year thirty-four the Pharaoh once more fought in Syria. At this time the area of conflict was Nukhashshe, a region south of Aleppo whose southern boundary stretched along the river Orontes. In other words, once more the focus of the Pharaoh was upon the western zone of the kingdom of Mitanni. Valuable items such as chairs of black wood, in addition to the expected horses and chariots, were taken from three cities. Since tent poles are mentioned as well, we can conclude that a battle took place during which the enemy lost its nerve in the melee. The foreign land of Isy, perhaps old Assuwa, then acknowledged the strength of the Egyptians in this region.

In year thirty-five a direct confrontation between the king of Mitanni and Thutmose took place. The importance of the encounter is reflected in the captured booty. We read of inlaid reins or possibly armor, bronze armor, 60 chariots and 180 horses (evenly three times the latter), 5 bronze helmets, and 5 Syrian bows.[12] These items were in addition to that which the king himself had obtained in battle. Significantly, even though the account points out that the Pharaoh fought against soldiers of the king of Mitanni, the enemy king is nowhere described. We must therefore assume that he avoided direct combat with Thutmose but instead sent his army westward against his opponent. The total number of chariots or horses indicates a conflict far less extreme than at Megiddo, and one can hypothesize that the full power of Mitanni was not released at this time.

The next series of campaigns of Thutmose III are more fragmentary. But in his thirty-eighth year the king was once more in the Mittanian-held territory of Nukhashshe. Owing to the extreme northern orientation of the war, both Cyprus and Alalakh supplied Thutmose with *inu* goods. The former sent two horses (but no chariots), but the latter avoided such dues. The next year saw another Shasu conflict, perhaps located near Beth Shan. In year forty-one the Hittites once more sent their special deliveries to Egypt, but we are unclear as to the extent of the king's campaigning. The final war of the king is to be placed in year forty-two. At this time the king traveled to Syria, possibly by sea. It is assumed that there was an uprising at this time, a not improbable interpretation.[13] The coastal region of Arqata was taken and Tunip subsequently seized once more. During his return journey, the Pharaoh reached the territory of Kadesh and successfully attacked three cities in that region. Some auxiliaries of the king of Naharain were also captured. Yet another peripheral region recognized the success because Tunnu, located in North Syria, is claimed to have sent special goods back to the king.

In the Pharaoh's campaign of year thirty-five Syrian bows are listed among the booty for the first time. Because the composite bow, of particular

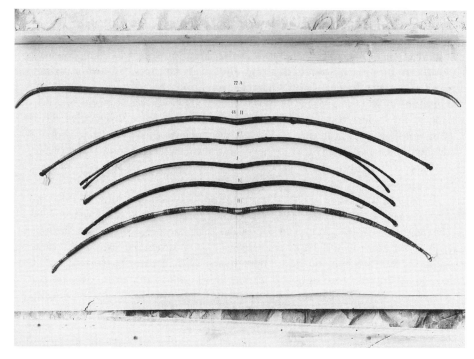

Figure 7.1   Group of bows on display in the Egyptian Museum from the tomb of Tutankhamun. Cairo. Photo The Griffith Institue, Ashmolean Museum, Oxford.

importance for large armies and most effective with chariots, was the decisive long-range weapon in the armies of the Late Bronze Age, was Syria rather than Palestine a center of manufacture?[14] It has been pointed out that select wood was necessary for such weaponry. General Yadin, for example, further indicated that two shapes of composite bows are known from this time: the triangular bow and the recurved one.[15] We can see these bows in tomb paintings dated to the reign of Thutmose III and Amunhotep II; they are among the gifts brought to Egyptian by Asiatics.

Though dated somewhat later in time, the reliefs on the chariot body of Thutmose IV reveal some interesting details concerning Asiatic warfare in mid Dynasty XVIII.[16] The king fights in an eight-spoke chariot while his enemies use vehicles with only four spokes. On one side Thutmose IV shoots with a typical recurved convex bow whereas on the other he holds a triangular compound bow. The Asiatics are depicted with helmets and armor. All the horses appear to belong to the second type of equid, the "short-

118

Figure 7.2 Right side of the chariot (exterior). *The Tomb of Thoutmôsis IV* by Howard Carter and Percy E. Newberry. Archibald Constable & Co. Ltd, 1904, pl. X. Photo © Bodleian Library, Oxford.

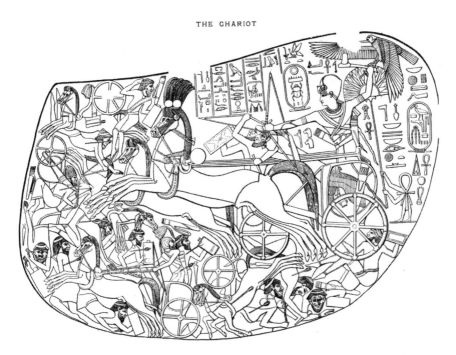

Figure 7.3 Left side of the chariot (exterior). *The Tomb of Thoutmôsis IV* by Howard Carter and Percy E. Newberry. Archibald Constable & Co. Ltd, 1904, pl. IX. Photo © Bodleian Library, Oxford.

lined type," which was common around this time. Of equal significance is the artistic representation. On the right side of the cab was the bow case that overlapped a quiver. On the left was a second quiver. Supplying even more arrows was a third quiver that was attached to the king's body. The arrows would be taken with the left hand.

But only in the accompanying scenes of carnage can the complete war situation be visualized. Once more, let me point out that these two scenes are dated somewhat later than the reign of Thutmose III.[17] Nonetheless, they may be used to establish the type of Egyptian preparedness for battle in mid Dynasty XVIII and at the same time to reveal the military ability of the Asiatic enemy. The king advances from the right to the left, ready to smite his foes with his battle-axe. The Pharaoh holds this weapon, originally imported to Egypt from Palestine and Syria, in his right hand. Hence, the triangular composite bow, held by the left hand, is not in use. The pose therefore reflects the earlier smiting scenes of the king with a pear-shaped mace. In the second scene Thutmose IV moves to the right. He shoots his arrows, many of which have penetrated both the enemy and their horses. Some but not all of his opponents have helmets, and various types of armor can be seen, undoubtedly made of leather and a metal (probably bronze).

The king's chariot is more curved in the rear than the Asiatics'.[18] The outer rim of the cab is made of wood that is thicker toward the base. The sides are not open but rather made of a softer material. Therefore, screening extended across from the rear of the box to the front. Extant chariot sidings are completely open, filled in as this one, or partly fenestrated. Canvas or thin wood, decorated in this case, filled the large gap. Most of the enemy horses have no padding and protection on their back and sides. Some have bow cases on the right side of the cab whereas none appear on the left. The Asiatics hold rectangular shields, not at all like the Egyptian one which had a rounded top somewhat wider than its base. There is little doubt that the Egyptian shield had developed from their earlier larger ones used in the Middle Kingdom. This shape was typical for the New Kingdom and appears to have been employed to protect the body and perhaps the face as well. From Dynasty XIX reliefs we can see that there was a strap for carrying the item on the inside, and that the sides had later become more parallel to each other.

These weapons, both protective and offensive, are often depicted in stereo-typical scenes of carnage. As has been mentioned earlier, the role of the solitary king in battle was a common pictorial theme for Egyptian wars. Generalized scenes of a triumphant Pharaoh hunting have to be considered separate from those of warfare.[19] With the former we are encapsulated within an atemporal setting: the king charging against animals and shooting his arrows. The war scenes, on the other hand, show many more details and often are located in time and place. Nonetheless, the depictions of weaponry may not indicate the actual conditions of combat but instead reflect the artistic temperament or an agreed-upon schema.

The iconography of the victorious Pharaoh with his reins tied behind his back resembles those scenes of hunting that the kings loved to recount from a visual point of view. Nevertheless, the use of the composite bows cannot be ignored. Both Thutmose IV and later Ramesses II employ a recurved type, but private tombs dated to Thutmose III (e.g., the vizier Rekhmire) and Amunhotep II (Kenamun) reveal the presence of bow cases that served triangular compound types. From the XIXth Dynasty reliefs the recurved compound bow had become preponderant. Earlier, however, we see regular bows in the battle reliefs of Ahmose. They appear to have been employed by the Egyptians. Among the fragments from Thutmose II's mortuary temple at Thebes are Asiatics with fenestrated axes of the duckbill type and bows whose type is difficult to determine. On the painted lid of Tutankhamun's wooden chest found in his tomb (late Dynasty XVIII), the Pharaoh hunts with a regular bow in a chariot with open sides. Clearly, this case cannot be employed to reconstruct the military aspects of the Pharaoh. Indeed, there are only six spokes on the wheels of the king's chariot, unlike the standard eight in early military scenes of Dynasty XVIII. We can assume that there was not that much need for protection during a hunt, and that the Pharaoh need not have used a bow of the compound type that was necessary in actual warfare.

This brief view of the military style in mid Dynasty XVIII complements the war records of Thutmose III. Even though it does not enable us to determine exactly how these Syrian bows were employed, there is little doubt that they were compound ones. A perceptible change occurred from the reign of Ahmose to Thutmose IV, a conclusion that is based upon the later presence of recurved bows in scenes of Dynasty XIX. First, the bows were developed from the simpler ones, either double-convex or large arc ones. (The latter were common in the Middle Kingdom.) We do not know when the change to the compound bow occurred within the Nile Valley. The Hyksos Period has traditionally been considered to be the time when a massive alteration of military technology came to pass in the Nile Valley. Yet the Ahmose reliefs indicate that at least the Hyksos (or possibly their Asiatic allies) still employed the simpler types. Composite bows required hardy woods, not the softer types found in Egypt. Egypt, with its natural deficiency in forests, was partly in an economic backwater, militarily speaking. Most certainly, however, as the scenes of Thutmose IV indicate, the king and his Asiatic opponents had mastered the new technique with their better bows. Both protagonists carry the triangular type. Thutmose IV's scene indicates that by mid Dynasty XVIII this type of bow as well as the double curved one was still in use. By Dynasty XIX the

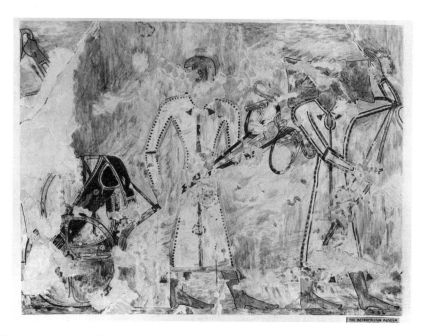

Figure 7.4a Detail of wall painting, Thebes, tomb of Rekhmire. Metropolitan Museum of Art, New York.

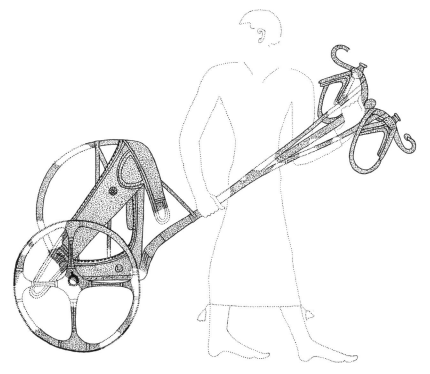

Figure 7.4b Drawing of 7.4a. From *Wheeled Vehicles and Ridden Animals in the Ancient Near East* by M. A. Littauer and J. H. Crouwel. Drawing by J. Morel. E. J. Brill, 1979, figure 43.

triangular compound bow had disappeared, at least from the official artistic repertoire.

These lags of technology in artistic representations should not surprise us. For example, the early Dynasty XVIII battle scenes contrast the king in a chariot with eight spokes against the enemy's four-spoked wheels.[20] Yet in one fragment from Thutmose II's mortuary temple an Asiatic might hold a compound bow. On the other hand, the enemy chariots reflect the earlier four-spoked type. Because Thutmose II is known to have campaigned against the Shasu Bedouin, can we assume that the battle scenes dated to his reign reflect this Asiatic conflict? Later evidence under Seti I indicates that the Shasu in the Sinai did not have horses and chariots, although the Asiatic enemies of Thutmose II in his reliefs used them. On the other hand, if the Shasu were in the Trans-Jordan, from which they also operated later, then this hypothesis might receive some support. Notwithstanding the quandary, and providing that the artistic representations are valid, it is clear that the Palestinian enemies had smaller and lighter chariots than the Egyptians.

Considering all of these imponderables, we still can conclude that by early Dynasty XVIII the Egyptian chariot arm was stronger than the Palestinian one. One fragment of Thutmose II, for example, apparently shows a six-spoked chariot wheel. I assume it to be Egyptian. Yet note the duckbilled axe carried by an Asiatic. This type of weapon was typical in the Middle Bronze Age, but had been replaced by more sophisticated axes by the time of Ahmose. Can we assume that the military technology of the Palestinians was not as advanced as, for example, their Syrian or Babylonian neighbors? However this question is answered, the Egyptians began to replace their triangular composite bows by recurved ones around the reign of Thutmose IV.

The two private scenes of Rekhmire and Kenamun referred to above reveal Asiatics with the triangular types, but the Egyptians also are shown with these weapons. Kenamun's depicts an Egyptian carrying a triangular case for the bow as well as a recurved composite bow, and we have noted the use of both by Thutmose IV. In fact, on a well-known block depicting Amunhotep II shooting at an ingot a four-spoked wheel is present in addition to a recurved compound bow.[21] Here, of course, no enemies are present, and it is not surprising to see that the sides of the chariot box are open. All in all, we cannot assume a strict linear development in the use of weapons of war. Lags, as I have already indicated, are always apparent, with the newer technology or details proceeding sometimes fast but also slowly, with the older types remaining in use for some years. But the singular occurrence of the mention of five Syrian bows in Thutmose III's "Annals" allows us to hypothesize that they were not only different from the Egyptians' but also from those in use in Palestine. We cannot tell, however, if recurved or triangular ones were meant.

EXCURSUS

1. In excursus 3 to chapter 5 the population of Palestine was estimated around 140,000 at 1600 BC. There was a wholesale drop to about 60,000–70,000 by 1200 BC. A settlement crisis in Palestine can be placed to the transition from Middle Bronze II to the Late Bronze Age. The studies listed in that Excursus point out the methodological constraints of the present archaeological record. In particular, there has been an emphasis upon Late Bronze cities, their functions, fortifications, public buildings, and the like. As Alexander Joffe has remarked to me, "even a huge site like Hazor had more than a few thousand residents" during this time, "and most sites far less." Owing to this, the scale of Egyptian imperial forces necessary to pacify the Palestine and the Levant was small.

For inland Syria no population estimates have been presented, but with regard to the kingdom of the Hittites in Asia Minor, Liverani observed the low natality of the countryside as well as the wars and plagues that decimated the population (*Prestige and Interest*, 148 and n. 22). The dating of the key text supporting this contention is fixed to the reign of Hattusilis III, a contemporary of Pharaoh Ramesses II (mid Dynasty XIX). We first hear of such plagues during the time of the Hittite king Suppiluliuma, who ruled around the time of Akhenaton and his immediate successors (late Dynasty XVIII).

2. From the reign of Thutmose III onward, the Pharaohs regularly "published" lists of foreign place names, a historiographic tradition that can already be seen to be at work in the Old and Middle Kingdoms. (See Johnson, *An Asiatic Battle Scene of Tutankhamun from Thebes*, 94–5, for an overview of the earlier use of these topographic name rings.) The foreign place name appears within a crenellated cartouche, which represents a fortress. The standard interpretation among Egyptologists is that these localities were considered to have been conquered by the Egyptian monarchs, although allowance for recopying and anachronisms is often mentioned. Donald B. Redford presented a new and useful hypothesis in his study, "A Bronze Age Itinerary in Transjordan (Nos. 89–101 of Thutmose III's List of Asiatic Toponyms)," *Journal of the Society for the Study of Egyptian Antiquities* 12 (1982), 55–74, and "Contact Between Egypt and Jordan in the New Kingdom: Some Comments on Sources," in Adnan Hadidi, ed., *Studies in the History and Archaeology of Jordan, Department of Antiquities*, Amman (1982), 115–19. His conclusion, with which I agree, is that many of the names can be placed together and the resultant portion appears to reflect a routier, or geographical itinerary. Hence, these lengthy topographical lists, which by the way are subdivided into northern (Asian) and southern (Nubian) lands, were copied from archival copies of official documents. Indeed, in Mesopotamia we find the same use of itineraries. For example, see W. W. Hallo, "The Road to Emar," *Journal of Cuneiform Studies* 15 (1964), 57–88. (Note the connections in Syria between Emar, Aleppo, Qatna, and then the road south to Hazor in Palestine.)

The geographical outline in P. Anastasi I, dated to Dynasty XIX, supports this argument. The master scribe sets out for his luckless underling a detailed political horizon of Syro-Palestine – the coastal cities of Syria, Palestine, and the east (Takhsy region in Syria and East Jordan): Fischer-Elfert, *Die satirische Streitschrift des Papyrus Anastasi I.*, XVI–XIX.

A useful approach to these toponym lists can now be found in Redford's study, *Egypt, Canaan, and Israel in Ancient Times*, 143 n. 61. His remarks must be read in conjunction with Aharoni's historical reconstructions of Egyptian campaigns (*The Land of the Bible*[2]). As a rule, Redford's conclusions tend to negate the topographical over-interpretations of Aharoni. From a historiographic viewpoint Helck's compendium, *Die Beziehungen Ägyptens zu Vorderasien*[2], chapter 14, is more accurate than Aharoni's, but we can now refer to the recent study of Redford, *The Wars in Syria and Palestine of Thutmose III*, 43–51.

3. The geography of Syria played a great role in determining the extent of Pharaonic control. We must keep in mind that the region was considerably further away from the home country than Palestine. In addition, major kingdoms flanked the region: the Hittites to the northwest in Anatolia and the Mitannians around the river Euphrates. Hence, it was considerably more difficult for Thutmose III and his successors to control permanently large portions of this territory.

Syria contains two mountain ranges that lie parallel to the coast. The first is the Ansariyeh, which runs north–south from the present-day northern frontier to the gap between modern Tripoli (somewhat south of the Nahr el-Kebir) and Homs. Therefore, one normally had to march in a northeasterly direction in order to reach Aleppo, for example. The second range is the Lebanon, which veers to the southwest from Homs to the present-day southern border. South of Homs the Anti-Lebanon and Mount Hermon massifs stretch southwest for more than 160 km. There are essentially two regions. Western Syria includes the coastal ranges, a depression (the Ghab and the Beqa Valley, where the Pharaoh often journeyed north to Kadesh on the Orontes), and the Anti-Lebanon plus the Mount Hermon massifs. To the east is a second zone that now includes steppe land and desert, the volcanic region of the Gebel Druze and the Hauran, the Euphrates Valley (where Thutmose I and III campaigned), and the Jezireh east of the Euphrates. The main routes in Syria naturally bypass the mountain ranges. In the middle of the western portion the Orontes basin forms a natural ecological zone.

Rainfall is most prominent near the coast, of course, though not exactly coterminous with it. East of Damascus and in a curved line running to the northeast, the amount of rain diminishes considerably. Beirut, for example, records 78 rain days/year and has a mean annual rainfall of 89 cm whereas Aleppo has 56 rain days/year and a mean annual figure of 38 cm; the records for Damascus indicate only 33 rain days/year and a mean annual figure of 48.26. We probably can allow the precipitation *contrasts* to have been roughly the same at the time of the New Kingdom as now. (The amount of fresh water was always a problem for the Egyptians when they traveled inland.) Moreover, downpours come in sharp showers here, and that there are also short spells of stormy or thundery weather. In Beirut, to take a case in point, the rainy season generally ends in the second half of May and recommences early in October. Owing to these constraints, it is not surprising that Thutmose III, and after him Amunhotep II, Seti I, and finally Ramesses II, moved upward to Syria from the center of Palestine. Evidently, control of the central King's Highway was of prime importance to the Egyptian warrior-kings. The coastal cities under Egyptian control reached through Byblos northward, but never so far as to include Ugarit in the little bay of Minet el Baida, located just a few kilometers north of Latakia. Ugarit did have close connections with Egypt around the time of Amunhotep III; however, it remained independent. Later, this port city was a politically independent client state (and so an ally) of the Hittites.

One of the best topographical works on Syria is that published by Great Britain during World War II, Naval Intelligence Division, *Syria²*, The Admiralty, London (1944). Even though now superseded, the 1:1,000,000 map remains excellent. In addition, note the lengthy study of Jean Sapin, "La Géographie humaine de la Syrie-Palestine au deuxième millénaire avant J.-C. comme voie de recherche historique," Journal *of the Economic and Social History of the Orient* 24 (1981), 1–62 and 25 (1982), 1–49.

NOTES

1 This portion of the historical records needs a careful and reevaluation which cannot be attempted here. Three useful and detailed analyses are Helck, *Die Beziehungen Ägyptens zu Vorderasien²*, 137–56; Aharoni, *The Land of the Bible²*, 152–66; and Redford, *The Wars in Syria and Palestine of Thutmose III*, chapters Five–Ten.

The main royal sources for this time period are the "Annals" of Thutmose III (Parts V–VI): Breasted, *Ancient Records of Egypt* II, 190–217; and Sethe, *Urkunden der 18. Dynastie*, 684–734. To this basic account can be added the well-known Armant Stela (Helck, *Urkunden der 18.* Dynastie, Akademie Verlag, Berlin [1955], 1243–7), as well as the Gebel Barkal Stela (pp. 1227–43 in the same volume). The latter two texts will be found in an adequate translation by Barbara Cumming, *Egyptian Historical Records of the Later Eighteenth Dynasty*, fascicle 1, Aris and Phillips, Warminster (1982), 1–7 (Gebel Barkal Stela) and 7–9 (Armant Stela).

2 Two studies have clarified the use of these terms: Jac. J. Janssen, "*B3kw*: from Work to Product," *Studien zur altägyptischen Kultur* 20 (1993), 81–94; and Anthony Spalinger, "From Local to Global: The Extension of an Egyptian Bureaucratic Term to the Empire," *Studien zur altägyptischen Kultur* 23 (1996), 353–76.

Edward Bleiberg, *The Official Gift in Ancient Egypt*, University of Oklahoma Press, Norman (1996), attempted a rigid definition for these words. The work of Liverani, *Prestige and Interest*, 255–66, often overlooked, remains fundamental.

He also presented a similar position in "Dono, tributo, commercio: Ideologia dello scambio nella tardo età del bronzo," *Istituto Italiano di Numismatica* 1979, 9–28.

Redford, *The Wars in Syria and Palestine of Thutmose III*, chapter Thirteen, has returned to the issue of "diplomatic gifts."

Stuart Tyson Smith, *Wretched Kush. Ethnic Identification and Boundaries in Egypt's Nubian Empire*, Routledge, London and New York (2003), discusses the term *inu*. See his argument on pp. 70–1 and 184–5. Unfortunately, his orientation is archaeological, and therefore he avoids the native Egyptian usages of this key word.

3 Conveniently, see Caminos, *Late Egyptian Miscellanies*, 431–46.

4 See now Kemp, *Ancient Egypt. Anatomy of a Civilization*, 195 for the New Kingdom. The earlier case is analyzed by him is on pages 172–8. Note also his study "Large Middle Kingdom Granary Buildings (and the archaeology of administration)," *Zeitschrift für ägyptische Sprache* 113 (1986), 123–36.

5 The classical study of this war is that of R. O. Faulkner, "The Euphrates Campaign of Thutmosis III," *Journal of Egyptian Archaeology* 32 (1946), 39–42. Useful data and an effective analysis of Thutmose's wars in this region were presented by Alan H. Gardiner, *Ancient Egyptian Onomastica* I, Oxford University Press, Oxford (1947), 153*–71*.

6 For this man's biography: Breasted, *Ancient Records of Egypt* II, (now very dated) 227–34 (reign of Thutmose III); and Sethe, *Urkunden der 18. Dynastie*, 890–5. See as well the sources listed in the last note.

7 The reference to the Gebel Barkal Stela is given in note 1 above. Add Liverani, *Prestige and Interest*, 259–60.

8 That is to say, in the "Annals" (Parts V–VI) each campaign is headed by a regnal year. One exception may be seen in the account of the seventh campaign. The "Annals" open with a full date: "Regnal year 31, first month of harvest (*shemu*), day 3. Summary of that which his majesty captured in this year": Breasted, *Ancient Records of Egypt* II 199, Sethe, *Urkunden der 18. Dynastie*, 690.14–15. It is self-evident that this record indicates the final totaling-up of the booty after the war was completed. (The date is the last day of the king's regnal year.)

9 The use of ships as the important factor in these later campaigns was first discussed by Breasted, *Ancient Records of Egypt* II, 194, 197, 198–9, and especially 201–2. Säve-Söderbergh, in his *The Navy of the Eighteenth Egyptian Dynasty*, 43–54, covers this matter in more detail.

10 Here I once more follow the conclusions of Na'aman, "Yeno'am," *Tel Aviv* 4 (1977), 168–77; add his "Pharaonic Lands in the Jezreel Valley in the Late Bronze Age," in M. Heltzer and E. Lipinski, eds., *Society and Economy in the Eastern Mediterranean (c. 1500–1000 BC)*, Uitgeverij Peters, Leuven (1988), 177–85.

I find his analysis of the economic results of Dynasty XVIII warfare in Palestine also very pertinent: "Economic Aspects of the Egyptian Occupation of Canaan," *Israel Exploration Journal* 31 (1981), 172–85.

11 The population of Syria in contrast to Palestine was considerably higher: excursus 3 to chapter 5.

12 For evidence of Asiatic (Syrian) helmets in the XVIIIth Dynasty, see Timothy Kendall, "*gurpišu ša awēli*: The Helmets of the Warriors at Nuzi," in M. A. Morrison and D. I. Owen, eds., *Studies on the Civilization and Culture of Nuzi and the Hurrians*, Eisenbrauns, Winnowa Lake (1981), 201–31. He links the Nuzi evidence with the Egyptian pictorial data from private tombs, but also covers the representations on the wooden chariot body from the tomb of Thutmose IV. On p. 222 there is the perspicacious comment that "most of the details of military dress represented here . . . suggest strongly that the Egyptian artist actually used as his models genuine articles of Asiatic armor, either those received by the court as gifts or those taken by the army as war booty."

13 Redford, *The Wars in Syria and Palestine of Thutmose III*, 238–40.

14 The repetitive nature of the military nature of the *inu* deliveries from Palestine and Syria to Egypt must be emphasized. This hallmark of Egyptian imperialism, at least in the XVIIIth Dynasty, has been ably commented upon by Na'aman in his study "Economic Aspects of the Egyptian Occupation of Canaan," cited in note 10 above. For the use of Lebanese shipbuilders in Egypt at this time, see Lucien Basch, "Le navire *mnš* et autres notes de voyage en Égypte," *The Mariner's Mirror* 64 (1978), 99–106, who discusses the earlier scholarly literature, in particular the analysis of Säve-Söderbergh.

15 *The Art of Warfare in Biblical Lands* I, 6–8, 80–3; and Partridge, *Fighting Pharaohs*, 42–6.

16 These details have been covered by Steven Harvey, *The Cults of King Ahmose at Abydos*, 303–72; see Yadin, *The Art of Warfare in Biblical Lands* I, 192–3, for a useful commentary.

17 The scholarly literature concerned with this pictorial evidence is listed in excursus 1 to chapter 6.

18 For the horses as well as the chariots, the compendium of Littauer and Crouwel, *Wheeled Vehicles and Ridden Animals in the Ancient Near* East, 75–97, is crucial; add the work of Herold, *Streitwagentechnologie in der Ramses-Stadt.*

19 The incomplete project of Eric Van Essche-Merchez must be cited in this context. He devoted his attention to the war reliefs of Ramesses III at the king's mortuary temple of Medinet Habu. See "La syntaxe formelle des reliefs et de la grande inscription de l'an 8 de Ramsès III à Médinet Habou," *Chronique d'Égypte* 67 (1992), 211–39, "Les discourse d'un text. Un extract de la Grande Inscription de l'an 8 de Ramsès III à Médinet Habou," in M. Broze and Ph. Talon, eds., *L'atelier de l'orfèvre. Mélanges offerts à Ph. Derchain*, Peeters, Leuven (1992), 169–81, "Pour une lecture 'stratigraphique' des parois du temple de Ramsès III à Médinet Habou," *Revue d'Égyptologie* 45 (1994), 87–116, "Quelques réflexions sur l'espace et le récit à Médinet Habou," *Annales d'histoire de l'art et d'archéologie* 11 (1989), 7–24, and "Ramsès III, le pouvoir et les dieux: recherches sur le plan de l'expression dans les reliefs 'historiques' de Médinet Habou," a study which was to appear in *Cahiers d'Argo* 1 (1993). The last analysis is particularly acute with regard to the use of Pharaonic hunting scenes and their interpolation within standard military ones.

I can now add the analysis of Heinz, "Wie wird ein Feldzug erzählt? Bildrepertoire, Anbringungsschema und Erzählform der Feldzugsreliefs im Neuen Reich," in Manfred Bietak and Mario Schwarz, eds., *Krieg und Sieg. Narrative*

Wanddarstellungen von Altägypten bis ins Mittelalter, Österreichischen Akademie der Wissenschaften, Vienna (2003), 43–67.
20 This is one of Harvey's important conclusions.
21 Conveniently, see Yadin, *The Art of Warfare in Biblical Lands* I, 200.

8

EGYPTIAN IMPERIALISM
AND THUTMOSE III

The second wave of Thutmose III's wars was mainly concentrated upon central and northern Syria. The repeated marches and cities taken and retaken indicate the strength of opposition. As many have seen, the real opponent was the king of Mitanni. The Pharaoh's ultimate strategic aim, however, is difficult to ascertain. Did he intend to carve out from this kingdom all of the lands from the Euphrates westward to the coast? The repeated recognition of his success reveals that the Egyptian ruler had full control of the Levant up to Arvad. Ugarit, nonetheless, appears to have been quasi-independent. In the hinterland the king had to deal with larger cities than those in Palestine, with the exception of Megiddo. For this warfare, a regularly supplied fleet was necessary, which demanded the necessary wood that could be supplied by the subservient city-states. The distances traveled were moderate. It is about 80 km from Arvad to present-day Hamath. This would have taken a mere four days. From Hamath to Aleppo the distance is about 121 km or 6 days of traveling. Finally, from Aleppo to Carchemish, following the normal route, the Egyptian army would have traversed about 113 km. All in all, the time it took to march from one key point to another was small. The major delays would therefore have occurred owing to armed resistance, and the threat from Mitanni surely forced Thutmose to bide his time.

Traveling would have been slower when he had his ships transported overland by oxen. These animals are very slow since they can only reach an average velocity of 3.2 km/hour and they can work only on the average for about 5 hours/day.[1] Moreover, it has been observed that their hooves are not suitable for covering long distances. Let us also add that a team of oxen requires ca. 45 kg food/day instead of a horse or a mule, both of which consume 4.5 kg of rations in addition to 4.5 kg of fodder.

We can hypothesize that when the king moved inland on his eighth campaign, he had to cover the distance from Byblos, Sumur, or Tripoli (unlikely) to Qatna. The distance was about 105 km and the time for the advance would have been, on the average, 7 days. Perhaps we can lengthen the journey northward, remembering that oxen were present. From Qatna to Hamath is another 51 km (ca. 3 days), and then we can add those distances listed earlier, but increase the time intervals owing to the pack animals. Because Thutmose fought at some of these sites, additional days would have passed in addition to the journey time. Nonetheless, the amount of time would not have exceeded a convoluted march from Egypt into Palestine. The food requirements, however, were probably greater owing to the necessity of feeding the oxen and transporting enough men and war material to meet up with the enemy in Mitanni. Here we can see the principle of strategic bifurcation referred to earlier. The Lebanese ports provided the base. Hence, they were not only strategically different from the Palestinian cities but they were also economically separate.

The Egyptian terms used for Asia are often unspecific.[2] From Dynasty XIX we find "Kharu" usually employed for Syria per se. Indeed, this came to replace "Upper Retjenu" or even "Retjenu." Let us remember that in his tenth campaign of year thirty-five Thutmose III obtained five bows from Kharu, and he fought against allies of Mitanni in Syria. More recent scholarship has identified Upper Retjenu with the mountainous region north of Eretz Israel.[3] This implies that our present designations of Syria and Palestine are not quite suitable. In the early XVIIIth Dynasty Djahy frequently indicated Palestine but included the territory inland of the coastal Lebanese ports, and the simple term Retjenu was the vaguer one. Because the latter often signified Upper Retjenu, we have to check the accounts carefully in order to determine where the king was.

This task is relatively simple when Thutmose III tells us that he was "in the land of Retjenu," and at the same time we see him advancing in Syria against the allies of Mitanni. Lebanon was separate, and therefore the coastal cities from Byblos northward can be disregarded. The difference lay with the inland territory west of the Euphrates and north of Megiddo. In year twenty-nine the Pharaoh was in Djahy, and one Lebanese port was captured. In year thirty Kadesh was taken, and as Retjenu is mentioned, this must indicate Upper Retjenu. The Euphrates campaign of Thutmose III is located in Retjenu (= Upper Retjenu), but then Djahy is mentioned in the attack against Nukhashshe during the following campaign, and also when Thutmose attacked the king of Mitanni in yet the next year. So Retjenu basically meant Asia, and Djahy Palestine plus the Lebanese coast inland to some unknown border. On one occasion we read of the annual *inu* delivery from the princes of Retjenu. But silver vessels as the work (*baku*) of Djahy are included. The more specific geographical term Upper Retjenu was simply avoided in the headings to king's "Annals" in the later sections dealing with regnal year 29 and following; only the *inu* of Retjenu is recorded.

This digression is important owing to the detailed records of the various *inu* deliveries that were annually given over to the Egyptians. If in year twenty-nine Thutmose indicates the felled trees, grain seed, wine, and the like from Djahy, I feel that the army went partly inland. After all, the account notes that the grain was on the terraces, and these should not have been too far from the coast. Perhaps some consignments went to the garrison cities in the Lebanon rather than directly to Egypt, but most surely were sent back home. It has been noted that many of the commodities mentioned in these Egyptian accounts from the port cities (bread, olive oil, incense, wine, honey, and fruit) are identical to the items sent back to Egypt as reported in the later Amarna Letters (time of Amunhotep III and IV).[4] Therefore, the detailed *inu* lists of Thutmose III do not relate to the provisioning of the Egyptian armies but rather bear witness to the Egyptian economic control over the north.

As most of this material concerns the administrative and political organization of the Empire that was founded in Dynasty XVIII rather than the Egyptian war machine, only a few salient points can be brought into the discussion. I believe that supplies for the army (food and equipment) are intended when the accounts notify us of towns being taken and their grain and fruit trees cut down.

The following is a list of the key items.

Year 29: Elite *teher* troops from Ullaza. The city was allied to Tunip, and so indirectly connected to Mitanni.
32 horses from the campaign in Djahy.

Year 30: 1,084 horses as *inu*.
40 various chariots as *inu*; they included inlaid ones (with gold and silver) as well as those painted.

Year 31: 26 horses from Ullaza.
13 chariots from Ullaza.
X horses as *inu*.
19 chariots inlaid with silver as *inu*.

Year 33: 260 horses as *inu*.
X chariots as *inu*.

Year 34: 40 horses taken in Syria.
15 chariots inlaid in silver and gold taken as well. (This may imply that there were 15 local kinglets who were present in the battle at Nukhashshe.) Other useful military supplies such as inlaid tent poles were also seized.
30 + *x* horses as *inu*.
90 (probably) chariots as *inu*.

Year 35: 180 horses seized in battle.
60 chariots also taken in the same battle.
Reins, corselets, and Syrian bows also seized.
226 horses as *inu*.
11 + *x* chariots; inlaid in gold and silver as *inu*.

Year 38: *X* horses in battle (in Nukhashshe).
X chariots in the same battle.

328 horses as *inu.*
70 chariots of various types as *inu.*
2 horses/teams of horses from Cyprus as gifts.
Year 39: 229 horses as *inu.*
X chariots.
Year 42: 48 horses in battle.
68 horses as *inu.*
Armor and various weapons of war as *inu.*

The war booty logically included horses, chariots, various weapons and other war material. Often wood was brought back to the harbors and then sent to Egypt if not dried and used there for building ships. Sometimes we can evaluate the significance of the battle such as the one in Thutmose's thirty-fifth regnal year.[5] On other occasions it is evident that the number of horses was logically twice that of the chariots. More important, I feel, are the figures relating to the deliveries of items to Egypt, which almost always included horses and chariots. In other words, the Egyptians required an annual delivery of the two most important elements of their chariotry arm. There was no regular delivery of corselets, bows, other weapons, or protective armor required by the Egyptian state. They could be easily manufactured at home. Chariots made of wood, however, belonged to the exclusive category of obligatory material. In addition, the Egyptians could decrease the potential of fractiousness among their subservient territories by appropriating these items.

Absent from the regular *inu* lists are grain totals as well as deliveries of precious woods. The latter were secured from the Lebanon and Syria. In the accounts covering years twenty-nine to forty-two, Thutmose refers to them in the context of actual successful battles or the capture of various northern cities. It would appear that the Pharaoh supplied his troops and his ports by means of these appropriations. Where the two different demands coincide is through the double mention of slaves (male and female) in addition to costly objects. From Nubia (Wawat and Kush) we can see the equally regular impost of slaves, cattle, and precious woods (ebony in particular).[6] When donkeys are mentioned, we find them only in the regular *inu* accounts for Syria and Palestine. Apparently, they were not normally taken after a battle.

The *inu* lists of Asia commence in year thirty and they contain a relatively large number of horses and chariots, normally far greater than what the king obtained in war in Syria. The detailed grain and wood list of Djahy referred to in the preceding year must indicate the results of Thutmose's campaign in that area. The *inu* deliveries are irregular in amount, and we can conclude that no specified total was required. This is yet another reason why we cannot translate *inu* as "tribute." The latter word implies a requirement, although to be fair it can be countered that such requisitions depended upon the demands of the day and so were irregular in number. Nonetheless, this section of the "Annals" must imply that horses and chariots were highly needed in Egypt.

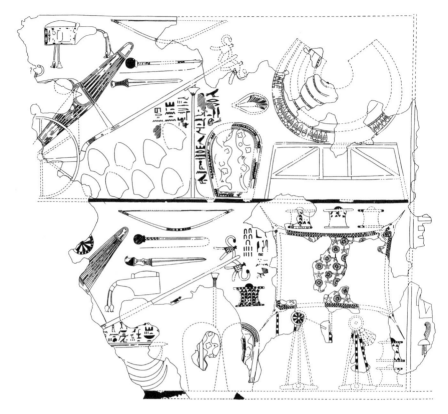

Figure 8.1 Military equipment from the tomb of Kenamun of Thebes. Norman de Garis Davies, *The Tomb of Ken-Amūn at Thebes*, Metropolitan Museum of Art, New York (1933) pl. XXII. Photo © British Library, London.

From the end of the XVIIIth Dynasty we have at our fingertips a series of deliveries referred to in the Amarna Letters.[7] Here as well the modern scholar is faced with the difficulty in ascertaining whether they were gifts or tribute. Among the items sent to Egypt under Amunhotep III and IV were silver, copper, bronze, glass, and wood from Amurru in Syria as well as from Tyre. Once more, Syria or rather Upper Retjenu provided the necessary raw material for chariots and other items. Various manufactured items were also transported south, and cattle as well as slaves are also mentioned. All of these coincide rather well with the lists of Thutmose III. One completely fitted chariot was sent by Gath-karmel in Palestine and the ruler of Ammiya was ordered to transport chariots and horses as a dowry to Pharaoh. Here, these items are gifts. It is possible that some military personnel were also dispatched. The kinglet of Taanach in central Palestine also was required by the king to send to him troops among which other military personnel were included.

134

The economic control over Palestine and portions of Syria was thus not that onerous. Foodstuffs are not listed in the Amarna Letters. The garrisons would have been supplied by the locals.[8] Gaza and Joppa in the south and along the coast were the effective staging points for any Egyptian thrust into Palestine. Both Ullaza Byblos and Sumur in Lebanon, and for a while Ugarit, performed the same function. They also were military bases and staging points from which the king could move inland. Once more we can visualize the bifurcation of Egyptian military policy. Two garrisons in the south and two others in the north were located on the borders of the inland territories of Palestine and Syria respectively. Separate from Israel we can add Beth Shan and possible Yeno'am, both cities positioned on the boundaries of Egyptian control. A further center, Kumidi, lay on the major crossroad of the Lebanese Beqa Valley. (Noteworthy is the absence in the Amarna Letters of parallel data relating to Megiddo, the key to the rebellion against Thutmose III in Palestine, and Kadesh, the other major opponent of the Egyptians.) The support given to these garrisons was mainly provided by the kinglets of Asia. Grain was secured from these cities, and the "Annals" of Thutmose III specifically mention that Egyptian inspectors controlled the harvest of three Trans-Jordanian cities (Yeno'am, Neges, and Khukkuri), and the number of wheat sacks, discussed earlier in this study, supports this analysis.[9] One later account refers to the triad as "yoked with work (*baku*) for the due of a year," and that the produce was to serve as offering for Amun in Karnak.[10] It may have been the case that these fields were regulated by the local Egyptian garrison at Beth Shan. The work was corvee labor, and it seems probable that the rulers situated in the border areas were responsible for this cultivation and harvesting. Last, we learn from the Amarna Letters that royal granaries were in operation at Joppa and that Sumur was provided with grain from Amurru. I am not confidant that the port garrison cities, those in southern Palestine, as well as the three located in the Trans-Jordan were directly incorporated into the Egyptian state. On the other hand, the Amarna Letters allow us to see that some Egyptian officials operated in Palestine and on the Phoenician coast, thereby indicating that these two regions were considered to belong to one administrative unit. From this data and other sources from the Ramesside Period Na'aman concluded that there were two provinces of Egyptian rule in Asia: Eretz Israel with Gaza as its center, and South Syria with its seat at Kumidi.[11]

The indirect control over Palestine and Asia did not require a large number of Egyptian troops. Palestine was permanently subdued through war, and only some garrisons were necessary. The localities around Beth Shan mainly indicate a threat from outside, a situation that arose later in the reign of Amunhotep II. The Lebanese ports were balanced inland by Kumidi, but even there the major cities were left alone. Kumidi, in fact, served as a staging point for any march upon Kadesh. The Egyptians once more preferred to control the major south–north arterial route that led into central

Syria. In sum, Egyptian imperialism in Asia was far less of a burden upon the locals than it was in Nubia.

With the port cities, however, Thutmose III and his successors could always march inland to subdue any rebellion in Upper Retjenu that might be aided by the king of Mitanni. Perhaps Lebanon and southern Palestine formed one administrative unit, but this is unclear. The system of control in both areas was nonetheless similar. Most certainly, southern Syria and northern Palestine formed a separate zone, one that was held more tenuously than these other two areas. It has been claimed that "The conquest of Canaan by kings of the 18th Dynasty marked the beginning of a process of Egyptian colonization."[12] This interpretation, however, goes against the actual historical setting. Palestine was comprised of a number of city-states and so was not a unity when the Pharaohs first advanced into that region. Subsequently, the local political arrangement was basically left alone. Cities, for example, remained independent of one another. There was no viceroy or one Egyptian commandant over this wide territory. The nature of the gifts and *inu* was large with respect to the shekels of silver, but small in number when slaves or cattle are recorded. True, the latter resemble the amount brought north from Nubia. But if these items were sent directly to the Egyptian court, then the men and women, as well as the chariots and horses, ended up in the Egyptian state and quite possibly its military.

One useful though fragmentary account dated to the reign of Amunhotep II provides additional data concerning the foreign troops of Asia. In a papyrus now in St. Petersburg a list of the food supplies for various *maryannu* is given in two portions.[13] One beer jug is recorded for each messenger (emissary) of various Palestinian lands. The city-states included Megiddo, Ashkelon, Hazor, Taanach, Sharon, Achshaph, Kinnereth, Shimron, and Mishal. In addition, a local prince may have been provided with the drink. There is no indication of war. Rather, this list refers to the provisions handed out to these "ambassadors," none of whom, it must be emphasized, came from Syria or the Levant. In other words, this section refers solely to the official representatives of these cities, all of whom were military men. Is it possible that they were connected with the local Egyptian administration over southern and central Palestine? The mention of Megiddo indicates the effective Egyptian control of that city, and the presence of Taanach denotes equal jurisdiction in this outlying region. Ashkalon moves us to the southern coast of Canaan and Hazor, another important inland entrepot, is also situated in southern Palestine. The absence of Gaza and Joppa is significant, especially as we know that both were major Egyptian centers. Hence, they would not have been represented in this group. Note that all of them are from Djahy. As this geographic term is embedded in an official administrative record, we can see once more how, in contrast, the royal hieroglyphic war records use such terms in a more indirect or general way than the administrative papyri.[14]

EXCURSUS

1. A useful Late Middle Kingdom (Dynasty XIII) parallel to the *maryannu* visit of mid Dynasty XVIII is recorded in P. St. Petersburg 1116A (see note 13 to this chapter) and may be seen in P. Bulaq 18: Alexander Scharff, "Ein Rechnungbuch des königlichen Hofes aus der 13. Dynastie," *Zeitschrift für ägyptische Sprache* [1923], 51–68 with pls. 13** and 21**); and Quirke, *The Administration of Egypt in the Late Middle Kingdom*, 19–22. In both cases provisions are issued for these foreign envoys.

In P. Bulaq 18 the envoys were Nubian, as befits the era, and arrived at the southern capital of Thebes. In the Dynasty XVIII example, dated to Amunhotep II, the men were from Palestine and (presumably) were fed at Memphis.

2. The supplementary information provided by the topographical lists has already been partially covered in excursus 2 to chapter 7. From Redford's preliminary work cited there we can conclude that the Egyptians, at least by the reign of Thutmose III, if not earlier, had at their fingertips a detailed knowledge of the major localities in Palestine, Syria, and also parts of the Trans-Jordan. I suspect that such *routiers* were present in the Middle Kingdom. After all, the so-called Execration Texts from that time are relatively detailed concerning the foreign princes and their localities, both in Asia as well as in Nubia. (On these documents, see the last important work of Georges Posener, *Cinque figurines d'envoûtment*, Cairo [1987], where all the pertinent information will be found.) The tradition goes back to at least the Old Kingdom, and I have little doubt that similar lists, concentrated upon Nubia, were present then.

This means that, at the chancellery, the Egyptian state possessed a well-organized list of place names, local potentates associated with the localities, and the routes on which one had to travel. Otherwise, I feel that it would have been very difficult for the Pharaohs after Thutmose I to have traversed Asia in person at the head of an army. Indeed, the well-organized campaign of Thutmose III to Megiddo reads as if all were pre-planned with regard to logistics and geography. As soon as the basic structure of Egyptian control over Palestine and subsequently into parts of Syria and Phoenicia had been established, such "maps" were *de rigueur*. If not, we would have to consider each Egyptian campaign into Asia as having been based upon a naïve conception of the local political and geographical structures. This I find impossible. Most certainly, by late Dynasty XVIII, as seen in the correspondence of the Amarna Letters, Egyptian knowledge of Palestine and Asia on the part of the court was great. (Compare the studious remarks of Na'aman in his studies cited in note 3 to this chapter.)

The mid Dynasty XIX document, P. Anastasi I, is worth revisiting in this context (Fischer-Elfert, *Die satirische Streitschrift des Papyrus Anastasi I.*, 190–3.) The editor discussed the topographical section of this important hieratic document and noted the exact order of the toponyms in chapters XVI–XIX. Fischer-Elfert also remarked that the section reveals an "intimate knowledge of the topography" (p. 190). Such a background implies its use for local administration by the Egyptians as well as for possible campaigns.

NOTES

1 A sketch map of this area may be found in Gardiner, *Ancient Egyptian Onomastica* I, 133*. For the exact details, I have consulted the 1:1,000,000 map in the volume of the Naval Intelligence Division, *Syria*[2] (see excursus 3 to chapter 7). It always should be kept in mind that east–west routes in Syria north of Damascus are not that common.

2 Gardiner attempted a clarification of the terms "Djahy," "Retjenu," "Upper (and Lower) Retjenu" in his *Ancient Egyptian Onomastica* I, 142*–9*. Others have argued that Retjenu refers to "the Levant in general" (Redford, *Egypt, Canaan, and Israel in Ancient Times*, 200). The problem in dealing with these key geographic terms *as they were used during the New Kingdom* is that one has to be careful where they are specifically mentioned. For example, are we dealing with mere headings to lists, is the inscription a private biography, does the royal narrative reflect a hymn of praise or is it historically oriented? It may not be mere coincidence that the famous *Lexikon der Ägyptologie* has no separate entry for either "Retjenu" or "Djahy."

Georges Posener, "Le pays Retenou au Moyen Empire," in *Actes du XXIe Congrès International des Orientalistes. Paris 23–31 Juillet 1948*, Société Asiatique de Paris, Paris (1949), 72–3, provides a useful overview of the term "Retjenu." Without an epithet this word is either an abbreviation of "Upper Retjenu" or refers to Syria and Palestine in Dynasty XVIII.

For the additional term "Kharu": Na'aman, "The Hurrians and the End of the Middle Bronze Age in Palestine," *Levant* 26 (1994), 177; and Gnirs, *Militär und Gesellschaft*, 31 and 78.

3 Note the studies of Na'aman that have been referred to earlier: "Pharaonic Lands in the Jezreel Valley in the Late Bronze Age" in *Society and Economy in the Eastern Mediterranean*, 177–85; "Economic Aspects of the Egyptian Occupation of Canaan," *Israel Exploration Journal* 31 (1981), 172–85 – a more sophisticated analysis than Shemuel Ahituv, "Economic Factors in the Egyptian Conquest of Canaan," *Israel Exploration Journal* 28 (1978), 93–105; Na'aman, "Historical-Geographical Aspects of the Amarna Letters" in *Ninth World Congress of Jewish Studies. Panel Sessions; Biblical Studies and Ancient Near East*, Magnes Press, Jerusalem (1988), 17–26; and his *The Political Disposition and Historical Development of Eretz-Israel According to the Amarna Letters*, Tel-Aviv University Dissertation, Tel Aviv (1975).

4 This is one of the important points stressed by Na'aman in his "Economic Aspects of the Egyptian Occupation of Canaan"; compare his remarks in chapters VII–VIII of his aforementioned dissertation. For two further up-to-date viewpoints, see Redford, *Egypt, Canaan, and Israel in Ancient Times*, chapter 7; and Liverani, *Prestige and Interest*, Part Three.

5 Sethe, *Urkunden der 18. Dynastie*, 709–14; and Breasted, *Ancient Records of Egypt* II, 207–9.

6 The terms *inu* and *baku* and their connection with Upper and Lower Nubia were crucial for Liverani in his analysis of the two words: see our comments in chapter 7 n. 2. He specifically pointed out the items sent to Egypt in the official

concluding section to the yearly reports of most of the subsections in Thutmose III's "Annals" (parts V–VI).

7 See Na'aman's extensive research listed in note 3 above, and add the recent studies of Redford and Liverani cited in note 4. I shall ignore the gifts and the like sent from the great powers (e.g., Babylon, Mitanni, and the Hittites) to Egypt.

The standard edition of the Amarna Letters, dated to the end of the reign of Amunhotep III through that of his son Akhenaton (Amunhotep IV), is that of William L. Moran, *Amarna Letters*, Johns Hopkins Press, Baltimore (1992).

8 This is one of the important points made by Na'aman in chapters VII–VIII of his dissertation, *The Political Disposition and Historical Development of Eretz-Israel According to the Amarna Letters*.

9 See chapter 5 with note 31. Add Redford, *The Wars in Syria and Palestine of Thutmose III*, 39–43, and chapter Fourteen. The latter outlines the early Dynasty XVIII Egyptian administration over Asia.

10 Sethe, *Urkunden der 18. Dynastie*, 744 ("Annals," Part VIII); and Breasted, *Ancient Records of Egypt* II, 223.

11 Na'aman, *The Political Disposition and Historical Development of Eretz-Israel According to the Amarna Letters*, chapter VII.

12 Eliezer D. Oren, "'Governors' Residencies' in Canaan under the New Kingdom: A Case Study of Egyptian Administration," *Journal of the Society for the Study of Egyptian Antiquities* 14 (1984), 37–56. The importance of this study for the military history of the Ramesside Period (Dynasties XIX–XX) will be covered later. However, there is no evidence of any massive Egyptian colonization in the New Kingdom.

13 W. Golénischeff, *Les papyrus hiératiques Nos. 1115, 1116A et 1116B de l'Ermitage impériale à St.-Petersbourg*, St. Petersburg (1913), pls. XVII and XXII; Helck, *Materialien zur Wirtschaftsgeschichte des Neuen Reiches* IV, Akademie der Wissenschaften und der Literatur in Mainz, Wiesbaden (1963), 623–4; Claire Epstein, "A New Appraisal of Some Lines from a Long-Known Papyrus," *Journal of Egyptian Archaeology* 49 (1963), 49–56; and Aharoni, *The Land of the Bible*², 165–6.

14 A series of chapters in Raymond Cohen and Raymond Westbrook, eds., *Amarna Diplomacy. The Beginnings of International Relations*, Johns Hopkins, Baltimore and London (2000) cover, in a very useful manner, the diplomatic relations among the various superpowers of the day (contemporary with Dynasty XVIII) as well as the maneuvering of their armies. Murnane, "Imperial Egypt and the Limits of Power" (pp. 101–11), touches upon some of the matters covered in this chapter, and Na'aman, "The Egyptian–Canaanite Correspondence" (pp. 125–38), presents a thoughtful survey of the Amarna correspondence, a theme which is covered in chapter 10 below. See as well Na'aman, "Dispatching Canaanite Maidservants to Pharaoh," *Ancient Near Eastern Studies* 39 (2002), 76–82.

9

DYNASTY XVIII: WARFARE
AND ECONOMY

Details of the remaining wars in Dynasty XVIII are sketchy in comparison
to the data surrounding those of Thutmose III. Nevertheless, the two campaigns of Amunhotep II in his seventh and ninth years cannot be ignored.[1]
Both are determined mainly from two royal stelae, neither of which is as
long as the official account of the king's father, Thutmose III. Even though
there are some textual problems associated with the redaction, the tactical
focus of the two is clear.[2] In his seventh regnal year the youthful Amunhotep
II set out on his first campaign of victory as sole king. We find the Pharaoh
already ensconced in central Syria at Shamash-Edom, west of the river
Orontes. This occurred on day twenty-five of the first month of the harvest
season, late April, a reasonable time considering the actual harvest of emmer
wheat in Egypt. We do not know how long it took Amunhotep II to reach
this area. In fact, it may be supposed that he traveled first by ship, and then
went by foot inland. But as his army later returned to Egypt through
Palestine, this speculation appears tenuous and we are left in the dark
regarding the actual preparations for war. It is possible that he may have
met up with divisions of the Egyptian army sent northward through Palestine. Nonetheless, it is significant that the king spent most of his time
campaigning to the west of the Euphrates, intensely preoccupying himself
with lands allied to the kingdom of Mitanni. He crossed the Orontes one
day later after he left Shamash-Edom and moved north. Most of the localities
cannot be identified with any certainty but it is interesting to see the
Pharaoh fighting in Labwi south of, yet near to, the city of Kadesh. During his
Syrian expedition some *maryannu* warriors were captured as well as horses
and chariots. Protective armor, quivers, and bows were also recovered from
the defeated enemy. The singular mention of reins should remind us that
there were also listed in the "Annals" of Thutmose III. Again, military
equipment was seized on the battlefield. During the king's southward
journey home he managed to capture an emissary of the king of Mitanni
at Khashabu, an unknown locality probably located in southern Syria. The
luckless man was placed on the king's chariot, a personal aspect of Amunhotep

that is seen in his battle reliefs as well as recorded elsewhere.[3] A further personal sidelight of the king's prowess is revealed when we read of him practicing archery near Kadesh. Unfortunately, many of the stops made by the Egyptian army are not listed, probably due to the limitations in size of the actual texts. After all, both are free-standing stelae and hence do not provide enough room for a very lengthy account such as the Battle of Megiddo. The time elapsed in the account was over forty days, and it seems probable that the Pharaoh reached Egypt soon after the sixth day of the third season.

The war booty is more useful to analyze as it provides some useful quantitative data. Five hundred and fifty *maryannu* were taken, and I suspect that most of these men, if not all, came from the confederates of Mitanni. It is probable that the men were brought back to Egypt as future soldiers because 240 of their wives are also listed. We may assume that many were originally stationed in the cities seized by Amunhotep II. Six hundred and forty Canaanites are also recorded, and here we cannot but conclude that the Pharaoh had to take care of some rebels in Palestine. Connected to the last are 232 of the children of the princes and 323 of their wives. Two hundred and seventy female singers are included, who brought along their musical implements. The Canaanites and the singers are a remarkable addition to a typical booty list. The account states that the latter came from the princes of every foreign land. Can we assume that they, in addition to the Canaanites, were not ordinary prisoners? I suspect that all of these peoples would have remained at the court in Memphis. After all, with their own families, these men would not have become slaves in the temples.

The lack of any other males recorded as prisoners except the *maryannu* indicates that one result was to take away important elite troops from Syria and possibly Palestine. Perhaps this detail indicates that all the captives taken on an Egyptian campaign were soldiers. Four hundred and ten horses (or teams of horses) and 730 chariots are also listed. This is a very large number, considering the accounts of Thutmose III in Syria. Granted that the figure of equids does not reach the over 2,200 caught at Megiddo by Thutmose III, the 892 chariots seized there matches well with Amunhotep's amount.

The second campaign of Amunhotep in year nine was more limited. It is likely that the king set out at roughly the same time that he did two years earlier.[4] The area was on the border of Egypt's control in the central portions of north Palestine. Except for two sidelights concerning the king's dream and devastation in Samaria, little can be offered concerning the chronology of the campaign. The war situation specifically highlights the (presumed) solitary vigil of Amunhotep over two ditches filled with the enemy. They were burnt alive, a cruel policy that may be seen in other sources of the king.

From this region the king obtained 34 princes, 57 *maryannu*, and 231 living Asiatics. The dead men amounted to 372, each of whom was listed by

Figure 9.1   Amunhotep II battle reliefs. Cairo Museum JE 36360.

Figure 9.2   Amunhotep II battle reliefs; drawings of Figure 9.1. From Abdel-Hamid Zayed, "Une representation inédite des campagnes d'Aménophis II," in *Mélanges Gamal Eddin Mokhtar*, ed. Posener-Kriéger, Institut Français d'Archéologie Orientale du Caire, 1985, 5–17, pl. II. Reprinted by permission of Archives Scientifiques IFAO.

means of his cut-off hand. (This we have seen earlier.). The total number of horses was 54 and chariots 54. It is clear that the first refers to the teams. Subsequently, Amunhotep obtained 17 *maryannu*, 6 children of the princes, and 68 Asiatics. These figures reflect the results of the conflict as well as that of the submissive kinglets who either were defeated in battles or who had supported the enemy. We further read of 123 dead, 7 good chariots and 7 teams of horses. (I am ignoring the cattle lists.) All in all, this campaign reveals the same results as the earlier one; namely, that elite soldiers were taken back to Egypt in addition to the normal military necessities obtained through the victories. The presence of *maryannu* wives additionally reinforces our supposition that these elite soldiers were probably enrolled into the Egyptian army.

One major problem for scholars has been the peculiar final list.[5] The title is simple: "List of the booty that his majesty brought back." Then follow 128 princes of Retjenu and 179 of their brothers. Can we assume that Amunhotep II replaced a large number of the local potentates with new men? Even if this assumption is followed, the lack of the other men, wives, and children carried away from at least two if not three sites is striking. For example, where are the *maryannu*? But to make things more confusing we have to analyze the following groups of people given in the account:

1,600 Apiru	15,070 living Neges people
15,200 living Shasu	30,652 associates
36,100 Kharu people	Total 89,600.

In all cases but one the numbers are neat round ones. This should make us a bit suspicious of their validity. Granted that the Shasu and the Apiru (cuneiform Khabiru) operated at the fringes of Asiatic settlements, perhaps their numbers are totally fictitious, being merely a reflection of the troublesome "eastern" peoples in the area around Yeno'am and Beth Shan. (This supposition is partly supported by the mention of Neges.) If so, then Amunhotep's second campaign indicates troubles on his borders near the Trans-Jordan. But the grand total is also egregious; the correct sum is 101,128 if we add the first two groups of princes plus brothers. One interesting possibility has been brought forth; namely, that the large figures represent a census of the local population. But where are the other Asiatics – the princes, their sons, and their wives? These, too, were captured by the Pharaoh. If the figures refer to the people residing in their households, then how was such a census undertaken? Finally, who, exactly, were these Kharu? If this did take place, it would be remarkable. Considering just the magnitude of the integers, these peoples could not have been brought to Egypt.

On the other hand the final amounts for other items are more reasonable. There are 60 gold and silver chariots, 1,032 painted chariots, and other weapons of war. For the final items we have a total of 13,500, another round integer with zeros. One supposition hitherto never entertained is that at least the first three refer to the normal *inu* or impost in this year. If this is assumed, then the figures referring to the groups of peoples could be estimates of local groups outside of direct Egyptian control. Although impossible to ascertain, this hypothesis at least allows us to interpret the troublesome Shasu, the Apiru, and even the Syrians not showing allegiance to Egypt. But the difficulty of these huge numbers still remains, and I must conclude that they cannot be trusted.

Two useful cuneiform letters have been connected to Egypt's military control over Palestine at the time of Amunhotep II, although their exact dating remains unclear.[6] They were discovered at Taanach in Palestine, but do not refer to any of Amunhotep II's known campaigns. A certain Amunhotep (not the king) had them sent to a local by the name of Talwishar. The Egyptian is the superior and the local, who bears a Hurrian (i.e., Mitannian) name, the underling. The overseer demands in Letter 5 that Talwishar send his brothers (or confederates?) with chariots as well as a designated quota of horses and "tribute," and more troops as well, to Megiddo. As Taanach is close to Megiddo (see the account of Thutmose III in his Megiddo battle report), the connection is reasonable. In Letter 6 Amunhotep states to Talwishar that there are no retainers of his present. Neither did the addressee nor his brothers come to him. Last, it is reported that at an earlier time Talwishar did not come to Amunhotep when the Egyptian superior was in Gaza. These two pieces of correspondence thus shed some additional light upon the military administration in Palestine through the presence of a garrison, the demand for troops, and the tribute requirement of horses. Simply put, Talwishar is the local potentate who had apparently failed to supply the local Egyptian superior with necessary items, all of which are military. There is no indication of an impending war or that one had already taken place. Rather, we are viewing the standard arrangements that the Egyptians established in Palestine.

The Egyptian Empire can thus be considered to have been a loosely held zone of warring city-states that was kept under control through a rather thin series of garrisons and not too many troops. Although this situation is best left for a subsequent analysis of Asia at the time of Amunhotep IV, some of its salient characteristics are worth mentioning at this point. For example, the population of Egypt vis-à-vis Palestine and Syria must be considered.[7] The Egyptian conquest of Canaan and its results may have led to devastation, with many sites left destroyed and deserted.[8] But problems with this analysis depend upon the precise dating of archaeological data, which then must be connected with the campaigns of the Pharaohs. We have seen that from year twenty-nine and following of Thutmose III, Palestine was virtually free from war because the king concentrated his activities in Upper Retjenu, Syria. Second, the amount of annual *inu* was considerable, but only if we take the grand total to heart. Individually, what did it represent per city?

Recent work has suggested that a decline in urban settlements in Palestine occurred in the sixteenth century BC.[9] On the other hand, a small but nonetheless noticeable pick-up is present in the following century, the one during which Thutmose III lived and warred. By the fourteenth century BC the number of settlements was considerably higher, doubling that of two hundred years earlier. There was an even greater expansion during the first half of the Ramesside Period (Dynasty XIX). Yet at this time the Pharaohs Seti I and Ramesses II waged numerous campaigns in southern Syria and across into the Trans-Jordan. Apparently, the population of Canaan grew even more, independent of the resumption of warfare. It would appear that a simple linear model of causation connecting Egyptian warfare in Asia with depopulation fails to meet the strict test of scientific proof. At best, we can state that the Egyptian economic domination may have restricted the flourishing of the Asiatic city-states.

But even here counterarguments can be proposed. For example, research by Na'aman has revealed that the urban culture of Palestine was in a state of decline at the time when Thutmose III moved against Megiddo.[10] According to him, the internal sector of this region was partly desolated by the time the Pharaoh advanced upon the enemy. Moreover, his wars in Palestine were limited. After all, how many of those inhabitants were killed and how many taken away into slavery? Furthermore, what specific cities were actually destroyed by the king? Solely from Thutmose III's accounts of war, very few if any in Palestine were plundered. In order to retain the devastation hypothesis we are forced to argue that the results of the Egyptian conquest weakened this region from an economic viewpoint. Otherwise, we have to argue that a deleterious birth-rate set in with the first series of Egyptian campaigns under Ahmose and Thutmose I. Yet the ability of the local Canaanite kinglets to supply the Pharaoh with precious metals (in shekels) and other expensive gifts argues that they could do this at the close of Dynasty XVIII. If the Egyptian policy of required deliveries was oppressive, then an economic analysis is needed, one based on calculable data. Unfortunately, this material is lacking.

Examination of the size of the Palestinian settlements has helped to clarify the situation to some degree. The percentage of small to medium-sized towns was roughly constant throughout the Late Bronze Age whereas the tiny ones increased quite remarkably. The number of large ones, on the other hand, fell in a considerable fashion, and even though there was a rebound in total area during the fourteenth and thirteenth centuries BC, the rapid decline in the sixteenth century was never overcome. But does size of settlement correlate with the size of total population? After all, these cities were citadels that controlled a region of plains and valleys where the farmers lived and worked. In order to estimate population in a region we must combine the urban population with the rural, taking into consideration that urbanism notably decreases population growth over time. It is from the areas outside of the palatine city that a greater population increase would occur. Therefore, we have to estimate total population of an entire region rather than depend solely upon cities or towns.

In the earlier Middle Bronze Period (IIA and IIB to be specific) the population of Palestine increased from 100,000 to 140,000.[11] This is a very rough estimate, and I wonder whether the effective density limit had been reached just before the beginning of Dynasty XVIII. To assume that the effect of Egyptian control in the southern coastal plain of Palestine and the Shephela region was oppressive is unclear. The assumption that the Egyptian demand for "mercenaries," other local troops, the indirect control through very few garrisons, and finally the annual deliveries of goods to Egypt drained off the economy of this region must remain an unproven hypothesis. Most certainly, after year twenty-three of Thutmose III, regular Egyptian attacking forces did not visit Southern Retjenu (Palestine). But for the sake of argument, we may assume about 140,000 inhabitants at 1600 BC, a figure that later shrunk to a considerable extent, say 60,000 to 70,00 by 1200 BC. This implies that Phoenicia and the Beqa Valley had about 100,000–200,000 in 1600 BC. Inland, we have to include more, perhaps 200,000 in central and east Syria. I do not think that we would be far off to hypothesize a maximum 450,000 people for all of these territories, and this is probably a high-end estimate.

Now let us turn to the population of Egypt.[12] Here we meet with a second decline during Dynasties XVIII to XX. Around 1290 BC (time of Seti I and Ramesses II) the population of Egypt was around 2.9 million. The Valley outweighed the Delta by 15/13. An era of declining population and productivity in the former region was present under the later Ramesside kings. The Delta population may have doubled in the early Ramesside era when the absolute level of population began to rival the Valley. The economic limits of growth were determined by the type of agriculture practiced within the latter region; namely, basin flooding. In addition, no new cereal or vegetable crops were introduced to Egypt until a considerably later period. The real problem for Pharaonic Egypt was that it lacked the necessary cash crops and summer cereals. The wheat and barley cycle ended by the beginning of April and sowing began at the beginning of October for wheat and at the beginning of December for barley.

The demographic expansion of Egypt appears to have taken off around 1500 BC when it has been estimated that about 2 million inhabitants lived in all of the land.[13] The highest point of ca. 3 million during the New Kingdom indicates a great increase up to ca. 1300 BC, 50 percent more to be precise. It is interesting that the more precise analyses of demographic change have tended to lower the figures for the total population of Egypt rather than to increase them. Still, we may take 2.5 to 3 million as a reasonable estimate. The most recent attempt raises this figure to 4 million, but incidentally lowers the area of agricultural land to 20,000 km²; this analysis, however, is not based on a rigorous demographic analysis.[14] Population figures for medieval Egypt, incidentally, support this approximation. From ca. 4.5 million in the first century AD, the numbers declined by around a third by the fourth century. The bottom was reached in the tenth and eleventh centuries when the total number of inhabitants leveled off at 1.7 million. Thereafter, a slight rise may be noted. At the time that the Turks took over in the sixteenth century the total populace was ca. 3.15– 3.6 million.

Solely for the sake of argument, let us fix the time at 1400 BC, some years after the death of Thutmose III. Egypt's control over Palestine was then complete, and the city-states in that region no longer a threat to the Pharaohs. (I will ignore Syria for the present.) Taking the rough estimate of 140,000 at the maximum we arrive at a 21-fold difference. But the ratio is purely one of populations. When we consider the number of available men sent out to deal with the locals, and the size of an army on a major campaign, then the difference becomes great indeed. How did the Egyptians manage to control the locals of Palestine without dispatching a large number of troops and administrative personnel to the region? The answer is roughly the same with regard to small nations that are located close to great powers. These tiny states either have a small military preparedness or are over-militarized, supported by a third and hostile power. By considering the tiny nature of the Palestinian city-states, their inherent divisiveness, and the lack of any great powers nearby, the situation becomes clearer. Yet outside factors were of equal if not greater importance – namely, the establishment of a large military machine in Egypt, one that could be assembled to include over 5,000 men, and one which could be supplied by the friendly (or coerced) local cities.

Remember that the distances within Palestine are not very great from Gaza or even Sile. From Gaza to Yehem, a 129 km journey, it took Thutmose III only six or seven days. And from there to Megiddo was considerably shorter. The Pharaoh left Sile and arrived at Gaza in a mere ten days. Equally short intervals of time may be seen in the Syrian war of Amunhotep II. Both the locals and the Egyptians were fully cognizant of the lengths of time an Egyptian army could march and the distance it could cover within one day. Only a long-lasting siege at a key city or the presence of a powerful outside enemy could cause the Pharaohs any difficulty. Finally, the control of the eastern Mediterranean meant that the Egyptians could organize the ports of the Levant.

The natural limits of Egyptian power were dependent upon its population base. True, we do not know how many troops at one time could be called into battle. There is some useful evidence from the Kadesh campaign of Ramesses II (Dynasty XIX) that can be analyzed. But this conflict, although a crucial one in which two superpowers were engaged, cannot be used as a paradigm for the regular control over Asia or for small wars. The large military actions of the XVIIIth Dynasty kings took place when the Pharaoh led his army. Otherwise, the local Egyptian garrisons and soldiers took care of minor problems such as incursions of semi-nomads or the like. The later wars of Thutmose III and the year seven campaign of Amunhotep II were aimed at securing control over the central portion of Syria, and their repetitive nature had to do with the presence of the nearby kingdom of Mitanni.

Individually, the local potentates could not oppose the might of the Egyptian army. Even collectively, they had to align themselves with a power far away. Hence, the minimum population ratio of 1:21 is misleading. Indeed, it does not even take into consideration the number of Egyptians who would be free to serve in the army on a regular basis. The size cannot be estimated with any degree of certainty. During the famous Battle of Kadesh under Ramesses II the Hittite enemy is credited with at least 3,500 chariots (7,500 men in this case) and two elite *teher* troops containing 18,000 and 19,000 men.[15] The last two are impossible. (Note once more the nice round nature of the integers.) At Megiddo, I have hypothesized an army of 5,000 men at the minimum. One can set the total number of Egyptian troops contained in Ramesses' five divisions at the Battle of Kadesh to be 25,000, each division containing ca. 5,000 troops. However, there are problems with this calculation. Somewhat later in time the famous satirical letter, P. Anastasi I, reports on a "host" (but not the more specific term "division" or "army") having 5,000 men.[16] Notwithstanding the didactic context of the text, this figure has often been used as the basis of the regular size of a full-scale Egyptian army. In "The Taking of Joppa," an Egyptian story set in the reign of Thutmose III, 500 Egyptian soldiers are reported.[17] But we cannot securely fix the size of a military unit larger than the company, and even there two possibilities remain: either 200 or 250 men. Finally, a large number of Egyptians in garrison service also saw duty in the south, for both Wawat and Kush had permanent garrisons of troops, and many soldiers came to live in the far south. Still, I do not believe that we can estimate more than 3,000 Egyptians *solely* performing military service in Nubia on a regular basis by the second half of Dynasty XVIII.

By standards of even the Roman Empire, the Egyptian army in Dynasty XVIII was not large.[18] For the moment, I am purposely ignoring the changes after the Amarna Period owing to the substantive alterations in the military set-up that occurred soon afterward. The economic ability of the state to have these men available for military service nonetheless remained crucial. In purely economic terms they were not primary producers. Hence, they performed tasks separate from the overwhelming number of cultivators and can be placed on a level that included bureaucrats and other officials, and the temple staffs as well.

Purely as an arithmetical exercise, if we assume a division to have amounted to 1,000, then at the Battle of Kadesh Ramesses had at least 5,000 combat troops.[19] This appears too small. Many would prefer to increase this number, assuming that the separate divisions amounted to 5,000 men apiece. The grand total would then have been 25,000, a figure that I have presented above with some trepidation. With a population in Egypt of around 3 million inhabitants at the most, the ratio of that army to population comes to either 1:120 or 1:600. Both ratios are quite high. Hence, we see the necessity for an objective analysis of the source material and the inherent limitations of a purely philological approach. What, then, about the Battle of Megiddo? Given at least 5,000 Egyptian troops, the result is 1:600. But in that case many prefer to estimate the number of soldiers in Thutmose III's army greater than I. Perhaps we would not be far from the truth by maintaining that the entire military organization through Dynasty XVIII had, at the minimum, a ratio of 1 soldier to 1,000 civilians. If so, and notwithstanding the uncertainties in our estimations, we are still left with the feeling that the army consisted of a remarkably large number of personnel. Indeed, it is far greater than in our present-day nation states. Observe that I have excluded military men whose duties were not of a combat nature; e.g., scribes, builders, followers, and the like.

The vast majority of ordinary Egyptian soldiers served in the army only part time. They would have returned home and supervised their plots of land. Earlier scholarly work, depending upon the abundant source material concerning private soldiers such as Ahmose son of Ebana, thus receives additional support. Moreover, the military organization of the New Kingdom was considerably more organized than earlier. It included a flotilla, and had a large chariot division. But the average soldier did not work full time in that profession. Egypt, in fact, could not afford to integrate all of its soldiery into an independent state-run military system.

Last but not least, let us consider the situation of field rations for an Egyptian army in the New Kingdom. In the satirical account dated to the reign of Ramesses II referred to earlier, P. Anastasi I, useful details concerning the military provisioning of a moderate sized group of 5,000 soldiers are presented.[20] It remains open whether this account reflects is realistic or not. Nonetheless, the number may be equivalent to an Egyptian division in the New Kingdom. The problem, although artificial, is not fanciful. The archers comprise 1,900 men and Sherden "mercenaries" total up to 520. There are as well 1,600 Qehek and Meshewsh troops, both of whom were Libyans in the pay of the Egyptian state.[21] Finally, 880 Nubians are present. (Again, the presence of these non-natives in Egyptian pay cannot be ignored.) Although this account is considerably later than mid XVIIIth Dynasty, a rough arithmetical analysis concerning the supplies can be attempted.

A master scribe, Hori, presents the example in a series of tests to his underling Amunemope. Various foods are given to the soldiers as a "peace gift."

However, the amount is stated to be too small for the soldiers. Included were 300 sweet breads (which I assume were baked with honey), 1,800 baked cakes, 120 cuts of meat from small cattle, and 30 wines. Although the containers of the latter are unspecified, we can assume either jugs or wine skins. The baked items are a crux because bread was a necessary part of the soldiers' rations. The army is to march at midday and reach its destination before nightfall. The foods were therefore handed out in the morning.

An attempt to determine the actual caloric intake of the breads can be hypothesized by turning to a second administrative papyrus. In one baking account of Seti I, Nubians, once more in the Egyptian army, are given breads.[22] Because the Amarna Letters provide explicit evidence that some Nubians were soldiers of Pharaoh, this conclusion appears reasonable. Each of the 85 receives one large bread apiece, which was prepared with a baking ratio of 15. This means that, on a standard, all such breads followed a set pattern in which the breads have to be divided by 15 in order to determine the amount of grain in liters. Can we utilize that information with our Anastasi I example in order to determine the caloric intake? Let us try.

The total number of baked items comes to 2,100. With a baking ratio dependent upon the *oipe* (1/4 of the sack), we arrive at 140 *oipe* or 35 sacks of grain. When milled, 1 kg of wheat will weigh 900 g and contain about 3,150 calories and 90 g of protein.[23] This figure roughly coincides with the number of calories necessary to sustain a solider in combat conditions. Actually it is somewhat lower, but we must remember that the troops received meat as well. An *oipe* weighs around 9.8 kg; 140 would weigh 1,374 kg. The caloric total comes to 441,000. Divided by the 5,000 troops we have 882 calories per man. Therefore alone, these breads would not have been sufficient to feed the army. But the Seti account specifically indicates that the measure was the sack (4 *oipe*). So we must conclude that, if these baked items roughly coincided in procession to the Nubians in Egypt, the troops could have been well fed.

From Dynasty XII there is archaeological evidence that is more explicit. The comparison is worth noting even though the date is earlier than the New Kingdom. In one fortress in Nubia we know that the soldiers possessed wooden tallies in the shape of their bread rations, and the amounts of wheat and barley or numbers of loaves were carved on them.[24] This example concerns troops on active duty but who were stationary; i.e., they were not engaged on a campaign. But it has been remarked that these tallies look like the soldier's checks on the value of their rations. I assume that a similar system of rations existed within the Egyptian army of the New Kingdom. Otherwise, such contemporary accounts as that of Seti I or the Anastasi example would make little sense.

Naturally, the scribal exercise in P. Anastasi I is purely demonstrative. I assume that each soldier was to receive the same amount as his fellow. The numbers, however, cannot be divided evenly into integer results. Portions of the meat could be handed out or cut up. On the other hand, it is difficult to conceive any of these men taking in their hands tiny parts. Hence, I suspect that the account is based upon an equal division where the amount of supplies would be expected to reflect a reasonable provision. Thirty wines, in whatever container, do not at all fit with 5,000 men. Clearly, the integers are not applicable, and the baked items were probably not typical Egyptian breads. The text supports this interpretation for it states that "The troop is too many while the delivered foods are underrated." In other words, the bread delivery must not be viewed as reflecting a real case; it is purely hypothetical. The Seti I example, however, is more useful as it can be used to estimate, in a rough and ready manner, the intake in calories of a soldier's bread ration.

The Anastasi citation further reveals that the locals in Asia were expected to supply the Egyptian army when on a campaign. (The enemy Shasu, who lived and plundered near the borders of the Egyptian Empire, are stated to be close.) Therefore, the Egyptian troops were fearful of attack from these marauding bedouins, friendly though they may have appeared. It is reasonable to locate this army near the Trans-Jordanian border of Egypt, a point that fits well with other details of the campaigns of mid Dynasty XIX. Note as well that this army division did not carry its own supplies, and we can assume that the distance covered was not a long one.

In sum, the soldier's trade in the New Kingdom remained a harsh one, a life that was enervating both emotionally as well as physically. Only a small number of men are able to perform the required tasks, among which we should not forget killing. The young and the strong fare best. They must travel long distances on rations of food and water unless they manage to despoil the enemy's territories for necessary sustenance. The hardy and well integrated can survive the battlefield, which includes not merely the risk of death or maiming but also involves the death of one's comrades. Perhaps in the first flush of victory against the Hyksos the Egyptian soldiers' enthusiasm overcame many of these hindrances. Later, however, regular discipline was needed. As a result, a hardened body of professionals was developed over time, and by the reigns of Thutmose III and Amunhotep II these men were the pick of the virile male youths of Egypt. Yet not until the early Ramesside Period (Dynasty XIX) do we see what was their social effect within the Nile Valley. It took time to coordinate a regular force of soldiers for major campaigns, and to set up an effective chariot arm.

EXCURSUS

1. Despite the relatively low population base of Pharaonic Egypt, an effective garrison system was relatively easy to man given Egypt's preponderance over

Palestine. Furthermore, a moderate size of the army was well within the ability of that archaic state to maintain. The crux for statisticians is to determine the aggregate size of the military that Egypt could produce during the New Kingdom. Following the detailed research of Butzer, it seems clear that in Dynasty XVIII the constraints of size were not too great (*Early Hydraulic Civilization in Egypt*). Difficulties appear to have occurred during the later era, Dynasties XIX and XX. With a population around 2.9 million by 1250 BC there may have been a greater need to enlist foreigners in the military than previously (Butzer, *Early Hydraulic Civilization in Egypt*, 83).

The difficulty is in estimating the number of boys born *who survived infant mortality* with respect to girls. Most of the useful historical studies concerned with this aspect of mortality, and its connection to "free and available" men fit for a military career at ca. 14 years of age, have yet to be employed. It is known that the true ratio of boys/girls at birth is 105.8/100, a remarkable fact discovered by Graunt in 1660. That is to say, despite common opinion, which feels that more girls are born than boys, especially in polygamous societies (Egypt was not one), the facts were to the contrary. (See Maurice Halbwachs, *Population and Society. Introduction to Social Morphology*, Otis Dudley Duncan and Harold W. Pfautz, trs., Free Press of Glencoe, Indiana [1960], 122–3.) But that statistic, a universal one, is highly dependent upon the absolute ages between the father and the mother. And with respect to Pharaonic Egypt, we simply do not know the facts.

When the difference of age between the parents is in favor of the father, it appears that the proportion of masculine births decreases. Halbwachs published an extensive analysis of this matter and proved that the number of boys per 100 daughters worked out unevenly ("Recherches statistiques sur la determination du sexe à la marriage," *Journal de la statistique de Paris*, May 1933, 164–95). If the given age of the father is less than one year of the mother, then the ratio is 92.74. On the other hand, if the interval is −1 to +1, then the ratio is 103.74. Finally, if the father's age is greater by one year or more than the mother, the number of boys is 100.75.

With these facts Halbwachs was able to prove that when the age differential between the parents diminishes within certain limits, then the proportion of male births augments; it diminishes when this limit is crossed. The real variations cease when the age difference is five years or greater. When the number of marriages increases, the proportion of male births also increases. It was therefore not surprising to Halbwachs to observe that in the countryside of France the number of male births was far greater than in the Seine. We should therefore expect the same situation within the rural sector of Pharaonic Egypt. Namely, that there were more male births per family than female outside of the cities, especially Memphis and Thebes, to take two well-known examples.

The ideal situation for male births within four European countries is presented by Halbwachs in his study. The facts are: fathers up to 25 years of age and mothers in the same category: 111.5/100. This number decreases slightly as the mother ages up to 35 years. But as the father ages, the ratio quickly diminishes.

It can be argued, so long as the rural base of the Egyptian population was healthy, that there would not only have been enough males to work as cultivators, but those individuals belonging to the relatively well-off "middle" sector would produce enough men for the war machine, while the others could supply the ordinary soldiers.

2. Lynn Meskell, *Archaeologies of Social Life. Age, Sex, Class et cetera in Ancient Egypt*, Blackwell, Malden (1999), 169–74, touches upon the female and male life expectancies during Ramesside times. Using the data from the workmen's village at Deir el Medineh in Western Thebes, she argues that a general life expectancy higher than that in Roman Egypt can be proven. Unfortunately, no detailed mathematical analysis is present. For the moment, I can refer to the economic study of Janssen, *Commodity Prices from the Ramessid Period*, 462–3. A monthly ration of grain would be amply sufficient for a family of about ten persons, "including some children" (p. 463). At the minimum, we can conclude that a relatively well-off state-paid manual laborer (artisan, draughtsman, painter) supported nine individuals. However, the problems of life expectancy and the gross population size of Egypt cannot be agued solely on the basis of this rather unique settlement.

Mark Lehner, "Fractal House of Pharaoh: Ancient Egypt as a Complex Adaptive System, a Trial Formulation," in Timothy A. Kohler and George J. Gumerman, *Dynamics in Human and Private Societies. Agent-Basing Modeling of Social and Spatial Processes*. Oxford University Press, New York and Oxford (2000), 283–6, discusses the common village household in ancient Egypt. Nonetheless, he cannot fix a relatively firm number of people per unit.

3. Kemp presented a worthwhile discussion connected to the nature of the rural landscape in Egypt in *Ancient Egypt. Anatomy of a Civilization*, 310–13. Relying for the most part upon the Dynasty XX text of P. Wilbour, he indicated that we only have a "hazy outline" of how much settlement lay outside of the towns. But Kemp showed that links from the court or cities with a provincial or a semi-rural base were not difficult to maintain. People at court or living in the capital "retained the provincial links of their origin and this inevitably included property rights and hopes of further inheritance" (p. 313). Therefore, we can assume that the soldiery, especially the officer class, was connected to the provincial sector of Egypt, even though specific figures are lacking for any mathematical analysis.

4. I shall discuss how useful P. Wilbour is for the situation of the military in Dynasty XX in Chapter 16. For the moment, let me observe that the number soldiers renting land in Middle Egypt on the basis of this papyrus was calculated to be 131 out of a grand total of 903 or 14.5 percent. The scribes came to 3.3 percent and the priests 12.4 percent, 15.7 percent in total. In other words, by the reign of Ramesses V, the date when this papyrus was written, the scribal officialdom was slightly higher than the native military in this section of the Nile Valley. But the same account reveals that 68 Sherden "mercenaries" also owned plots of land. Their percentage is therefore 7.5. In other words, the regular Egyptian army formed twice the size of these foreigners, but both together amounted to about one-third more than the older professions of priest and scribe.

5.   Julius Beloch was the first scholar to prepare a scientific basis for any population analysis concerned with Egypt: *Die Bevölkerung der griechisch-roemischen Welt*, Duncker and Humblot, Leipzig (1886), 254–60. See as well his "Die Bevölkerung im Altertum," *Zeitschrift für Sozialwissenschaft* 2 (1899), 600–1. Butzer's work, used in this chapter, took a different approach, but one that was necessary owing to the paucity of primary data.

6.   The natural and human-devised conditions of population control may be found in Josiah Cox Russell, *The Control of Late Ancient and Medieval Population*, American Philosophical Society, Philadelphia (1985). He maintained: "if the number of basic sources of income can be ascertained, an estimate of population can be made. If a city is more than seven times its basic sources of income, it is obviously overpopulated" (p. 11). Unfortunately, for the most part such necessary data are absent from Pharaonic Egypt. But it is useful to note that Butzer argued for a doubling of the population of the Delta population during the early Ramesside Period (*Early Hydraulic Civilization in Egypt*, 95). He felt that the absolute level of population density came to rival that of the Nile Valley, narrowly speaking. What this means is that in the north there had occurred a preponderant shift in settlement patterns allowing this region to become more politically and socially important than Egypt south of Memphis.

During our time period the Egyptian population base was most dense between Aswan and Quft in Upper Egypt, and also in the Fayum and Memphis regions (Butzer, *Early Hydraulic Civilization in Egypt*, 80). This means that the evidence from P. Wilbour must be taken with some degree of caution, as it cannot be extrapolated to other regions of Egypt. Nonetheless, it is reasonable to locate the families of later New Kingdom soldiers within the higher density sectors.

7.   One final point can be drawn with regard to this population density. Russell, in his "Demographic Comparison of Egyptian and English Cities in the Later Middle Ages," *Taius* 2 (1969), 64–72, reflected upon the metropolitan city of Cairo in the late medieval period. It comprised ca. 60,000 inhabitants, and therefore formed the expected normal 1.5 percent of the total population in an agrarian society. He also provides a useful table of the population estimates for fifteen other Egyptian cities around 1340 AD. If we follow his argumentation, and taking into consideration the necessary disparities between this era and that of the New Kingdom, ancient Memphis would not have had a population more than ca. 45,000.

8.   The size of a division within the Egyptian army has been partly covered in note 16. A useful summary may now be found in Kitchen, *Ramesside Inscriptions. Translated and Annotated, Notes and Comments* II, 39–40. I agree with him that the infantry and chariotry together may have been included in the division total of 5,000 men. If so, this would have been very unusual from relatively modern conditions because both contingents have different operational viewpoints that prevent them from being integrated with each other.

Kitchen refers to Faulkner's basic analysis of the army units, "Egyptian Military Organization," *Journal of Egyptian Archaeology* 39 (1953), 32–47, where a 5,000-man division was argued. (Breasted earlier hypothesized this.) Of course, the figure is an ideal one because the actual manpower of any military unit is always below its defined number. Schulman, on the other hand, felt that the infantry division had no fixed strength (*Military Rank, Title, and Organization in the Egyptian New Kingdom*, 15). Yet the figure of 5,000 fits neatly into the available evidence. For example, the companies (*sa*) were lead by a "chief of fifty" (Schulman, pp. 26–30), but see Faulkner's remarks on p. 45. If we maintain that each division theoretically contained 5,000 soldiers, then at the Battle of Kadesh Ramesses II personally led 20,000 troops into Syria, with a fifth division also present. This situation will be covered in excursus 1 to chapter 13, but note the important text of Seti I referred to in excursus 4 to chapter 2 where the expedition encompassed 1,000 men.

9.   Schulman ignored the importance of the so-called "deputy" in the military, the *idenu*. Subsequently, Yoyotte and Lopez laid emphasis upon the high-ranking nature of this man in "L'organisation de l'armée et les titulaires de soldats au nouvel empire égyptien," *Bibliotheca Orientalis* 26 (1969), 6–7, a point that later Gnirs returned to in her *Militär und Gesellschaft*; see especially pp. 31–2 in her study. Faulkner's position was that a regiment contained 200 men in the early Ramesside Period, although this may be queried. On pp. 26–30 of Schulman's work the supporting data for 250 (+ 3) troops are presented. Whereas his argumentation has weaknesses, many of which Yoyotte and Lopez revealed, one might still accept his conclusions. Nonetheless, both his subtotal of 250 and that of Faulkner (200 men/company) divide evenly into the presumed division strength of 5,000; 253 does not. A split into four, nonetheless, seems more reasonable. The hierarchy of the system would have operated as follows: 4 divisions (which at the battle of Kadesh accompanied the king); 200 men per company; the "chief of 50," and then the lowly soldier (the *wa'au*). (50 × 4 = 200.) The exact system of army organization has yet to be written. That it changed over time is self-evident. Indeed, this was one of the telling points by Yoyotte-Lopez against Schulman. The *idenu* (Gnirs' "field marshals") were considerably superior to the "standard-bearers" of each company, and there were separate ones for the chariotry and infantry. The "generals" were subordinate to "generalissimos." Finally, note that Schulman's "group marshals" (*tjesu pedjet*) were actually those men who were responsible for the tactical dispositions of the troops and determined the route to be taken. The reader should understand that I follow the system of Gnirs with respect to the high officials of the army.

NOTES

1   Der Manuelian, *Studies in the Reign of Amenophis II*, chapter II, presents an excellent analysis of the warfare. The basic texts are presented in Helck, *Urkunden der 18. Dynastie*, 1287–99 (Amada Stela, recording an earlier cam-

paign in the king's third year when he was coregent with his father, Thutmose III), 1299–1309 (Memphis Stela), and 1310–16 (Karnak Stela). Translations will be found in Cumming, *Egyptian Historical Records of the Later Eighteenth Dynasty*, 19–35.

2   Helck, "Das Verfassen einer Königsinschrift," in Jan Assmann, Erika Feucht, and Reinhard Grieshammer, eds., *Fragen an die altägyptische Literatur*, Ludwig Reichert, Wiesbaden (1977), 241–56. He attempted to reconcile the divergent presentations in the two accounts of the Karnak and Memphis stelae.

3   For these battle reliefs, see Zayed's study, "Une représentation inédite des campagnes d'Aménophis II," in Posener-Kriéger, ed., *Mélanges Gamal Eddin Mokhtar* I, 5–17. Liverani discusses the personal aspects of valor of Amunhotep II in connection with other rulers of Western Asia at this time in *Prestige and Interest*, 121–3.

4   The peculiarities of the booty list to this campaign have remained an interesting problem. *Inter alia*, see Der Manuelian, *Studies in the Reign of Amenophis II*, 76–7; Spalinger, "The Historical Implications of the Year 9 Campaign of Amenophis II," *Journal of the Society for the Study of Egyptian Antiquities* 13 (1983), 89–101; and Liverani, *Prestige and Interest*, 147 with n. 21. Amin A. M. A. Amer, "Asiatic Prisoners Taken in the Reign of Amenophis II," *Scripta Mediterranea* 5 (1984), 27–8, ignores the situation of gravely exaggerated (and neatly rounded) integers.

5   See the sources cited in the previous note.

6   Der Manuelian, *Studies in the Reign of Amenophis II*, 83–90. Na'aman has presented some pertinent comments regarding Taanach at this time and later in the XVIIIth Dynasty: "Economic Aspects of the Egyptian Occupation of Canaan," *Israel Exploration Journal* 31 (1981), 179. The language of the correspondence was covered by Anson F. Rainey, "Verbal Usages in Taanach Texts," *Israel Oriental Studies* 7 (1977), 33–64.

In this context it should not be overlooked that "About one third of the personal names in the Taanach tablets are of northern, mainly Hurrian origin" (Na'aman, "The Hurrians and the End of the Middle Bronze Age in Palestine," *Levant* 26 [1994], 177). As this scholar indicates, there was a distinctive Hurrian element in the area of Taanach during the XVIIIth Dynasty. (Hurrian was the language of the kingdom of Mitanni.) He also indicated that one Egyptian term for Syria–Palestine from the reign of Thutmose III onward, Kharu, points to this northern influence.

It was earlier believed that many of the names in the later Amarna Letters reflect an Indo-Aryan language. As Na'aman indicates in his study, this is an incorrect assumption. I therefore cannot follow the interpretation of Redford in *Egypt, Canaan, and Israel in Ancient Times*, 137.

Owing to this Hurrian influence, it is not surprising that the coalition of Asiatics opposing Thutmose III at Megiddo were not only connected with Kadesh in Syria, but also had indirect support from Mitanni. See chapter 5.

7   See the list of basic studies in excursus 3 to chapter 5.

8   An argument against this position was presented by Na'aman, "The Hurrians and the End of the Middle Bronze Age in Palestine," *Levant* 26 (1994), 175–87. On the other hand, Dever strongly objected to the hypothesis: "Hurrian Incursions and the End of the Middle-Bronze Age in Syria-Palestine: A

Rejoinder to Nadav Na'aman," in Leonard H., Lesko, ed., *Ancient Egyptian and Mediterranean Studies in Memory of William A. Ward*, 91–110. See our remarks in note 7 to chapter 3.

9 The citations are to be found in the last note plus excursus 3 to chapter 5.

10 Na'aman, "The Hurrians and the End of the Middle Bronze Age in Palestine," *Levant* 26 (1994), 175–87.

11 See excursus 3 to chapter 5.

12 Butzer, *Early Hydraulic Civilization in Egypt*, chapter 7. This analysis is the most scientifically based work on the topic of ancient Egyptian populations that I have read.

In his "The Low Price of Land in Ancient Egypt," *Journal of the American Research Center in Egypt* 1 (1962), 44, Klaus Baer had estimated a total population of 4.5 million in Rameside times, but cautioned that there was a "very sizeable margin of error each way." Subsequently, he reduced that figure by a considerable percentage, estimating 2.4 to 3.6 million inhabitants for all of Ramesside Egypt (p. 76 in Butzer).

For Medieval Egypt, Josiah C. Russell, "The Population of Medieval Egypt', *Journal of the American Research Center in Egypt* 5 (1966), 69–82, remains basic. This study was reprinted in his *Medieval Demography. Essays by Josiah C. Russell*, AMS Press, New York (1987), 75–98. His figures are as follows: ca. 4.4 million at the time of Christ; 3.4 million ca. AD 300; a slight rise to 3.6 million in the late fifth century followed by a leveling off; a decline to less than 2.4 million ca. AD 740 followed by an increase to ca. 2.75 million shortly after AD 800.

It is clear that such population estimates are fragile. Nonetheless, the attempts of Butzer and Russell are based upon a host of factors, including the total amount of acreage. As a salutary introduction I can recommend Russell's "Demographic Pattern in History," *Population Studies* 1 (1948), 388–404. His voluminous research on this topic is too well known to list here.

13 Butzer, *Early Hydraulic Civilization in Egypt*, 82–5.

14 Pierre Grandet, *Le Papyrus Harris I (BM 9999)* I, Institut Français d'Archéologie Orientale, Cairo (1994), 128, attempted a reconciliation among the figures given by various scholars.

15 See chapter 2 n. 14.

16 Fischer-Elfert, *Die satirische Streitschrift des Papyrus Anastasi I.*, 148–57 (17.4–5, chapter XV). The author covers in exemplary detail the previous scholarly work on this passage.

Faulkner, "Egyptian Military Organization," *Journal of Egyptian Archaeology* 39 (1953), 45, argued that in the XIXth Dynasty the main unit of the Pharaonic army was a company of 200 men with a commander. Schulman, on the contrary, felt that it was a 50-man unit and not the company that was the "principal and tactical unit." He also concluded that "the normal strength of a company was 250 men": *Military Rank, Title, and Organization in the Egyptian New Kingdom*, 26–30, especially p. 27. Yoyotte and Lopez, however, showed that there were problems with Schulman's analysis in "L'organisation de l'armée et les titulaires de soldats au nouvel empire égyptien," *Bibliotheca Orientalis* 26 (1969), 2–7.

The total of 5,000 for a division of the army was presented by Breasted, *Ancient Records of Egypt* III, 127 and 153 n. a; see excursus 1 to chapter 13 and our remarks under excurses 8–9 in this chapter.

17 For a translation, see Wente, in William K. Simpson, ed., *The Literature of Ancient Egypt²*, 81–4; the text is in Gardiner, *Late Egyptian Stories*, 82–5. The precise passage is 2,7.

18 This conclusion includes the Egyptian soldiers associated with garrison duty in Asia. For the latter situation, see the remarks of Na'aman, "Economic Aspects of the Egyptian Occupation of Canaan," *Israel Exploration Journal* 31 (1981), 172–85, with his *The Political Disposition and Historical Development of Eretz-Israel According to the Amarna Letters*, chapters VII–VIII. Compare the remarks of Liverani, "Farsi Habiru," *Vicino Oriente* 2 (1978), 65–77.

19 There were five divisions present. Four marched with the Pharaoh and a fifth came across from the west. See chapter 13.

20 Fischer-Elfert (note 16 above) covers this situation.

21 The importance of the Libyans within Ramesside military society will be discussed later. This passage would appear to indicate that they were either captured or, more probably, joined the Egyptian army as "mercenaries" after Seti I's campaigns to the west of the Nile: see our remarks in chapter 13 below.

22 K. A. Kitchen, *Ramesside Inscriptions* I, 260ff. for the text; see my commentary in "Baking During the Reign of Seti I," *Bulletin de l'Institut Français d'Archéologie Orientale* 86 (1986), 307–52. There is an additional study of this material in Kitchen's *Ramesside Inscriptions, Translated and Annotated. Notes and Comments*, I, 173. He feels that because these "Nubians belong to the 'New Land of tribute',” this "suggests that they were cultivators of that land (perhaps soldiers [Spalinger's conjecture] settled on it)."

On p. 180 of his *Ramesside Inscriptions, Translated and Annotated. Notes and Comments* I, Kitchen further points out that in a subsequent section of these accounts of Seti I, a group of Nubians is listed where all of them "appear to be the personal servants of various officers and officials." In particular, they are the underlings of charioteers as well as scribes, a chamberlain, and a royal cupbearer. The Nubians, all of whom bear Egyptian names, were summoned for inspection.

A very useful translation of this material will be found in Kitchen, *Ramesside Inscriptions. Translated and Annotated. Translations* I, 207–30.

23 This data was presented in my study referred to in the last note. Kitchen expanded upon some of those analyses in his *Ramesside Inscriptions, Translated and Annotated. Notes and Comments* I, 166–76.

24 Kemp, *Ancient Egypt. Anatomy of a Civilization*, 124–6.

10

THE AMARNA LETTERS
AND WAR

Until we reach Dynasty XIX the details of further campaigns of the Pharaohs are few at best.[1] From the vantage point of interpreting the Pharaonic war machine it is therefore necessary to turn to the Amarna archive, dated to Amunhotep III and IV. Among those documents, a series of letters placed within the latter years of Amunhotep IV (Akhenaton) read as if an Egyptian campaign was in process.[2] The preparations are military, and the correspondence from the vassals always indicates that the loyal potentate has established the foods and supplies for Egyptian troops. Horses and chariots are repeatedly jotted down, but also native bodies of soldiers are mentioned. Foods such as corn, drink, oil, and the like can be found listed in one letter from Ashkelon. The phrase "tents of the soldiers," i.e., of the infantry, may be found on another. Levantine ports are included in this group because Sidon and Beirut are listed. Indeed, a large number of these letters present reports of a similar vein. Lachish, Ashkelon, Acco, and possibly Megiddo – all in Palestine – are included in the dossier. It has been argued that similar war preparations took place earlier under Amunhotep III because some letters from Qatna and Amurru in Syria reveal parallel matters. This, however, is incorrect. The famous Qatna Letter (No. 55 of the Amarna dossier) is actually dated to the very end of the Amarna correspondence, and it seems not to belong to the select group of letters specifically dealing with a forthcoming Egyptian attack.[3] But the refrain is concentrated upon the words "make ready for the soldiers of the king." Nowhere is it stated that Pharaoh, whoever he may be, is expected. This point should be emphasized as some have argued that the Pharaoh himself was to arrive in Asia. Moreover, not a few letters state that captives are being sent down to Egypt or that local razzias, raids, have already taken place.

We must be on our guard not to over-interpret these repetitive series of military accounts lest we fall into the position of viewing every single one as indicative of a major war. Yet many of these letters note the advance preparations for military conflict in which the king's troops were expected. The latter are called "archer-troops," and we must assume that they were not mere simple footsoldiers in the pay of the Egyptian state. The term for the latter is quite different. In fact, it is a direct transcription of the Egyptian word for "soldier," or to be more precise "footsoldier."[4] I prefer instead to regard them as well-practiced and professional warriors. It is not clear enough to conclude that these men were mere units of the regular (Egyptian) army. To handle an impending major war required well-trained and experienced troops. Infantry they were, but simple privates I suspect not. These men would be effective in attacks from citadels, walls of cities, and perhaps also in chariots. But as it is necessary to cover the specific historical situation in Asia at this time, I will discuss these men later.

A more detailed study of these letters from a purely military viewpoint is in order.[5] In this correspondence one sees the local princes in Palestine repeatedly stressing their loyalty to Pharaoh and going at great lengths to point out that they are keeping everything in tip-top military condition. The city is well guarded; provisions are stored and ready for delivery to the expected Egyptian soldiers. Some of the letters are very late in time, and we can assume that the preparations for war were a result of the successful pro-Hittite maneuvers in Syria. The Beirut correspondence, for example, was written after the loss of Byblos to the Hittite side. Two Egyptian officials, indeed the famous Maya, are named in the archive.[6] (Maya was appointed high commissioner of Palestine in the final years of Amunhotep IV.) Reevaluation of the letters containing these effective military preparations indicates that the subgroup belongs to the very end of the extant correspondence. Among the writers we may point out a chief of the king's stable. Horses, once more, are connected to these events. Other men included various Egyptian officials in Asia. But the role of Maya, who may have replaced a certain Yankhamu as governor, was a crucial one as he controlled most of Palestine for the Pharaoh. His role is most important for us because we can see more clearly the Egyptian military set-up in Asia.

Sometime between Thutmose III and the middle years of Amunhotep IV a controller of the north was established. Unfortunately, only the Amarna Letters provide the evidence and even that is slim. Can we conclude that the increasing troubles that the Egyptians faced in the north led to a stricter control over Palestine? This hypothesis must remain unclear. But we can see that Amunhotep IV was ready to intervene in this territory. To take a case in point, one Amarna Letter from the king of Tyre (No. 147, a long one) uses the unusual phrase "great army." Evidently, not just a few or even one hundred troops were meant. In that letter the local prince expected the arrival of the Pharaoh. Earlier, the king's own commissioner, Khani, had been sent to Palestine and the Levant to make ready the campaign.

From the early letters in this archive conflicts were also discussed, even though there was no direct Egyptian response concerning a possible departure of the king to Asia. The frequent jostlings in Syria, especially in the region of Amurru, Kadesh, and Byblos, were a threat to Egyptian control.

Sometimes we read of a task force sent to this region to effect a punitive result. On other occasions the anti-Egyptian maneuverings of Aziru of Amurru were recognized and that prince warned of retaliation. As that portion of the correspondence is enlightening with regard to the Egyptian military, additional factors may be presented at this juncture.

Abdi-Ashita of Amurru, the father of Aziru, attempted to switch sides. He aligned himself with the Hittites and kept up relentless attack on Rib-Addi of Byblos.[7] Byblos was still in Egyptian hands. Abdi-Ashirta was finally beheaded for his treachery and Aziru replaced him. Yet the Pharaoh eventually countered the machinations of this man. Aziru feared the Egyptian counterattack and so suddenly became friendly, even offering to travel to Egypt, undoubtedly by way of Byblos.

Supplementary information on this affair has sometimes been connected to the famous "Letter of the General" found at Ugarit.[8] The difficulty, however, in using this single piece of correspondence is that the date of redaction is unclear. The major problem is whether this letter should be located to the epoch of the Amarna Letters or else within the years following the Battle of Kadesh under Ramesses II. On the other hand, the military strategy involved concerns the Egyptians in Syria, and therefore the overall consistent aims of Egyptian Pharaohs in Syria can be revealed.[9] We find no major divergences between the northern advances of earlier Dynasty XVIII monarchs, or even those who ruled at the beginning of Dynasty XIX, and the events recounted by an enemy in this missive. Hence, this letter can still be brought into discussion with regard to Syria during the Amarna Period when the Egyptians were about to lose all control over Amurru to the Hittites, but only from a strategic geographical viewpoint. The addressee, Sumiyanu, was an army commander in Amurru, and certain scholars, on the weight of internal evidence, place the letter along with the earliest Amarna texts from that region. General Sumiyanu received news of the impending Egyptian military attack from a captive. As I shall return to the situation of spies and the dissemination of military secrets later, I wish only to reemphasize the situation concerning the predictability of impending war. It was well nigh impossible to hide the preparations.

The letter is written to the "lord" of Sumiyanu, a man yet to be identified. The following are the remarks of the correspondent. War material is to be sent to Aleppo; three chariot pairs should be maintained for conflict; and hopefully supplies and ancillary troops are ready. The military dispositions of Sumiyanu are very important. He had already secured the region. We hear that he guarded the roads and the entrances into Amurru. The general then declares: "Half of my chariots are stationed in front of the Lebanon Mountains." It is clear that some of the Lebanese ports were still on the side of Egypt. The account is somewhat hyperbolic in tone and the rhetoric indicates a pleading if not desperate man. Sumiyanu had actually arranged his forces well, although attacks on the coast had taken place. See, for example, the problems at Ardat. In addition, a captive in that city revealed that the Pharaoh was planning to go north, "but he is leaving unaccompanied." Does this mean that the king intended an attack on the Lebanon alone? Are we dealing with affairs slightly later in the reign of Tutankhamun when Horemheb fought in Asia, or, as now argued, under Ramesses II? It is evident that a date to Amunhotep IV seems improbable even if the Egyptian military dispositions tended to follow a tried-and-true pattern.

This move of the Egyptians is presented in great detail. First, the military equipment of the Egyptians is to arrive and then the troops. The letter proceeds as follows: "Perhaps the king of the land of Egypt does not come himself, but if it is the 'archer-troops' that will come, then I will overpower by force." The prospective orientation of the report implies that an attack was expected, but it is left open whether the Pharaoh will be present. The geographic zone included the Nahr el-Kebir (the Classical Eleutherus River), and it was the coastal plain along that river which was protected. Whatever our interpretations of this crucial document may be, the welcome light that it throws upon the Egyptian preparations for warfare fits neatly with Thutmose III's later Syrian wars and, as we shall recount later, with those of Seti I and Ramesses II. In other words, the general strategic situation in Syria remained the same over many years.

A few additional remarks can supplement the above analysis. In the Amarna archive we hear from time to time of Nubian troops in the Egyptian army. Letter No. 117 from Byblos indicates that Amunhotep III had previously sent Nubian soldiers northward to that city. We also hear of various Egyptian political officers apparently resident in Asia and in charge of the various Syrian potentates such as Abdi-Ashirta of Amurru, his son Aziru, and Etqama of Kadesh who also became hostile to Egypt. In two additional letters, Rib-Addi of Byblos remarks upon the presence of Sherden who have been killed in Byblos by the Egyptian official Pakharu. In the later Ramesside Period some of the Sherden became "mercenaries" in the Egyptian army, but at this time they were very troublesome sea raiders who, with their ships, did more damage than merely pestering the harbors of Lebanon and Cyprus.[10] One Egyptian commissioner, a certain Pakhamnata, had his headquarters at Simyra, also on the coast. His zone of control included the region immediately to the east of Phoenicia, north of Kadesh, or quite possibly included that key city, and the territory that led up to Qatna. It would appear from his words that full control of the coast north of Byblos had not yet fallen away from Egypt. This is, in fact, one good reason why it has been reasonable to date the "Letter to the General" to the reign of Amunhotep IV rather than later.

Local difficulties in political control abound in the reports of the princes in these letters. Sometimes the kinglet states that he will wait until the political official arrives in order to quell the difficulties. In others, Egyptians are asked to march against a local enemy. Notwithstanding all of these complaints, most of which should not be summarily disregarded, the type of Egyptian administration remains unclear. As stated earlier, these letters provide a great amount of information concerning Egyptian political officials, the need for small bodies of troops, and the presence of garrison towns. From the archive it would appear that the Egyptian policy had grown more complicated since the middle of Dynasty XVIII. But we still see the lack of major Egyptian military settlements in either Palestine or Syria.

The Egyptian army, the force behind its northern imperialism, was not permanently stationed in Asia. Local Egyptian garrisons still remained the major means of controlling local disturbances. For a major war, it was necessary to provide the supplies (material and provisions), to strengthen the fortifications (walls of cities, for example), and to control the roads. In the Amarna Letters chariot warriors are not listed among the troops desired. Were these men resident Egyptians living far away in the Nile Valley? This seems rather far-fetched, especially as many letters concerning the possible Egyptian campaign indicate that the local prince had made ready both horses and vehicles. Evidently, the Egyptian "archer-troops" included charioteers, both drivers and the second man, and this is what occurred at Kadesh, but that is a story more concerned with the Hittite threat in early Dynasty XIX.

Finally, the role of the Egyptian navy at this time must not be disregarded.[11] With regard to the affairs in Syria, along the Lebanese coast (e.g., at Byblos) as well as inland (Amurru), the Egyptian navy was expected to join forces with the fleets of Tyre, Sidon, and Beirut. The aim was to suppress the growing danger of Abdi-Ashirta who controlled most of the inland of central Syria and was threatening the Lebanese ports that were allied to Egypt. An Egyptian representative, in fact, was to be dispatched to these three mercantile cities in order to arrange cooperation from the locals. In other words, the Egyptian navy with the support of the key seaports formed an effective base, both logistically and military, against any threats from the hinterland of Syria. This policy, so well revealed in the Amarna dossier, enables us to understand one result among the long-ranging consequences of Thutmose III's later wars in Asia.

EXCURSUS

1. Even though the logistic situation within the Asiatic territories of the Egyptian Empire has yet to be written, some of its parameters can be described. By the second half of Dynasty XVIII the Egyptians had established the support for their defensive and offensive strategies, and they understood the limitations inherent in the use of pack animals and vehicles drawn by oxen or horses. In most cases we can assume that the lines of supply and fortified locations, as evident in the Amarna Letters, were not of so recent a date. The venerable bureaucratic society of Pharaonic Egypt no doubt helped to handle

the normal situations satisfactorily. This is why we find so few locally based Egyptian troops in Asia. The expected problems were simply not of a magnitude that would have entailed garrisons of over one hundred soldiers, if not even fewer men.

In fact, the Pharaohs seem to have been risk-adverse. The caution of Amunhotep IV (Akhenaton) when he witnessed the gradual erosion of former supporters in Syria (e.g., Amurru and Kadesh) supports this contention. I believe that his attitude, often chided by Egyptologists, was based upon an established policy of reducing the number of potentially uncertain and expensive campaigns that had to be led by the Pharaoh. The Egyptians, at least in the second half of Dynasty XVIII, appear to have followed a practice of preserving, or only altering modestly, the status quo in Asia. (The control over Palestine, which was a serious matter, has to be viewed separately from Asia as a whole.) The political situation in the Ramesside Period, to the contrary, demanded a more pro-active approach, and this will be discussed later.

Supply bases for the Egyptian army were necessary, and the system described here and earlier provided the Egyptians with an effective means of moving their major armies north. By utilizing the local cities in Palestine, the Pharaohs avoided the problems of slowness of movement and that of supplies. We have also seen that from regnal year twenty-nine onward Thutmose III laid the basis for his power in central Syria by means of a tight policy over the Lebanese ports.

Nevertheless, one can regard extortion to have been the norm. Cities, towns, and entire districts footed the bill and supplied food for the passing or occupying Egyptian army. This dependence meant that many of the localities served as supply magazines, quite probably at great cost to the locals. It is perhaps not a mere curiosity that in the battle reliefs and inscriptions we neither see nor read of supply columns. This is not to say that such necessary food items as breads and water were not carried along, but that the local cities were forced to take care of the major load of provisioning.

Additional ramifications in connection to the marches of large armies include the consequences of the policy of "living off the country." Green fodder especially had to be gathered on a campaign if there was no city or town close by where the necessary requisitions could be made. Such food is the equivalent of today's fuel, and although search parties could quickly gather the necessary forage, this was not effective when the army was stalled. Lengthy sieges, for example, entail the use of dry fodder. Excluding this "fuel," an army had to sustain its human element with other supplies, and these had to be either laboriously brought up from the rear or taken from cities.

Because the Egyptian monarchs were not out to exterminate their enemies, even the major ones, their struggles were over territory and limited advantages. Therefore, their major wars were not of a long duration; the armies departed from Asia to Egypt after a maximum of three to four months. But the kings did not leave behind them a series of fortifications in key locations. This would have entailed the mobilization of substantial resources to provide the necessary logistic supports to build these assets, and then to maintain the structure and the troops. Warfare at this time was determined, as always, by the physical, technological, and social constraints of the age. The basic studies on the administrative system of the Egyptian Empire in Asia have been listed in the second and third notes to this chapter. The logistic situation may be viewed from both a theoretical as well a practical viewpoint in the following two works: John A. Lynn, ed., *Feeding Mars. Logistics in Western Warfare from the Middle Ages to the Present*, Westview Press, Boulder, San Francisco, and Oxford (1993); and James A. Huston, *The Sinews of War: Army Logistics 1775–1953*, United States Army, Washington (1966), chapter XXXV (theoretical section).

NOTES

1 For the background data, see Betsy M. Bryan, *The Reign of Thutmose IV*, Johns Hopkins University Press, Baltimore and London (1991), 332–47. The evidence collected is ample for generalizations, but except for Thutmose IV's Konosso Stela, discussed by the author on pp. 334–6, little can be presented that directly involves the theme of this volume. This is due to the limited corpus of Dynasty XVIII military inscriptions after the reign of Amunhotep II, a situation that probably was partly caused by the decreasing importance of foreign wars.

Yoyotte and Lopez, "L'organisation de l'armée et les titulaires de soldats au nouvel empire égyptien," *Bibliotheca Orientalis* 26 (1969), 5, presented an important evaluation of the king's army on the march on the basis of the Konosso Stela. The chariotry were normally the farthest removed from the Pharaoh, and were at the front of the army. Moreover, the elite warriors (the "strong-of-arm") were placed on the flanks of the mass of ordinary soldiers.

2 The term Amarna refers to the new capital in Middle Egypt established by Amunhotep IV (Akhenaton) in his fifth regnal year. Found in that city was a major archive of cuneiform letters. The missives refer to various city-states in Palestine and Syria as well as the major kingdoms of the day (e.g., Babylon and Mitanni). We possess letters from these potentates to Amunhotep III and IV as well as copies of those sent out by the Egyptian chancellery.

William Moran's standard edition of the Amarna Letters has already been referred to earlier in note 7 to chapter 8. For its importance, see the comments of Anson F. Rainey, "A New Translation of the Amarna Letters – after 100 Years," *Archiv für Orientforschung* 36/37 (1989/1990), 56–75, concerning Moran's earlier edition in French, *Les letters d'El-Amarna. Correspondence diplomatique du pharaon*, Les Éditions du Cerf, Paris (1987).

The study of Mario Liverani, "Political Lexicon and Political Ideologies in the Amarna Letters," *Berytus* 31 (1983), 41–56, should be read in the context of the political and social aspects of these official missives. He emphasizes the denotive and connotative levels of various key words in Egyptian, Akkadian, and Canaanite. To that article can be added his compendium, *Three Amarna Essays*, Undena Publications, Malibu (1979). Of particular importance is the discussion " 'Irrational' Elements in the Amarna Trade."

The work of Cohen and Westbrook, ed., *Amarna Diplomacy*, referred to in note 14 to chapter 8, can be cited as it provides some elegant summaries of the diplomatic and military affairs of this period.

3   I concur with Nadav Na'aman, "Praises to the Pharaoh in Response to his Plans for a campaign in Canaan," in Tzvi Abush, John Huehnergard , and Peter Steinkeller, eds., *Lingering Over Words. Studies in Ancient Near Eastern Literature in Honor of William L. Moran*, Scholars Press, Atlanta (1990), 397–405. The expected war was not to be directed against the Hittites in Syria. An earlier analysis will be found in Schulman, "Some Observations on the Military Background of the Amarna Period," *Journal of the American Research Center in Egypt* 3 (1964), 51–69.

Other studies of Na'aman concerning this correspondence have been cited earlier. *Inter alia*, see "Economic Aspects of Egyptian Occupation in Canaan," *Israel Exploration Journal* 31 (1981), 172–85, and "Historical-Geographical Aspects of the Amarna Tablets," in *Proceedings of the Ninth World Congress of Jewish Studies. Panel Sessions Biblical Studies and Ancient Near East*, Moshe Goshen-Gottstein, ed., Magnes Press, Jerusalem (1988), 17–26.

4   The Akkadian term is *ṣābē piṭāti*. Useful for any evaluation concerning the military background as reflected in this correspondence is Edward Fay Cambell, Jr., *The Chronology of the Amarna Letters. With Special Reference to the Hypothetical Coregency of Amenophis III and Akhenaten*, Johns Hopkins Press, Baltimore (1959); and Kitchen, *Suppiluliuma and the Amarna Pharaohs. A Study in Relative Chronology*, Liverpool University Press, Liverpool (1962), chapters IV–V in particular (for Syrian affairs). Liverani's *Prestige and Interest* can be cited as well, because the entire work is permeated with inter-state relations of the Late Bronze Age.

5   I rely heavily upon the unpublished dissertation of Na'aman, *The Political Disposition and Historical Development of Eretz-Israel According to the Amarna Letters*. His later study, "The Contribution of the Amarna Letters to the Debate on Jerusalem's Political Position in the Tenth Century BCE," *Bulletin of the American Schools of Oriental Research* 304 (1996), 17–27, refines some if his ideas in chapter IV of the earlier work. See now his "The Seat of Three Disputed Canaanite Rulers According to Petroglyphic Investigations of the Amarna Letters," *Tel Aviv* 29 (2002), 221–37.

An overview is presented by Donald Redford, *Akhenaten. The Heretic King*, Princeton University Press, Princeton (1984), chapter Eleven.

6   Jacobus Van Dijk provides a detailed study on this man in *The New Kingdom Necropolis of Memphis. Historical and Iconographical Studies*, Rijksuniversiteit Groningen, Groningen (1993), chapter 2.

7   There is a study of this individual and his family in Na'aman's works cited in notes 3 and 5. In particular, see chapter IX of his dissertation, *The Political Disposition and Historical Development of Eretz Israel According to the Amarna Letters*. A recent discussion is by Liverani, "How to Kill Abdi-Ashirta. EA 101, Once Again," *Israel Oriental Studies* 18 (1998), 387–94.

8   Shlomo Izre'el, "When Was the 'General's Letter' from Ugarit Written?," in *Society and Economy in the Eastern Mediterranean (c. 1500–1000 bc)*, M. Heltzer and E. Lipinski, eds., Uitgeverij Peeters, Leuven (1988), 160–75, argued for a time frame during the Amarna Period of late Dynasty XVIII. The follow-up

study by him and Itamar Singer is *The General's Letter from Ugarit. A Linguistic and Historical Reevaluation of RS 20.33 (Ugaritica V, No. 20)*, Tel Aviv University, Tel Aviv, (1990). Pages 155–59 cover the main reasons for their historical dating. See as well his chapter, "A Concise History of Amurru," in Shlomo Izre'el, *Amurru Akkadian: A Linguistic Study*, Scholars Press, Atlanta (1991), 135–95.

Singer's analysis with respect to the political jockeying in Syria during the Amarna Period was rejected by Manfred L. G. Dietrich, "Der Ugariter Sumiyanu an der südsyrischen Front gegen den Pharaoh: Zu den Nachwehen der Schlacht bei Qades 1275 v. Chr," in Anke Ilona Blöbaum, Jochem Kahl, and Simon D. Schweitzer, eds., *Ägypten – Münster. Kulturwissenschaftliche Studien zu Ägypten, dem Vorderen Orient und verwandten Gebieten*, Harrassowitz, Wiesbaden (2003), 45–74. He argues that the confrontation between the port city of Ugarit and the Egyptian ruler must imply a date around the famous battle of Kadesh (Ramesses II, regnal year five). Otherwise, to place it during the Amarna Period is unreasonable because no known confrontation between Ugarit and Egypt is known from so early a time. I tend to agree with the author that this letter should be placed sometime after the Kadesh conflict of Ramesses II and Muwatallis, the Hittite king.

9   For the naval situation at this time, see Liverani, "How to Kill Abdi-Ashirta. EA 101, Once Again," *Israel Oriental Studies* 18 (1998), 398–401. He stresses the Egyptian fleet's inability to land in Amurru. From this (and other details in the Amarna Letters) we learn that the Egyptians maintained their flotilla in ready condition in order to oppose the expansion of the kingdom of Amurru. On p. 392 Liverani notes that Abdi-Ashirta's kingdom had once separated the area of Mitanni from the Egyptian-held ones in Sumur and the coastal area.

10 See Na'aman, *The Political Disposition and Historical development of Eretz-Israel According to the Amarna Letters*, chapters VIII–IX. Add Rainey, "The Amânnah Texts a Century after Flinders Petrie," *Ancient Near Eastern Studies* 39 (2002), 66–8. Pages 62–5 cover the historical geography.

11 See Liverani's analysis cited above in note 7. I follow his analysis. On the province of Canaan at this time, see Na'aman, "Four Notes on the size of Late Bronze Age Canaan," *Bulletin of the American Schools of Oriental Research* 313 (1999), 31–7.

11

THE INFLUENCE OF THE EGYPTIAN MILITARY FROM LATE DYNASTY XVIII TO DYNASTY XIX

Because the Egyptian military administration in Asia consisted of military personnel as well as civilian officials, the responsibility of control always involved the threat of troops.[1] Some of the high administrators who worked in Palestine also served in the Levant. Even though Amurru was separate from Byblos, it would appear that the Phoenician coast was closely associated with the core of Palestine. Kumidi would have served as the major control center in southern Syria, with Gaza performing the same role on the Palestine–Lebanon coast. There was rotation of the high officials, and it has been argued that this was a result of the preparations undertaken by Amunhotep IV for war. The two Akkadian terms in common use at this time were *rabisu* ("inspector" or "supervisor") and *shakin mati* ("commissioner"). The second term is not found in the Amarna Letters that came from Palestine. The first, on the other hand, is employed for all ranks in that region (and Ugarit as well) without referring to any specific rank. The title held by the local potentates, *khazannu*, indicates that these men controlled their city-sates with the expressed approval of Pharaoh. This must indicate the personal oath that each was to perform upon taking over the office. Yet, as we have seen, the local ruler was allowed to exercise his power through the principle of dynastic succession.

Troubles were frequent in Palestine at the close of the Amarna Period, notwithstanding the difficulties that the Egyptians had in Syria. Indeed, the threat to the peace must have resulted from the nature of the indirect Egyptian control over the region. Unrest can be pinpointed to the south and central areas. The city of Gezer is one clear-cut case where the ruler disappeared. Jerusalem with its lord, Abdi-Kheba, reveals another. Lachish and perhaps Ashkelon can be added to our list. There was a reformation of the Shechem-Gezer axis, with added woes in the northern plains and the Trans-Jordan. Finally, Milkilu of Gezer proved to be difficult in the Shephelah

169

and the Plain of Sharon. New rulers appear in the southern cities when the preparations were set into force for a military expedition: at Gezer, Ashkelon, and Lachish, to name three important localities.

Additional difficulties are reported concerning the nasty Apiru.[2] The latter were not mere rebels but instead a particular grouping of peoples who brought about a social and political crisis in Palestine. When considering these enemies, Na'aman placed emphasis upon the tendentiousness of the correspondence from the Amarna archive. He considered the major problem for modern interpretations of these peoples to lie in the subjective zone of "blurring." To put it simply, a scribe might refer to any tribal group working outside of an urban center as an Apiru. But these peoples were not formed into tribes. They may have been semi-nomadic or transhumant as archaeologists believe, but we have to be on our guard before accepting in an automatic fashion what the literate scribes wrote to their overlord in Egypt. Any frequently bothersome tribal entity could easily be labeled by the pejorative term Apiru. Nonetheless, it remains clear that there was a deterioration of internal control in Palestine, and that the reorganization alluded to earlier helped to stop this disintegration.

Disparaging terms such as Apiru remind us of the conflicts that previous Pharaohs had with elements on the periphery of the borders in Asia. One such group, the Shasu, first turn up in the reign of Thutmose II. Ahmose Pen-Nekhbet reports on a war against these peoples during which numerous captives were obtained.[3] Thutmose III fought against them in his thirty-ninth year. It is highly probable that the term encompassed many distinct elements: tribes, marauders, raiders, and the like. From later data in the reign of Seti I we can place some at the Trans-Jordanian boundary near Beth Shan and others around the Sinai. In his mid Dynasty XVIII biography Amunemheb recounts that he fought in the Negev region when his king, Thutmose III, was already in the far north.[4] Perhaps he encountered such Shasu. The text, however, merely refers to three "Asiatic" prisoners caught by the warrior. Horemheb, as well, fought against them.

I have brought the Shasu group into discussion because they became a thorn in the side of the Egyptians at the close of the XVIIIth Dynasty. True, they were quite different than the Apiru owing to their zones of operation and, apparently, their organization. The latter, after all, may be found operating within Palestine; the Shasu did not. Yet the report of Amunhotep II at the end of his ninth campaign refers to both in that odd booty list of captives that we have surveyed previously.[5] It is possible that both troubled Egyptian domination at the eastern Palestinian boundary with the Trans-Jordan. Most certainly, they menaced the stability of Egyptian control in the south. Naturally, they could not oppose the Egyptians en mass or even threaten the total disintegration of the Egyptian control over the local city-states. But the danger was clear. The reorganization of Palestine preceding the planned Egyptian campaign under Amunhotep IV

(Akhenaton) indicates a switch by the Pharaoh in his policy over this region.

In the second half of the XVIIIth Dynasty the military arm of the state had reached a position of great importance.[6] The regular infantry were divided into those serving in a campaign and those performing local garrison duty abroad, whether in the south or in the north. Small numbers of troops, especially in comparison to those amassed in an army led by the king, took care of the various internal problems existing in Palestine and perhaps Syria. From the Amarna Letters we see that a regular chain of communications by post had been set up in order to insure that the court became aware of the local perturbations in the foreign lands. Naturally, this was not in "real time." The lag between event and report plus that between reaction and result were great by our standards. Yet this was commonplace during the Late Bronze Age. Massive incursions by a major enemy or the gradual shifting of political allegiance on the part of some city-states (e.g., Amurru or Kadesh) could be addressed since these events also took some time to transpire.

I have already covered the situation of "mercenaries" in the Egyptian army during the New Kingdom when I emphasized that this word is a misnomer. By this time some Nubians, the Asiatic Apiru, and later the Sherden belonged to the Egyptian army. Although separate in many respects from the natives, they were also soldiers of the Egyptians who lived and died within the Nile Valley. A further group of "mercenaries" began to play a role in the Egyptian army from the middle of Dynasty XVIII, but more particularly in the Ramesside Period. These were the *teheru* who first turn up in Egyptian sources in the Annals of Thutmose III.[7] At the Battle of Kadesh we see them protecting the Hittite king, and the title "chief/great one of the *teheru*" is known from those records. These warriors were of foreign extraction, and some of them ended their lives in Egypt. One "great one of the *teheru*" is known to have been associated with a fortress in Egypt in the Late Ramesside Period. A second, dated to the reign of Ramesses III, was associated with a garrison of that king. By Dynasty XX these soldiers belonged to the middle level of the military society. They owned land, apparently mainly in Middle Egypt although this is somewhat unclear, and they also dealt with trade. (The known localities of the *teheru* officials were somewhat south of Memphis, around the Fayum and near Herakleopolis Magna.) The Sherden are known to have settled in the region of Middle Egypt as well, and subsequently Libyan troops as well are known from this region. As an aside, if we look at the "commanders" of late Dynasty XX, the connection between the chiefs of the *teheru* and the term "commanders" seems close.

Many scholars have argued that the takeover of the state by the ruling military class occurred at the end of the Amarna Period. This, however, is to misunderstand the ancient society. The Pharaoh was the head of state, a god and a king. He was also the supreme commander. As war leader he learnt the profession of a soldier from early age, and as head of state he was the commander-in-chief. At the end of Dynasty XVIII and into Dynasty XIX military men such as Horemheb and his successor Ramesses I became Pharaohs. This does not automatically imply that the army seized power. Indeed, it is a misreading of the Egyptian structure of monarchy.

When we see the rise of such Pharaohs after Amunhotep IV such as Ay, Horemheb, and Ramesses I, all of whom were military men, we are apt to forget where they came from.[8] All three belonged to prominent families in the land. All had served in the army. Some may have actually fought with their Pharaoh, albeit in a high-ranking position in the army. But the king, as well, was a warrior. True, by the reigns of Amunhotep III and IV the need for continual warfare had greatly decreased. Palestine and Nubia had reached a position of subjugation that allowed the monarchs to avoid personal involvement in a war on a repetitive basis. Nevertheless, this does not mean that either of those two rulers were cowards, pacifists, or men who eschewed combat. Their feats on the battlefield may have been minimal at best – I fear nonexistent – but this was not due to a weakness of heart but rather to the absence of a major enemy.

Although the Egyptian army did not self-consciously seek to take up the reins of power, its influence had increased over the centuries. Horemheb, for example, was as equally adept in administration (he was a vizier) as he was on the battlefield. His importance also lay in the area of personal relationships. He was married to the sister of Nefertity, the wife of Pharaoh Amunhotep IV. Ay, aged when he took over the office of Pharaoh, came from a prominent military family, but one that was intimately connected to the royal family. Even the future Ramesses I, also a warrior, eventually became vizier.

Typically, when discussing the takeover of a civilian state by the military occurs, various gradations of control are examined.[9] The gamut runs from simple persuasion through blackmail, heightens to displacement, and then finally ends up as supplantation. It is worth while to examine these conditions with respect to the question of a possible seizure of power by the military elite in late Dynasty XVIII Egypt. Here, I am referring to the entire military apparatus. As with every social system, the ancient Egyptian war machine had its own rules of entry, its particular hierarchy, its implicit and explicit self-differentiation from another entity (e.g., the officialdom or the priesthood), and its unique definition of self-identity. The heroic ideal that we see frequently in the royal inscriptions can likewise be read in the accounts of the some private biographies (e.g., those of Ahmose son of Ebana and Amunemheb.) But the level of society as a whole, that is to say Pharaonic Egypt in the Late Bronze Age, must be approached critically. The country had a subsistence-based economy containing a thin elite of non-producers. Among the latter were, traditionally, the officials of the state who are best called civilians. The strict differentiation between civilian professionals and army men in the later Ramesside Period became notable in the second half of Dynasty XVIII. Earlier, this was not the case. The growing importance of the chariot arm, the use of hardier horses, and the constant need for permanent garrisons led to this more complex form of the military.

Such a society in which the people of Egypt lived at this time might be best labeled as "proto-dynastic." This term I have borrowed by Samuel Finer in his study of the military class and its effect upon civilian government.[10] He describes the cement of personal loyalty to the state as one where allegiance is shown to the dynasty. There is no social consensus, per se. Hence, there cannot be an active and organized force of the public. Opinion remains traditionally structured and dependent upon family (but not clan) and village communities. At the same time there are elites performing designated services. But the latter are directed to maintaining the king, his family (including both near and distant relatives), the court, the whole apparatus of extraction (taxation in its broadest sense), internal security, and work projects. All of this can be seen from the nascent Old Kingdom onward, and at this level of development soldiers were needed mainly for internal pacification of some internal regions and a few campaigns abroad. In fact, the functions of the earlier army covered diverse activities such as construction and mining expeditions as well as warfare. Later in the Middle Kingdom, and subsequent to the Nubian campaigns of the Pharaohs, troops were used for garrison duty in Nubia. If internecine war broke out, this indicated that Egypt was subject to a collapse of leadership. Especially then, warfare became a necessity and troops were levied in larger numbers than normal.

With the expansion of horizons beyond the limitations of the land, such as we see at the beginning of Dynasty XVIII, the need for an army larger than previously came into being. The wars of the Thebans of Dynasty XVII against the Hyksos were its genesis. Eventually successful at home, the Egyptian state found a reasonably sized army at its fingertips, and one that could also be used to re-conquer its older Nubian territories. But this well-prepared fighting machine could be employed to strike out even further, whence the creation of a vast area of subjected territories. The army served this purpose, although in its wake came administrators, tax masters, accompanying civilians, and even the priesthood. Egyptian temples, it must be mentioned, were built in Asia and Nubia.

The social system of interpersonal relationships among the elite was not as complex as today, nor did it involve a chain of very many people. The ruling class in Dynasty XVIII was small, the members of which either were on close personal terms with one another or were related. The administrators and priesthood were also closely intertwined. The same is true when we add the ingredient of the army or, to be exact, the high officers in the army. Andrea Gnirs' research into the social structure of the military of the first half of Dynasty XVIII has revealed just how interwoven these connections were.[11] For example, a man could rise to great heights in the army, yet he remained dependent upon the importance of his family. These upward mobile army men were able to move laterally into higher positions, from one segment of the state (army) into another (administration).

Throughout most of Dynasty XVIII there was no need for the military to see itself contesting for the highest position in the land. Descent from the male ruler, the Pharaoh, was the only way to kingship. Naturally, if the lineage could not be perpetuated, there would be difficulties, and it is this factor that loomed so greatly at the end of the reign of Amunhotep IV. But even at this point the contest for Pharaonic status was played out among very few families. There was no struggle between civilians and soldiers. The commander-in-chief of the army was the king. His immediate inferiors in the army belonged to the most important families. Most had connections at court and quite a number had male relatives in the officialdom. One might argue that the new demands placed upon Egypt in Asia owing to the growing successes of the Hittites in Syria, a point to which we shall return later, forced the appointment of a military man as king when the old lineage ended. General Horemheb, later vizier, is usually brought forward to support this contention, especially if he was connected to the famous Zannanza affair.[12]

Yet Horemheb's rise to Pharaonic status does not mean that the army won in a contest between officialdom and the military. There was simply no battle for power aligned on an axis of civilian versus military. Rewording Samuel Finer's useful remarks, we may liken the king to a man running a great civilian and military hive, in which the Pharaoh was the Queen Bee, even down to his prerogative of selecting his successor, the latter within defined limits, of course. Because all Egyptian rulers had to be proficient in war, or at least be able to lead the army, Horemheb's advancement makes perfect sense. But he also had been the highest-ranking civilian in the land. As vizier he was expert in the mechanics of civil government. Furthermore, Horemheb came from a very important family – a "right" one. Ay, the successor of Tutankhamun, also a general and vizier, was a member of the royal lineage. The only defect to the latter's "nomination" as Pharaoh was his old age. Nevertheless, the three facets of Ay's persona were enough to enable him to act as ruler. He was acceptable to the ruling elite, although I am sure that all knew that his reign was to be a short one owing to advanced age.

It was necessary that the rule of succession be definite, precise, and strictly observed. Egypt of Dynasty XVIII, however, was not so strongly legalized that the absence of a male heir was explicitly defined. The eldest son of the main wife had precedence, a situation that may have been bolstered earlier in the Late Middle Kingdom when the term "great wife of the king" first came into use.[13] But problems would occur when that woman bore no male heirs. The choice in succession should have devolved upon the sons of lesser wives, but this meant some degree of indecision. Indeed, there was already a crisis at the death of Amunhotep I. Thutmose I was not born of the main wife but of a lesser one. Thutmose III, to examine another case, was not born of Thutmose II's chief wife Hatshepsut, but rather was the offspring of a secondary lady. As Ferraro states in his work on the principles of power, "Like the sovereign, the potential successor must be universally known and recognized without hesitation or difference of opinion."[14] We can see the difficulties that would have occurred at the death of Amunhotep IV and immediately afterwards. A clique, consisting of very few high officials, many at the court, as well as the living members of the royal family – the women – had to determine the succession, or else the possibility of violence would ensue. This did happen, but only later at the close of the XIXth Dynasty.

Of the various possibilities open to political change effected by the military, none of them aptly fits within this type of archaic society. Most certainly, persuasion was one that would automatically come from the highest-ranking generals. But they already belonged to influential families. This I concede, but with the caveat that the army, as a unit, did not really affect the state. It had as of yet no rigid self-image as a corporate entity opposed to the state. In addition, there was no strict legal procedure for transferring power in New Kingdom Egypt that allowed for change in extraordinary circumstances. The crucial decision would have to be made when a dynastic line was about to end or had already ceased. At that point legitimacy had to be carried through by means of some family connection.[15] If not, civil war would probably result.

We can thus dismiss the presence of the common levels of military intervention that modern political scientists list. Blackmail, the first, does not apply to the Egyptian society at the close of Dynasty XVIII or, in fact, previous to this era. There were also no large-scale offensives against the civilian elements of the state. To go higher, there was also no possibility of displacement. The Egyptian military prior to the reign of Horemheb never threatened non-cooperation with the civilian authorities. Likewise they did not fail to defend them against violence. Only supplantation of the civilian regime appears possible, but even here this argument presumes a strict division between a professional army and the state. How could that be? There were no sharp lines drawn between these two presumed different subsystems of the Egyptian elite. There was a Pharaonic regime, and it included civilians and warriors alike.

If one wants to make a comparison of societies later in time, perhaps the warlord kings of feudal Europe can be brought into discussion. Here, at least, a king had to be successful in arms. If not, his retainers, especially the great barons, dukes, and margraves, would be leery of supporting a weakling. Yet this society was so different from Pharaonic Egypt that to suppose a resemblance seems far-fetched. We must therefore return to the roles that the important families played in Egypt.

The rise and fall of powerful land-based families is one well known to the historians of the Late Middle Kingdom and the Second Intermediate Period.[16] Here we see the ever-fluid and always competitive nature of their role. Some of them managed to secure the throne for one of their males but only to see the hopeful dynasty cease in a short period of time. With the re-establishment of the kingship by one family, that of the Theban ruling house in late Dynasty XVII, among which we can place Seqenenre, Kamose, and finally Ahmose, stability had returned. And with the security of a ruling house, the state was solid. But the additional ethos of a warrior king rendered the New Kingdom significantly different from those of earlier times.

At best, we may consider the motive of "national interest" to be the one that impelled the highest level of Pharaonic society at the close of Dynasty XVIII to insure that their Pharaohs had a military background. Tutankhamun, in his Restoration Inscription, places some emphasis upon the lack of Egyptian military success abroad.[17] Naturally, his account is tendentious, but it nonetheless reveals, quite surprisingly, an attitude of failure on the part of the Egyptian state. This feeling was undoubtedly due to the loss of Syria to the Hittites, especially after the successful campaigns of the Hittite king Suppiluliuma in the north. With the defection of Kadesh and Amurru, and the loss of the Levantine ports south to and including Byblos, Egypt no longer had a toe in this region. But an argument proposing that the corporate self-interest of the military played a role in the appointment of a new Pharaoh (Ay, Horemheb, and the later Ramesses I) is too modern a concept.

With the rise of Horemheb to Pharaonic status, and then with his successor, the vizier and general Paramesses, military affairs became quite preponderant. Indeed, from mid Dynasty XVIII to Dynasty XIX the elite sector of the army can be more narrowly pinpointed. In the language of war, for example, the most common word, *seneny*, referred to the "charioteer," and we know of many "chiefs of the charioteers" during this time.[18] The term was borrowed from Asia, indeed it is Hurrian and therefore of Mitannian origin. Again, we are thrown into the area of Syria as a focus for the chariotry division. The shield-bearer, Egyptian *qer'iu*, is derived from another foreign word signifying "shield." This man was the second warrior who stood in the cab of the chariot and protected the "charioteer." Protocols such as "shield-bearer of Pharaoh" or "shield-bearer of his majesty" are common enough. But our examples mainly date from the second half of Dynasty XIX and XX, and at this later period the title "chief of the shield-bearer troops" also occurs, as does "a man of the shield-bearer troops." And even after the fall of the New Kingdom terms such as "shield-bearers and their superiors" also can be found.

A third term, Egyptian *kedjen*, is derived from the Akkadian *guzu*. This word signifies the "chariot driver." First mentioned in the reign of Thutmose III, the *kedjen* appears to have been originally the personal "driver" of a very important official. The designation "first *kedjen* of his majesty" may be found dated to the reign of Amunhotep IV. The simple *kedjen*'s of subaltern status are frequent enough from the reign of Seti I onward. The word *seneny* as a title is unknown after the beginning of the reign of Ramesses II. To be more precise, outside of literary texts or ones with a healthy literary flavoring, *seneny* disappeared as an official designation, and in the texts narrating the Battle of Kadesh under Ramesses II, *seneny* is apparently used as a synonym for "shield-bearer." But how did all three terms connect with a chariot having only two men?

This diachronic evidence can be pieced together. When the pictorial representations show the army on march, one of the chariot soldiers carries a shield and the second is the driver of the vehicle. The *kedjen* is the man who conducts the vehicle and the *qer'iu* is the "shield-bearer." In battle, they both were in the cab and therefore their roles changed somewhat. The XVIIIth Dynasty knew only the *seneny*, "charioteers," whose superiors were the "chiefs of charioteers," and bore the rank of "standard-bearers." It has been remarked that the texts of this period show no distinction between the two types of chariot soldiers: all were *seneny*. From the Amarna Period of late Dynasty XVIII the term *kedjen* was introduced, and later in the Ramesside Period (Dynasties XIX–XX) it became commonplace. By then these warriors were the more important men connected with the chariotry, with the less expert chariot men, or cadets, labeled as *qer'iu*. (The Medieval division between *chevalier* and *écuyer* has been proposed to render the later distinction.) In the course of the Ramesside Period *qer'iu* was applied to the lower-level men of the chariotry and the old term *seneny* disappeared. Such an evolution naturally implies an alteration within the military institution.

I suspect that the development was gradual, occurring with greater and greater force from the end of the reign of Thutmose III until late Dynasty XVIII. By the Amarna Period the marshals, whose military training was with horses, appear very prominent in the historical record. For example, a certain Parennefer was the brother of the treasurer Maya. Both men can be dated to the reign of Tutankhamun and Horemheb. The vizier Paramesses, the later Ramesses I, had a career quite similar to king Ay before the latter was crowned. It is noteworthy that Paramesses' father was a troop commander. Both men were connected to the chariotry and both had become marshals. Although their carriers can be traced with some difficulty, we can note the advance from the position of "overseers of troops" to marshal, and then finally to general. In addition to these warriors, a similar career can be traced for the Amarna generals Nakhtmin and Horemheb. But Paramesses' titles represent a newer form.[19] He was the "first *kedjen* of his majesty," a royal messenger (a diplomat in this case), in charge of the fortress of Sile, and an officer of the archers, all roles that automatically imply a final move to marshal. Paramesses also describes his military career before switching to the final civilian role that he played so importantly. The man was a field commander and, as already noted, the commander of Sile. Hence, he was intimately associated with the northeast. As field commander Paramesses' son, Seti, later Pharaoh Seti I, had been a marshal and commandant of Sile as well. From evidence subsequent to this period both men's military *cursus honorum* were not that common. The position of marshal did not automatically lead to that of general.

In addition, we see both the viceroy of Kush Paser (time of Ay and Horemheb) and his father Amunhotep/Huy connected to the chariotry as well. The son of Paser also held a career of field officer. The continuance of a military career through man, son, and grandson is clear, thus confirming our earlier remarks concerning the importance of the family as a social unit with Pharaonic Egypt. But other families, such as those of Paramesses, were also very important, indeed so powerful that their background in Asiatic careers (commandant of Sile, royal messenger to foreign lands) automatically reveals a thorough grounding in northern affairs, so much needed at the close of the Amarna Period and onward.

Ay, as "god's father" to the ruling lineage, cannot be overlooked. His wife Teye was of extraordinary importance within the Pharaonic house. Ay's intimate connection to the end of the lineage of Pharaoh Ahmose undoubtedly led him to be the successor of Tutankhamun, or at least a legitimate one. The lineage difficulties of Amunhotep IV were the basis for the problems of royal succession, not the desire to provide a pure military rule to the country. Amunhotep IV, having no son, effectively closed one possibility. Tutankhamun, whose relation to the royal family still remains murky, provided no sons to succeed him. Ay was too old and, in fact, had no male heirs. Horemheb, likewise, is not known to have had any living offspring. Clearly, the move to Paramesses was conditioned upon a series of factors, among which we can nominate his military background, but he had a son who also was well versed in war.

In this connection, a brief look at the Ramesside princes of the royal family is worth while to examine on the basis of the titles that the young men held.[20] Not surprisingly, the earlier tradition of Dynasty XVIII was continued. The first son of Ramesses II, Amunherkhepeshef, was a general. He thus followed his father in the same role. Indeed, Ramesses II tells us in his Dedicatory Inscription that when his father was alive he had been chief of the infantry and chariotry. The second son of this Pharaoh, Ramesses, was also a general. The third was a charioteer, a *kedjen*. Montuherkhepeshef, yet another of the king's brood, was a marshal, and even later Merenptah, the eventual successor of Ramesses II, claimed military status as a general. This situation was to continue to middle of Dynasty XX. Two sons of Merenptah, for example, were generals, as was Ramesses III himself. One of the latter's sons was a marshal, as were also Ramesses IV and VI before they became Pharaohs. Additional male offspring of Ramesses III, two in this case, held key positions in the chariotry. Subsequently, we can mention a son of Ramesses IX who was a general, and finally a certain Anchef, the eldest son of Hrihor, who exercised the duty of a marshal. In so far as we have reached the end of the New Kingdom, an era when a different military set-up existed within Egypt, it is best to return to our earlier theme.

Future kings such as Ay and Horemheb were once viziers. Later, even Ramesses II referred to his nonmilitary positions while crown prince, and so did Ramesses III. Future rulers were expected to deal with important civil matters as well as military ones. The Pharaoh was not merely a war leader. In all of the cases listed, as well as others, the princes were connected only with the chariot army of the war machine. This is to be expected because that sector was the elite one. Therefore, it is more accurate to claim that royal sons were expected to be chariot warriors, and such a policy was not just prevalent in late Dynasty XVIII onward. Amunhotep II warred in Asia before his father, Thutmose III, died, and he also boasted of his ability with horses and chariots while still a prince and heir. Prince Wadjmose, the eldest son of Thutmose I, can be brought in as well owing to his versatility with the chariot.[21] Not surprisingly, in the Ramesside story of "The Doomed Prince," set in Dynasty XVIII, the hero calls himself a *seneny*, and thus has a military orientation.[22] In another Ramesside tale, the "Story of the Two Brothers," the king's son becomes Viceroy of Kush and later prince. Here, however, no reference to the chariot arm is presented, although the man's early career remained oriented to the military. In sum, the necessity of leadership on the battlefield continued in full strength throughout the New Kingdom. The Pharaonic ethos included official civil duties at home on the part of the heir apparent, but these nonmilitary roles were preceded by a period of time during which the virile young prince moved up in the chariotry division.

The career of Horemheb is most illuminating because it enables us to trace not only the steps of his career, but also to see in a precise way the growing importance of this military man.[23] Before he was crowned Pharaoh he was a scribe and a chief registrar of recruits. In another important role Horemheb served as the royal messenger, or diplomat, to foreign lands, undoubtedly in the north. In his tomb we see reliefs indicating that he was in charge of the booty from Asia, and these included captured northern enemies. I assume that these functions reflect the continual Hittite aggression in Syria. Unfortunately, precise details are lacking. One of his titles is that of "royal messenger" at the front of his army to the southern and northern lands. (The "his" refers to an unnamed king.) Perhaps Horemheb had served in the army during the attack of Egypt against the Nubians under the reign of Amunhotep IV. This would permit us to link the reference to the south with his title. A fragmentary inscription from Zizinia in modern Alexandria allows us to extend this analysis.[24] The first part refers to Egyptian attacks as far as the "sun disk" (the Aten) shines, clearly indicating an Amarna dating for this reference, and a brief mention of the land of the Hittites points undoubtedly to full-scale warfare in Syria. Subsequent to these murky events, the account refers to a new but unknown king, and Horemheb is referred to as "regent" of the land. That is to say, he then stood in the number two position in Egypt, and was the designated successor to the living Pharaoh. I presume that Ay is meant. In his Saqqara tomb, which was constructed and decorated before Horemheb became Pharaoh, there are clear-cut references to both Asia and Nubia, and the owner indicates that he received numerous captives. But in the Zizinian fragment Horemheb is referred to in terms that leave no doubt that he was a field commander.

We are in the dark with regard to the actual dating of the northern career of Horemheb. It may be supposed that he dealt with the collapse of Egyptian control over Syria, especially in the Amka region in the central zone of that territory. Indeed, the Hittites had gained control over Carchemish from Mitanni, Kadesh and Amurru from the Egyptians, as well as Byblos. But the tomb scenes themselves stress the role of Horemheb as the king's diplomat. There, the man is already the regent, and thus his role was no longer merely that of commander-in-chief or generalissimo.

The enemy captives that are carved in Horemheb's tomb included Asiatics as well as Nubians.[25] In his reliefs that are probably dated to king Tutankhamun, the northerners, with one or two exceptions, are definitely not Hittites. Traditionally, these peoples are shown clean-shaven, unlike the Asiatics with their beards. Their hair is long, their foreheads sloping, and they appear to have puffier faces than the Palestinians or Syrians. Most of the presumed representations of Hittites in Horemheb's tomb appear doubtful. Recent analysis has shown that at least one may have been a *maryannu*, a representative of the elite chariots soldiers in Asia. Indeed, some of the "grooms" depicted in Horemheb's tomb may have been members of this group, but then we have to allow for them being dependents of the luckless Asiatic chiefs who came groveling to the Egyptians. But at least two depictions of Hittites stand out, one being a beardless northerner seen below the Window of Appearances of the king and the second a groveling Asiatic. The other captive northerners are not Hittites.

Can we assume that the Egyptians captured these people during the few years separating Amunhotep IV and Horemheb as king? This seems to be the case, especially when we consider the additional inscriptional evidence from the Memphite tomb of Horemheb in conjunction with the Zizinian fragment. The large number of Asiatics indicates a major push by the Egyptians to reconquer lost territory and to strengthen their control over Palestine if not the coast of Lebanon. A few foreigners in Horemheb's tomb may have been Cretans, possibly indicating some connections with this sea kingdom of the eastern Mediterranean. However, even these figures are hard to specify. Two so-called "mixed Phoenicians" may represent the rules of captured port cities north of Palestine. If so, they would allow us to reconstruct the naval policy of Egypt at this time. But there is no indication in

Horemheb's tomb of a flotilla or even ships. John Darnell has suggested that these ambiguous representations could reflect the increasing problems that Egypt had with sea pirates at this time.[26] From the Amarna Letters we learn that the Sherden were troublesome, although not to the Egyptians. The Nile mouths had, nonetheless, come under closer administration in the reign of Amunhotep III, and from a list of "conquered" foreigners in one of his temples various principalities in Crete and even mainland Greece are mentioned. If one wanted to sum up all of this pictorial evidence of Horemheb in combination with the slim textual sources the result would be tentative, perhaps even disappointing. Suffice it to say that little from a military vantage point can be gleaned solely from the native Egyptian evidence in the man's tomb.

Finally, additional pictorial evidence, probably from the reign of Tutankhamun, may be brought into discussion because it indicates the common theme of king in chariot and sheds welcome light on the continual warfare in the far north at this time.[27] One set of blocks can be discerned that deals with an Asiatic war. The narrative development parallels what we know from Dynasties XIX and XX in so far as various episodes may be discerned: battle, presentation of prisoners and booty to the king, return home, and presentation of the spoil to Amun. The scenes depicting the

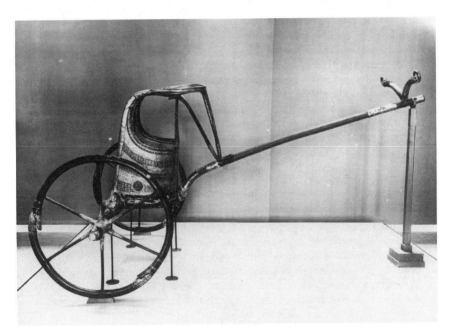

Figure 11.1   Chariot A1 (Obj no. 122). Cairo Musuem JE 61990. Photo The Griffith Institute, Ashmolean Museum, Oxford.

northerners reveal Asiatics and not Hittites. The Pharaoh attacks an enemy citadel, a common pictorial theme of the Ramesside Period, and from the aftermath we can see marching captive soldiers plus horses. On the other hand, two different types of chariot groups are depicted. The Egyptians have two men to their chariots and their vehicles still retain the common six spokes. The better part of a three-man Asiatic chariot is present, thereby allowing us to hypothesize that this conflict took place in the far north, undoubtedly against some of the local supporters of the Hittites.[28] Moreover, two separate types of enemies are present. In addition to the common Canaanite types there are some that resemble Syrian or Hurro-Mitannians.[29] All in all, we may hypothesize that yet another undated conflict took place in Syria, when the Pharaoh once more marched out with his army. At this time, however, the Hittite monarch did not engage his foe personally but instead left the resistance in the hands of his Syrian allies.[30]

EXCURSUS

1. The fully developed chariot–footsoldier Egyptian army was present at the end of the XVIIIth Dynasty. Gnirs' *Militär und Gesellschaft*, a work frequently cited in this volume, will provide the reader with a wealth of information on this subject. She advances new and compelling data to refine much of which Schulman presented in his "Some Observations on the Military Background of the Amarna Period," *Journal of the American Research Center in Egypt* 3 (1964), 51–69. Hence, we are better able to link the rise of field marshals (in the chariotry division) with the royal personages at the end of Dynasty XVIII and the new ruling house of the XIXth.

Schulman, who continued the direction of research first presented by Helck in 1939 (*Der Einfluß der Militärführer*), nonetheless felt that "there was no break in the Amarna period with the earlier military traditions of the Dynasty" (p. 51). Because this interpretation has been challenged by Gnirs, I feel that his following comments need to be rewritten in a more circumscribed sense: "the army . . . not only determined the royal policies, but installed its own leaders on the throne." This chapter and the preceding ones have presented reasons for qualifying much of this theory; see in particular excursus 2 to chapter 4.

Marc Gabolde, in his volume, *D'Akhenaton à Toutânkhamon*, Boccard, Paris (1998), views the late period of Akhenaton's reign and the opening years of his successors in a detailed and considerate perspective, one that includes both the problems of royal succession as well as the military situation in Asia. M. Eaton-Krauss and Rolf Krauss, however, have written a critical review of the work in *Bibliotheca Orientalis* 58 (2001), 91–7, which nevertheless includes many positive remarks. Murnane's study, "The End of the Amarna Period Once Again," *Orientalistische Literaturzeitung* 96 (2001), 9–22, is a highly judicious commentary.

THE INFLUENCE OF THE EGYPTIAN MILITARY

2.   Gabolde's study should be consulted with the more general analysis of Helck, *Politische Gegensätze im alten Ägypten*, a work that I discussed in excursus 3 to chapter 4. He argued that the settlements of soldiers formed a counterweight to the officialdom already at the beginning of Dynasty XVIII (p. 47), and by the reign of Ay, the immediate predecessor of Horemheb, a "Soldatenkaisertum" came into being (p. 63). This analysis I find too one-sided. To view the military corporation as the "motor of the state" is to overemphasize the differences of profession and career within the New Kingdom. Gnirs, for example, has presented a more nuanced approach. While agreeing with Schulman and to a lesser degree with Helck, I find no sharp differentiation between the elite officer class of the Egyptian war machine and the royalty. The society of the Nile Valley was run by an interconnected body of professional men, both civilian and military, a point well presented by Gnirs. Granted that the chariot arm "took off" in the second half of Dynasty XVIII. It did not, however, become a closed cast that eventually was able to "elect" a Pharaoh. Let us not forget general Horemheb's nonmilitary background; the same may be said for king Ay.

3.   A second point emphasized by Helck in his *Politische Gegensätze* is an assumed conflict between conservatives and progressives within Egyptian society of the New Kingdom. To a lesser degree this interpretation may be found in his study, "Überlegungen zur Geschichte der 18. Dynastie," *Oriens Antiquus* 8 (1969), 281–327. The contention of this scholar was that among the court elite a sharp division existed between those men who viewed Egyptian society, and in particular foreign affairs, with a more global and aggressive perspective than those whom we could call "stay-at-homes." Here, too, we come upon too modern an interpretation. I prefer to interpret any possible conflict with regard to warfare in Asia or Nubia as resting not upon defined ideologies, but rather more upon chance, individual career patterns, the motive of "liberation" (late Dynasty XVII–early Dynasty XVIII), and the rapid if not easy success of Egyptian arms abroad under Amunhotep I, Thutmose I, and even Thutmose III. Later, it was necessary for Egypt to defend and consolidate her newly won territories, and from that point of time a relatively simple administrative system was put in place in Asia. (See Na'aman's studies that I have cited in previous chapters.)

Sharply defined social groups that, by their individuality, see themselves in conflict with one another did belong to Pharaonic society in Dynasty XVIII. I am fully in agreement with many researchers who have placed emphasis on the growing military aspect of the early New Kingdom and its ramifications within native society. On the other hand, the political level of Egypt had yet to approach a complex system in which various social groups were large and powerful enough to view themselves in latent opposition to each other, and to have sharply differentiated ideological goals. To do so is, I believe, to fall into an anachronistic interpretation that draws parallels from modern times (ca. AD 1500 onward) to the remote past. It is best to view Dynasty XVIII society as one in which some groups (bureaucracy/officialdom; priesthood; military) existed, and when the war machine had become important. To consider such

183

corporations unified entities capable of wresting the power of the land from civilians is to stretch the data.

At the risk of repeating myself, all Pharaohs were war leaders. Horemheb and Paramesses, the future Ramesses I, fit perfectly into this pattern. Indeed, both can be viewed as close parallels to Seqenenre and Kamose many centuries earlier, both of whom lived at a time when a new lineage was about to come into being with the warrior-king Ahmose. At the close of Dynasty XVIII Egypt needed firm and capable leadership at a time when it had lost territory in Syria to the Hittites during the reign of Amunhotep IV. Horemheb, who did not have a male heir to succeed him, was the most likely candidate owing to his connections at court, his ability as an administrator (vizier), and his early career in the army as general.

For the situation of New Kingdom kingship, two useful studies may be found in David O'Connor and David Silverman, eds., *Ancient Egyptian Kingship*, E. J. Brill, Leiden, New York, and Cologne (1995): Redford, "The Concept of Kingship during the Eighteenth Dynasty," 157–84; and Murnane, "The Kingship of the Nineteenth Dynasty: A Study in the Resilience of an Institution," 185–217.

NOTES

1 Na'aman, *The Political Disposition and Historical Development of Eretz-Israel According to the Amarna Letters*, chapter VII; and Murnane, *The Road to Kadesh*, appendix 6 ("Syria in the Amarna Age: Problems and Perspectives").
2 Ibid., chapter VI.
3 Sethe, *Urkunden der 18. Dynastie*, 36.13; Breasted, *Ancient Records of Egypt* II, 51. Note as well Raphael Giveon, *Les bédouins Shosou des documents égyptiens*, E. J. Brill, Leiden (1971); and the review of this work by William A. Ward, "The Shasu 'Bedouin'," *Journal of the Economic and Social History of the Orient* 15 (1972), 35–60. Murnane has provided a new interpretation of the Shasu during the reign of Seti I in his *The Road to Kadesh*, 55–9; see also Redford, *Egypt, Canaan, and Israel in Ancient Times*, 269–75.
4 Sethe, *Urkunden der 18. Dynastie*, 890.14–15; Breasted, *Ancient Records of Egypt* II, 231; and Gardiner, *Ancient Egyptian Onomastica* I, 155*–6*.
5 Der Manuelian, *Studies in the Reign of Amenophis II*, 76–7.
6 Gnirs, *Militär und Gesellschaft*, 17–28, especially p. 21. On the marshals at this time, see pp. 29–31.
7 Ibid., 57–8.
8 Ibid., 44–53 (regarding general Horemheb, the later Pharaoh), 69–71, and 91–116; see excursus 1 to chapter 1.
9 I can refer to Finer, *The Man on Horseback*, for these details.
10 Ibid., chapter Nine. He separates countries of "low minimal culture" from those of "minimum political culture." But his analysis covers only societies "in transition from a static and transitional culture" to a more dynamic one. Ancient Egypt, even in the New Kingdom, was quite different than those

countries discussed by Finer. Nonetheless, we can adhere to his further remarks concerning those societies which "are placid, coherent and still predominantly traditionalist . . . which indulge their ruling élites in their struggle for power without feeling at all involved in it." See the excursus to this chapter.

Ancient Egypt formed one land in which the "antediluvian class" operates; see Finer's remarks in note 2 to p. 89 concerning these "proto-dynastic societies." The "public, as an active and organized force, does not exist."

11 *Militär und Gesellschaft,* especially pp. 40–79.

12 In this case scholars have assumed that general (or possibly vizier) Horemheb supported the more nationalistic sectors in Egypt who were opposed to the Egyptian queen's desire to marry the son of the Hittite king Suppiluliuma after the death of her husband. See the helpful analysis of Van Dijk. *The New Kingdom Necropolis of Memphis,* 48–54, who, however, proceeds to speculate beyond what the evidence warrants. I adhere to the present scholarly opinion as identify the queen as Tutankhamun's wife, Ankhesenpaamun.

13 Lana Troy, *Patterns of Queenship in ancient Egyptian myth and history,* Almqvist and Wiksell, Uppsala (1986), 83, 102, 104, and cases C2/5 (with *wrt*).

14 Guglielmo Ferrero, *The Principles of Power. The Great Political Crises of History,* Theodore R. Jaeckel, trs., G. P. Putnam's Sons, New York (1942), 147.

15 Ibid.

16 Ryholt, *The Political Situation in Egypt during the Second Intermediate Period,* Part III.

17 Helck, *Urkunden der 18. Dynastie,* 2025–32; John Bennett, "The Restoration Inscription of Tut'ankhamun," *Journal of Egyptian Archaeology* 25 (1939), 8–15; Benedict G. Davies, *Egyptian Historical Records of the Later Eighteenth Dynasty,* fasc. 6, Aris and Phillips, Warminster (1995), 30–3; Gabolde, "Ay, Toutankhamon et les martelages de la Stèle de la Restauration de Karnak (CG 34183)," *Bulletin de la Société Égyptologie de Genève* 11 (1987), 37–61; and Murnane, *Texts from the Amarna Period of Egypt,* Scholars Press, Atlanta (1995), 212–14.

For evidence of warfare in Asia and Nubia under Tutankhamun, see Johnson, *An Asiatic Battle Scene of Tutankhamun from Thebes,* and our comments in the following chapter.

18 For these terms: Gnirs, *Militär und Gesellschaft,* 19–23; Schulman, "The Egyptian Chariotry: A Reexamination," *Journal of the American Research Center in Egypt* 2 (1963), 75–98, and Military *Rank, Title and Organization in the Egyptian New Kingdom,* 59–62 (*seneny*), 67–8 (*qer'iu* and *guzu*); with Yoyotte and Lopez, "L'organisation de l'armée et les titulaires de soldats au nouvel empire égyptien," *Bibliotheca Orientalis* (1969), 10–11.

The term *seneny,* either employed alone or with "*seneny* of his majesty," covers almost all of the reigns of Dynasty XVIII. Its first occurrence is under Thutmose I.

19 Gnirs, *Militär und Gesellschaft,* 67–70; and Eugene Cruz-Uribe, "The Father of Ramses I: OI 11456," *Journal of Near Eastern Studies* 37 (1978), 237–44, for an analysis of this man's family.

20 Marjorie M. Fischer, *The Sons of Ramesses II,* Harrassowitz, Wiesbaden (2001), provides an up-to-date study of the numerous male offspring of Ramesses II and covers the connections between this man and his father Seti I.

21 Sethe, *Urkunden der 18. Dynastie*, 91; and Breasted, *Ancient Records of Egypt* II, 321.

22 For this literary composition as well as the following, see Lichtheim, *Ancient Egyptian Literature* II, 200–14.
   Helck provided a study of the Doomed Prince in "Die Erzählung von Verwunschenen Prinzen," in Jürgen Osing and Günter Dreyer, eds., *Form und Maß. Beiträge zur Literatur, Sprache und Kunst des alten Ägypten. Festschrift für Gerhard Fecht zum 65. Geburtstag am 6. Februar 1987*, Harrassowitz, Wiesbaden (1987), 218–25. Although our copy of the composition was written down at the beginning of Dynasty XIX, the mention of the king of Naharain (Mitanni) places the narrative of the tale to the second half of the preceding Dynasty.

23 Van Dijk, *The New Kingdom Necropolis of Memphis*, chapter 1; and Gnirs, *Militär und Gesellschaft*, 41, 44–51. The basic study of the man in the context of his northern tomb at Saqqara is by Geoffrey Thorndike Martin, *The Memphite Tomb of Horemheb. Commander-in-Chief of Tut'ankhamun* I, Egypt Exploration Society, London (1989).

24 Gnirs, *Militär und Gesellschaft*, 46–7.

25 John Coleman Darnell, "Supposed Depictions of Hittites in the Amarna Period," *Studien zur altägyptischen Kultur* 18 (1991), 113–40, discusses the representations of foreigners in Horemheb's Saqqara tomb.

26 Ibid.

27 Johnson, *An Asiatic Battle Scene of Tutankhamun from Thebes*. He argues that the blocks under consideration originally came from the king's mortuary temple, probably on the west bank of Thebes. Pages 59–64 are crucial for this discussion.

28 The Hittites are well known to have employed a three man to a chariot system at the battle of Kadesh, dated to the fifth regnal year of Ramesses II (Dynasty XIX); see chapter 13. Notes 16–17 in chapter 12 refer to Beal's unproven hypothesis that this arrangement occurred only after the reign of Seti I.

29 Ibid., 59–60.

30 Yet the presence of a three-man chariot implies that Hittite assistance was forthcoming.

12

EARLY DYNASTY XIX

The next phase of the Egyptian war machine can be reconstructed owing to the detailed pictorial evidence of Seti I.[1] On the northern exterior wall of the Hypostyle Court at Karnak, between Pylons II and III, a series of six registers present his wars against Asia and Libya. The accompanying inscriptions are mere captions, although they help us to focus attention upon the reliefs. The organization is neatly divided into three registers on the left (east) and three on the right (west), with a doorway located in the middle. Known to scholars for a long period of time, this evidence is fundamental in evaluating the early Ramesside approach to warfare. Each register may indicate a solitary campaign; there are, however, some difficulties with this interpretation. To read the entire system has also been difficult, but it is now agreed that one proceeds from bottom up. We must begin with the dates of regnal year one in the lowest register to the left. There are no others. Hence, it is difficult to ascertain when the other five wars took place, although given an eleven-year reign for Seti, and additional evidence that shall be covered later, it seems reasonable that these wars ended in regnal year six of Seti or thereabouts.

Before proceeding with a strategic analysis of these campaigns a brief art historical background is necessary. Until recently, it was argued that battle reliefs became one of the major ways that a Pharaoh could broadcast his wars, and that this policy, in contrast to the narrative textual approach of Dynasty XVIII, took over in the Ramesside Period.[2] But this opinion was based upon the scanty war material hitherto known from the earlier time. With the discovery of Ahmose's battle reliefs, the reevaluation of those of Thutmose II, the publication of blocks of Amunhotep II and those of Tutankhamun, it is now clear that all the standard artistic practices of Dynasties XIX and XX were planned and executed considerably earlier. Seti I, Ramesses II, Merenptah, and Ramesses III followed the practice of adhering to a standard repertoire of Pharaoh preparing for war, mustering his army, advancing against the enemy, combating his foe, returning (usually from Asia), and presenting his spoils to the gods of Thebes (Amun in particular). Constraints of space in conjunction with the idiosyncrasies of the master designer or Pharaoh meant that some of these portions could be omitted. There was no rule that all be incorporated into the final product. Finally, we should not forget that often large spaces on various temple walls were available for carving, and when the heroic nature of the reigning Pharaoh, so uppermost in the royal ideology, had to be "published," the blank spaces could be filled with numerous scenes of battle. Thus side by side with the royal narrative there existed a second means of presenting a war, the pictorial record.

At the same time we witness a growing development of war-like stories and tales. It is from the Ramesside Period that such texts as "The Doomed Prince" or "The Capture of Joppa" are known.[3] Additional military accounts on papyri have come down to us from the same era, and I can mention a fragmentary tale set in the reign of Thutmose III. One newly published papyrus narrative deals with a war against the Libyans; it probably refers to a campaign of Ramesses III. Combined with this literary evidence, we also have various reflexes of military affairs. The so-called "Testament of Ramesses IV," a gigantic papyrus document dated to Ramesses IV, refers to the past military activities of his father, Ramesses III.[4] Others could be added, especially as many royal narrative accounts in hieroglyphic betoken a strong literary interest. All in all, it would appear that in Dynasties XIX and XX there was a strong interest in military accounts of a literary nature. But whether this is simply a reflection of the dearth of similar material dated to Dynasty XVIII that refers to war is another matter. As with the presumed development of pictorial military art of the Ramesside Period, we must caution ourselves not to over-interpret the sources. Much may have been lost, especially if it was originally written on papyrus, a very fragile medium.

With this background to the sources at hand, let us now turn to Seti's war reliefs.[5] The lowest resister on the left twice refers to a campaign in the king's first year. Evidently, the newly crowned Pharaoh wished to combat his foes as quickly as possible. In this case the king is depicted leaving Egypt at the border fortress of Sile. This was a common motif; see, for example the beginning of the Megiddo campaign of Thutmose III. Seti then traversed the inhospitable Sinai. Forts and wells are listed, and the latter prove that the Egyptians depended upon water supplies in this region as has been surmised earlier. The inscriptions are brief and the captions often purely rhetorical; the reliefs tell all. Seti advances with his army. He receives the "tribute" of one town whose name is now lost. We note the name of his horse, also common as well in war reliefs of Ramesses II and later. King, royal chariot, and his equids are paramount, as befits the chariot orientation of the day.

The first enemy encountered was the ever-present Shasu, the seminomadic marauders and troublesome tribal units that operated on the fringes of civilization.[6] They have no horses and chariots, and most assuredly posed no major threat to the Pharaoh and his army. At this time Seti was marching north to Gaza, and I suspect that he did not intend to defeat only these peoples. The focus of the campaign, its strategic goal, must have been somewhere else, otherwise why travel north just to Gaza (the city of Pa-Canaan mentioned later) and then return? I feel that this register does not tell the whole story.

According to Seti's relief, the zone in which the Shasu operated lay between Sile and the city of Pa-Canaan. The Shasu could interfere with the mobility of the army but not destroy it. Hence, both overtly and dramatically, this record of victory indicates an army of an advanced state smashing a minor foe. The enemy could have caused a great deal of trouble, but it lacked the effective war material of an urban society. Perhaps their numbers should be considered. Unfortunately, in this case the accompanying text and reliefs are silent. We only view the king shooting his arrow into a miserable foe.

Further along in the same register a more important battle took place, this time outside of Pa-Canaan. It is generally assumed that the locality was Gaza. The account is still dated to year one, and the Shasu again are mentioned. At this point we must run our eye to the right (west) where the triumphal return of the king to Egypt is depicted. Following upon it comes the presentation of the captives and booty to Amun of Karnak.

Pictorially, the organization of the campaign is divided into two portions. The advance into the Sinai commences in the middle of the first register. It continues eastward, or to the left, and turns around the corner. There are three such scenes. The two scenes that depict the return and presentation run from the middle to the right and end at a topographic list of captured lands that flank the doorway. The movement of the figures indicates the direction of the narrative: one follows the right or left depending upon the action, but there is no divider marking the division. Perhaps the right-facing king and captives were meant to literally enter the door to the Hypostyle Court. If this hypothesis is followed, then at least the double direction makes perfect sense: outward or away from the entrance denotes the advance, and inward or rightward to the doorway betokens the return.

The greatest difficulty of interpretation arises in connection to a historical analysis of these reliefs.[7] The second register presents Seti already in Asia, first against Yeno'am, close to the Trans-Jordan, and later in the Lebanon. Because this group is separate from the first, many have argued that it depicts a campaign separate from that of the first. I do not believe that this conclusion is without difficulties. The main reason for this comes from at least one small freestanding stela that the Pharaoh had set up at Beth Shan, not far from Yeno'am.[8] The account is dated to regnal year one, the third month of harvest, day 1. Allowing for some uncertainties in the absolute chronology of this time, we can fix the time at the conclusion of his first regnal year to the early portion of April. This temporal setting must imply that early to middle of March (the latter at the latest) the king set out from

Egypt, because Beth Shan is located far to the east in Palestine. We probably should assume that Seti made no prolonged halts on the way, either at
cities or towns, or in the field.

The narrative portion of the stela is relatively short. A report was presented to Seti on the day that the inscription designates. The center of
the foe was in Hamath, close by to Beth Shan. The enemy seized Beth
Shan and united themselves with "those of Pella," an additional city in the
vicinity. As a result, the prince of Rehob was prevented from going out.
Then Seti replied by sending his division, "Amun-Powerful-of-Bows,"
against Hamath. His division of Pre was directed to move against Beth
Shan, and that of Seth against Yeno'am. The results were completely
successful according to the account.

Nowhere in this short narration do we learn where, exactly, was the
Pharaoh. I think that any attempt to argue that he was near to Beth Shan
needs conclusive evidence. But the mention of the king's three divisions –
we shall hear of four in Ramesses II's time – provides us with some clues.
These were the core groups, although a fourth may have remained with
their monarch. Seti realized that the disturbances were threatening his control over the eastern sector of Palestine, and so acted quickly to quell the
revolt. It was, nonetheless, local in so far as no outside assistance is indicated. It is quite possible that the king found out these things when he was
in the middle of the country, say at Megiddo. Clearly, he had taken a land
journey northward.[9]

Yeno'am is also mentioned in register two on the left side of his Karnak
war monument. Is this mere coincidence or were there two separate campaigns to the Beth Shan region? Before proceeding, let us survey that
portion of the war record. We are now at the extreme west portion of the
outer wall: the king this time charges against Yeno'am, holding two foes in
one hand. Hyperbole, to be sure, but the presence of Seti can be used as
an argument that he was present. The Pharaoh directed an attack against
the stronghold. In the Beth Shan Stela we saw that he sent his three
divisions to this region but the account is unclear whether he went there or
not, or whether he was present but let his divisions do all of the carnage.
Indeed, this dated Beth Shan text does not mention Yeno'am at all.

Although the king was in East Palestine, we later find him far north in the
Lebanon. This scene is on the eastern side of the north wing in the second
register, and around the corner. One fortress is named. There are four
chiefs who cut timber for Seti while others, the local princes, render
homage to him. At the right front side the expected return of Pharaoh is
indicated, and there is a second presentation scene. The Theban triad of
Amun, his consort Mut, and their son Khonsu are present as, in fact, they
were below in the first register.

How did the king move to Lebanon?[10] Since he is earlier located at
Yeno'am we must presume that his journey was by foot, possibly across to

Megiddo and then north until he reached the coastal road, the Via Maris. But the Lebanese scene is a peaceful one, and should indicate that Seti had begun to prepare his harbors in the Levant for an inland attack, just as Thutmose III did many years ago.

There are many difficulties in reconstructing the extent of the campaign depicted in the second register, not the least of which is the supposition that it must have taken place after the year one campaign carved just below. Let us examine the strategic situation:

Two Campaigns Hypothesis

A. Year One
1. This rests mainly upon the division of registers, i.e., one register equals one war.
2. The First Beth Shan Stela appears to belong to the year one campaign even though the Karnak reliefs ignore the area of conflict recounted in the small inscription. Because the inscription states that the king sent his divisions to this area, he may not have been there at all.
3. In the reliefs that war effort ended at Gaza or thereabouts, if the equation of Pa-Canaan = Gaza is accepted.
4. The enemy were Shasu, bedouin types, who were not as technologically able as the Egyptians.
5. The presentation scene in register one refers to the Shasu. But note that the land of Retjenu is referred to as well as princes. The Shasu are depicted (with captions) separate from the other northerners.
6. There is a separate return and presentation scene for this war, and year one is recorded once more.
7. The first register is the only one with regnal year dates (year one).
8. Present in that register, both in text and depiction, is Mehy, whose figure was later replaced by a prince.[11] In the second register an original person was replaced by Mehy, only to be later altered into a titular fan-bearer.
9. The horse in the lower register bears a name different from that in the second. In my opinion, this seemingly unimportant fact may very well prove that the two registers do not belong together.

B. Year X
1. The war went to the area near Beth Shan, but the only city mentioned is Yeno'am.
2. The king may have gone on foot and not by ship to the Lebanon. This cross-country journey is very unusual. If correct, this is the first indication of such travel by a king of Egypt in Palestine. On the other hand, was the king really in Lebanon? Artistic license may call into question his presence there.

3. Connected with the war may be the account on a second stela from Beth Shan.[12] The date is lost, however. But the account deals with the Apiru who also operated on the borders of Egyptian-held territory. Thus, the area of Beth Shan fits perfectly with the enemy. The account is decidedly in variance with the historical record of the First Beth Shan Stela.

4. The presentation scene refers to the foreign land of Retjenu and princes are also referred to. There is no mention of the Shasu.

But this evidence, though strong, contains some problems. First, there is the strategic situation. Was Seti merely content to smash the luckless Shasu at or in the vicinity of Gaza and avoided advancing further? If so, is this a "real campaign"? It would have been short, restricted to a small region, and not coordinated with any other. William Murnane hypothesized that this short war was preceded by one under Ramesses I, Seti's father, during which he fought against the Fenchu Lands, i.e., Lebanon.[13] He also felt that the year-one campaign was solely concentrated upon the Shasu.

Why was the war of such a short duration? And if it was not, why is Beth Shan and the surrounding area that included Yeno'am not covered in the first register at Karnak? Moreover, why is register one the only section in which we have a specific regnal date? Did it also refer to the middle register where Yeno'am appears? Complicating the scenario is the mention of Yeno'am in the First Beth Shan Stela as well as in the second register (east side) of the Karnak reliefs. If they do not belong together then we must assume further outbreaks in the same region, a point indicated in the second stela at the same site.

One way out of the dilemma is to posit the first campaign of year one as having taken place soon after the king's coronation. He became Pharaoh at the end of the eleventh civil month of the Egyptian year. A short Shasu campaign took place soon after the coronation. This can be argued, and a useful parallel can be drawn from the commencement of the reign of Thutmose III as sole king after the death of Hatshepsut, his stepmother who also ruled with him for a long time. Approximately 85 days after her death Thutmose III was ready at Sile to march into Asia. Evidently, all war preparations had been made during the final months of the life of the queen.

If this parallel is accepted, Seti I could have marched from Sile north simply to curb the local yet threatening disturbances caused by the Shasu. Subsequently, he then moved into Palestine whole-heartedly at the close of his first regnal year. The evidence for this derives from the First Beth Shan Stela which is dated to the tenth day of the third month of harvest, not many days before his second regnal year began. With this hypothesis we can at least understand better the limited nature of the Shasu campaign. I have no qualms about connecting the Second Beth Shan

192

Stela with the same encounter, although this inscription can be used to argue the other case.

A further alternative is that the Shasu encounter actually took place under Ramesses I. Murnane was the first to raise the possibility that the Shasu might have been attacked when Seti was the crown prince, regent, and commander-in-chief of the army, basing his reasons on a few key sentences in a lengthy dedicatory stela of the king found at Abydos.[14] There, rebellious Fenchu lands (Lebanon) are mentioned in addition to fractious foreign peoples. Do these oblique remarks refer to yet another Asiatic campaign undertaken by Seti occurring before he was crowned, and do they then relate to the relatively minor Shasu campaign?

These complications arise because the Karnak material is undated except for the first register on the left (east side of the north wall). But it is perturbing that the king is depicted only as far as Pa-Canaan and not placed in the center of Palestine at Beth Shan. This should be expected if the aforementioned first stela belongs to this war. Otherwise, the inscription may be connected with register two. If so, the second campaign would have lasted some months longer than the first, perhaps over a half-year. But we must then hypothesize that Seti campaigned to Yeno'am, as Karnak reveals, and also marched to the Lebanon. Marcus Müller felt that the structure of the scenes indicated that the first register and the second belong together, if only to allow a resolution of the Yeno'am conundrum.[15] Speculating further, some may feel that Seti never reached the area of Beth Shan in his first year, preferring instead to send his three divisions and remaining at Gaza. When the Second Beth Shan Stela was carved must remain open, although I prefer it to be connected to Seti's march into Yeno'am as depicted in the middle register on the east.

Seen together, the two registers indicate the strategic aim of Seti I soon after he became king. The king's intent is not difficult to ascertain. He first dealt with troubles that affected the well-being of his empire, namely the Shasu and the difficulties in the Beth Shan region. If the tenor of these accounts and the accompanying stela as well is taken into consideration, then it would appear that the local princes found it very hard not to request Egyptian assistance. If the two-campaign position is argued, then these incursions and attacks appear to have been more serious than hitherto expected. This may have been why Seti brought into play a major army comprising of at least three divisions.

The king's subsequent march to the Lebanon is also troublesome. True, it fits neatly with the presumed grand strategy of settling disturbances in Palestine and then preparing the northern port cities – all to make ready a major campaign in central Syria, Amurru in particular (see below). But how did he get there? With Thutmose III the reasonable supposition is that the king went on at least one occasion with his flotilla, but further reinforcements could have been sent northward by land. In the case of Seti we must

Figure 12.1 Seti I against the Libyans [Thebes, Karnak: Exterior of north wall to Hypostyle Court]. *The Battle Reliefs of King Sety I* by the Epigraphic Survey. The University of Chicago Oriental Institute Publications, vol. 107. Reliefs and Inscriptions at Karnak, vol. 4, 1986, pl. 28/29. Courtesy of the Oriental Institute of the University of Chicago.

physically move him overland from Yeno'am to Lebanon. As noted earlier, however, the pictorial representation idealizes the submission of Lebanon through the image of the Pharaoh, but he may not actually have been there. Because "Upper Retjenu" is also mentioned within the short captions of presentation, evidently some of the local princes in this region recognized the might of Egypt. Unfortunately, the upshot of this matter cannot be immediately discerned because the third register on the left is lost.

We must therefore turn to the right (west side) and examine the scenes at the bottom. Here, we are once more placed in Asia. It is as if the march from Sile depicted on the left is assumed to apply for all subsequent journeys of the king. The new enemy was the Hittites, and their defeat represented a major turning point in the foreign relations of Egypt. Under their king Suppiluliuma they took Amurru at the close of Dynasty XVIII. Seti appears to have finally avenged the loss in that region. But in the key scene the superhuman Hittite enemy is most definitely not the king of the Hittites nor, I should emphasize, his son and viceroy who resided at Carchemish.[16] It is equally impossible to determine whether or not the man was yet another Hittite commander stationed at Aleppo. The king's horse, interestingly enough, is not the same as the one named in the year one campaign. Nor is the animal identical to the one in the second register on the left. (The latter's name was recarved and the superimposed name is a new one. However, neither is identical to the horse in the Hittite scene.)

For some students of Hittite military affairs this scene is a crucial one as it reveals a system of two Hittites per chariot.[17] Because it is a well-known fact that at the Battle of Kadesh Muwatallis, Ramesses II's opponent, fought with three men to a chariot, it might appear that there was a change in tactics by the enemy from the reign of Seti I to that of Ramesses II. The presentation scene specifically mentions Hittites. Indeed, they are to be found willy-nilly in the scene of the king's victory. The encounter was not between Seti and only the Syrian allies of the Hittites. The accompanying scene also makes this explicit. I presume that the combat took place on an open plain in Syria, but any further specification must remain speculative. One final point is worth stressing. The captives were brought back to "fill the workhouse" of Amun. That is to say, they now would be serf workers in the greatest temple in Egypt. It may be noteworthy that this is not recorded in the previous two extant registers to the left.

Previous to the conflict the Egyptian army must have advanced into Syria. Wars in this territory were frequent, as also may be seen in the topmost register on the right side. There, Seti I attacks and defeats the enemy outside Kadesh.[18] But a better parallel may be seen in the depictions of the copious wars of Ramesses II subsequent to his unsuccessful campaign to retake the same city. The Pharaoh was back again in Syria on at least two subsequent occasions. They proved to have no end, mainly because the local Syrian princes in that region lived close to the Hittite sphere of influence

Figure 12.2 Seti I against the Hittites [Thebes, Karnak: Exterior of north wall to Hypostyle Court]. *The Battle Reliefs of King Sety I* by the Epigraphic Survey. The University of Chicago Oriental Institute Publications, vol. 107. Reliefs and Inscriptions at Karnak, vol. 4, 1986, pl. 34/35. Courtesy of the Oriental Institute of the University of Chicago.

if not within it. Ugarit, an independent port city north on the Levantine coast, remained loyal to the Hittites. Moreover, the foe could send his troops south with little delay, either from Carchemish or from Aleppo. For these reasons the Egyptians were placed at a strategically geographic disadvantage in Syria.

The order of progression led up to Kadesh. We can therefore assume that Seti first struck in Amurru from his base in the Lebanon and, quite probably, inland through Palestine. Most certainly, Ramesses II utilized a two-pronged advance to Kadesh in his fifth regnal year, allowing four major divisions to march with him but also keeping a fifth separate. The latter moved across Syria from west to east. The reason why he and his father followed identical military tactics can be seen in the terrain of the area as well as in the strategic necessity of capturing Kadesh. That city lay in the middle of the Beqa Valley and controlled the road going northward to Aleppo and Carchemish. Earlier, Thutmose III had secured its submission before marching into Mitanni even though his trans-Euphratean campaign saw him avoiding that region until the north was effectively brought into submission. But the control of the Lebanese seaports had been reduced to such a degree that Seti and his son were forced to concentrate on lengthy inland marches.

A Libyan war separates the two Syrian wars of Seti.[19] Here the enemy is labeled by a traditional and age-old ethnic term, Tehenu, and if only for this reason the details of the campaign are unclear. We see Seti spearing the chief and not shooting him dead with his gigantic bow and arrow. Unfortunately, the captions include few additional details. Significantly, earlier under Amunhotep III a group of Libyan tribes, the Meshwesh, first appear.[20] In Dynasty XIX they and another new tribal entity, the Libu (whence the modern term Libya), became very troublesome to the Egyptians. Indeed, it has been remarked that these Libyans sought to settle in the fertile lands of the north where they could remain with their cattle, which they brought along with them.

Causes for the Libyan threat are generally considered to be climatic, but also overcrowding has to be considered to have been an impetus. The warfare of the Egyptians did not change despite the threat of this new enemy. All that was needed were troops and plenty of them. But the demand for more soldiers and the need to have a permanent army stationed somewhere on the northwest were not easy to fulfill. The second requirement meant that a series of guard-posts or garrisons would have to be built, a project completed during the later years of Seti's son, Ramesses II.[21] But fortresses merely delay rather than block infiltration. Indeed, the Libyans were able to circumvent these permanent control points near the end of Dynasty XIX. But the size of the army had to be expanded, and this must have placed a great expense upon the state. Perhaps for this reason we hear more and more at this time of Sherden "mercenaries" working for the

Egyptian war machine, both within Egypt and outside. Then too, let us not forget that with the foundation of Dynasty XIX the capital was moved north from Memphis to Avaris in the East Delta. Owing to this, the most important city of Egypt, at least politically, could be under direct threat if the Libyans managed to reach the area around Memphis and Heliopolis in the Central Delta.

Two additional factors relating to pictorial reliefs such as Seti's, both of which apply to texts as well, must be recognized. First, there is always a lag between a new invention and its wholesale use. Second, there is likewise a further delay in its presence within pictures. It is difficult to say which side of the historical record is more conservative. Sometimes the literature shows great reluctance to embrace new words or new ideas. Ideology as well definitely plays a key factor. On the other hand, the innate dominance of a "Classical" style hindered the appearance of new motifs, sudden changes in styles, and the like. Despite the wealth of information that is presented by these Ramesside war reliefs one has to be very cautious not to over-interpret the data. For example, the standard arrangement of Egyptian relief work meant that a more accurate depiction always occurred when the movement was to the right. Hence, depictions of warfare directed to the left are not as valid for purposes of exactitude. The superhuman size of the Pharaoh and the very large size of his single opponent or fortress have to be considered as well. Hence, we have to be as careful with the scenes as philologists are with the texts.

In the first register on the left side of Seti's monument we see the king shooting at the enemy with his bow. His two horses charge ahead of him to the left. The weapon is, as expected, the composite bow. At the city of Pa-Canaan the effects of this action are dramatic. Arrows kill the enemy, or else the foes are crushed under the king's horses and chariot. Some of the Asiatics attempt to surmount the tell of this city; others are dying, but not one of them has a horse or a chariot. A few carry fenestrated axes similar to the earlier period of the Middle Bronze Age in Palestine while male elders (?) beseech the Pharaoh for peace. One breaks his staff while another holds his intact. These northerners possess long spears, and some of them have rudimentary protection around the waist. No "true" armor is recorded and the headdresses appear feebly designed. All in all, the pictorial evidence supports the textual. If these men are indeed the Shasu, as it would seem, although not emaciated in body they are weak in armament.

The king's chariot is the only one present. The typical six spokes are retained as well as the curved back of the cab. Another scene in the same register reveals the militarily secure ruler holding his sickle sword in his left hand which also grasps the reins. The bow case is drawn to the rear side of the cab and it is shown at the front. Javelins or spears may also be seen in a holder. A second depiction reveals the same set-up as in the first. Seti once more fires his arrows against his foes. Here, as well, the monarch does not wear any body armor. Indeed, he is lacking a helmet. He shoots in a relaxed position because the chariot has stopped. This is obvious because his right leg is partly angled with the knee jutting out; his left leg is more vertical but is not completely perpendicular to the base of the cab. The requirement that the reins be strapped around the waist of the archer is overtly recorded. Noteworthy are the sides of the chariot. The last scene reveals an open side on the war vehicle whereas the first does not. In fact, there are problems with these two representations, not the least of which is the depiction of the king's arrow case because it overlaps the top rail of the cab but then slides behind his left foot.

On the way back with his captured enemy Seti holds the reins in his right hand and also grasps a bow. The depiction is meant to indicate that although all is peaceful the Pharaoh remains the victorious war leader. The quiver that is carved at his back is empty. Seti grasps the sickle sword in his right hand, an action that is intended to reflect military determination rather than actual combat.

In the second register it is the battle at Yeno'am that is so important. The enemy also possessed horses and chariots. Moreover, Seti's opponents may wear helmets, thereby indicating in a striking fashion their difference from the Shasu.[22] Once more the direction is to the left and we see the open side of the royal chariot. Here, his right leg is far more flexed than in the scenes in register one. The typical depiction of Pharaoh as archer is repeated. In addition, the enemy chariots are six-spoked, as are Seti's, and two men are contained within each vehicle. The cheek bands of the bridle are bifurcated, as those of the Pharaoh's horses. There are clearly two reins. The manes of Seti's horses are naturally well groomed and combed; those of the enemy are simpler in presentation. In the scene of the submission of the Lebanese chiefs the horses are leaping somewhat, but definitely not in a fearsome mood. The king holds his bow, which is in relaxed position, and has the requisite quiver on his back. In the final scene of the return with captives Seti's chariot now reveals an open side. Two spear-holders may also be seen.

The carnage in the Hittite register is most illuminating. The representations of king in chariot, archer as hero with reins tied to his waist, and open side of the cab (direction right) are repeated. His left leg is partly flexed but the pose of the monarch is somehow more sedate than in the previous reliefs. As has been pointed out, the Hittite enemy in his chariot, large in size but not dwarfing the Pharaoh, has only one companion. His chariot appears to be identical in design to the king's, and I surmise that this reflects artistic license rather than reality. The Hittites have their typical helmets and head cloths. There are other chariots, and we can see a scout or a signalman riding his horse in the rear position, typical of the day. (He does not have any protection, such as a blanket, under his rear end.) One spear or javelin transfixes the body of a Hittite chariot man who carries a rectangular shield. The sides of the enemy cabs are not open and their horses have a bifurcated bridle; however, it is difficult to know whether the artistic representations of the Hittite chariot system copy the Egyptians'. The design of the vehicles look Egyptian and the presence of two men to a chariot is troublesome, if only because the enemy employed three men to a chariot during the later Battle of Kadesh.

At the point of departing from this battlefield Seti steps into his chariot and the direction is to the left. The side is once more open. Perhaps this was rendered in order to show the posture of his right leg, which is flexed for mounting the war vehicle. In this scene we see the sickle sword once more. It is never used in the Asiatic reliefs when the act of carnage is performed. Here, it serves as a symbol of the virile war leader, but is avoided in the scene of the attack.

The last (top) register dealing with the northern wars is that of the attack upon Kadesh. At this point all the common motifs of charging Pharaoh are repeated. The enemy with their horses and chariots wear helmets that differ from those of the Hittites even if their garments are similar. Square shields, nevertheless, identical to those of the Hittites, can be recognized. The king's attack is represented through his role as archer.

In the middle register on the right side, the Libyan campaign, things are not the same. The scenes of the defeat of the enemy reveal different aspects such as the lack of an opposing armed chariot division. The enemy's swords, physiognomy, and clothes are also at variance to the Asiatics and Hittites. In one depiction the archetypical posture of killing the enemy chieftain is shown. The Pharaoh holds his bow in his right hand; it is not flexed for shooting. In the left is the sickle sword. Evidently, with these opponents, the Egyptian artist had recourse to an all too common artistic motif. This time, however, it has been updated to reveal Seti standing within his chariot instead of on the ground, although the monarch does not use his bow. Nevertheless, the entire depiction follows an older pattern. The king's left foot moves up the chariot pole and his right steadies him from behind.

In the second useful scene narrating this western campaign the king, shown with intricately carved sandals, strikes out at a Libyan foeman. His right foot crushes the head of one enemy while the other is up in the air. While Seti grasps his opponent's arm, an arrow pierces the Libyan chief. The traditional motif of the smiting king has now been set within a contemporary setting, but in this case the Pharaoh hurls a spear with his right hand at his Libyan opponent. The victory is highly schematic or too stereotypical. No specific topography is rendered. Neither the battlefield nor the time is indicated. In many ways the entire Libyan series presents separate depictions, which although not exactly traditional, conform to the more static representation of the victorious king.

The key depiction in this register presents Seti ready to kill his Libyan enemy with a spear. Instead of the Pharaoh in a chariot, killing his foe by an arrow, the symbolic representation presents the major foe killed by a spear shot by the Pharaoh. The enemy, in fact, lacks a chariot, and is thus on a lower technological level than the Egyptians. Hence, a long sword, effective for impaling, was sufficient. Mighty Pharaoh has become a leaping sword-bearing war commander.

With the exception of the Libyan war, the key ingredient is the archer-king in chariot. Again and again, we see the positioning of the Pharaoh as a superhuman shooting his arrows.[23] Even the foes that are transfixed by spears do not matter. Instead of smiting with a mace, the Pharaoh, as chariot warrior and archer par excellence, defeats his solitary opponent. Later, when we cover the war scenes of Ramesses II and Merenptah, we shall note how stereotypical these ingredients are.

Seti I also had to deal with troubles in the desert away from the Nile River in southern Nubia. The major inscriptions associated with this minor war, one in which the king did not go in person, indicate that it was probably later than the Asiatic campaigns. Probably in year eight, and during the coolest time of the season, the Pharaoh dispatched his forces south to a region called Irem.[24] Unfortunately, the exact location of this area is still in dispute, but it is clear from the tenor of the account that the campaign was far less important than any of the king's to the north. It is significant that the Pharaoh did not lead his army. Leaving the river, the troops moved up into the desert, eventually capturing five wells and 400 people. As we shall see, under Ramesses II, Seti's son and successor, a further campaign was needed to secure this region from hostile control.

But the orientation of the Pharaonic war machine was primarily directed northward. In fact, when we examine the Ramesside administration in Palestine a situation different from that of Dynasty XVIII is revealed.[25] It is unfortunate that the dating of the so-called "governors' residences" in Canaan is unclear, if only as they are located in such districts as Beth Shan, which we have seen played such an important role in the opening years of Seti I. During the XIXth and XXth Dynasties this area continued to show intense Egyptian influences, among which we many single out the presence of an Egyptian temple. Eliezer Oren concluded that the entire region between Nahal Besor in the south and Nahal Shiqmah in the north was part of a zone centered upon the Egyptian administrative capital of Gaza.[26] This area became the focus of Egyptian rule during Dynasty XIX, and the term "Pa-Canaan" probably refers to it. There was an intensive integration of Canaanite elements into the Egyptian administration, and not surprisingly the main arterial route from Sile to Gaza and northward remained the crucial road for the army as well as civilians. Governors' residences can be found somewhat inland in the southern border area of Palestine; e.g., at Tel Masos, Tell el-Far'a, Tell el-Ajjul, and the like. Further north was Tell el-Hesi and, of course, Beth Shan. In addition, a few fortresses were built, such as those found at Beth Shan, Tel Mor on the central coastline, and Deir el-Balah in the south. All in all, the archaeological evidence indicates that a more intense system of foreign control came to be the norm in Palestine. This could have been a result of constant external pressure from the Shasu and other "outsiders," if not sea pirates as well. On the other hand, the city-states in Palestine may also have become harder to control owing to the military requirements for wars in Syria and defensive measures against Libya.

EXCURSUS

1. The Libyan threat to Egypt – in particular to the West Delta – has been discussed by Kitchen and O'Connor, whose studies are cited in note 20. On pp. 66–76 the latter scholar directs our attention to the military organization of the enemies, placing attention on their war leader, the *wer* (an Egyptian word), which in this context is best rendered as "leader" or "war chief." Pages 81–9, however, provide the grist for the military historian's mill. O'Connor deals with the data on the swords of the Libyans captured during the reign of Merenptah, and describes the "lightly armed troops" and archers who accompanied their ruler. He does note, however, the small nature of the chariotry contingent among the Libyans. During the reign of Ramesses III the following useful details are elaborated: about 5–10 percent of the enemy army included chariots; 25–35 percent of the forces were swordsmen; and over 50 percent foot archers.

The conclusion that O'Connor makes, with which I concur, is that these Libyans "were neither as unstructured nor as functionally simple as the Egyptian sources might at first suggest" (p. 85). Hence, the military effectiveness of the enemy must not be disregarded by modern interpreters of the data, nor should it be underestimated. In particular, O'Connor adds, the Libyans may not have been able "to prevail in a major pitched battle with a large and first-class Egyptian army," but they could be effective. After all, had not these peoples "a long tradition of service within the Egyptian army"?

I feel that one additional point can be offered concerning the Libyans in the Ramesside Period. We seem to be dealing with communities fundamentally organized for war, with martial values predominant and where the links between social organization and the army were close. One of the major functions of the "chief" was to provide war-leadership. In contrast, the military system of Egypt required a permanent army, maintained by the state at the expense of the rest of the population. This indicates a military and civil bureaucracy that used written orders and archives. Yet the ratio of combatants to civilian population must have been low, a point that I have brought into discussion earlier.

For the Late Roman Empire the fraction has been estimated *in practice* to be 1/400; the theoretical order was 1/100: Philippe Contamine, *War in the Middle Ages*, Michael Jones, trs., Basil Blackwell, New York (1984), 12. In contrast, the army of Frederick William I of Prussia was 1 in 25 of the population when the army of France was around 1 in 150 (G. Barraclough, *The Origins of Modern Germany*, Basil Blackwell, Oxford [1966], 400 n. 1). By 1789 the regular army of Prussia was 162,00 men, which rose to ca. 250,000 in time of war, and the French army was 173,000, which could be increased to 211,000, or 287,000 with the militia. It is important to recognize that the population of Prussia was less than one-third that of France. In this extreme case, however, we are dealing with a militarized society.

Despite the Libyans' rudimentary tactics in comparison to the Egyptian professional army, a contrast was present between their military efficacy – a point stressed by O'Connor – and that of Egypt. Was the Libyan society one that demanded the employment of all adult males around fifteen years of age until their physical strength greatly declined? Contamine felt that Germanic society could present a fighting force of around 20 to 25 percent of the total population. Delbrück also maintained similar ideas in his *The Barbarian Invasions* (*History of the Art of War*, vol. II), Walter J. Renfoe, Jr., trs., University of Nebraska Press, Lincoln and London (1980), Book I.

We must be on guard not to take on face value the Egyptian reflections in scenes or in text. That this goes without saying for all sectors of Pharaonic society needs no emphasis here. But, as O'Connor notes, many of the Libyan–Egyptian clashes at the end of Dynasty XIX and the two in Ramesses III's reign reveal that the western enemies were able to provide a large number of warrior males in order to invade Egypt. Moreover, the Libyans did not merely form armies but were whole peoples on the move. It is useful to quote Contamine in the context of the Germanic armies: "carts, baggage, livestock, women, children and the old, whom they took with them, reduced their mobility and continually forced on them the tasks of surveillance and protection" (p. 12). Once their initial thrust miscarried, the Libyans were easily overcome by the efficacy and discipline of the Egyptian army. In small bands, and this was a problem later on in Dynasty XX, the Libyans were able to scour the countryside, as the Nile Valley was not well protected by numerous fortifications or organized defenses.

As the repeated attempts by the Libyans to enter Egypt indicate, the threat to the Egyptians was real. The enemy could be stopped at the borders of the Western Delta by a mass of Egyptian troops, and the usefulness of the Egyptian chariotry was one of the decisive advantages to the natives. But it remained a problem whether the limited resources of the Late New Kingdom could provide a large enough *defensive* force to prohibit Libyan incursions.

Once more we are forced back upon the question of how large was the effective (not theoretical) Egyptian war machine within Egypt. This cannot be answered with any degree of statistical probability. Given the 3 million or so inhabitants in Egypt at this time (chapter 9, excursus 1 with notes 12–13), we can only hypothesize the size of the army within the confines of Egypt. If we follow Contamine, then that would have been 30,000, and this figure is based on his lower estimate, one that takes into consideration any possible soldier. I do not see any reasons why this result should be *greatly* augmented when New Kingdom Egypt is taken into consideration.

On the other hand, the Egyptian soldier was a landowning cultivator who was required to serve in the army when the Pharaoh demanded service. As such, these men were not full-time soldiers paid by the state for a 365-day service. If we can estimate the amount of time per year that they served (or were demanded to serve), then I feel that 1/3 to 1/4 per year was required of them. This might imply a further multiplicative factor with respect to the standard data. That is to say, we should expect a larger ratio than $1/100 \times 3,000,000 = 30,000$.

But I do not believe that the Egyptian army, even with any augmentation of ordinary troops, could produce an army in excess of 40,000. The economy could not allow such an increase.

2. As assembled by O'Connor, the totals of Libyans include captured peoples. Hence, not all of them were warriors. Delbrück, *The Barbarian Invasions*, 226–29, 242 n. 30, who compared the population of the Roman Empire ca. AD 200–300 with that of the army, felt that out of ca. 90 to 100 million inhabitants, one could estimate about 250,000 soldiers at the time of the Severi. Recent studies have not progressed much in this direction. This leads to a ratio of military/civilians = 1/400. If the army amounted to around 550,000–600,000 about the time of Diocletian, as now claimed, then the result is 1/200 (Pat Southern and Karen Ramsey Dixon, *The Late Roman Army*, B. T. Batsford, London [1996], 56; these figures include the *foederati* of non-Roman origin).

The above data are dependent upon the assumed total population for the Roman Empire ca. AD 300. The classical study on the matter is that of Beloch, "Die Bevölkerung im Altertum," *Archiv für Sozial-Wissenschaft* 2 (1899), 600–21, especially pp. 619–20 (100 million during reign of Caracalla). During the reign of Augustus he estimated 54 million (*Die Bevölkerung der griechisch-roemischen Welt*, 507. Russell, "Medieval Population," *Social Forces* 15 (1937), 504, and *The Control of Late Ancient and Medieval Population*, 36, provides a smaller estimate of 32.8 million for the same era. See his *Late Ancient and Medieval Population*, Philadelphia [1958], 148.

Russell's analyses, however, tend to be to extreme on the lower end: Colin Wells, *The Roman Empire*[2], Fontana Press, London (1992), 305. Nonetheless, if the data are to be followed, then the military participation ratio for the Roman Empire ca. AD 200–300 will have to be significantly increased from the assumed 1/200–1/400, even though the problem of the high percentage of German troops remains. See our comments regarding the similar situation at the end of the New Kingdom in the excursus to chapter 16.

3. A rudimentary statistical analysis of the percentage of the elite warrior class in the Ramesside Period in comparison to the civilian officials and priests can be obtained from the volumes of Kitchen, *Ramesside Inscriptions*. I have used the data for the reigns of Ramesses II and III because these two Pharaohs ruled for ca. 66 and 31 years respectively. Hence, the evidence is large enough to claim some type of validity. Concentrating solely upon the men who were significant enough to leave behind them some evidence of their careers, and excluding the workmen at western Thebes, the following

rough percentages can be marshaled. The upper echelons of the military counted for 17.3 or 25 percent of the elite during the reign of Ramesses II, and 15.9 or 22.5 percent during that of Ramesses III. The second and larger figure for each king includes the viceroy of Nubia and his underlings.

Solely from this rough estimation it appears that the elite of the military during the Ramesside Period held a very important role within society, one that I shall discuss later in Chapter 16. These two results, nonetheless, do not enable us to calculate the percentage of all the soldiers/all the civilians.

4. The veracity of the war reliefs of Seti I and his successors has been only partly discussed in this study. The interested reader may reexamine the comments of Heinz, *Die Feldzugdarstellungen des Neuen Reiches* and the other works listed in note 1 to this chapter. Artistic sensibilities involved the proper layout of the scene desired, the necessity of locating the central figure (Pharaoh) in a key position, the schematic rendering of certain localities (cities, rivers), and a realistic but not necessarily accurate depiction of the enemies and their war material.

The following two studies begin to address these parameters: Heinz, "Wie wird ein Feldzug erzählt?"; in Bietak and Schwarz, eds., *Krieg und Sieg*, 43–67; and Anthony J. Spalinger "Epigraphs in the Battle of Kadesh Reliefs," *Eretz Israel* 27 (2003), 222*–39*.

NOTES

1 Epigraphic Survey, *Reliefs and Inscriptions at Karnak, Vol. IV: The Battle Reliefs of King Sety I*, Oriental Institute, Chicago (1986); Murnane, *The Road to Kadesh*; Müller, *Die Thematik der Schlachtenreliefs*, chapter 6; and the later analysis of Gonzala M. Sanchez, "A Neurosurgeon's View of The Battle Reliefs of King Sety I: Aspects of Neurological Importance," *Journal of the American Research Center in Egypt* 37 (2000), 143–65.

The texts will be found in Kitchen's edition, *Ramesside Inscriptions* I, 6–32, and VII, 422–7. He provides a translation in *Ramesside Inscriptions. Translated and Annotated. Translations* I, 6–26, and a commentary in *Ramesside Inscriptions. Translated and Annotated, Notes and Comments* I, 10–42 (includes all texts).

A recent attempt to determine the role, function, mechanism, and effect of Egypt's empire over Asia in the Ramesside Period is that of Michael G. Hasel, *Domination and Resistance: Egyptian Military Activity in the Southern Levant, 1300–1185 BC*, Brill, Leiden, Boston, and Cologne (1998). The nuts and bolts of military *factors* are not dealt with although the volume provides a useful overview of the pertinent data and includes a worthwhile section on the naval bases of the Egyptian Empire in Dynasties XIX–XX.

2 For the background data to this argument, see the discussion in notes 25–6 and 31–2 to chapter 1 and notes 12–13 in chapter 4.

3 See Spalinger, *The Transformation of an Ancient Egyptian Narrative*, chapter XI, for these texts and the following literary examples.

4   Conveniently, Grandet, *Papyrus Harris I* (BM 9999).

5   I have used the sources cited in note 1 above.

6   Shlomo Bunimovitz, "On the Edge of Empires – Late Bronze Age (1500–1200 BCE)," in Thomas E. Levy, ed., *The Archaeology of Society in the Holy Land*, Leicester University Press, London (1998), 327–8. He maintains that the frontier zones of Canaan were "populated by nomads and other non-sedentary groups." This explanation for the troubles of the Apiru and Shasu, first evident in the Egyptian textual record from the Amarna Letters, helps us better to understand the Pharaohs' concerns about the marginal areas of Sile to Gaza, the Trans-Jordan, and eastern Palestine.

7   Murnane, in *The Road to Kadesh*, and in the analysis presented in the Epigraphic Survey volume referred to in note 1, splits the events depicted in the bottom and center register of the east side of the exterior wall of the hypostyle court. Earlier, Gaballa, following Kitchen, had done the same: *Narrative in Egyptian Art*, 103–06. Müller, on the other hand, did not; see his *Die Thematik der Schlachtenreliefs*, chapter 6 and pp. 48–58.

8   This inscription is now called "The First Beth Shan Stela." The standard work on the site of Beth Shan in the Ramesside Period is that of Francis W. James and Patrick E. McGovern, eds., *The Late Bronze Egyptian Garrison at Beth Shan: A Study of Levels VII and VIII*, University Museum, Philadelphia (1993). In the work a full analysis of Egyptian garrisons is covered. See as well our comments in note 25 below.

9   The warfare of Seti follows the pattern of Thutmose III: first Palestine, then the Lebanon, and finally Syria. This was so because the logistic and strategic aims were similar. Murnane, *The Road to Kadesh*, 75, sees a "grand design" in the wars of Seti I.

10   Kitchen, *Ramesside Inscriptions* I, 13, places the campaign to Yeno'am and Karnak to "Year 1 or Later."

11   For the enigmatic Mehy, see Murnane's analysis in his "The Kingship of the Nineteenth Dynasty," 199–203.

12   The events recounted in the Second Beth Shan Stela are distinct from those in the first.

13   *The Road to Kadesh*, 70–4. Murnane pointed out that the original version of the prisoners in the first register contained both settled Asiatics and Shasu. The latter were subsequently recarved into Shasu for the final version. Were those Asiatic princes merely delivering to Egypt tokens of submission, possibly as a recognition of their deliverance from these marauders? This cannot be ascertained.

14   Ibid.

15   This was one of Müller's arguments against the position of Murnane: *Die Thematik der Schlachtenreliefs*, 49–58.

16   This scene was of prime importance for Richard H. Beal, *The Organisation of the Hittite Military*, C. Winter, Heidelberg (1992), 148–51. See plate 34 in Epigraphic Survey, *The Battle Reliefs of King Sety I*.

     Notes 28–9 in chapter 11 provide the counter-argument of Johnson, *An Asiatic Battle Scene of Tutankhamun from Thebes*, especially p. 59.

17   Beal remarks on this in study referred to in the last note. See our comments later on in this chapter.

18   Kitchen, *Ramesside Inscriptions* I, 25. For a summary of the king's success, see the work of Murnane cited in note 1.
19   Epigraphic Survey, *The Battle Reliefs of King Sety I*, Pls. 29–31 (middle [second] register, west side).
20   There are two important studies on the Libyans in the New Kingdom in Anthony Leahy, ed., *Libya and Egypt, c. 1300–750 BC*, School of Oriental and African Studies, London (1990): Kitchen, "The Arrival of the Libyans in Late New Kingdom Egypt," 15–27; and O'Connor, "The Nature of the Tjemhu (Libyan) Society in the Later New Kingdom," 29–113.
21   Labib Habachi, "The Military Posts of Ramesses II on the Coastal Road and the Western Part of the Delta," *Bulletin de l'Institut Français d'Archéologie Orientale* 80 (1980), 13–30; and Kitchen, "The Arrival of the Libyans in Late New Kingdom Egypt," in Leahy, ed., *Libya and Egypt c. 1300–750 BC*, 18–19.
22   For evidence of Asiatic helmets in the XVIIIth Dynasty, see again Kendall, "*ǧurpišu ša awēli*: The Helmets of the Warriors at Nuzi," 201–31.
23   The symbol of the archer-warrior is a common one in the war reliefs of the New Kingdom. A more detailed study of its development in connection to the war equipment is necessary; compare Heinz, *Die Feldzugdarstellungen des Neuen Reiches*, 69–93.
24   Kitchen, *Ramesside Inscriptions, Translated and Annotated. Notes and Comments* I, 81–90. For the historical background to this war, see as well Spalinger, "The Northern Wars of Seti I: An Integrative Approach," *Journal of the American Research Center in Egypt* 16 (1979), 29–47, with "Historical Observations on the Military Reliefs of Abu Simbel and other Ramesside Temples in Nubia," *Journal of Egyptian Archaeology* 66 (1980), 83–9. Both studies link the later years of Seti with this campaign.

       According to Kitchen (p. 90), Irem was "not exactly part of the Egyptian domain, but something of a client-state." He felt that the threat from the south was probably directed at vital wells and trade routes. The later campaign under Ramesses II directed to the same region led to a large number of prisoners being brought back. Kitchen, "Historical Observations on Ramesside Nubia," in Endesfelder et al., eds., *Ägypten und Kusch*, 213–25, provides the background data. Note that his remarks are also concerned with the problem of the location of Irem, and he refers to O'Connor's two studies cited above in note 33 to chapter 3.

       Jean Vercoutter, "Le pays Irem et la penetration égyptienne en Afrique (Stéle de Saï S. 579)," in *Livre du Centenaire de l'IFAO (1880–1980)*, Institut Français d'Archéologie Orientale, Cairo (1980), 157–78, provides a further helpful analysis of Seti's Nubian war in which Irem is discussed.
25   The basic studies are: Oren, "'Governors' Residences' in Canaan under the New Kingdom: A Case Study of Egyptian Administration," *Journal of the Society for the Study of Egyptian Antiquities* 14 (1984), 37–56, with his "Palaces and Patrician Houses in the Middle and Late Bronze Ages," in Aharon Kempinski and Ronny Reich, eds., *The Architecture of Ancient Israel from the Prehistoric to the Persian Periods*, Israel Exploration Society, Jerusalem (1992), 117–20; Singer, "An Egyptian 'Governor's Residency' at Gezer?," *Tel* Aviv 13 (1986), 26–31; Aren M. Maeir, "Remarks on a Supposed 'Egyptian Residency' at Gezer," *Tel Aviv* 15–16 (1988–89), 65–7; and Shlomo Bunimovitz, "An Egyptian

'Governors Residency' at Gezer? – Another Suggestion," *Tel Aviv* 15–16 (1988–89), 68–76.

A summary of the data will be found in Redford, *Egypt, Canaan, and Israel in Ancient Times*, 203–07 (Dynasties XVIII–XIX); and Bunimovitz, "On the Edge of Empires – Late Bronze Age (1500–1200 BCE)," in Thomas E. Levy, ed., *The Archaeology of Society in the Holy Land*, 324–6.

26 See his two studies cited in the previous note.

13

TO KADESH AND AFTER

The final and decisive Egyptian battle in Asia, a turning point equal to that of Megiddo under Thutmose III, took place in year five of Ramesses II at the city of Kadesh in central Syria.[1] Yet this was the second northern campaign of Ramesses II because a preparatory advance had occurred one year earlier. A stela of the king, set up at the Nahr el Kelb on the southern coast of Lebanon, probably bears witness to Ramesses' first preparations for the major war.[2] We can presume that the Pharaoh followed the earlier practice of his father (and Thutmose III) in first assuring control over the coast before marching inland. Noteworthy is the presence of Sherden "mercenaries" within the Egyptian army at Kadesh in the king's fifth regnal year.[3] They are referred to in the main inscriptions that recount this war as well as in the reliefs. The latter differentiate these warriors from the Egyptians by means of their round shields, long swords that are wide close to the haft, and their cap-like helmets surmounted by two prongs and a small sphere. Because the Egyptians had fought some of these sea pirates at the mouths of the Nile earlier than the fourth year of Ramesses, it seems reasonable that not a few had now become a staple ingredient within the Egyptian military. Their absence in the battle reliefs of Seti supports this contention.

Ramesses II ordered an account of the Battle of Kadesh to be inscribed and drawn on the walls of various temples.[4] Abydos, probably the earliest, reveals only the lowermost portions of the war owing to the fragmentary condition of the temple.[5] At Karnak two versions are still extant while at Luxor three may be found, although one of them presents only the two main narrative accounts. The king's mortuary temple to the west of Thebes, the Ramesseum, has two versions as well, and Abu Simbel in Nubia presents a more condensed version.

The importance of the detailed account, the so-called "Poem," and its shorter companion, the "Bulletin" is balanced, if not dwarfed, by the pictorial record.[6] Indeed, the latter may be said to provide the fullest visual information concerning the Egyptian military in Dynasty XIX. As noted earlier, all campaigns were divided into various portions. By and large some of these episodes are present in all of the temples. On the other hand, Ramesses

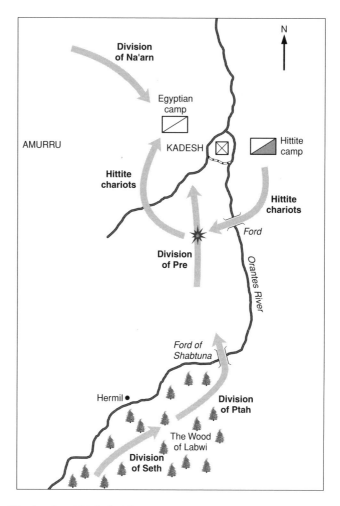

Map 5 The battle of Kadesh: The Hittite attack

wished to highlight four main events in this campaign: the camp and the war council, the battle itself, the spoils and captives, and the second presentation at home to the gods.

Note once more the war council. In the narrative of the Megiddo battle this was a prominent portion of the account, and the same may be said for the opening section of Kamose's war record. But the reason for Ramesses' interest lies in the fact that, after the king settled down in his camp to the west of the city of Kadesh, he received news that the Hittites were close by and not far away in Aleppo as he had originally thought. After the spies

210

of the Hittites were beaten and forced to tell the truth, the attack of the numerous enemy chariots occurred. The pictorial representations cover these two interlocked events as well as the arrival of the Pharaoh's fifth division, the Na'arn. The latter traversed southern Syria by foot, undoubtedly leaving the ports of the Lebanon in order to meet up with the king and his four main divisions, all of which had advanced northward through the Beqa Valley.[7] If this elite division left Tripoli, to take a case in point, then approximately 121 km would have been traversed before they met up with Ramesses. Hence, it would have taken them more than $9\frac{1}{2}$ days to reach their destination, providing that there were no delays. Although this is not a long duration, the coordination of the Na'arn with the king's other four divisions is remarkable, and one is left with the feeling that Ramesses earlier had been in communication with these additional troops, probably by messenger, in order to effect the juncture of the Na'arn with his army. If these men had arrived earlier they would have been isolated. If they came later, then the entire composite army would been prepared as a large unit at least one day after Ramesses' arrival at Kadesh. I feel that the coincidence is too great to allow for chance.

The second episode draws together the attempt of the king to hasten his other divisions that had followed the first where he was at the front. The all-mighty king is carved in superhuman size charging on his chariot against the foe and, of course, shooting his arrows. Since this portion is highly detailed, I shall leave it for a more detailed analysis below. The remaining two episodes are more straightforward but present interesting details of their own.

Globally, Ramesses II intended to retake the city of Kadesh which had switched sides after the withdrawal of the large Egyptian army under Seti I. His strategy was a simple one: march to the city and take it. From the background to the eventual combat it is clear that Ramesses with his four divisions did not intend to meet the Hittites.[8] The "Poem" begins the narration at the departure from Sile, and then continues with the arrival at a royal fortress in the "Valley of Cedar." There was no opposition in Palestine; combat was expected only in Syria. He is then described as crossing the ford of the Orontes, which was south of the city and at a point where the river coursed in a westward direction, perpendicular to the march of the king.

Earlier, Ramesses had received false information from two Shasu at the town of Shabtuna (modern Ribla), who stated that his Hittite opponent, Muwatallis, with his army, was in Aleppo, north of Tunip. In other words, the king felt that he could reach Kadesh unopposed and settle for a battle or a siege. A series of background points can now be made. The first is the simplest, and one that I have referred to on more than one occasion. The war was known to all and sundry. Both the local princes in Palestine and Syria as well as the leaders of the two great states of Hatti and Egypt could not hide their feelings, their war preparations, indeed their war aims. The journey of Ramesses, though not rapid by today's standards, nonetheless covered the same number of miles per day as, for example, Thutmose III did when approaching Megiddo. The march was thus ca. 12.5 miles/day and no lengthy delays occurred. If we allow about 10 days from Sile to Gaza, and then about 12 days to get to Megiddo, we can place him in central Palestine about three weeks after his departure from Egypt. He left Egypt approximately at the close of March to early April, following the practice of his Dynasty XVIII predecessors. On day nine of the third month of the harvest season he was at Shabtuna south of Kadesh, and about one month had passed. (The departure from Sile is dated exactly one month before the arrival at Shabtuna.) At this point he received the false news that the Hittites were not around the city of Kadesh. The Egyptians were approximately 14 km from Kadesh. Ramesses then advanced, and it would have taken at most half of a day for the first division to set up camp opposite the city.

More details help to elucidate the final stages of the march to Kadesh. In the morning the king awoke and prepared his troops for the march. Sometime after that the army reached Shabtuna. This would have taken time. Ramesses's extended army was composed of four divisions, all marching separately and behind one another; the advance would have been slow. The temporary halt at Shabtuna did not last long. Moreover, the king discussed with his commanders the oral evidence of two Shasu "deserters" who falsely reported that the Hittites were not at Kadesh but away in the north. Again, we can assume the passing of time, at least one hour, but probably more. One line of the "Poem" (P 60) states that a distance of 1 Egyptian *iter* separated that ford south of Shabtuna from the position of Ramesses when the second division (Pre) was crossing the Orontes.[9] The distance from the ford to the camp, or even to Kadesh, was at most 16.5 km. To march it would have taken $^3/_5$ of a day. I cannot but assume that the time when Ramesses settled peacefully in his camp must have been in the afternoon. One final point needs to be brought into the discussion; namely, the length of the Egyptian *iter*. There were two: a larger one of about 10.5 km and a smaller, of approximately 2.65 km. It is evident that the former was employed here.

We can perhaps better understand why the Egyptian monarch failed to take cognizance of the Hittites.[10] According to the Poem the latter were "concealed and ready to the northeast" of Kadesh. The first division of the Egyptians was at the northwest of the city, settled beside a local brook that was so necessary for the animals and men. They had pitched the tents, and from the scenes of relaxation the army had already settled down for the day. However, as one relief caption indicates, they were not completely finished with the preliminary tasks of pitching the camp (R 11).

But no attack by Ramesses was planned on day nine. The city of Kadesh was not directly approached. Indeed, the king settled down on the west, across the Orontes, and arranged his camp for the arrival of the following divisions. We must assume that either he expected a military encounter with the enemy forces stationed within Kadesh on at least the following day or that he intended a siege of the citadel. The second alternative is a secure and economical way to victory, provided that time is not of the essence. Such a blockage prevents additional men from supporting the enemy, and eventually the lack of food and water becomes a major problem for the defenders. Yet in this case there is no evidence that Ramesses immediately proceeded to invest Kadesh. Indeed, he was somewhat removed from that citadel. The topography of the region indicates that west of the city and around the Orontes there was a relatively level plain, one suitable for chariot warfare.[11] The Egyptian camp and the advancing three other divisions were well placed to suit their purposes. If this analysis is accepted, then we may very well wonder if once more the possibility of a "pre-arranged" battle was understood. That is to say, soon after dawn on the following day, the clash of the Egyptians and the foes within Kadesh was expected, provided that no surrender took place.

The Hittites, as all now know, were hidden. The less detailed but highly useful account of the "Bulletin" twice says "behind" Kadesh whereas the "Poem" is more specific, locating Muwatallis, the Hittite monarch, and his army at the "northeast of the town of Kadesh." This report also uses the word "behind" but adds that the enemy's chariots charged from the "south side of Kadesh" and broke into the second division of Pre that was still marching north to meet Ramesses. Either the Pharaoh had not used advance chariotry or scouts of his own to size up the strategic situation at Kadesh, and this appears the correct solution, or the Hittite king arrived after any Egyptian scouts had left. Considering the location of the enemy, the depictions of their camp, and the prepared state of Kadesh, the second alternative must be rejected. But the crucial question remains: how could Ramesses have not seen or heard the enemy?

Armies such as Muwatallis' had horses, and we know that his chariots and troops were prepared. Do not horses neigh and create dust clouds by their moving hooves? How can one hide them? Was the grass very high? Or was the enemy simply too far away for traces of their presence to be noted? Evidently, the Egyptian king had not sent a reconnaissance party across the river to the east. This may have been due to the fact that his first division was just on the point of settling down, and that the sun had begun to dip faster in the mid afternoon.[12] Nonetheless, Ramesses thought that the coast was clear because the two Shasu had deceived him concerning his opponent's whereabouts. Was the hour of the day a factor? We have calculated, albeit in a tentative way, that before Ramesses reached his desired spot a considerable amount of time had passed. Sunset occurred around 6 p.m. local time, and I doubt if evening twilight had already occurred at the point when the Hittite chariots were sent directly across the Orontes. The Poem helps us further when it states that Muwatallis and his soldiers were hidden "behind" Kadesh. The mound and the city itself therefore provided the necessary cover.

A few additional remarks concerning this deception can be offered, not in order to excuse the mistake of the Egyptian monarch, but rather to indicate how armies that are at close quarters are unable to perceive each other. It may be possible to surprise small forces but with large ones it becomes increasingly difficult to obtain. The Baron de Jomini observed "As armies at the present day [1838] seldom camp in tents when on a march, prearranged surprises are rare and difficult, because in order to plan one it becomes necessary to have an accurate knowledge of the enemy's camp."[13] Surprisingly, this sentence fits neatly with the tactics of Muwatallis. He allowed Ramesses to settle down, or at least to begin pitch the tents, before he moved his forces across the river. In addition, he waited for the second division of Ramesses to advance sufficiently so that he could smash it and hence isolate the first division at the camp.

Muwatallis must have known about the Na'arn, the fifth division, when he sent his chariots ahead. As stated before, these armies had reasonable knowledge of the strategic goals of their enemy. In the case of the Hittites, their basic situation was better than the Egyptians. They already held the area and had sufficient reconnaissance to enable them to understand the enemy's advance. If so, they should have known of the incoming fifth division. Muwatallis was also able to send two Shasu south to meet up with the main Egyptian force. He realized that his plans had succeeded. Otherwise, Ramesses would not have acted the way he did.

The numbers of chariots said to have been employed by Muwatallis belie the truth. Once more we meet nice rounded integers: 2,500 in the first wave, the one that reached the Egyptian camp, and another 1,000 later on.[14] We could add the 19,000 *and* an additional 18,000 *teher* warriors said by the Egyptian account to have remained with their leader. But let us return to the force of chariots. As the Hittites followed a system of three men to a chariot in this battle, 7,500 men are implied. Following the data, we arrive at an area of 27,941 m^2; in a square the sides would be 167 m or about 548 feet, 10 percent of a mile.[15]

These calculations have avoided any other soldiers in the Hittite army. Even though the Hittite chariots were somewhat different from the Egyptians', their length (including the horse) was about the same. The only other problem is that with three men in the vehicle the width would have been greater. Hence, we ought to increase our result by a few meters although we cannot assume that the chariots were set up neatly in a square. The type of fighting as well as the width of a chariot arm would have depended upon the area in which they could maneuver. We cannot assume that the chariots attacked en mass with no depth. For the original 2,500 the space would not have allowed it.

214

If a camp for a Roman legion totaled 6,000 men, then the area would be approximately 60 acres.[16] For a mere 7,500 men we have 75 acres or .12 miles². Muwatallis certainly did not require such a large area because the city of Kadesh could have supplied him with provisions. The Hittite monarch had already camped there before Ramesses arrived, and his tactical situation was excellent. But given the figures of the enemy troops in the text, especially those of the 37,000 *teher* warriors, it would have been remarkable if the Hittite king could have not been observed from a distance. I believe that we must discount all of the numbers in Ramesses' account of the battle of Kadesh.

Yet this does not mean that the battle cannot be analyzed. In particular, we have to ask ourselves: what was the original intention of Muwatallis when he sent his chariots across the Orontes? The lack of footsoldiers is the key. He did not intend to fight for a long time. The infantry were kept behind. Hence, the purpose of the attack was to run through division number two, that of Pre, and to get to the camp of his foe as soon as possible. Muwatallis also knew that the Pharaoh was just settling down. He did not delay, for that would mean that the Egyptians could assemble with double the number of troops. Considering his action, we may suppose that he felt, with about 75 percent of the enemy army still marching north, the odds were certainly in his favor. Nonetheless, he did not commit himself to full force: additional chariots were left behind.

At this juncture there are a series of imponderables. Was the second group of Hittite chariots, fewer in number than the first, a strategic reserve or only the remaining ones that Muwatallis had? We do not know. In addition, what happened to the division of Pre? If most of the Hittite chariots sped quickly upon the Egyptian camp, then it would appear that they did not bother to wipe out that division. For if they did, the time element would have been squandered. From the pictorial evidence I must conclude that the enemy burst through the marching column of Egyptians, sped north, and although killing some of the soldiers, did not bother to stop. It was sufficient to give them a mauling; the aim was not to liquidate the vast majority of the second division. Strategically, Muwatallis' goal remained focused upon the camp of Ramesses.

The attack of the enemy chariotry upon the second division of Pre took place south of Kadesh. Major Burne assumed that these men were, at most, about 2.4 km from Ramesses' camp.[17] This might be discounted as it is based on his analysis of the size of the king's main army (20,000 soldiers).[18] More useful, however, is his argument that the enemy crossed a ford south of Kadesh. This seems reasonable; otherwise the chariotry could not have easily gotten through the waters. But should we argue that the front of the Hittite chariot line was relatively small because of the width of the ford? Most certainly, the scenes of later carnage at the Orontes as well as those of the Hittite attack indicate that the passage was not difficult.

The number of Hittite chariots that reached Ramesses' camp also remains a thorny issue. Most certainly, the Pharaoh was able to dispatch some of his high officials south in order to warn the remaining divisions of what was transpiring. Actually, only the third division (Ptah) is specifically mentioned; the situation of the fourth (Seth) is left aside. Allowing the distances assumed by previous historical research, one interesting question is whether those men reached the actual melee at the Orontes or not. One additional remark indicates that the enemy forces reached Ramesses with Hittites and peoples from Arzawa, Masa, and Pidassa (P 85–6). Can we assume that at some point the enemy had organized itself into four groups?[19]

Yet they were repulsed. Subsequently Muwatallis sent another, albeit smaller, wave of chariots westward, and we must credit Ramesses for being able to repel all of them. This might have appeared impossible. But the Pharaoh, with the troops of the first division and the relief support given to him by the arrival of the contingents of the Na'arn, found his resources sufficient to repulse the advancing enemy chariots. His success must have depended upon three factors. The first was the number of Hittite chariots that reached the camp, the second the presumed destruction of the division of Pre, and the third the possibility that many Hittite chariots were still fighting against those Egyptian troops. Indeed, one relief caption notes that the Hittite king had also sent forward some of his infantry. The latter would have arrived at the battlefield somewhat later than the faster-moving chariots, and they may have ended up only on the immediate west side of the Orontes.

The type of combat appears to have been mainly based upon chariots. Else, Ramesses could not have repelled the attacks of his enemy. The roles of the Pharaoh's footsoldiers and those of Muwatallis are not described. Because the reliefs show the king's attack in a chariot, a common theme of New Kingdom war representations, we cannot evaluate the service that the Egyptian infantry performed at Kadesh. All that we are left with is an assumption of the size of both armies, and that is based upon the evidence of the texts (Hittite chariotry and *teher* footsoldiers) and the probable size of an Egyptian division (5,000). I feel that all of these figures are open to question.

If Muwatallis sent 2,500 chariots and if Ramesses had the same number in his first division, then unless the former were held up by the carnage of Pre, the Pharaoh's immediate success makes sense. With an additional 1,000 chariots on the enemy side, and the lack of reinforcements from the third division of Ptah, the Hittites would have had a numerical advantage. Moreover, the relief captions note the presence of Hittite infantry. All in all, unless we argue that the second division was not massacred, or that it held up the Hittite charge, one is thrown back upon the role of the Na'arn in the fifth division. Earlier Egyptologists had noted their crucial presence, and we cannot but follow their analyses.

One lengthy caption in five versions refers to a pictorial representation of arriving infantry and chariotry. These are the Na'arn, and with them the king was able to charge into the foe. Although they might have been tired from marching, by no means were they exhausted. In fact, they were ready to fight like Pickett's men. Unlike General Lee, Ramesses immediately used them, and with this advantage in chariots – I assume double that which he first had – the enemy was repulsed. Did Muwatallis have some idea that the Na'arn were nearby, and thereby decided to attack the Egyptians as quickly as possible before these reinforcements could have come into play?

Even though much ink has been spilled in analyzing the battle, some details can be reconstructed. The account of the second day, however, has left everyone in suspense. It is only given in the account of the Poem, but the high-blown verbiage is impenetrable, or not of any use to the military historian. I believe that further combat took place, "prearranged," so to speak. The king was able to marshal his ranks. Hence, at daybreak of the following day the two armies met once more. Granted that this section of the Poem is short, it nonetheless provides some support for my contention that often battles were fought on plains, normally soon after dawn, with the tacit agreement of both war leaders.

When we turn to the scenes of this battle, many useful military details can be ascertained. We see the Na'arn arriving. They are Egyptians, and hold their long shields in the same manner as the natives, whether on foot on in a chariot. The third men in the enemy chariots hold spears or javelins. Sherden are present acting as a guard around Ramesses on the occasion when he ordered the Hittite scouts to be beaten. Clearly, these men served as an elite guard whose duty was primarily to their liege lord. The Hittite parallel is the group of *teher* warriors who surrounded Muwatallis. The same set-up was carved for Ramesses' camp except here more specific details are conveyed, even to the point of indicating the relaxed mood of the Egyptian troops. In the enemy camp pack animals are shown. The oxen of the Hittites pull wagons with six spokes; donkeys are also laden with provisions.[20] The similarity to the Egyptian camp is self-evident.

Returning to the Egyptian army, a series of significant military aspects can be noted. The army of the Na'arn marched as follows: first a line of chariots, then soldiers, and then another line of chariots. This point, hitherto unnoticed, provides a useful estimate for the size of a brigade. In particular, three chariots lead the force. Behind each of them are two columns of ten men. There are thus forty footsoldiers and twelve men on the chariots, making a grand total of fifty-two. Was this the way that Egyptian armies were organized when marching, or do the reliefs follow artistic license? Whatever are our conclusions, it appears from the Kadesh scenes, but not from the literary narrative of the Megiddo battle, that the Egyptian army used oblong squares.[21]

At Abydos we see a column of fifteen men proceeding in front of one chariot.[22] Further to the forward position there is another group of chariots.[23]

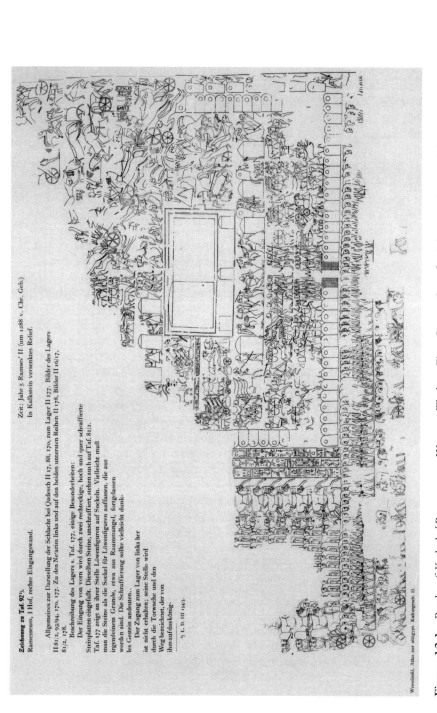

Figure 13.1 Battle of Kadesh [Ramesseum, Western Thebes, First Court; Camp]. *Atlas zur altaegyptischen Kulturgeschichte* by Walter Wreszinski, vol. II. Geneva-Paris: Slatkine Reprints, 1988, pl. 92a. Originally published by

Figure 13.2 Battle of Kadesh – reliefs from the Temple of Ramesses II at Abydos, Temple of Ramesses II, Exterior Wall. Counting hands. Courtesy of Ch. Leblanc.

Figure 13.3 Battle of Kadesh – reliefs from the Temple of Ramesses II at Abydos, Temple of Ramesses II, Exterior Wall. Hittite Guards of *Teher* Warriors. Courtesy of Ch. Leblanc.

Figure 13.4 Battle of Kadesh – reliefs from the Temple of Ramesses II at Abydos, Temple of Ramesses II, Exterior Wall. Attacking Hittites. Courtesy of Ch. Leblanc.

Figure 13.5 Battle of Kadesh – reliefs from the Temple of Ramesses II at Abydos, Temple of Ramesses II, Exterior Wall. Advancing chariots. Courtesy of Ch. Leblanc.

Clearly, the arrangement is different. Can we assume that the artists worked to a specific pattern, one that depended upon a predetermined artistic interpretation rather than solely upon the actual events? Furthermore, in these reliefs there is a bottom row of marching chariots, apparently serving as a protective wing for the footsoldiers. But when we survey the approach to battle, the system alters. Abydos shows the following. When marching in normal order, normally two men are placed on the side of, or within the protection of, one chariot. But as we near the expected danger zone the two footsoldiers are now depicted with shields, and they have raised them for protection. Finally, there is the charge of the chariots, and, as may be expected, the infantry disappear because the rapidly moving vehicles have outpaced them. The onslaught is also indicated by the upward direction of the horses: a true charge into the fray is present.

Version L1 at Luxor reveals the same pattern but also with a contrast.[24] The number of Na'arn footsoldiers appears to be six or seven. R1, one of the Ramesseum variants, has ten men between the two sections of chariots, yet they are marching with at least seventy footsoldiers. Its companion (R2) does not help us very much. But all accounts indicate that the Egyptian counterattack was made up of chariots; the soldiers on foot must have followed soon after.

The precise if limited pictorial subsections dealing with the army of Ptah likewise are useful for our analysis of Egyptian marching order. Two speedy officials reach this division, and at Abu Simbel we see two distinct sectors of the group. One is composed of archers and the others of spearmen. The latter are identical to the marching Na'arn at Abydos. In a Luxor version (L1) the lagging division is led by five standard-bearers and the division leader. Behind all of them are three footsoldiers preceding a chariot.

Other subtle contrasts among these pictorial representations show that a hard and fast rule concerning the number of combat soldiers per subsection in a division is impossible to determine. Yet we can notice the variances in tactics. When marching, for example, the footsoldiers were protected by chariots. This is most clearly seen with the Na'arn. The advancing division of Ptah, for example, is shown in a more relaxed mode. Because the footsoldiers and the standard-bearers are at the head of the division with the division leader in front of them, it is evident that they did not expect any danger. So we must separate out those representations that indicate a relaxed but careful march from the advance to combat, the immediate attack, and the actual melee.

The mopping up of the Hittite attack is not recorded. Instead, the oversized figure of Ramesses on his chariot plunges into the Hittite host of chariots. But there are many ancillary points worthwhile indicating. Above all is the repulse to the Orontes. This is most evident by the specific details of Hittite dead in the river and the figure of the luckless prince of Aleppo rescued from the waters. Evidently, Ramesses' charge pushed the chariot

Figure 13.6a Battle of Kadesh [Luxor, First Pylon (East); Attack on the Enemy]. *Atlas zur altaegyptischen Kulturgeschichte* by Walter Wreszinski, vol. II. Geneva-Paris: Slatkine Reprints, 1988, pl. 83. Originally published by Leipzig: J. C. Hinrichs, 1935, 1923–40. Photo © British Library, London.

Figure 13.6b Battle of Kadesh [Luxor, First Pylon (East); Attack on the Enemy]. *Atlas zur altaegyptischen Kulturgeschichte* by Walter Wreszinski, vol. II. Geneva-Paris: Slatkine Reprints, 1988, pl. 84. Line drawing of figure 13.6a. Originally published by Leipzig: J. C. Hinrichs, 1935, 1923–40, figure 42. Photo © British Library, London.

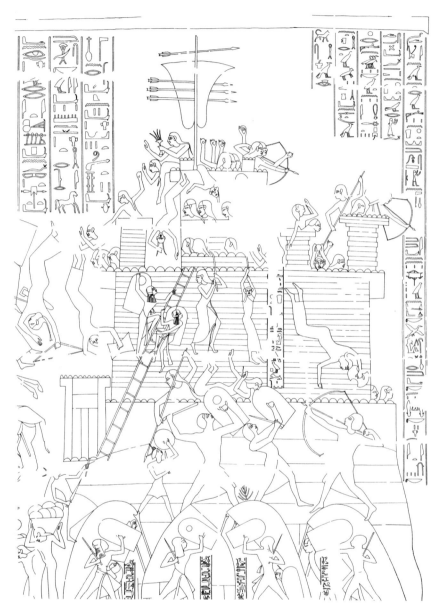

Figure 13.7   Ramesses II: Attack against Dapur. [Ramesseum, Western Thebes]. A. A.-H. Youssef, Ch. Leblanc, and M. Maher, *Le Ramesseum IV. Les batailles de Tounip et de Dapour, Centre d'Étude et de Documentation sur l'ancienne Égypte*, Cairo (1977), pl. XXII. Reprinted by permission of Archives Scientifiques IFAO.

Figure 13.8 Ramesses III: Siege of Tunip. Epigraphic survey, Oriental Institute, University of Chicago. *Medinet Habu*, vol. II, Chicago, 1934, pls. 88 and 89. Courtesy of the Oriental Institute of the University of Chicago. Copy of Ramesses II.

divisions of the enemy backward. If the full power of the first chariot wave had reached the Egyptian camp I feel that this would have been impossible. It would have taken some time for the Pharaoh to recover from his initial surprise and to prepare his troops for combat. But with the arrival of the Na'arn Ramesses had on hand an additional chariot force ready for battle. They must have seen the attack of the Hittites, and I believe that not many of the enemy's chariots had attained their desired aim. In other words, the king's division of Amun plus the Na'arn first blunted and then ended the tactical superiority of Muwatallis. Hence, Muwatallis had to send another wave of chariots forward in order to hold his own lines.

But this support failed. The evidence of Egyptian success may be read from the captions that accompany the figures of many Hittites. There is little doubt that the names and titles of these men were written down by the military scribes who accompanied the king. Enemy charioteers as well as troop-captains and a shieldbearer are listed together with two brothers of Muwatallis and two chiefs of the enemy's *teher*. A dispatch-writer and a "chief of the suite" of Muwatallis may also be found. Note that these are all prominent men; none are mere footsoldiers. This befits the type of military action that took place in which high-ranking men were responsible for the carnage. We can assume that after the battle these men were identified, but their names and titles could only have been determined with the help of the enemy. Whether this list was drawn up with the aid of captured Hittites or, following the melee, with the assistance of Muwatallis, is unclear.[25] Perhaps after the subsequent fighting on day two an official list of enemy dead on both sides was determined. As the dead Hittites were prominent men I cannot but conclude that their bodies were examined, their names recorded, and the corpses sent back to the camp of the foe.

On the second day the result of the carnage must have been clear to all. Ramesses had won the battle; his tactics were superb. On the other hand, he was forced to withdraw from the field because he was unable to dislodge the Hittites. Losing the strategic aim of the campaign, Ramesses left the field having failed to take Kadesh. No wonder, then, that the Egyptian monarch was forced to return to Asia soon thereafter. Hence, additional wars of Ramesses in Syria are known from various sources in Egypt. The accounts are mainly pictorial and their representations stereotypical.[26] From the scanty data that is preserved it is clear that the Egyptian king personally went into Syria at least twice. He fought there in his eighth and tenth regnal years, but if the advances of the Egyptian army are impossible to determine, it is easy to conclude that Ramesses went by land. On one occasion we read that he fought without donning his armor at Dapur, a very heroic situation that further reinforces our opinion of the king as a doughty war leader. In addition, there appears to have been more fighting in the Trans-Jordan.[27] Here as well the evidence is merely one of place names and generalized artistic representations. Whether or not a general uprising took place within Egyptian-held territory is a moot point. A war directed against incursions from the east does not provide automatic support for this hypothesis.[28] The towns captured by the Pharaoh in year eight include Palestinian ones, but the presence of Yeno'am again indicates a zone in the east close to the Trans-Jordan.[29] In year ten a stela was erected at the Nahr el Kelb, thus once more emphasizing Ramesses' interest in Syria or at least at his northwest border. A further one erected in Beth Shan in the king's eighteenth regnal year is purely rhetorical. By and large, the undated war scenes are hard to place into a chronological framework, although those referring to a Trans-Jordanian war can be securely set into the king's early second decade.

Later in the reign of Ramesses II, most probably in his third decade as Pharaoh, the peaceful relations between Egypt and the Hittites had grown to such an extent that diplomatic marriages took place. On two occasions the Hittite monarch, Hattusilis III, sent one of his daughters to the Egyptian court. The intense political activity between the two states may be read on the various cuneiform tablets that are still preserved. But within Egypt, in particular at the Delta capital of Avaris, Egyptian–Hittite interconnections are overt. Recent archaeological discoveries at Qantir, located just opposite the capital of Avaris, have allowed us to reconstruct the military setting of this northeast Delta capital.[30] Shield molds with Hittite motifs explicitly indicate that a foundry was established there for the production of these defensive weapons. Archaeologists have concluded that Hittites themselves were producing and repairing Hittite shields. This leads to the supposition that there were Hittite "mercenaries" or guards at Avaris. Tools of these foreigners were also discovered, further proving that the large site of Avaris-Qantir was the major military center in the northeast. Parts of chariots such as fittings, harness pieces, bronze foundries, javelins, arrow tips, horse bits, short swords, projectile tips, scales of coats of mail, and even stables indicate the warlike nature of the capital. A large number of vast buildings point to a chariot garrison that contained an exercise (or training) court, adjoining workshops, and horses' stables. It has been estimated that, at the minimum, 350 horses could have been housed. But whether this was done for contingents within the entire Egyptian army, or solely for the foreigners, must remain an open question. None of the later battle reliefs of Merenptah or Ramesses III point to any Hittite sector of the native war machine.

A leather roll, now in the Louvre, adds welcome data with regard to the importance of these stables.[31] This text is an account papyrus dated to year five of Ramesses II. It deals with "The Great Stable of Ramesses II" in which four stablemasters are listed. One of the supervisors in fact bore a good Hurrian name, Hurrian being the language of the kingdom of Mitanni in Syria. Hence, we see once more the presence of Asiatics within the Egyptian military. Under the overseers were gangs of men who were put to work making bricks. This indicates temple-building projects if not also domestic structures for the state, and the mention of wooden beams and bundles of reeds implies the construction of scaffolding. For our purposes, however, we can view in a striking fashion the intimate connection of the military with work projects, a point made more than once in this volume.

Various small literary compositions of Dynasty XIX called Late Egyptian Miscellanies shed additional light upon these recent discoveries.[32] P. Anastasi II contains a typical eulogy of praise to the new Delta capital of Avaris (Pi-Ramesses), and from internal data it can be dated to the same time as those Hittite shield molds described in the previous paragraph; i.e., to the third decade of Ramesses II. One subsection in P. Anastasi III, dated to the reign of Merenptah, forcefully points out the military importance of Avaris. The encomium equates the city to a "marshaling place of your chariotry, the mustering pace of your army, and the mooring place of your ships' troops." We can envisage the Pharaoh standing above his army at the Window of Appearances or on a dais and surveying his warriors. Additional praises include the "corps of archers marching along." In fact, the tone of the account is fearsome and warlike. P. Koller, another of these Miscellanies, reports upon the equipment for an expedition into Asia. Although this text will be covered in detail later, it would appear that the letter was sent from the Delta capital abroad. All of these so-called Miscellanies fit the second half of the XIXth Dynasty, after the Hittite threat had ceased but also when the Eastern Mediterranean and Palestine had become somewhat troublesome.

Above all, it is the martial flavor of the accounts that bears examination. In conjunction with the archaeological evidence from Qantir-Avaris, these compositions indicate a very developed military set-up at the capital. The warlike nature of the age, concentrated in the very north of Egypt, is no better appreciated than from these data. The king as army commander lived and ruled surrounded by soldiers. I suspect that this was also the case in Dynasty XVIII when Memphis was the capital, but one can better understand the decision to move the base of operations from the apex of the Delta – Memphis – to the northeast at Avaris. Its proximity to the Asia as well as to the sea meant that a large contingent of his troops could be sent more quickly by land to the north. Finally, any violent disturbances in the Mediterranean could be met by rapidly dispatching warships to the coast. The Pharaoh's civilian entourage was balanced, if not dominated, by his army.

Finally, the Nubian situation under Ramesses II deserves some amplification. Although the wars there were not as extensive as in the north and the enemy not overtly threatening to the Egyptian state, we can see how offensive raids were still necessary. The exact date of Ramesses' Irem war in Upper Nubia is unclear although it is relatively easy to place it in the middle of the king's second decade.[33] As briefly noted in the last chapter, the number of captured Nubians was not small. In fact, we can argue that the Pharaoh realized once more the danger to his trade routes, a point that might be equally argued from a later offensive raid into the southern oases led by the viceroy of Kush, Setau; Irem is once more mentioned. These military actions may have presaged the more serious Nubian rebellion that took place under Ramesses II's successor, Merenptah, when Lower Egypt (or Wawat) revolted at a time when the north was threatened by a Libyan invasion. Even later under Ramesses III, we hear of disturbances in the south, thereby indicating that although the core areas of Nubia were maintained, persistent troubles with the state of Irem remained.[34]

EXCURSUS

1. We have observed the low estimate of Keegan regarding the number of Egyptian troops that were present at this famous and decisive battle in note 18 to this chapter. The figure of 5,000 men per division, first presented by Breasted in 1905 (*Ancient Records of Egypt* III, 127, 153 n. a, and earlier in "The Battle of Kadesh," 10: 25,000 to 30,000 men at the maximum) and then supported by Faulkner, indicates that Ramesses had with him 20,000 infantry and chariotry. See Kitchen, *Ramesside Inscriptions. Translated and Annotated, Notes and Comments* II, 39–40; and our comments in excursus 8 to chapter 9 with note 16. Keegan, *A History of Warfare*, 176, argued for fifty chariots and 5,000 soldiers, totals that are too small.

In excursus 1 to chapter 12 I estimated that the maximum number of regular troops in the Egyptian army during the New Kingdom was around the order of 40,000 at the most, although I prefer the lower figure of 30,000. The second figure would exclude, however, "mercenaries" such as the Sherden. Therefore, if we add an approximate 2,000 or so Na'arn, or even a theoretical 5,000, the grand total of Egyptian fighters would come close to the theoretical maximum that New Kingdom Egypt could produce. Delbrück made similar calculations in his *Warfare in Antiquity*, 38–50, concerning Athenian resistance to Persia in 431 BC. Granted that this study is now dated; nevertheless, it indicates the need of the military historian to attempt some numerical qualification.

The data on the enemy, outside of the presumed chariots totals covered in note 14, included 18,000 plus 19,000 *teher* warriors (Reliefs, R 43–4). This would indicate an enemy having at the minimum 44,500. That is to say, the Egyptian account indicates a ratio of Hittites/Egyptians at around 1.8. Because none of these figures can be accepted at face value, it is sufficient to state that the official report of the Egyptian account tends to place a two to one preponderance of the enemy over the home troops.

If we accept the basic analysis of Breasted concerning a maximum of ca. 20,000 men in the four main Egyptian divisions personally led by their king, then this figure would indicate that the limits of the native Egyptian war machine had been approximated. Perhaps this would explain the exhaustion of Egyptian military potential relatively soon after this battle. Most certainly, the cost in equipping these soldiers and having them supplied by the local cities in Palestine would have been considerable.

2. The slow march of the second, third, and fourth divisions of Ramesses makes better sense when seen from this light. If the divisions had about 5,000 men, then their column or columns would have been rather long. (See already, Kitchen, *Ramesside Inscriptions, Translated and Annotated. Notes and Comments* II, 41–2.) The first division of Amun, which had already settled down and was "at peace," would have had enough men to stand up to the first Hittite chariot attack. Indeed, from the reliefs, these men had already disencumbered their horses from the chariots, presumably had eaten, and were relaxing at the time that the enemy attacked. (Note Keegan's comments in his *A History of Warfare*, 301: "When a body of men join together to perform a day's task, they will need at the very least to eat once between sunrise and sunset.") Naturally, we cannot interpret the pictorial account of the battle in a naïve fashion. It should be left open for further discussion whether or not the first division was as surprised as the reliefs indicate. I personally find it hard to believe that none of them, and this includes the Pharaoh, were ignorant of the swift chariot attack of the Hittites. The melee to the west of the Orontes caused by the Hittite encounter with the second of Pre would have held up some of the enemy chariots for a period of time. My understanding of the pictorial depictions includes a healthy skepticism with regard to their historical veracity. They have to be read carefully, perhaps with an approach similar to that of Van Essche-Merchez; see note 19 to Chapter 7.

NOTES

1 The most recent Egyptological analyses are the presentations by Kitchen, *Ramesside Inscriptions, Translated and Annotated, Translated* II, 2–26, and his commentary in *Ramesside Inscriptions, Translated and Annotated. Notes and Comments* II, 3–55. The latter remarks must be read in conjunction with the earlier scholarly treatments, among which we may cite: Alan Gardiner, *The Kadesh Inscriptions of Ramesses II*, Oxford (1960); Thomas von der Way, *Die Textüberlieferung Ramses' II. zur Qades-Schlacht*, Gerstenberg Verlag, Hildesheim (1984); and Hans Goedicke, ed., *Perspectives on the Battle of Kadesh*, Halgo, Baltimore (1985) – four separate studies.

A recent study on this battle is that of Walter Mayer and Ronald Mayer-Opificius, "Die Schlacht bei Qades. Der Versuch einer neuen Rekonstruktion," *Ugarit Forschungen* 26 (1994), 321–68.

The numbers following "P" indicate the presently accepted scholarly agreement on the lines of the Poem. They are artificial.

2 Conveniently, see Kitchen, *Ramesside Inscriptions, Translated and Annotated. Translations* II, 2–26, with his *Ramesside Inscriptions, Translated and Annotated. Notes and Comments* II, 1–2.

3 Murnane, *The Road to Kadesh*, covers the intense political jockeying that led up to the crucial encounter between the Egyptians and the Hittites.

4 Conveniently, see Gaballa, *Narrative in Egyptian Art*, 113–19; Spalinger "Notes on the Reliefs of the Battle of Kadesh," in Goedicke, ed., *Perspectives on the Battle of Kadesh*, 1–42; Kitchen's comments in *Ramesside Inscriptions, Translated and Annotated. Notes and Comments* II, 5–10; Heinz, *Die Feldzugsdarstellungen des Neuen Reiches, passim*, especially pp. 126–44; and Müller, *Die Thematik der Schlachtenreliefs*, 79–83, 91–2, and 96–8, with his *Der König als Feldherr*, chapter IX.

5 Spalinger, "Historical Observations on the Military Reliefs of Abu Simbel, and other Ramesside Temples in Nubia," *Journal of Egyptian Archaeology* 66 (1980), 83–99.

6 Gardiner, *The Kadesh Inscriptions of Ramesses* II, 1–4, saw that the "Bulletin" was a lengthy caption of one specific scene – namely, a legend "which served to explain the accompanying reliefs" (p. 4).

Von der Way (note 1 above) covers the Bulletin as well as the Poem in a literary and philological study, with emphasis upon the personal piety of Ramesses. With regard to the latter situation, see the important lengthy article of Jan Assmann, "Krieg und Frieden im alten Ägypten," *Mannheimer Forum* 83/4 (1984), 175–321.

My study, *The Transformation of an Ancient Egyptian Narrative: P. Sallier III and the Battle of Kadesh*, Harrassowitz, Wiesbaden (2002), covers the later papyrus versions of the account.

7 See now Kitchen, *Ramesside Inscriptions, Translated and Annotated. Notes and Comments* II, 37–8.

8 The situation of the king's march, especially its duration and composition, is presented by Kitchen in *Ramesside Inscriptions, Translated and Annotated. Notes and Comments* II, 41–2.

9 On the *iter* see Adelheid Schlott-Schwab, *Die Ausmasse Ägyptens nach altägyptischen Texten*, Harrassowitz, Wiesbaden (1981), 118–22. She argues that this distance was 10.5 km if we understand the figure as an average one, determined by the distance of 900 km (Nile length of Upper Egypt).

Additional studies are: Erhart Graefe, "Einige Bemerkungen zur Angabe der *Stꜣt*–Grösse auf der Weissen Kapelle Sesostris I.," *Journal of Egyptian Archaeology* 59 (1979), 72–6; P. Vernus, review of Schlott-Schwab's 1969 Dissertation on the same subject, in *Revue d'Égyptologie* 30 (1978), 189–93; and Schlott-Schwab, "Atlägyptische Texte über die Ausmasse Ägyptens," *Mitteilungen des Deutschen Archäologischen Instituts, Abteilung Kairo* 28 (1972), 109–13.

10 On the element of surprise, the classic military remarks are those of Jomini, *The Art of War*, 190–1; note as well Turney-High, *The Military*, 57–9. There are enough examples in history of armies failing to see one another even though they were close by. Dust, clouds, not to mention problems caused by the terrain, have had remarkable effects upon the failure of a war leader to recognize that his enemies were near.

We also have to take into account the time of day. Kitchen discusses these afternoon events in *Ramesside Inscriptions, Translated and Annotated. Notes and Comments* II, 43–7.

11 The best analysis of the topography remains that of Breasted, "The Battle of Kadesh. A Study in the Earliest Known Military Strategy," *The Decennial Publications of the University of Chicago* 5, Chicago (1904), 81–126. Later work on the subject has refined this analysis.

12 See note 8.

13 This is also discussed in Kitchen's general comments cited in note 8.

14 These were the Hittite chariots attacks: P 84, P 132, and P 153. The Poem (P 221) indicates that Ramesses entered (on his chariot) into the enemy six times.

15 The data for these calculations have been presented in earlier chapters. The arithmetic works as follows. (1) 7,500 men, allowing 3 feet per person with a space in between, means a line of about 6,858 m long. Let us assume a depth of 91 m. The area is 6241 m^2. In a square, that means that each side is 79 m. (2) The width of Egyptian chariots is approximately a bit over 1 m. We can assume that the Hittite chariots were roughly the same size as the Egyptian ones. The reliefs, for what they are worth, indicate this. (3) Cab plus draught pole equals 3 m. But we must deduct from that result ca. 0.5 m because the pole ran under the floor of the cab all the way back. Hence, outside of the chariots they were about 2.5 m long. (4) But it is easier to work with the diameter of the wheel, ca. 1 m. The result is that the length one chariot and horse occupied was 3.25 m or so. 3.25 m × 1 m = 3.25 m^2. (5) If there were 3,500 chariots then the total area would have been 11,375 m^2. (6) Allowing 61 m between them standing in a file and when situated side by side, this means an area per chariot of 1.61 m × 3.86 m or 6.2 m^2. (7) So (5) becomes 21,700 m^2. (8) Adding (1) and (7) results in 27,941 m^2. In a square the sides would be 167 m or 548 feet, about 10 percent of a mile.

16 Verbruggen, *The Art of Warfare in Western Europe during the Middle Ages*, 10; see the text to note 16 in chapter 5.

17 Major A. H. Burne, "Some Notes on the Battle of Kadesh," *Journal of Egyptian Archaeology* 7 (1921), 191–5.

18 Kitchen, *Ramesside Inscriptions, Translated and Annotated. Notes and Comments* II, 39–40. Breasted was the first to maintain that the four divisions consisted of about 20,000 men: see excursus 1 to this chapter. John Keegan felt that "the Egyptian army appears to have had fifty chariots and 5000 soldiers": *A History of Warfare*, 176. Both of his figures are too small. He observed that with 2,500 chariots, the enemy's front of attack would have been "8000 yards wide," about 7,315 km. I follow Kitchen.

19 Later in the account (P 149ff.), and at the time that the second Hittite chariot attack occurred, a more detailed and significantly different enumeration of the Hittite allies is given. The leaders of this follow-up attack were high-ranking members of the enemy coalition.

20 Elmer Edel, "Kleinasiatische und semitische Namen und Wörter aus den Texten der Qadesschlacht in hieroglyphischer Umschrift," 99–105.

21 Machiavelli, *The Art of War*, Lynch, trs., 102 (Book V 13ff.). Kitchen discusses this situation in *Ramesside Inscriptions, Translated and Annotated. Notes and*

Comments II, 41–2. Classical generals were accustomed to operate with oblong squares, a tactic which the writers of the Renaissance, such as Machiavelli, modified.

22 Wreszinski, *Atlas zur altägyptischen Kulturgeschichte* II, Pls. 16–24; Charles Kuentz, *La bataille de Qadech*, Institut Français d'Archéologie Orientale, Cairo (1928–34), pls. XVII–XXIII; and Edouard Naville, *Détails relevés dans les ruines de quelques temples égyptiens*, Librarie Orientaliste Paul Geuthner, Paris (1930), pls. V–XXII (his drawing are sometimes inaccurate).

23 The following remarks are dependent upon my study of these chariot scenes, "The Battle of Kadesh: The Chariot Frieze at Abydos," *Ägypten und Levante* 13 (2003), 163–99.

24 The designations of the variants are taken from Kitchen, *Ramesside Inscriptions* II, 2; the scenes may be found in Wreszinski's study referred to in note 22.

25 Edel, "Hethitische Personnennamen in hieroglyphischen Umschrift," in Erich Neu and Christel Rüster, eds., *Festschrift Heinrich Otten*, Harrassowitz, Wiesbaden (1973), 59–70.

26 A summary will be found in Kitchen, *Pharaoh Triumphant. The Life and Times of Ramesses II*, Aris and Philips, Warminster (1982), 64–70. His translations and commentaries of the inscriptions can be found in the two works cited in note 1 to the present chapter. David Warburton provides an overview of Egyptian–Hittite relations in his chapter, "Love and War in the Late Bronze Age: Egypt and Hatti," in Roger Matthews and Cornelia Roemer, ed., *Ancient Perspectives on Egypt*, UCL Press, London (2003), 75–100.

27 See Kitchen, " Some New Light on the Asiatic Wars of Ramesses II," *Journal of Egyptian Archaeology* 50 (1964), 47–70; Peter W. Haider, "Zum Moab-Feldzug Ramses' II," *Studien zur altägyptischen Kultur* 14 (1987), 107–23; and John Coleman Darnell and Richard Jasnow, "On the Moabite Inscriptions of Ramesses II at Luxor Temple," *Journal of Near Eastern Studies* 52 (1993), 263–74.

28 I cannot but conclude that the cost to the state was significant; see our comments in excursus 1.

29 The war to the east of Palestine indicates that the traditional Egyptian military administration was not that successful in dealing with these new groups of enemies. Noteworthy is the data presented in P. Anastasi I: Fischer-Elfert, *Die satirische Streitschrift des Papyrus Anastasi I*, Chapter XIXa. There, portions of the East Jordan are covered. This information partially allows one to support the editor's date for this composition up to year five of Ramesses II (pp. 261–7). However, I place the time of redaction into an interval commencing with the Kadesh campaign of this Pharaoh and ending around Ramesses II's twelfth regnal year.

30 The following three studies are useful: Edgar B. Pusch, " 'Pi-Ramesses-Beloved-of-Amun. Headquarters of the Chariotry'. Egyptians and Hittites in the Delta Residence of the Ramessides," in Arne Eggebrecht, ed., *Pelizaeus-Museum Hildesheim Guidebook. The Egyptian Collection*, Phillip von Zabern, Mainz, (1996), 126–44, with his "High Temperature Industries in the Late Bronze Age Capital of Piramesses (Qantir)," in *Proceedings of the First International Conference on Ancient Egyptian Mining and Metallurgy and Conservation of Metallic Artifacts*, Ministry of Culture, Supreme Council of Antiquities, Cairo (1996), 121–32; and Herold, "Piramesses – the Northern Capital: Chariots,

Horses and Foreign Gods," in Joan Goodnick Westenholz, *Capital Cities: Urban Planning and Spiritual Dimensions*, Bible Lands Museum, Jerusalem (1998), 129–44.

Memphis, however, remained a major production center of armaments at this time: Serge Sauneron, "La manufacture d'armes de Memphis," *Bulletin de l'Institut Français d'Archéologie Orientale* 54 (1954), 7–12.

31 Kitchen, *Ramesside Inscriptions* II, 789–99 and VII, 435–7, with his *Ramesside Inscriptions, Translated and Annotated, Translated* II, 519–26, *Ramesside Inscriptions, Translated and Annotated. Notes and Comments* II, 518–21, and "From the Brickfields of Egypt," *Tyndale Bulletin* 27 (1976), 141–3.

32 The standard editions are Alan H. Gardiner (text), *Late Egyptian Miscellanies*, Fondation Égyptologique Reine Élisabeth, Brussels (1937); and Caminos (translation and commentary), *Late Egyptian Miscellanies*.

33 Kitchen, "Historical Observations on Ramesside Nubia," in Endesfelder et al., eds., *Ägypten und Kusch*, 220–1 (for Ramesses II, but the whole discussion is important). The inscriptions at Abydos and Amarah West will be found in the author's *Ramesside Inscriptions* II, 192–3 and 218–22. There is a helpful commentary by him as well in *Ramesside Inscriptions. Translated and Annotated, Notes and Comments* II, 104–05 and 130–33.

34 See Kitchen's discussion on this matter in the article cited in the last note (pp. 224–5). The Deir el Medineh stela mentioned by him will be found in *Ramesside Inscriptions* V, Blackwell, Oxford (1983), 90–1.

14

MERENPTAH AND
RAMESSES III

The successor of Ramesses II, his thirteenth son Merenptah, provides a wealth of information concerning the Egyptian military and its importance at the end of Dynasty XIX. For the moment, let me concentrate upon his Libyan war of year five before turning to Asia.[1] Here we are lucky to possess a series of narrative and literary texts, all written in hieroglyphic; pictorial evidence is lacking. The longest of these is a lengthy historical inscription carved at Karnak. There, the title to the work indicates that a coalition of foes comprising Meshwesh Libyans as well as Sea Peoples attacked the Western Delta. We have already met both of these peoples earlier and have noted the presence of Mediterranean Sherden mercenaries within the Egyptian army. This invasion was aimed at settlement rather than plunder. Although it is possible that these westerners planned to establish a "Libyan state," there is no doubt that their role was identical to the later Gothic and other Germanic tribes who moved across the boundaries of the Roman Empire.[2] The Libyans brought along their families, provisions, and living utensils. Their alliance with the Sea Peoples was crucial because they obtained necessary advanced weapons from them. Moreover, the support of these pirates meant that the coastline of the Delta was threatened, although we hear of no naval encounter. The Sea Peoples associated with the land-based troops of the advancing Libyan armies included the Akyawash (perhaps the same ethnic designation as the Akhkhiyawa, who were enemies of the Hittites, the name of which has been linked to the Achaeans of Homer), Teresh, Luka (Lycians), Sherden, and the Shekelesh (often equated with the later Sicilians).[3] The first move was to take over the age-old land of the Libyan Tehenu bordering upon Egypt proper and to encroach upon the western boundary.

From a military viewpoint this war reveals the static defense posture of Egypt. During the later years of Ramesses II a series of fortresses were built well beyond the inhabitable territory of Egypt.[4] As we have observed, these defensive measures have their limitations as well as their strengths. Just as the famous Alamo, they can hold up an enemy army but cannot supply the necessary men to defeat a large hostile force. In this case one of the local commandants of a western fortress reported the flight of the enemy chief after Merenptah's victory. Apparently he had not been able to block the attackers earlier. In addition, the Libyans seized control of the western oasis routes to the south, and thereby had potential entrance into the southern portions of the Nile Valley without control from any fortified garrison. It is thus not surprising to read of a Nubian revolt that occurred not too soon after the Libyan attack.[5]

The type of combat indicated by the main narrative account is not that easy to interpret. Merenptah sent his infantry and heavily armed troops westward.[6] Archers, chariots, and scouts are also listed among his warriors. Significant is the passage wherein armed contingents lead the archers. The reason for this is easy to determine: archers must be protected from attack because they are unprotected. They have to put down their shields, if they have any, in order to fire. But perhaps more pertinent was the type of combat that Merenptah expected; namely, an infantry attack. As we shall see, the Libyans relied upon their numerous footsoldiers, and well-protected infantry divisions could ably withstand the attack.

The king marched with his army. The chariotry and infantry were camped opposite the Libyans. Merenptah took his sickle sword, or so says the Karnak text, a fact indicated by other contemporary sources; a bow is not mentioned. We are thus reminded of one of Seti's war scenes in which he prepares himself to decapitate the Libyan chief with such a weapon. (Let us not forget that in this relief the Libyan enemy had no chariots.[7]) But once more the situation of impending combat shows a structural form identical to previous wars. The king and foe were within sight of each other. The date of combat is given as the third day of the third season, approximately the beginning of April, again a useful time for combat. The march to battle, at any rate, seems to have taken fourteen days, but this figure may also refer to the preliminary mustering and assembling of the Egyptian soldiers.[8] There is an oblique reference to the night of day one, and I presume, unless this refers to the Libyans, that the Pharaoh had reached his destination at that time. But the actual combat took place *two* days later when the enemy actually arrived. In other words, the king remained in his camp ready for defense and did not plan to move further westward. The battle was thus predetermined as to location. The time was set and the protagonists could see each other. After dawn Merneptah advanced.

The Karnak text describes six hours of carnage, a lengthy period of time.[9] Although the foe was numerous and strong, and the combat intense, the enemy chieftain was defeated and fled. The main account emphasizes his loss of sandals, bow and arrow, but not any chariot. With the precipitate flight of their leader, the Libyans broke ranks in panic. Egyptians on horses, the *seneny*, chased after their opponents. In fact, the Karnak text appears to indicate that they used their bows and shot at the enemy, thereby massacring them. The passage in which this highly important statement occurs is, however, broken, and we cannot be sure whether these Egyptians were actually horse riders with bows. If so, then this encounter could reveal an important facet of late New Kingdom warfare as practiced by the Egyptians. The desperate Libyan chief, no longer supported by his clan leaders owing to his cowardice, passed by the western fortress in the night. Whether or not the slow infiltration of the Libyan peoples into the Delta had led to overconfidence on his part is a hypothesis that we are unable to confirm. The Karnak Inscription puts some emphasis upon this aspect, but as it is included in a detailed literary prologue, its historicity may be questioned. Perhaps it is best to leave such matters unresolved.

During the return home, the Egyptian army marched in chariot and infantry divisions. The heavily armed troops are again referred to as well as the archer captains.[10] The list of captives and slain is given. These totals do not quite match other sources recounting the war but all of the accounts are reasonably close to one another. The Libyans, among whom were the children of the enemy chief, and those of his confederate leaders as well as the ordinary soldiers, are listed separately from the Sea Peoples.[11] The total is somewhat above 6,000. (All of the war records provide unrounded integers, owing to which we may argue that these numbers are accurate.) The Sea Peoples, both captured or killed, amounted to about 2,400, i.e., they comprised around 3/8 of the opponents, a very large percentage. The figures also prove that this large army was highly dependent upon the Sea Peoples as confederates. Finally, the grand total of more than 9,000 listed must be set side by side with an assumed greater number of Egyptians soldiers. I feel we will not be far wrong if we assume that the opposition totaled over 16,000 (see below). The main forces of the army apparently were either killed or caught alive.

The Sea Peoples and the Libyans came mainly by foot. The former seem not to have been accustomed to chariot warfare, a point that is explicable if we keep in mind their naval orientation. And the captured war booty reveals the same situation. The Karnak Inscription notes only 12 pairs of horses that were used by the Libyan chief and his children. We could assume that they rode in chariots as the account lists six of the latter, but this is somewhat questionable. An additional inscription from Heliopolis, albeit short, lists 44 horses, which some may regard as indicating only 22 chariots.[12] Over 9,000 swords were taken. As this number roughly equals the grand total of slain or captured, we do not err in assuming that this figure as well can be used to estimate the total number of opponents. (It has also been observed that the Tjemhu Libyans are rarely shown with both swords and bows.) The total number of the enemy can be hypothesized to be over 16,000. But with regard to the total of 128,660 quivers and arrows, I once more feel that grave doubt must be placed upon such figures.[13] We can at least argue that the Libyans relied heavily upon their archers, a point supported by the later pictorial and written evidence under Ramesses III.

What metal was used for the weapons of the Libyans?[14] The specific word has to be translated as "copper" instead of "bronze." Although to use copper at this time for a sword might appear foolhardy – indeed a retrograde step considering the military technology of the day – the reading "copper" is secure. We can assume that these weapons consisted of arsenical copper. But the enemy Sea Peoples, who also were present, perhaps did not fight with copper swords. Finally, the presence of the large numbers of arrows and quivers taken by Merenptah's troops – even if the enormous grand total cannot be trusted – indicates that the enemy footsoldiers were accustomed to light armed combat in which the archers, standing somewhat removed from the melee, provided the main force.

Turning to the Libyan campaigns of Ramesses III in early Dynasty XX, two different sizes of swords are listed in the second report of the king's western campaign that is dated to his eleventh regnal year.[15] They were 3 and 4 cubits in length, approximately 1.6 m and 2.1 m. Hence, they were long and powerful weapons. Of some importance is the explicit notation that 184 horses were brought with the Meshwesh in that same war, a figure that fits perfectly with the 92 chariots recorded.[16] It is obvious that the Libyans had acquired some of the technology of Egypt and possibly the ability to utilize these chariots in war. But the total number is not large. Merenptah captured only 44 horses in his campaign and no chariots are listed unless we argue that only 22 were present. But considering the numerous bows and arrows, it is evident that the Libyan army was an infantry one that relied heavily upon its archers. David O'Connor estimated that at least 16,000 enemies participated in the attack, but can we trust these numbers?

Further analysis of the totals in Ramesses III's second Libyan war leads to the conclusion that the number of bows retrieved by the Egyptian was small (123), and because the slain Meshwesh amounted to 2,175, this threat was not as serious as the one under Merenptah.[17] Last but not least, the detailed and separate list of the various animals (steers of all sort, asses, goats, and sheep) allows us to conclude that the foe, although relatively small in comparison to his first war (see below), were composed of one major block of Libyans, perhaps indicating that they were a wholesale contingent of related clans who decided to march into the West Delta. In other words, the year eleven war of Ramesses III was directed by a new incursion of Libyans who, although not as dangerous as the earlier groups, nevertheless had to be repelled. The total number of slain plus captives (including women and children) came to 4,227, a substantial number but one that was not overwhelming. Owing to this, I suspect that the victory, although publicized as a major success for the Pharaoh, was not a great one.

Merenptah had summoned the Egyptian contingents from Egypt for active duty at the western border. This was not a one-month march into foreign territory. In fact, the Pharaoh did not advance beyond the pasturelands. He wisely stayed within a zone of protection and also had the time to assemble his troops. Whatever the total number of soldiers that went with him was, we can assume that that figure would have been, at the most, roughly equivalent to the assumed 20,000–25,000 Egyptian troops at Kadesh under Ramesses II. Furthermore, Merenptah did not have to depend upon semi-arid conditions far away from home. Provisions and water were not as great a difficulty to obtain when, for example, an Egyptian king had to march far north into Syria.

From the famous Israel Stela of Merenptah, a hymn of victory over the Libyans, we read that some of the key northern Delta cities had closed their gates. Hence, this invasion was taken seriously. On the other hand, with the numerous Sherden "strongholds" in Egypt in conjunction with a free means of advancing, the Egyptian monarch's logistic problems were not that serious. Indeed, he only had to fear defeat in battle.[18] The supply route was well protected, the strategic bases secure, and the advance could be accomplished in a rapid fashion.

It is sufficient to reiterate the image of Pharaoh. Merenptah was given the sickle sword of victory by the god Ptah of Memphis in a dream, and this image is followed through in the various accounts of the war. It is reasonable to claim that he was in his war chariot but, as indicated by the earlier Seti relief, the encounter with the Libyans was of a nature different than that shown in the accounts of Asiatic campaigns. Merenptah knew that the Libyan coalition was intent upon seizing and retaining Egyptian land. He also was cognizant of the type of warfare that they would use. The Libyans did not dash forward with chariots but rather brought along their families – the women and young children assuredly proceeding somewhat to the rear of their men – and pack animals laden with necessary goods.

But the presence of Egyptian chariots must have been always the deciding factor against the Libyans. Otherwise, the battles would have seen footsoldier against footsoldier, and I do not believe that this can be argued. The duration of the melee at the time of Merenptah, nonetheless, speaks for a serious and enervating encounter, one that was not decided solely by those war vehicles. Therefore, we must conclude that the number of troops that the Pharaoh brought with him did not exceed by too much that of his opponent. As stated above, I would place a cap of 25,000, although this figure may still be too great.[19]

The numbers presented in the historical inscriptions of Ramesses III have recently undergone yet a further analysis.[20] However we interpret the data concerning this Merenptah's war, I follow O'Connor in retaining a healthy skepticism with regard to the figures associated with Ramesses III's first Libyan campaign in his fifth regnal year. The two groups of 63,000 plus and 24,000 men (both round numbers) for this conflict are impossible unless, as has been noted, these grand totals refer to the *entire* society of Libyans.[21] No one has attempted to estimate the size of the opposing army in square meters, and even if we assume a nice geometrical figure in order to work out the physical size of the enemy, all falls to ruination. For example, the first and larger figure indicates a square with a size of 73 m, but then we are assuming a compact group of soldiers, which, in this case, did not occur.

Needless to say, with such figures it would take more than a few hours to defeat the enemy. O'Connor, who has covered the improbability of these integers, quite wisely turned to the account of Ramesses III's year eleven war in which slightly more than 2,000 slain Libyans and an equal number of captured foes are listed.[22] He arrived at a figure of 4,227 people (slain and living) for this campaign and felt 19,020 (another round number) to be a reasonable figure. O'Connor concluded that in Merenptah's time there were 30,588 opponents (soldiers plus noncombatants) and for Ramesses III in his eleventh year 19,020. Although these numbers do not indicate the size of the opposing army, I believe that they are impressive. We do not know how many tribespeople accompanied the soldiers of the Libyans. If we neglect the noncombatants, the total size of the enemy at the place of battle in year eleven of Ramesses III appears reasonable, especially in contrast to the baseline figures presented for the Libyan invasion in his fifth regnal year. If the latter are considered valid, then I must assume that the Egyptian army, although possessing more troops than their opponents, would have occupied too long a column.

Were the Libyan noncombatants strung out in columns or in an amorphous series of files meekly following their virile men? This is possible. But were they distant from the scene of battle, a possibility that appears more reasonable in light of the eight *iters* of carnage recorded by Ramesses III in the account of his year eleven campaign?[23] The narrative unfortunately does not list the total number of Libyans in the vicinity of battle. Then too, how many chariots would have been necessary to crush the enemy soldiers if, for example, we set the number of those men above 24,000? The head-on smash of the combatants would have slowed up the Egyptian charge. Indeed, the Egyptian chariots would have stopped advancing so that their bowmen could shoot their arrows at the foes. But this would only have been effective against the first lines of the foe. Those deeper would not have been affected by the charge of the Egyptians. True, they could have fled, but then this implies that the Egyptian footsoldiers would have mopped up the first line of enemy soldiers and those immediately behind. I prefer to take the figures for the year eleven account as reasonable. Let us not forget that any figure given in a military account need not be accurate. Indeed, historiographic analysis has revealed that even the presumed "exact" lists of dead and captured are liable to great distortion by the victor. For the year five campaign we either have 63,000 plus slain or else about 24,000. O'Connor used this data in order to estimate the sizes of the Libyan tribes, but the larger figure remains a quandary.[24]

I have left out Merenptah's Canaanite war until now, as the continual Libyan threat was so much greater.[25] Chronologically, this campaign is to be dated at least two if not three years earlier. The action was localized to Palestine and the regions included the southern port cities as well as the border zone to the east. The enemies appear to include Israelites and other tribal elements such as the Shasu.[26] In other words, this conflict arose not from a general revolt in the area but as a result of population pressure that affected the more unstable zones of Egyptian control. Parallels can be seen in the early campaigns of Seti I and at least one during the reign of Ramesses II; Horemheb might be added as well. We have already observed a tightening of control by the early Ramesside kings in southern Palestine, no doubt a by-product of the potential instability. Under Ramesses II strongholds and administrative centers were established in strategic locations such as at Ashdod and Aphek as well as in other towns along the Via Maris.[27] This policy of more direct involvement also may have been a result of the troubled Mediterranean. With roving Sea Peoples, Egypt had now to watch out for raids along the coast and possible attacks upon her port cities. It is assumed that by the reign of Merenptah the last semi-independent Canaanite city-kingdoms such as Ashkelon and Gezer were already eliminated. Indeed, from P. Anastasi III it is clear that the Egyptians had an interest in the hill country leading off the major route from Sile to Gaza.[28] Merenptah's reconquest of Gezer was a necessary prerequisite to further campaigning in the north of Palestine. All in all, military strongholds were probably established around every 20 km at locations from Aphek down to Gaza. Thus the "Ways of Horus," the coastal road out of Egypt, was made more secure.

Merenptah, if he campaigned in person, seems to have moved from Gezer to Yeno'am.[29] We hear of the following defeated cities or peoples: Ashkelon, Gezer, Yeno'am, and Israel. The last, a tribal entity at this time, may have been in the area northeast of Yeno'am. Let us remember that they were semi-nomads or perhaps tribal units that could threaten the Egyptian peace but could not conquer major centers. They perennially threatened any urban area, but so long as the Egyptians remained vigilant, the political situation was under control. Along with those four named peoples and places Merenptah fought against the Shasu. It has been noted that he is not depicted in reliefs at Karnak fighting these peoples but only binding them.[30] This may mean that a subordinate, possibly the crown prince Seti-Merenptah or Khaemwase, another member of the royal family, conducted the attack against the Shasu. One hypothetical reconstruction envisages the Pharaoh

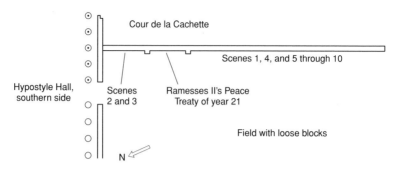

Figure 14.1a Position of Merenptah's Canaanite Campaign reliefs in the temple of Karnak, at Luxor. Frank J. Yurco, *Journal of the American Research Center in Egypt* vol. XXIII, 1986, p. 191. Reprinted by permission of Dianne Yurco.

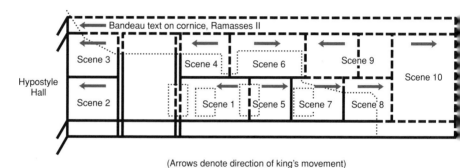

Figure 14.1b Layout and disposition of scenes of Merenptah's Canaanite Campaign reliefs at Karnak. Scene 9 based upon reconstruction of Le Saout, *Cahiers de Karnak* VII (1978–81), 352, pl. IV, no 4b. Frank J. Yurco, *Journal of the American Research Center in Egypt* vol. XXIII, 1986, p. 191. Reprinted by permission of Dianne Yurco.

personally moving against Israel after reconquering Gezer, Ashkelon, and then Yeno'am. At the same time his son would have attacked the Shasu. In the Gezer scene of Merenptah at Karnak Khaemwase figures prominently. But all of this is speculation as we must rely upon various military scenes and a few tantalizing remarks in the other war inscriptions of the king. The Israel Stela, drawn up in Merenptah's fifth regnal year, mentions the Israelites among other cities (Ashkelon, Gezer and Yeno'am), but only in a final poetical coda.[31] Finally, a second Miscellany, P. Anastasi II, appears to refer to the victorious king's later voyage to Thebes, soon after the war.[32]

Figure 14.2a   Scene 1, Lower register. Merenptah besieges Ashkelon. Frank J. Yurco, *Journal of the American Research Center in Egypt* vol. XXIII, 1986, p. 192. Reprinted by permission of Dianne Yurco.

Figure 14.2b   Scene 2, Lower register. Merenptah besieges an unnamed town, probably Gezer. Traces of water from earlier reliefs visible at bottom center. *Journal of the American Research Center in Egypt* vol. XXIII, 1986, p. 192. Reprinted by permission of Dianne Yurco.

EXCURSUS

1. O'Connor discusses the military structure of the enemy Libyans in "The Nature of Tjemhu (Libyan) Society in the Later New Kingdom," 66–89. His study should be read with that of Detlef Franke, *Altägyptische Verwandts-chaftbeziehungen im Mittleren Reich*, Borg Gmbh, Hamburg (1983), 197–203. Here, we are faced with a situation similar to that which Delbrück and others have exposed. Namely, that these "pastoral nomads" were able to harness a greater number of fighting men per population base than their sedentary (and civilized) opponents. See our comments in excursus 1 to chapter 12.

The technological level of the Libyans must be viewed independently of their strategic aims and their tactical competence. It is one thing to maintain that the Egyptian sources are, owing to their inherent bias, one-sided and dramatic in viewpoint and another to claim that these peoples "were neither as unstructured nor as functionally simple as the Egyptian sources might at first suggest" (p. 85 in O'Connor's work). Were the Libyans "warrior peoples" whose military organization was intimately related to their social and political order? It is interesting to note that Keegan follows the footsteps of Andreski (*Military Organization and Society*[2]) by recognizing that Egypt was spared "the burden of maintaining a standing army until late in its civilised life" (*A History of Warfare*, 225, but see pp. 224–9 for useful military data supporting O'Connor's thesis). Although I would qualify some of his claims – see chapter 1 in this volume, for example – Keegan's point is well made. Success on the battlefield relies heavily upon generalship, but it is also a result of "who gets there fastest with the mostest." Given the threat of the Libyans, and the kings' knowledge of their direction and aims (strategy), Merenptah, and subsequently Ramesses III, were able to counter the invasions. The predominance of the chariot arm on the part of Egypt was able to offset the large forces of the enemy. As I have commented above, if we accept those large figures of killed and captured Libyans that the Egyptian sources write, then the Pharaonic victories must have been a result of their better military preparedness. Otherwise, we will have to elevate the number of the native forces to ca. 35,000 during the reign of Merenptah and perhaps even greater under Ramesses III (year five: 30,000 or 65,000): see O'Connor, "The Nature of Tjemhu (Libyan) Society in the Later New Kingdom," in Leahy, ed., *Libya and Egypt c 1300–750 BC*, 42–44, for his estimates of the Libyan enemies. This I find impossible to do owing to the inherent limitations of the sedentary civilization's military/civilian ratio.

2. We are left with the seminal ideas of Andreski who coined the phrase "military participation ratio" in order to elucidate the situation of a state or polity which attempts to attain the maximum military strength (*Military Organisation and Society*[2], 33–4). Concerning one Libyan attack, O'Connor notes that 25 to 35 percent of the enemy were swordsmen, over 50 percent foot archers, and a mere 5–10 percent charioteers ("The Nature of Tjemhu (Libyan) Society in the Later New Kingdom," 85). But if virtually all

able-bodied Libyan men were warriors led by the clan leaders, then the ability of these peoples to threaten settled regions such as Egypt was great indeed.

An extension of military service tends to sharpen bellicosity, and even though cohesion and subordination may not have played major roles in Libyan pastoral society, these tribes were able to unite in order to invade the Delta. Perhaps the best parallel, though only mentioned here for comparative purposes, is that of the German tribes east of the Rhine. Despite their low population base in comparison to the Roman Empire, these peoples were nonetheless warlike and dangerous. They could assemble large numbers of men intent upon moving west. In both cases, the invaders were able to effect major changes within the sedentary populations of their foes.

NOTES

1   Two key contributions to the Libyan situation during the Ramesside Period are Kitchen, "The Arrival of the Libyans in Late New Kingdom Egypt," in Leahy, ed., *Libya and Egypt c. 1300–750 BC*, 15–27; and O'Connor "The Nature of Tjemhu (Libyan) Society in the Later New Kingdom," 29–113 in the same volume. Steven Snape, "The Emergence of Libya on the Horizon of Egypt," in O'Connor and Quirke, eds., *Mysterious Lands*, 93–106, provides a recent summary of the pertinent data concerning these western peoples' relations to the Nile Valley.

The main texts (covering the coincidental Nubian revolt) are in Kitchen, *Ramesside Inscriptions* IV, Blackwell, Oxford (1982), 1–24, 33–41, VII 446; and there is an old and dated translation of the historical inscriptions by Breasted, *Ancient Records of Egypt* III, 238–64. Note the analysis of portions of the Karnak account by Schulman, "The Great Historical Inscription of Merenptah at Karnak: A Partial Reappraisal," *Journal of the American Research Center in Egypt* 24 (1987), 21–34. I have also used a series of photographs taken by Wolfgang Helck, to whom I am indebted. Nonetheless, the edition of Colleen Manassa, *The Great Karnak Inscription of Merneptah: Grand Strategy in the 13th Century BC*, Yale Egyptological Seminar, New Haven (2003), replaces all other earlier studies of the key historical narrative relating Merenptah's war against the Libyans.

Manassa discusses the Libyan chariots on pp. 89–90 of her work.

2   This is the argument of O'Connor. The military background of the Egyptians and the Libyans is ably described by Manassa in *The Great Karnak Inscription of Merneptah*, Chapter 3. I am not convinced, however, that there was a "grand strategy" on the part of either the Egyptians – they were acting defensively – or the Libyans. The latter were taking advantage of the weakened Egyptian state.

3   The most recent treatment on the Sea Peoples is the volume of Eliezer D. Oren, ed., *The Sea Peoples and Their World: A Reassessment*, University Museum, Philadelphia (2000). Two chapters are crucial for our analysis: Redford, "Egypt and Western Asia in the Late New Kingdom: An Overview," 1–20; and O'Connor, "The Sea Peoples and the Egyptian Sources," 85–102.

4 Habachi, "The Military Posts of Ramesses II on the Coastal Road and the Western Part of the Delta," *Bulletin de l'Institut Français d'Archéologie Orientale* 80 (1980), 13–30. See as well Kitchen, "Ramesside Egypt's Delta defense routes – the SE sector," *Studi di egittologia e di antichità puniche* 18 (1998), 33–8. He points out the establishment of the Libyan defense-line under Ramesses II in addition to the erection of military control posts in the area just east of the Delta.

5 Kitchen, "Historical Observations on Ramesside Nubia," in Endesfelder et al., eds., *Ägypten und Kusch*, 213–25, can be read with profit; pp. 221–4 cover the reign of Merenptah. He points out "the remarkable synchronism of the Nubian revolt with the Libyan invasion of Egypt," and accentuates this stratagem, one that Kamose had to face centuries earlier (p. 223).

6 The account at Karnak indicates that the Libyans took their time in advancing: see lines 19ff.

7 For chariots with the Libyans, see O'Connor, "The Nature of Tjemhu (Libyan) Society in the Later New Kingdom," 57. Horses with the Meshwesh Libyans are indicated in the year eleven campaign of Ramesses III as well as in this earlier war of Merenptah. O'Connor felt that some Libyan chariots were present during both attacks although they were not many. Indeed, he pointed out that these vehicles "are not included in the booty lists" of Merenptah. The evidence with regard to the year five campaign of Ramesses III is indirect.

8 If the figure of 14 days is understood as the actual distance covered, then should 280 km of travel be argued as an average distance?

9 Line 33. For the battle at Perire, see Manassa, *The Great Karnak Inscription of Merneptah*, 103–7.

We have already seen that at Kadesh the actual encounter at Ramesses II's camp must have taken place in mid-afternoon. Kitchen, *Ramesside Inscriptions, Translated and Annotated. Notes and Comments* II, 45, felt that the king's camp was attacked around 3.30 p.m. With evening twilight close to 6.00 p.m., we can assume that Ramesses fought for about two and a half hours. In the case of Merenptah, the fighting occurred early in the day.

At Kadesh, both the Egyptians and the Hittites relied upon chariots. Merenptah and Ramesses III, on the other hand, faced large numbers of Libyan infantry who were not so easily dispersed by those war vehicles.

10 In line 12 the Great Karnak Inscription states that the heavily armed troops led the archers. The latter, of course, would have had to be protected by troops because they lacked the protective shields that ordinary infantrymen carried. To shoot, even if you carry a shield, means that you become exposed. This passage, however, refers to the king's accession and not the actual march against the Libyans.

On the other hand, line 27 indicates that that the leaders of the archers were in the front.

11 O'Connor, "The Nature of Tjemhu (Libyan) Society in the Later New Kingdom," 41, argued that at least 70 percent of the captured or slain foes were Libyans; the rest were the Sea Peoples. He felt that the total force was greater than the some 16,128 who lost their weapons. Can we assume that the Pharaoh had about the same number of soldiers with him that Ramesses II is presumed to have accompanied to Kadesh? If so, that number, 20,000, would

indicate the immensity of the threat and the dire necessity of the Egyptian state to defend itself. Once more, I am led to the conclusion that the military and economic capabilities of Egypt were stretched to their limits.

12 Kitchen, *Ramesside Inscriptions* IV, 38.5; see note 7 above for O'Connor's comments on this figure.

13 In fact, can we assume that all of these were counted?

14 O'Connor, "The Nature of Tjemhu (Libyan) Society in the Later New Kingdom," 56–7, observed that in the booty lists of Merenptah the weapons of the Libyans are mixed together with those of the Sea Peoples. The "copper swords" of the Libyan Meshwesh are only referred to in line 58 of the Karnak text: see Manassa, 56 and 163. Note that the Meshwesh were not present in the earlier attack on Egypt under Merenptah. O'Connor further refers to a possible Sea Peoples' origin for these swords.

　　See W. V. Davies. *Catalogue of Egyptian Antiquities in the British Museum VII. Tools and Weapons*, British Museum (1987), 97–8.

15 See O'Connor's remarks cited in the previous note. For translations of the wars of Ramesses III, see William F. Edgerton and John A. Wilson, *Historical Records of Ramses III. The Texts in Medinet Habu Volumes I and II*, University of Chicago Press, Chicago (1936). The texts will be found in Kitchen, *Ramesside Inscriptions* V.

16 Edgerton and Wilson, *Historical Records of Ramses III*, 66 and 68. See note 7 above.

17 O'Connor, "The Nature of Tjemhu (Libyan) Society in the Later New Kingdom," discusses the pastoral nomadic aspects of the Libyan society. The presence of these animals fits perfectly into his thesis.

18 Grandet, *Le Papyrus Harris I (BM 9999)* II, 243 (n. 919).

19 See note 11 above.

20 O'Connor, "The Nature of Tjemhu (Libyan) Society in the Later New Kingdom," 41–5, tends to follow all the figures given in the Egyptian accounts.

21 As a healthy antidote to trusting war record totals, see Delbrück, *Numbers in History*, University of London Press, London (1913).

22 Ibid.

23 Conveniently, Edgerton and Wilson, *Historical Records of Ramses III*, 61 with n. 1b. See note 9 to Chapter 13. Hence 84 km is indicated. Does this mean that the Egyptians gave up pursuing and killing the enemy at a lengthy distance from the battlefield?

24 Redford, *The Wars in Syria and Palestine of Thutmose III*, 196–7, discusses the size of state armies at this time. His analyses are referred to in note 22 to chapter 5. The Libyans, on the other hand, had a tribal society quite different from those of the agriculturally based kingdoms that Redford covers.

25 Yurco, "Merenptah's Canaanite War," *Journal of the American Research Center in Egypt* 23 (1986), 189–215. There are two later analyses by him: "Merenptah's Canaanite Campaign and Israel's Origins," in Ernest S. Frerichs and Leonard H. Lesko, eds., *Exodus: The Egyptian Evidence*, Eisenbrauns, Winona Lake (1997), 27–55 – the other authors in the same volume may be consulted – and "Merenptah's Wars, the 'Sea Peoples', and Israel's Origins," in Jacke Phillips, ed., *Ancient Egypt, the Aegean, and the Near East. Studies in Honour of Martha Rhodes Bell*, Van Siclen Books, San Antonio (1997), 497–506.

26 I can refer to the theory of Bunimovitz, "On the Edge of Empires – Late Bronze Age (1500–1200 BCE)," in Thomas E. Levy, ed., *The Archaeology of Society in the Holy Land*, 327–8, concerning his theory of the "shifting frontier."

27 Singer, "Merneptah's Campaign to Canaan and the Egyptian Occupation of the Southern Coastal Road of Palestine in the Ramesside Period," *Bulletin of the American Schools of Oriental Research* 269 (1988), 1–10; and Lawrence E. Stager, "Merenptah, Israel and Sea Peoples. New Light on an Old Relief," *Eretz Israel* 18 (1985), 56*–64*.

Add Kitchen, "Ramesside Egypt's Delta defense routes – the SE sector," *Studi di egittologia e di antichità puniche* 18 (1998), 33–8.

28 Caminos, *Late Egyptian Miscellanies*, 108–13. Singer discusses this and other evidence in his article cited in the previous note. Egyptian control over the Via Maris and other key routes was of primary importance. But Singer also felt that the Egyptians eliminated the last remaining Canaanite city-kingdoms in southern Palestine. This led to an even stricter Egyptian control over that region.

29 The Gezer scene of this war depicts a member of the royal family, Khaemwase, in charge of the army. Can we assume that he, and not the Pharaoh, was the actual commander-in-chief? That is to say, is it possible that Merenptah never led the army northward? See the following remarks.

30 See Yurco's article in *Journal of the American Research Center in Egypt* referred to in note 25.

31 Conveniently, see Lichtheim, *Ancient Egyptian Literature* II, 73–8.

32 Caminos, *Late Egyptian Miscellanies*, 44–5. I owe this interpretation to Andrea Gnirs.

15

EGYPT ON THE DEFENSIVE

In undertaking his Asiatic campaign not too long after he was crowned, Merenptah attempted to retighten Egyptian control over the strategic parts of Palestine in response to a general weakening of Egyptian authority during the twilight years of Ramesses II. During early Dynasty XX Ramesses III continued this policy. During his reign three main campaigns of the Pharaoh took place, all of which were defensive in nature.[1] As we have seen, in years five and eleven he fought against the Libyans, and the area of combat was roughly the same as recounted by Merenptah. The enemy were the Meshwesh, but by now the Libu tribes, first mentioned in the reign of Ramesses II, appear on the horizon. Between these two bloody encounters was a further attack in the king's eighth regnal year, this time by the Sea Peoples. This additional event, comprising two separate attacks by land and sea, was a result of the enemy presence hovering along the settled coastline of the eastern Mediterranean and also moving overland through Asia Minor and Syria. As with the Libyans, the warfare resulted from their attempt to settle in the Egyptian-held territory. In the case of the Sea Peoples we witness the next stage of their bellicose policy. These foes of Egypt were actually originally soldiers of fortune but also traders. Like the Norsemen, and the Islamic pirates of the western Mediterranean who threatened Italy and Spain, the Sea Peoples would trade if they had to. But if a port city was undefended or even unfortified, then it was easy prey to these raiders.

By and large the sources for all of these defensive wars are found in the mortuary temple of Ramesses III at Medinet Habu, located to the west of the city of Thebes.[2] On the walls of that religious building we see and read the accounts of battle. Significantly, the Sea Peoples appear in at least three guises, all of which can be determined by their headdresses. Some have feathers on their helmets whereas other used horns. A third type is depicted with thick caps. Some of them turn up in the scenes of both the Libyan wars under Ramesses III. The confederacy of these pirates included the Peleshet (the later Philistines), Shekelesh, Sherden, Weshesh, and the Denyen. Beside the reappearance of the Sherden on the opposite side of battle was the last group who appear to have come from southeastern

Anatolia. The other ethnic units of this amorphous group have been identified earlier.

The lengthy Year Eight Inscription of Ramesses III at Medinet Habu outlines the Sea Peoples' threat.[3] A background to the two-pronged advance upon the Delta is reported, but this portion of the historical narrative is very vague and, in fact, lacking in historical exactitude. For example, the opening baldly states "The foreign lands made a confederacy in their islands."[4] If we accept this Egyptian account then we must assume that some type of military alliance among many of the Sea Peoples had come to pass. It was in the far north, and led to success against the various kingdoms and city-states in Anatolia and Syria. The allies of the Hittites – Qadi and Carchemish in North Syria as well as Arzawa in southwest Anatolia and Cyprus (Alashiya) – were taken. The Hittite empire fell. Somewhat earlier, accounts from the northern Lebanese port of Ugarit indicate a series of naval preparations and battles at sea just before that crucial city was taken by the enemy, thereby indicating that this massive success could not have been sudden.[5]

The confederacy reassembled in the middle of Amurru in northern Syria and then moved down by land into Palestine. We can presume that the attack was directed along the coast if only because a fleet of Sea Peoples later made its way to one of the Nile mouths in the Eastern Delta. The threat was severe and the local military and civilian Egyptian administrations of Palestine could not deal with it. Scenes at Medinet Habu show Ramesses marching in his chariot out against the enemy accompanied by his native troops as well as foreign ones (e.g., Sherden); the final charge on the battlefield was with the chariotry. The Sea Peoples had arrived with footsoldiers as well as their women, children, and baggage train, the latter pulled by oxen. The attempt was aimed at settlement along the coast of Southern Palestine and possibly in the more lush regions of northern Egypt.

At this time the population of the Delta had expanded more rapidly in Dynasties XIX–XX than in the Nile Valley, and therefore this region had become more important.[6] This is best seen in the transference of the capital from Memphis to Avaris in the early Ramesside Period, and may also be observed in the subsequent move to Tanis at the close of the New Kingdom. The topographic layout of the Delta in Dynasties XIX and XX has been ably reconstructed so that we are able to understand the geographical ramifications of the Sea Peoples' naval attack as well as the persistent Libyan threat. North of Memphis there were three main Nile arms, two of which branched off in the middle of the Delta.[7] The Western River, located east of the actual desert tract of Libya, split into two arms further north, roughly at the site of Kom el Hisn. It formed an effective boundary. The age-old city of Sais, also in the west, was located on the Water of Ptah, the second branch. In the center of the Delta was the Great River. According the Great Karnak Inscription of Merenptah, the Libyans had at an earlier time crossed

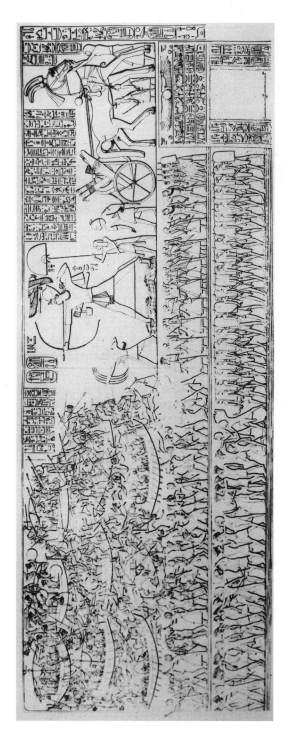

Figure 15.1 Ramesses III: Naval battle against the Sea Peoples, Medinet Habu, Western Thebes. Epigraphic survey, Oriental Institute, University of Chicago. *Medinet Habu*, vol. I, Chicago, 1930, pl. 36ff. Courtesy of the Oriental Institute of the University of Chicago.

Figure 15.2 Ramesses III: Land battle against the Sea Peoples, Medinet Habu, Western Thebes. Epigraphic survey, Oriental Institute, University of Chicago. *Medinet Habu*, vol. I, Chicago, 1930, pl. 32ff. Courtesy of the Oriental Institute of the University of Chicago.

this key zone. To the east were respectively the Water of Amun and the Water of Re. Both Avaris, modern Tell ed-Daba, and Bubastis, somewhat upstream, were situated on the second branch. Heliopolis had its own canal, called Ity, and even here the Libyans threatened the Egyptians in Merenptah's time. Lastly, at the egresses of Egypt to the northeast were the famous Bitter Lakes, the Biblical Sea of Reeds, and Shi-Hor, the name of a lake as well as the most eastern arm of the Nile. Various canals later connected the Nile arms of the Delta, thereby horizontally linking all key Delta cities, but it is unclear whether such a complex system existed in the New Kingdom.

Especially perturbing is the absence of any direct reference to these Nile arms or canals. On the other hand, the purposeful avoidance of any well-known cities or localities allows us to hypothesize that the naval battle occurred either directly on the Mediterranean coast or not too far away. The Egyptian soldiers were able to stand and operate from the shore. No quays are recorded in the inscriptions or depicted in the scenes; neither do we see any signs of habitation or human construction. In other words, the locality was probably somewhat north of the capital of Avaris if, indeed, the battle took place in the east as generally assumed. Yet there remains the possibility that this naval encounter was in the west. After all, were not the Sea Peoples and the Libyans allies at an earlier time when Merenptah ruled, and is it not reasonable to see the enemy flotilla aiming at the same region that the Libyans did? These questions must remain unanswered at the present time, owing to the dearth of explicit data.

In the lengthy narrative of the Sea Peoples' war one common subsection is oriented to a royal address of Ramesses III.[8] We find this literary approach pinpointing the organization of Egypt. A list of the key officials and military men who heard their king's encouraging words of success against the enemy is included. The military classes of Egypt are mentioned as well as the king's sons and royal officials. An additional scene presents this outlook in pictorial format. Ramesses III addressed his "leaders of the infantry and chariotry" before setting out on the campaign. War equipment was handed out to the army, thus indicating that most of the weapons were owned by the state. Included were helmets, sickle swords, corselets, quivers, spears, and bows. This evidence further reinforces our contention that the state virtually controlled the entire economic organization of the army. Horses are not present, a point well worth stressing as we shall examine this situation later. The eldest king's son and heir is in charge of the distribution, and from him the commands descend to the army commanders and the lower combat officers. This first scene of the Sea Peoples' war paints the opening call to arms. The army is prepared, and we may assume that, because Ramesses III is standing on a rostrum, this was the occasion when the king spoke to his troops just before marching. The following depiction reflects the march into Asia (Djahy). On land he pressed the enemy and defeated them.

The narrative inscription provides the necessary detailed written account.[9] The backdrop to the war, however, merely limns the causes of the attack. The frontier in Palestine was organized. Can we presume that the king met these invaders far south of Byblos at the coast in southern Palestine or was the battle close to the old northern border? The inscription, at any rate, later adds that the enemy was met at the frontier and crushed. Ramesses' princes, garrison commanders, and the elite *maryannu* formed the bulk of the officer class who were ordered to provide an effective defense. Evidently, enough time remained for the Pharaoh to face his enemies. The whole body of troops is specified. Within the chariotry were "runners," although there is scholarly dispute concerning the exact significance of this term. "Picked men" and chariot warriors are also listed. This interesting sidelight therefore indicates that three separate contingents of soldiers composed the chariot arm of the state even though two men remained on the war vehicles.

A second series of reliefs adds to this account, and the accompanying lengthy historical inscription likewise provides welcome support to our analysis. A further contingent of Sea Peoples came by water. The text states that there was a naval encounter at the mouths of the Nile in the Delta. The king's defensive measures included a stockade of lances that was set up on the shore to impede the enemy ships. At the minimum, this was done to prevent the Sea Peoples from landing their troops. In the accompanying reliefs, perhaps reflecting artistic sensibility, only four Egyptian ships attack five Sea Peoples war vessels. The king remained on land while his archers provided the necessary attack force. No chariots were employed because the battle was fought from shore to ship and from ship to ship. The naval victory was celebrated at a coast fortress. Ramesses III indicates the types of ships employed in this defense, and that they were also divided into three groups: ordinary transporters, galleys, and coasters. The first term was the most common one, and we can assume that the king requisitioned all types of Nile-bound vessels in order to provide his defense. The second refers to cargo ships whereas the third was employed for naval vessels undertaking lengthy voyages in the Mediterranean along the eastern coastline of Palestine and Syria.

Ramesses IV provides supplementary information concerning the Sea Peoples in the Great P. Harris, written soon after his accession.[10] But the account of his father's wars does not indicate much besides a list of the names of the Sea Peoples. Tjeker, Peleshet, Weshesh, and Sherden are named. The latter two are subsumed under the rubric of "Peoples of the Sea." This narration further reveals the organization of the Egyptian army in the king's reign. Infantry and chariots are logically separated as earlier, and Sherden and Qeheq (a Libyan tribe) soldiers are named. Once more the necessity of employing foreign elite men within the Egyptian war machine is stressed.

The naval battle, quite rightfully, has been the subject of much study.[11] The ships of the enemy reflect an Aegean tradition, one that was based on relatively long sea voyages across a large extent of water. In other words, they were not mere coasters or trading vessels. The hulls of the enemy fleet were angular and the prows and sternposts vertical. In addition, it seems that the Egyptian fleet blockaded the river outlets in order to prevent the enemy from escaping. This novel interpretation implies that Ramesses purposely waited until the enemy was close to disembarking and then, after having trapped them between shore and sea, attacked. In the scenes of battle, the enemy ships are stationary and within range of the land-based archers. Their vessels appear slender and lower in the water than the Egyptian ones, but a problem remains concerning the artistic impression. The Egyptian ships, on the other hand, reveal quite astounding details. Their high angular sternpost has no native parallel. The aftercastles were built with two stories, thereby providing a higher base for the naval archers and giving the helmsman a better position. But the high bulwark that protects the rowers is not known in the Nile Valley even though it was commonplace among the Aegean Bronze Age galleys. The low prow may imply the practice of ramming and therefore reflect a technological defense against the maritime activities of the Sea Peoples. This interpretation, however, seems questionable.

Under Ramesses II and III the Egyptians began to employ a type of merchant ship hitherto unknown within the Nile Valley.[12] These ships, called *menesh*, were probably built in the royal dockyards. But they were not developed from local sailing vessels known to the Egyptian for many centuries earlier. Lucien Basch has proposed that these *menesh* were derived from the north, and he pinpoints Syria, although Phoenicia is meant, as the origin. Known from the early years of Ramesses II, these ships were also present in the naval battle of Ramesses III against the Sea Peoples but operated as well in the Red Sea for voyages to the fabulous land of Punt, inland from the Somali coast or, as has been recently argued, along the southern coastline of Arabia. By and large, it seems reasonable that in Dynasty XIX, if not somewhat earlier, the flotilla of Egypt was reorganized according to the naval traditions of the Phoenicians. Their ports had close connections with various peoples traversing the eastern Mediterranean, and possibly their shipwrights had developed the high prows and sterns of other foreign sea cruisers. Moreover, these high prows were also common in scenes of the Syrian ships that unloaded their produce at Thebes in Dynasty XVIII. It appears reasonable to conclude that the Egyptian state improved its own merchant and combat navy during the second half of Dynasty XVIII and the first part of the succeeding dynasty in order to transport soldiers and to deliver "tribute" from Asia. Later, however, they would be used in sea combat.

The reliefs show that the fighting was mainly hand-to-hand, notwithstanding the presence of Egyptian archers on land and in the ships. Many of the Sherden and other enemies are carved in the position of captives. Their hands are constrained within wooden shackles. Some Egyptians have spears whereas others brandish swords. The Peleshet, Sherden, and other sea enemies mainly depended upon spears, swords, and protective shields. The reliefs depict one enemy ship captured by Sherden "mercenaries," and we can see their round shields, medium but thick swords, and distinctive helmets. (Note that the Sherden do not appear to have been part of the archer contingent of the Egyptian army.) Here, an Egyptian with shield is about to climb into an enemy ship. In another location one vessel has already been seized. Avner Raban, after subjecting the scenes of warfare, concluded that Ramesses' flotilla may have been built upon the lines of the Sea Peoples' fleet.[13] We can add that it is equally possible that the Egyptians, with the Sherden for instance, may have reorganized their ships along more up-to-date military lines. Whether or not this was a contemporary innovation must remain open, especially because the encounter between Ramesses II and the Sea Peoples early in his reign could have provided such an impetus. At any rate, the juxtaposition of both fleets is so close that we must conclude that only the final hour of the battle is pictorially recorded. The melee appears similar to a land battle, with the tactics of the Egyptian navy dependent upon the use of archers, thereby reflecting the New Kingdom tradition of the composite bow. In other words, just as with chariots, bows and arrows provided the main element of fighting.

In the account of the first Libyan war in year five of Ramesses III the arrangement of the battle reliefs is similar to that of the Sea Peoples' encounter. The king leaves with the sickle sword of victory.[14] One account states that the enemy was composed of three separate groups: the Libu, Seped, and Meshwesh. Here, the king mounts his chariot for attack, and there is little doubt that the relief indicates the actual march to battle. The main contingents of the war machine are presented visually and in writing: charioteers, *meshkeb* officers who were connected to the chariotry, and shieldbearers. Note the tripartite separation, exactly as is reported with regard to the chariot division in the later Sea Peoples' account of year eight. The king was surrounded by these men who served in his bodyguard, as did other soldiers. While on the march the foreign "mercenaries" advanced in their own groups, and thus were separate from the Egyptians and any other foreign contingents. The battle scene reveals a chariot attack at a hillside. The number of dead was recorded at around 13,000, but as noted earlier, this figure is extraordinarily large and it is possible that the number included troops and civilians.[15] Indeed, one wonders whether this number is correct, but let us keep in mind that the enemy were composed of footsoldiers and not chariotry. Many of them were brought back alive to Egypt as captives, with the Libyans far outnumbering the Sea Peoples.

In the lengthy historical account of the same war the facts are once more blurry. The advancing Libyan coalition is claimed to have "assembled in one place" and been led by a chosen war commander. But the report includes facts directly relating to the Sea Peoples' campaign of three years later in a later section. Although combined, both wars must be separated. Whether or not there was some planned joint action or at least tacit collusion between these two foes is hard to tell, although in light of Merenptah's earlier defensive success in the west this possibility is not mere speculation. Yet the literary account and the scenes of Ramesses' first Libyan war are less specific than those of the year eight campaign against the Sea Peoples, and the scenes of the victory are not as useful for analysis as those depicting the Sea Peoples' encounter.

From this pictorial evidence there is no doubt that the Egyptian army had become more polyethnic, a conclusion that must reflect the contemporary need for more soldiers if not better equipped and technologically advanced troops. The shields, bows, chariots, and armor of the Egyptians remain the same as in Dynasty XIX. Yet the Sherden are easily picked out, because their round shields and helmets are so distinctive in comparison to the Egyptians; they remain footsoldiers.

The narrative of the year eleven campaign of Ramesses III against the Libyans is the most reliable of all three war accounts at Medinet Habu. This is overtly rendered by means of the inclusion of year, month, and day.[16] More importantly, the scenes that accompany the lengthy royal narrative are far more realistic with regard to the numbers of enemy slain or captured. In one depiction the Pharaoh has dismounted from his chariot in order to bind two Libyans. Here we witness the end of the battle. Charioteers and shield-bearers, the two groups of men who ran the elite division of the Egyptian army, are singled out. The slaughter is situated at one of the western fortresses of the king: "The Town of Ramesses III which is upon the Mountain of the Horn of the Earth." (I do not think we can equate this location with the town of "Ramesses is the Repeller of the Tjemhu" mentioned in the first Libyan war of year five.) The location of the year eleven campaign is connected to the actual military clash, and thus the account sheds welcome light upon the system of border posts that were established earlier under Ramesses II.

The Pharaoh is also carved pursuing the fleeing enemy, a scene not present in the reliefs of the first Libyan war, and the exact locality is recorded. The battlefield, including the later westward advance by the Pharaoh in his mopping-up, is supposed to have covered eight *iters* of length between the minor yet topographically significant locality Hut-sha and the fortress town of Ramesses. As an *iter* is 10.5 km, the total distance was rather long: 84 km.[17] The victory ended up being a drawn-out massacre.

Ramesses III's success in this second Libyan war was different than in the first, with the battle depictions and accompanying captions more vivid. Particularly interesting is the stress upon the battle and the results. In the earlier Libyan campaign we view the preparations for battle, the march, the engagement, and finally the victory celebrations. Then come the return of the triumphant army and the final presentation to the Theban triad. Here, on the other hand, the pictorial aspect is concentrated solely upon the carnage, the return march, and the presentation. Animals are also listed in detail, with captured quadrupeds including various steers, cows, asses, goats, and sheep. This is a very different means of recounting the results of a campaign, one that reveals a greater extent of accuracy. About 43,000 animals are recorded, a huge sum, and one that would have slowed up any army.

It seems that in year eleven Ramesses III fought against a marching group of Libyan clans who had fewer troops than on the previous occasions. The invaders were mainly composed of families with their household paraphernalia, although they included a reasonable number of footsoldiers, albeit not as many as in the king's fifth regnal year. If this is accepted, and I believe that the textual evidence in combination with the pictorial supports such an interpretation, these Libyans were less of a military threat than earlier. Their desire to enter Egypt and live there, however, still indicated a massive population movement, one far more threatening to the Delta than the flotilla of the Sea Peoples. After all, warriors manned the ships of those peoples; no families appear in those scenes. Evidently, the naval attack was not aimed at settlement.

In later times the Libyans slowly managed to carve out a territory in the West Delta. This gradual development is best seen from ca. 850 BC onward although it occurred many centuries earlier. It is particularly striking that in the middle of the Third Intermediate Period (Dynasties XXIII–IV) the Libu rather than the Meshwesh coalesced around a leader centered at Sais in the West Delta. In order to explain this situation, it has been assumed that during after the reign of Ramesses III the Libyans continued to infiltrate into the northwest of Egypt.[18] I believe it is only part of the answer. The apparently inexorable upward social and political movement of their war leaders within Egyptian society, so noticeable at the end of Dynasty XXI, was also present at the close of the Ramesside Period. These results will be covered in the next chapter.

Under Merenptah the Libu are associated with villages, although one city of the ruler of the Libu is mentioned. But by year eleven of Ramesses III enemy cities as well as settlements are recorded. It would appear that these Libyans were not merely semi-nomadic folk, wandering around the small fertile areas of the coast of the Mediterranean and somewhat inland. They probably lived to the immediate west of the Delta, and although subdivided into tribes, nonetheless knew settled life. Therefore, in sufficient numbers, they may have been allowed to settle within Egypt in a fashion similar to the policy of the Late Roman Empire. Because Rome needed able troops to defend her boundaries, the emperors of the third and fourth centuries AD allowed various Germanic tribes to reside within their territory and to defend the borders. Declining population within the Empire inhibited the ability of the Roman state to supply an ever-growing need of soldiers. Did the same problem exist in Egypt at the beginning of Dynasty XX?

Even though this parallel lacks substantial data, can we hypothesize a similar case with regard to Dynasty XX and the Libyans? In other words, were they allowed to settle within the West Delta near to the line of demarcation, the supposed reason being that the Pharaohs needed soldiers in this zone? This hypothesis may partly explain why the Libyans subsequently rose to importance in the northwest. Schematically, the military situation could have progressed as follows: (1) increasing difficulties with the Libyans (Seti I); (2) internal defensive measures such as the construction of fortresses in the west (Ramesses II); (3) wholesale attacks (Merenptah to Ramesses III); and (4) Libyans allowed to settle in the West Delta and thereby control the border.

This had occurred in Palestine. Subsequent to the campaigns of Ramesses III, many of the Sea Peoples settled down on the coast of southern Palestine, the famous Biblical five cities of the Philistines being a written reminder of this policy. From archaeological evidence and the account of Wenamun, a literary text dated to the end of Dynasty XX that is historically based, it is evident that many of the Sea Peoples became federated allies of the weakened Egyptian state.[19] Was there an identical Egyptian political strategy relating to both Asia and Libya?

The principal sites in Canaan that show Philistine influence cover a great amount of territory, stretching from El-Zuweyd and Deir el-Balah on the southern coast of Palestine up to the ports of Dor and Akko.[20] Inland, evidence of Philistine contacts has been found in Hazor and Dan (in the northeast), and Beth Shan. This influence runs down in a slight southwesterly direction to encompass Beit Mirsim, Beersheba, and Masos. Trade with mainland Greece took place: the local pottery made at Ashdod follows the ceramic traditions of the Mycenaeans. But it is also interesting that there were strong Egyptian stylistic influences and traditions with respect to the Philistine tombs. The use of anthropoid coffins at Deir el Balah, an intrusive tradition, is mixed with distinctive Egyptian objects, and it is assumed that Philistine "mercenaries" or civilians may have adopted Egyptian funerary rites in this region. At other towns, however, foreign Aegean burial traditions predominated.

It is probably necessary to separate the defeat of the Sea Peoples by Ramesses III from the later Philistine settlements in Palestine. As with the Libyans, the military failure of the invaders did not end their influence. Both groups were impelled to settle in areas that were suitable for farming and trade. In the north, along the coastline of Palestine, more and more Sea Peoples held the balance of power. The Egyptian army could not dislodge them, and some type of *foederati* system took over from the older Ramesside policy of local Egyptian governors. The assumption that a "symbiosis" of Philistine–Egyptian interaction after year eight of Ramesses III appears to be buttressed by the ceramic evidence, and perhaps the rapid decline of Egyptian power in Canaan was a result of the inability of the Pharaohs to prevent the Sea Peoples from settling along the southern coast. As "associates" or even *foederati*, these seafarers, and in particular the Peleshet-Philistines, quickly managed to wrest the actual power from the Egyptians over these regions. Later, they expanded their strength inland.

EXCURSUS

1. O'Connor, "The Sea Peoples and the Egyptian Sources," in Oren, ed., *The Sea Peoples and their World: A Reassessment*, 94–100, provides a useful introduction to the historiographic basis of the war reliefs of Ramesses II at Medinet Habu (his mortuary temple). In addition, the detailed works of Essche-Merchez have provided a formal basis for explicit investigation into the arrangement of the scenes of war; see note 19 to chapter 7. The pictorial direction of the various scenes (preparation, departure from Egypt, battle encounter, return) in conjunction with the "plan of expression" were resolved by him in a striking and novel way. Essche-Merchez not only placed great emphasis upon the direction of the scenes and their culmination, often at the center of a whole series of episodes, but also covered the kernel scene in each of the pictorial war records. The additional studies of Müller and Heinz have been discussed previously.

2. The number of possible Egyptian (plus mercenary) soldiers encountering the Egyptian armies has been previously adumbrated. In the cases of these Libyan wars of Ramesses III we can estimate around 30,000–40,000 resisting troops at the maximum. See chapter 12 excursus 1 and chapter 13 excursus 1. We have to take into consideration the economic state of Egypt at the time, its maximum population (3 million), and the nature of the army. Soldiers would be absent from home, normally commencing just before mid April till early May, and then for around four months or so. Possibly excluding some "mercenaries," Pharaonic Egypt during the Ramesside Period had no full-time regular army on service for 365 days in the year.

As an example, we can refer to P. Anastasi III wherein the chariot warrior has to buy his chariot (Section 7; Caminos, *Late Egyptian Miscellanies*, 95–9). This man is assigned to the stables, economically supported by the state, and horses are "provided for him." Nonetheless, even though the steeds appear to have been given to the prospective charioteer by the central bureaucracy, the vehicles were privately bought. Therefore, the state exercised a predominant but not total economic control over the elite branch of the army. Owing to this, I believe that ratio of 1/200–1/400 for military versus civilians, as presented in excursus 1 to chapter 12, might be altered somewhat.

For the situation of the Libyan and Sea Peoples as soldiers within Egypt, see the excursus to the following chapter.

NOTES

1 The main studies are listed in notes 14–15 to chapter 14.
2 Redford, "Egypt and Western Asia in the Late New Kingdom: An Overview," in Oren, ed., *The Sea Peoples and their World: A Reassessment*, 1–20, is a very helpful presentation of the key material and its historiographic background. This analysis is concentrated solely upon the Sea Peoples.

Expanding my *Aspects of the Military Documents of the Ancient Egyptians*, Barbara Cifola, "Ramses III and the Sea Peoples: A Structural Analysis of the Medinet Habu Inscriptions," *Orientalia* 57 (1988), 245–74, and "The Terminology of Ramses III's Historical Records with a Formal Analysis of the War Scenes," *Orientalia* 60 (1991), 9–57, added useful comments. See now O'Connor, "The Sea Peoples and the Egyptian Sources," in Oren, ed., *The Sea Peoples and their World: A Reassessment*, 85–102. His most recent summary (with Eric H. Cline) is "The Mystery of the 'Sea Peoples'," in O'Connor and Quirke, eds. *Mysterious Lands*, 107–38.

3 To those studies connected with this war listed in the preceding note add Werner Widmer, "Zur Darstellung der Seevölker am großen Tempel von Medinet Habu," *Zeitschrift für ägyptische Sprache* 102 (1975), 67–77; Avner Raban, "The Medinet Habu ships: another interpretation," *International Journal of Nautical Archaeology and Underwater Exploration* 18 (1989), 163–71; Elmar Edel, "Der Seevölkerbericht aus dem 8. Jahr Ramses' III (*MH* II, pl. 46, 15–18)" in *Mélanges Gamal Eddin Mokhtar* I, 223–37; and Manfred Bietak, "The Sea Peoples and the End of the Egyptian Administration in Canaan," in *Biblical Archaeology Today, 1990. Proceedings of the Second International Congress on Biblical Archaeology*, Israel Academy of Sciences and Humanities, Jerusalem (1993), 292–306.

Trude Dothan and Moshe Dothan, *People of the Sea. The Search for the Philistines*, Macmillan, New York (1992), provide an overview of the data relating to the settlements of the Peleshet-Philistines in Palestine. We must, however, include the seminal articles of Van Essche-Merchez discussed in note 19 to chapter 7.

Bojana Mojsov, *The Sculpture and Relief of Ramesses III*, New York University Dissertation, New York (1992), 36–41 and 69–107, outlines the various reliefs present at Medinet Habu. Heinz, *Die Feldzugsdarstellungen des Neuen Reiches*, nonetheless remains fundamental.

4 Edel's study cited in the previous note discusses the historical "prologue" to the year eight campaign of Ramesses III.
5 Annie Caubet, "Ras Shamra-Ugarit Before the Sea Peoples," in Oren, ed., *The Sea Peoples and their World: A Reassessment*, 35–49, is a helpful archaeological and historical overview.
6 Butzer, *Early Hydraulic Civilization in Egypt*, 85 (fig. 13), 95.
7 Here I am following the research of Bietak, *Tell el-Daba II; der Fundort im Rahmen einer archäologische-geographischen Untersuchung über das ägyptische Ostdelta*. Vienna (1975). See as well his "Historical Geography in the Eastern Nile Delta," *Bulletin de l'Institut d'Égypte* 60/61 (1978/80 = 1983), 71–94.

8 Spalinger, *Aspects of the Military Documents of the Ancient Egyptians*, 96 n. 64; see Redford, "Egypt and Western Asia in the Late New Kingdom: An Overview," in Oren, ed., *The Sea Peoples and their World: A Reassessment*, 10–13.

9 O'Connor, "The Sea Peoples and the Egyptian Sources," in Oren, ed., *The Sea Peoples and their World: A Reassessment*, 94–100, is an up-to-date analysis of this narrative.

10 See Grandet, P. *Harris I (BM 9999)* I, 335–42. We can add a new, albeit fragmentary, hieratic account published in Spalinger, *The Transformation of an Ancient Egyptian Narrative: P. Sallier III and the Battle of Kadesh*, chapter XI. The narrative appears to reflect upon the Libyan wars of Ramesses III.

11 Most recently see Shelly Wachsmann, "To the Sea of the Philistines," in Oren, ed., *The Sea Peoples and their World: A Reassessment*, 104–43.

12 Basch, "Le navire *mnš* et autres notes de voyage en Égypte," *The Mariner's Mirror* 64 (1978), 99–123.

13 The study is cited in note 3 above.

14 For the two Libyan wars of Ramesses III see Kitchen and O'Connor's studies, both in the volume edited by Leahy, *Libya and Egypt c. 1300–750 BC*, referred to in Chapter 14 n. 1.

15 See our remarks in Chapter 14 n. 1 and the accompanying discussion. O'Connor discusses these figures on pp. 39–45 in "The Nature of Tjemhu (Libyan) Society in the Later New Kingdom," in Leahy, ed., *Libya and Egypt c. 1300–750 BC*.

16 A short discussion of the veracity of this account with regard to the actual carving of the scenes and inscriptions at Medinet Habu, which was the most contemporary of all the king's three wars at Medinet Habu, is in my *The Transformation of an Ancient Egyptian Narrative: P. Sallier III and the Battle of Kadesh*, chapter XI; and "Sothis and 'Official' Calendar Texts," in Charles C. Van Siclen III, ed., *Jubilate Conlegae. Studies in Memory of Abdel Aziz Sadek*, Part I, *Varia Aegyptiaca* 10 1995 (= 1997), 182–3. The narrative accounts of the earlier two wars merely give the year.

17 See note 23 to chapter 14. If, however, we take the *iter* as equivalent to 2.65 km, a figure that also occurs in one Egyptian text, then the distance would be 21 km, another reasonable integer. But considering the time it would take to repulse over 2,000 soldiers and remembering that the families of the Libyan tribes were also following behind their men, the longer distance seems reasonable.

18 A summary of the Libyan movements into Egypt subsequent to the wars of Ramesses III is by Kitchen, "The Arrival of the Libyans in Late New Kingdom Egypt," in Leahy, ed., *Libya and Egypt c. 1300–750 BC*, ed., 21–4, and "La suite des guerres libyennes de Ramsès III," *Revue d'Égyptologie* 36 (1985), 177–9. Leahy's contribution to this subject is "The Libyan Period in Egypt: An Essay in Interpretation," *Libyan Studies* 16 (1985), 51–65; see as well Gnirs, *Militär und Gesellschaft*, 206–9.

19 For a handy translation of this composition, see Lichtheim, *Ancient Egyptian Literature* II, 224–30.

20 For this data and the following discussion there have been many detailed archaeological studies. In addition to Trude and Moshe Dothan's volume referred to in note 3 above, see Singer, "The Beginning of Philistine Settlement in

Canaan and the Northern Boundary of Philistia," *Tel Aviv* 12 (1985), 109–122; Raban, "The Philistines in the Western Jezreel Valley," *Bulletin of the American Schools of Oriental Research* 284 (1991), 17–28; Lawrence Stager, "The Impact of the Sea Peoples in Canaan (1185–1050 BCE)," in Levy, ed., *The Archaeology of Society in the Holy Land*, 332–48; and the following chapters in Oren, ed., *The Sea Peoples and their World: A Reassessment:* Trude Dothan, "Reflections on the Initial Phase of Philistine Settlement," 145–58; Israel Finkelstein, "The Philistine Settlements: When, Where and How Many?," 159–180; and Ephraim Stern, "The Settlement of the Sea Peoples in Northern Israel," 197–212. The subject is voluminous.

16

THE SOCIAL SYSTEM OF THE MILITARY IN THE RAMESSIDE PERIOD

Within Egypt one major source dealing with land ownership sheds welcome light upon the later organization of the Egyptian military. P. Wilbour, dated to Ramesses V, covers the measurement and assessment of various plots of land for the purposes of some type of taxation.[1] The extant papyrus deals mainly with Middle Egypt around the Fayum and further south. In certain zones "soldiers" occur frequently, especially to the south in the regions administrated by Sepermeru and Hardai. The second controlled a region that was very densely settled. The "soldiers" are purposely separated from the Sherden, and once more the presence of this non-Egyptian ethnic group within the country is overtly recognized. In the four zones that can be ascertained, and running from north to south, the percentages of the military classes are as follows:

	Stable-masters	Soldiers	Sherden
Zone I	4.3	1.4	4.3
Zone II	30.8	9.6	4.2
Zone III	33.9	21	4.8
Zone IV	24.2	19.7	2.4

The importance of horses is evident in the more southern regions while the core of the ordinary native Egyptian military men was even further upstream. The Sherden are situated more to the north, perhaps owing to their greater importance as an elite component of the Egyptian army whose service was concentrated in southern Palestine, the Delta coastline, and the western border. Further research by Barry Kemp has provided an interesting social profile of all of these landowners. The Sherden, just as the Egyptians, were settled upon the land. The cemetery of Sedment, close to Herakleopolis in the XXth Nome of Upper Egypt, and hence within this Middle Egyptian zone, provides additional supporting archaeological evidence for this practice. The percentages of ownership run in this descending order:

Stable-master	22	Small farmer	12
Soldier	17	Herdsman	11.3
Lady	14.5	Sherden	7.5
Priest	12.4	Scribe	3.3

Granted that the data come from a limited region within Middle Egypt, and that the Sherden might be overrepresented in this area, it is still useful to see that the literate scribes comprised a very minor number of land-owners. There is also an absence of the highest ranks in the Egyptian army. Stable-masters form the largest group, thereby indicating their importance for the army. If we add this group with the native soldiers, the figure reaches 39 percent, and if the Sherden are included, the total becomes almost one half of the total of landowners. Does this not imply a military preponder-ance in northern Middle Egypt? By themselves, the Sherden amount to 44 percent of the combat troops, excluding the stable-masters.

I do not believe that the facts in P. Wilbour can be employed to estimate the size of the Egyptian army. As Kemp saw, the number of soldiers very well may be a local peculiarity. It is impossible that the Sherden composed 225,000 and the Egyptian warriors 510,000 within a total population of ca. three million. This would reveal an incredible number of male warriors. To a degree this bias may be eased since these four zones were relatively populous, especially in comparison with the nomes of Upper Egypt. Actu-ally, the number of individuals owning land is rather small, and the statistics in the previous two charts do not reflect this factor. For example, in zone I we have 6 Sherden. Zones II, III, and IV contain respectively 18, 30, and 9. Thus the percentages have to be viewed from the actual figures. Furthermore, we must not forget that landowners were an elite group. In P. Wilbour they are sometimes called "cultivating agents" or more simply, "agents."[2]

Only a small amount (10 percent) of the total agricultural land is recorded in P. Wilbour. If we take that figure and multiply it by the integers presented in the previous two charts, the soldiers plus Sherden owned about 2.5 percent of the total land in the specified four zones. On a one-to-one basis this might indicate that the grand total of the army was at least 75,000 men. Notwithstanding the fragility of this assumption, we are at least within striking distance of a reasonable approximation. The settlements of Sherden further indicate that free land was available for the Pharaohs to allow their "mercenaries" a permanent home and a secure means of life. Therefore, many of them lived, as did the native combat troop, by owning lands which they may have cultivated when not engaged in war stationed abroad. But it remains striking that so many warriors are represented in this area. The need for the Egyptian state to have a large number of troops settled in this area must point to some instability in the north, with Libya and the East Mediterranean being the logical focal points for defense.

Within the Nile Valley the gradual developments that led to this land-owning policy are reflected in the various satires that were written down in Dynasty XIX. These small texts, called Miscellanies, indicate the social setting in which the soldiers lived.[3] Particularly striking is the presence of tractates that deprecated the life of the military. These compositions are particularly informative as they purposely separate the common footsoldier from the charioteer and reveal a stage in which the latter were the more important sector of the Egyptian war machine. These compositions were written from the point of view of the officialdom, which now had to enclose itself within a protective ideological setting, one that was not opposed to war, but rather to the career of a military man.

A key Miscellany, P. Anastasi III, can be summarized as it presents the common themes of the scribal hierarchy's antipathy toward the soldiers.[4] The first section deals with the boy who is inducted into the army in order to be a footsoldier. He is first sent to the state barracks for military training where he is beaten and subjected to harsh discipline. Subsequently, he sees active duty in Asia, and it is worth while to remark that the foreign climes in these satires are always those of the north. Clearly, Nubia was not worth mentioning because the danger was insignificant. In Asia the soldier goes on patrols and is continually exhausted. He is virtually a pack animal, and when he returns to Egypt his physical condition is hopeless; even his clothes are stolen and his attendant runs away. Interestingly, a brief notice in P. Bologna 1094 proves that young men designated to be ordinary priests could be conscripted into the army against the order of the vizier.[5] This official letter sheds additional light upon the status of footsoldiers and may in fact reveal the growing need of the state to obtain more combat troops by not so legal means.

The second group to be satirized is the chariot warriors. At this point the writer becomes more careful with his perorations. Owing to some personal influence – after all, chariot warriors belonged to a social level above that of the infantry – the recruit is assigned to the royal stable. There he acquires the necessary horses from the military camp. Thus we see that at least the animals belonged to the state and were not bought and sold at a market. Nonetheless, the luckless boy has to buy his chariot. The man's inability to ride horses is less significant than his ineptitude with the war vehicles. He ends up physically ruining his body because he cannot control the movement of the horses tethered to the chariot.

A further example from P. Lansing is even more instructive in elucidating the social distance between literate scribe (official) and weary soldier.[6] In this satire the infantryman is placed in the bottom rung of a highly graded series of military officials. He is called up for Asia and received his weapons at Sile. The war is about to begin. The long marches, brackish water, and tedious but minor military encounters exhaust the man. There is no glory but instead sickness and exhaustion. Other satires point out that the real life of a footsoldier involves minor forays against an enemy that hides in the hills or who is dangerous only at the limits of Egyptian control. No great campaigns exist. There is no glory in this tedious and dangerous life. The result is not worth the gain of military renown.

It is true that among these Miscellanies the scribal class is quick to point out other professions that are abhorrent. Thus the cultivator's life is despised. But once more the assumptions are laid clear. The scribe is a superior. He follows no orders and avoids physical labor. Even the stable-master is not worthy of recognition and lowly priests receive their comeuppance in these writings. Yet even though scribal satires were already popular among the literate class, at least from the beginning of Dynasty XII, the inclusion of the military profession is new. Therefore, these compositions have to be viewed in light of the different social make-up of the New Kingdom, one in which the career of a soldier had come to be significant.

The state officials in the New Kingdom, and especially in the Ramesside Period, now included the military. It was the growing importance of this arm of war that led to these virulent attacks. Earlier, when the army was not that significant, such as in Dynasty XII, the profession of the warrior was not attacked. Now it became commonplace. Side by side with the officialdom now loomed the warrior. These tractates were not written to dissuade a young man from the career in the military. Composed, copied, and read by the literate officials, they served to bolster the self-awareness of the scribal elite as a corporation different from the military. It is true that many facets of the scribe's life were overlooked or misconstrued, such as the patent lie that a scribe is independent. Did he not follow the orders of superiors? In addition, the accounts of exhaustion and warfare are flagrant exaggerations. But for purposes of contrast the soldier's life was depicted as yet another wretched profession. It may not be out of place to point out that the owners of these Miscellanies were predominately treasury officials. Was it solely in this sector of the royal administration that a very strong antipathy was prevalent? We do not know. Nevertheless, the strength of vituperation leaves little doubt that these officials viewed the ordinary military men in a very lowly light.

The Miscellanies include other sections that report on military events in a sober and realistic manner. These facts were, however, not included in the satires. Some of them have to do with the reports of the border officials in the northeast Delta. A second case, a eulogy, covers the praise of Pharaoh Merenptah (P. Anastasi II).[7] It seems that the king had just returned from an expedition, probably in Asia. The writing must therefore reflect upon Merenptah's Palestinian campaign. Enemy *maryannu* are reported to have been destroyed, and the Sherden turn up again as the elite sector of the Egyptian army. In fact, the king is reported to have departed to Thebes with his chariot "bowed down with hands" while pinioned chieftains go in front of him. Was there a victorious march from north to south through the countryside?

A further useful example is reported in P. Koller.[8] The equipment for an Asiatic expedition is listed. Hence, we can visualize the actual preparations for war. The stable-masters and grooms for the horses come first in the account. Noteworthy is the mention of the provisions for men and animals. The equids have straw and the soldiers are given special kyllestis-breads, items that are also recorded in one of the baking accounts under Seti I that were discussed earlier. Two men take care of the donkeys. The weapons are stacked in the chariots, and the items include arrows, swords, lances, bows, cuirasses, tent poles, and other associated military paraphernalia. Also worthy of mention is the presence of a Hittite javelin, the key weapon that was held by the third man in the enemy chariots at the Battle of Kadesh.

Another satire, P. Anastasi I, is actually different in tone and orientation from the anti-military tractates. The text is a literary one, written in the form of a letter from a master to his scribal underling.[9] The exact date of the composition is unclear, but one editor has set it to a time before year five of Ramesses II. Although this is uncertain, the composition is most certainly a product of the first half of Dynasty XIX. For our purposes the numerous Asiatic localities, foreign (Semitic) words, and general understanding of the political geography is Asia are paramount. We are given a detailed "world picture" of Asia in the XIXth Dynasty in this composition. The regions specified are in a logical geographic order, and they encompass the coast of the Lebanon, a few inland cities in Syria, and a series of localities in Palestine. To the north the knowledge of the coast runs from Tyre and Byblos, and then even further. The inland cities of Syria include Kadesh, Tubuhi, and Hermon. The latter two were south of the first, but the geographic orientation reflects a date when Egypt no longer controlled any portion of Syria. In Palestine the localities mentioned include Rehob, Marun er-Ras (?), Der'a, Megiddo, Aduruna, Hazor, and Shechem. Of equal importance is the concentration upon these settled zones. One group is located near to the Jordan River while a second covers the eastern regions of Syria south of Kadesh and in north Palestine.

From this satire we can determine just how extensive the Egyptian knowledge was of the north. The account concentrates mainly upon the territory held by Egypt, and it also emphasizes those cities on the borders of Palestine and the coast. I feel that this orientation, probably derived from well-known "routiers" of Asia kept in archives at home, indicates the places of key importance to the Egyptian administrators, emissaries, and soldiers. In other words, P. Anastasi I provides us with a political geography that is focused upon those areas where the Egyptians had to maintain strict vigilance. This would explain the presence of large or more important cities in the center of Palestine such as Shechem, Hazor, and Hamath and the lack of southern ones.

In the last paragraph I mentioned the presence of Egyptian road maps or "routiers."[10] To administer their northern territories and to dispatch armies into these regions the Pharaohs had to possess lists of the key cities if not the lesser ones. Rivers and mountains also would have to be included. From lengthy lists of "conquered" foes set up in the temples it appears that the

Egyptians possessed a great knowledge of the political set-up of Asia. Earlier I pointed out that one hypothesis maintains that sections of these lists indicate specific directions such as north–south or east–west. By analyzing such portions we can see that some type of geographical arrangement holds. In fact, the Syrian localities are usually separated from the Palestinian ones; places in the Trans-Jordan similarly form a unified whole. The evidence from P. Anastasi I supports this hypothesis. At the capital and perhaps in other important Egyptian cities the king, vizier, diplomats, soldiers, and other high officials had at their fingertips a reasonably detailed geopolitical outline of Asia. How else could such a lengthy and detailed account such as this one, satirical though it is, have been composed without the help of some first-hand knowledge of the north? More importantly, how did the Pharaohs know where to send their troops if the case should arise, or even know where to march? As always, a general staff needs maps and lists of the foreign lands for future attacks.

By the time these satires were composed stabilization of the higher ranks in the military had been accomplished. We have pointed out the growing alterations that occurred in this corporate unit by the time of the Amarna Period, yet the necessity of dealing with the Asiatic situation meant that a more direct system of administrative control came to pass in Palestine. The role of kings' sons, the marshals, and their superiors the generals, increased in importance from mid Dynasty XVIII until later a solidification set in. A further leveling-off of this social movement is reflected by the connection of royal princes with the chariotry and various non-royal families associated with the position of viceroy in Kush.[11] For example, princes who were marshals proliferate in the inscriptional material of late Dynasty XIX and Dynasty XX. Among them we can note the future Ramesses VI and VIII, but also one son of Ramesses IX, a general, and the eldest son of Hrihor (end of Dynasty XX), who was a marshal.

Thus the military connections of the highest officials of the day remained in play, and the viceroys of the Ramesside Period were likewise connected to the chariotry. At the close of Dynasty XX, Hrihor, and his temporary "successor" Piankh, were both generals. But many of the army officers were connected to temple administration as well. We can see this most clearly under the reigns of Ramesses II and Merenptah. A certain Mai, who was not really a "pure" warrior, was also in charge of architectural work and the prophets of a temple. Various other middle-ranking soldiers were in charge of work at Karnak or at Memphis. By Dynasty XX, and proceeding into the early Third Intermediate Period, the close association of the military with the state became standard. It is true that this connection is noticeable under the reigns of Amunhotep II and III, to signal out two Pharaohs of the second half of Dynasty XVIII. Subsequently, Amunemint, a generalissimo and successor of Horemheb, was associated with a temple of Thutmose III, and other individuals owed their successful careers to their family connections with the priesthood. But increasingly in the Late Ramesside Period the warp and woof of Egyptian society was becoming militarized.

The reason why war officers were affiliated with civilian positions is not hard to fathom. Their ability and experience in running a large organization automatically made them acceptable for advancement outside of the military. They could easily transfer their knowledge to work projects, which also demanded the running of a large number of men. By and large, the non-royal officer class tended to remain in the army although various local governors often had previous military careers.

But the second half of Dynasty XX reveals an acceleration of the military factor in the social fabric of the state. The growing power of the south with its center at Thebes meant that the local High Priest of Amun had to be a military man. Piankh, the successor of Hrihor at Thebes, was a leader of troops, marshal, and also a priest. His contemporary Panehesy, who later was an opponent of the state, had also been a warlord. By the end of Dynasty XX many of these high-ranking men possessed a series of military titles, almost as if they accumulated them at whim. Hrihor, to take a case in point, began his career in the military. He was a general and war commander. Eventually, he took over the control of Nubia and thus ruled there. But his sacerdotal powers as High Priest of Amun under Ramesses XI were as important, if not greater in significance, than his military ones. Not merely did this man run the entire province of Nubia, but he also controlled Upper Egypt through his military and religious functions. Subsequently, Piankh became High Priest of Amun, and as we have seen, was also a general.

In Dynasty XX, and definitely after the death of Ramesses III, the degree of military particularism became more and more prominent. The preponderant sector of the Egyptian army was now based in Egypt owing to the inevitable loss of the Asiatic empire. We have already mentioned the Sherden and their "strongholds," and P. Wilbour reveals that in portions of Middle Egypt these "mercenaries" and the native Egyptian soldiers were numerous landowners.[12] Consider the situation after the last major war of Ramesses III. In Asia Sea Peoples, including the Peleshet-Philistines, had been allowed to settle on the southern coast of Palestine. Later, they extended their influence inland, but for the moment their influence in Palestine had superseded the Pharaoh's. Egyptian control faded bit by bit during the reigns of Ramesses IV to VI. Granted that this was a short period of time – about twenty years – the repercussions were important. No longer did Egyptian troops and their "mercenaries" fight in local or major wars in Asia. Hence, the soldiers, although well versed in the art of combat, remained at home.

The state thus contained a large number of men who were not only employed to repel disturbances in Nubia but also assigned to control the internal polity. In this case, the attempt of the local viceroy Panehesy under Ramesses XI to carve out a domain of his own, if not a kingdom, was paradigmatic. Ultimately, it failed, but only due to the perseverance of the

270

High Priests of Amun who, it must be remembered, were also military men. At least the Pharaoh – Ramesses XI in this case – could send his troops upstream to aid the faithful. But for all practical purposes, the war machine had become introverted, and this occurred when Libyans still continued to infiltrate the Nile Valley. The latter adversely affected the Theban area at the time of Ramesses IX, but earlier, under Ramesses VI, these peoples had already become troublesome. Indeed, a settlement of Meshwesh Libyans is known from the Delta at this time; any blocking of the routes into Egypt from the west was ineffective.

Not surprisingly, many of the Libyan men turn up in the military. Although the data are scanty, enough information remains to allow us to conclude that a career in the Egyptian war machine was one way that the Libyan warriors could practice a profession that was still in demand by the state. Hrihor, in fact, may have been of Libyan blood. If we turn to the historical development of late Dynasty XXI this influence is even more prominent. Why did this occur?

Demographic reasons are often cited to be the cause why the Libyans moved eastward. The consistent pressure, which resulted in four major wars during the Ramesside Period, did not abate after the death of Ramesses III. As a case in point we may remark that the ruling house of Bubastis, which took over Egypt at the end of Dynasty XXII, was not merely Libyan in origin, but it was also military-based. The Libyans clans may have persisted in retaining their ethnic identity through their names and bloodlines. Nonetheless, it is more important for this discussion to cast light upon their warlike careers. Was the number of native Egyptian soldiers relatively small by mid Dynasty XX? And even if we include the Sherden and Nubian "mercenaries," exactly how great was the population of Egypt vis-à-vis the professional soldiers at this time?

Previously, we have covered the conflicting hypotheses relating to the population of New Kingdom Egypt. By the end of Dynasty XX it had shrunk from a high point of 3 million to around 2.9 million.[13] There was a strong trend to urbanization, as well as rural emigration to more densely populated areas. In the long run this would lead to a decrease in the total number of inhabitants in the Nile Valley. Yet the settlements in the Delta grew at the same time, and it was mainly in the western tracts that the Libyans settled and expanded. A definite limit to the native population had been reached in Dynasty XVIII and a slight decline had taken place by Dynasty XX, the time when the Libyans started to reside in Egypt. Was the growing thinness in the north connected to the rapid advancement of these peoples within the Egyptian war machine?

At the close of Dynasty XX the military situation had altered, and the control of Upper Egypt had essentially passed into the hands of the High Priests of Amun. Their ability to administer the southern nomes of Egypt as well as the central portions of the Nile Valley was buttressed immensely by their military preparedness. Not only do their titles indicate this, but also the careers of such men as Hrihor and Piankh reveal the new character of the age. In the north, and especially in the West Delta, some Libyan chiefs had established themselves in various districts, and the social background of these men indicates a strong military character. True, one does not see the triumph of the Libyans until the end of Dynasty XXI, yet their importance was nonetheless growing throughout the Late New Kingdom in Dynasty XX. Localism, as well, played a crucial role in the advancement of these clans. Turned in upon themselves, such military men found success within their particular zones of influence, and regions such as Bubastis and later Sais gradually became centers of Libyan preponderance. In sum, the type of military society represented at the close of the New Kingdom was a more accentuated form of what had preceded during Dynasties XIX to XX.[14]

It will not be out of place to conclude this work with a recapitulation of the main social forces that were at work from the point of view of the military. The structure that was bequeathed to Ahmose at the commencement of the New Kingdom was one in which there was a low military participation ratio. There also was high subordination. The footsoldiers, low-ranking officers, middle-level warriors, and generals were ultimately dependent upon their war leader who was also the Pharaoh. Yet at no time within this epoch, even at its close, was Egypt a warrior society.[15] And although the cohesion of the military class was relatively closely knit and tightly organized, the rank and file of the soldiery remained connected to civilian society. Their dependence upon land ownership was perhaps the key factor in this configuration. The anti-military tractates of Dynasty XIX indicate that the lowest ranks of the military came from towns just as the other major professions such as the officialdom and the clergy.

Yet there were centers of military preponderance, at least among the Sherden "mercenaries" as well as the natives. This is paramount in the land register of P. Wilbour, described earlier, although it has to be stressed that the document is dated to the middle of Dynasty XX, and so reveals a landowning situation near the end of our time period. Hence, it may not be applicable to an earlier epoch, and I suspect that at the beginning of the New Kingdom there was a preponderance of warriors from the old Theban area of Dynasty XVII. Later, the chariot arm became preponderant, at least with regard to its superior social status. But even in Dynasty XVIII the existence of a military career was not sharply differentiated from the civilian professions. Only in the second half of that era, and then accelerating during the Amarna Period, did the chariot sector of the army become very much one of an enclosed corporation.

Then came the scribal attacks upon the military. It may not be mere coincidence that these tractates were written down in the middle of Dynasty XIX. This was a time when the Egyptian state had to exert itself to the fullest in order to resist the Hittite threat and subsequently to deal with serious problems in Palestine and Libya. As a result, the war machine became even more important for the survival of the Egyptian state. The presence of the Sherden acting as separate units within the army further highlights the Ramesside Period's growing dependence upon military men, even if they were ethnically different from the Egyptians.

The upward social mobility of the soldiers can be traced with a degree of confidence only with respect to the high-ranking members of the army. Yet the basic structure of Egypt did not appreciably change until late Dynasty XX, and even then the essential framework of the state remained the same. No social revolution took place. This was due to the preexistent structure of a powerful and socially hierarchized kingdom. In the absence of any major wars after Ramesses III, notwithstanding the serious troubles with the viceroy of Nubia at the end of the New Kingdom, military talents were, if not wasted, at least circumscribed. After all, it is war that promotes vertical mobility within armed forces, not its absence. But we can be assured that the importance of the army and the chances for promotion in Dynasties XVIII and XIX meant that there was a relatively free upward movement of promotion. Lacking any significant technical progress, Late New Kingdom Egypt remained on the same basic economic and political level that it was during the reign of Ahmose. Monocracy was the rule, even during the subsequent weakened conditions of Dynasty XXI.

The Egyptian military organization coexisted within a society whose internal unity had been and remained one that consisted of various cohesive elements. The priesthood and the scribal officialdom are two obvious cases in point. New Kingdom Egypt, although possessing a well-organized war machine, still contained elite elements that were separate from the soldier's profession. The privileged stratum did not merely consist of warriors. During the Third Intermediate Period, however, there was a change in emphasis, one that can be traced back to the second half of Dynasty XX. Perhaps we could label the period from Dynasty XXII to XXIV as semi-feudalized, a land in which the Libyan warriors, now dispersed over a relatively wide area, and after some ethnic amalgamation with the locals, tended to emancipate themselves from the Pharaoh's control. This is most evident in the weakening of political control within Dynasty XXII. And we must not forget that these warriors of Libyan descent, whose influence was the greatest in the Delta, were in the privileged stratum of society.

The Pharaoh was the war leader of the New Kingdom Egypt. He reigned supreme over the military just as he did over the officialdom and even over the clergy. Was he not as well the son of Amun, the major deity in Egypt? Yet what would happen when wars ceased and the king no longer was seen to be a champion of his state? This aspect, perhaps put in too modern a guise, nevertheless serves to epitomize the role of the kings after the death of Ramesses III. Was it mere coincidence that the last Pharaoh of the New Kingdom saw his temporal control, and thus his military role, replaced by new men in the south such as Hrihor? And even if the High Priests of Amun did not repeat the grandiose campaigns of the earlier monarchs of Egypt, they still managed to take over a large amount of military control in the south. The second half of Dynasty XX witnessed this switch of emphasis, one that coexisted with the growing power of the local Libyan families. But the period was a transitional one, and it lasted throughout most of the succeeding Dynasty. The military of the New Kingdom, nonetheless, was gradually encapsulating into a ruling warrior class, and by the death of Ramesses XI it had become further removed from civilian life than earlier.

EXCURSUS

1. Previous discussions have centered upon the military participation ratio of the New Kingdom. The final issue concerns the percentage of non-Egyptians in the Egyptian army around the reign of Ramesses III. This bears upon the presumed 1/200 to 1/400 ratio for the late Roman Empire, a massive state that had quite a number of non-Roman *foederati* within its military forces (Germans in particular). The comparison of Ramesside Egypt with Rome ca. AD 300 is worth while owing to the increase in the number of Libyans and Sea Peoples within the Egyptian forces.

A useful series of historical references may be found in the Great Harris Papyrus as well as in the Medinet Habu inscriptions of Ramesses III. (They are conveniently summarized by Grandet, *Le Papyrus Harris I [BM 9999]* II, 242–6.) We can see that after his defensive wars, this Pharaoh claimed to have reorganized the military and administrative sectors of the land (Grandet, ibid., 265–7). Whether this can be accepted on its face value is crucial. On the other hand, additional passages from the literary account of P. Harris indicate that Ramesses III placed the "leaders" of the captured Libyans (and perhaps others who joined the king) in his "strongholds." These military establishments were presumably in the Delta. The king also gave to them "archer captains" and various Libyans as their underlings and "slaves."

In other words, these "strongholds" were filled with Libyans whose purpose was military. Ramesses III also settled various Sea Peoples into other "strongholds." Unfortunately, we have no information where these men were located. Both the Eastern Delta and the coast of Palestine remain strong possibilities. (If the latter possibility is envisaged, then we have some additional evidence concerning the early occupation of the Peleshet "allies" in Palestine.) Finally, the same account indicates that these foreigners were supplied with clothing and grain by the state.

It is thus clear that early in Dynasty XX the Egyptian army was in the process of becoming polyethnic in a way that parallels the situation of the later Roman Empire ca. AD 300. Grandet, in his *Ramsès III. Histoire d'un règne*, Pygmalion/Gérard Watelet, Paris (1993), 170–9, summarizes this accentuated military policy of the Pharaoh. See now Kemp, "An Egyptian

Perspective," in *Cambridge Archaeological Review* 13 (2003), 126, who discusses the reorganization of Egyptian society by Ramesses III into royal butlers and military groups that included Libyan Qeheq as well as Sherden. He bases his arguments upon the Great Papyrus Harris and also notes the same king's official address to the "dignitaries, leaders of the land, infantry, chariotry, Sherden, ordinary troops, and every citizen of the land of Egypt."

2.   Kemp discussed the high military percentages reported in P. Wilbour and summarized at the beginning of this chapter. As he maintained, the northern geographic concentration of the Sherden in that document cannot be overlooked even though the region is south of Memphis. I follow his analysis, and the rough statistical analysis based on the extant monuments presented in excursus 3 to chapter 12 can be added. Although this information is representative of the elite during the reigns of Ramesses II and III, it nevertheless points to a relatively sizeable war machine during the Late New Kingdom. For the time of Ramesses III the army may have comprised about 15.9 percent of the elite grand total, and this figure excludes the military administration in Nubia.

3.   Our comments with regard to the military participation ratio within Egypt at this time must be modified when we consider the increasing Egyptian reliance upon foreigners. This appears to be symptomatic of the XIXth Dynasty as well, but the evidence is considerably less forthcoming than those of the following period. By and large, if Egypt was able to muster more than 20,000 troops at the Battle of Kadesh and over 30,000 against the Libyans – both figures have been discussed earlier – then I feel that the army had to include a reasonable number of non-Egyptians. By itself, the country could not supply the requisite number of men to sustain such wars.

The increasing number of Libyans settled in Egypt under Ramesses III (if not Merenptah) must be one of the basic reasons why their influence within the later phase of Dynasty XX, and then subsequently, grew in importance. The increased Libyan preponderance in the Western Delta during Dynasties XXI–XXIV can be partially explained by this early military strategy.

As a conclusion, let me quote the sober words of Turney-High: "In general, it seems that the basic cause of mercenarism is a gap between the offensive or defensive goals of a state and the qualitative or quantitative military potential of its manhood" (*The Military*, 273).

4.   Recent scholarship has revealed a large number of military men centered at Assiut (Upper Egyptian nome XIII) who can be dated to the Ramesside Period and Dynasty XVIII. In particular, see Terry DuQuesne, "Hathor of Medjed," *Discussions in Egyptology* 54 (2002), 39–60 with pp. 42–3; and Nicole Durisch, "Culte des canidés à Assiout: Trois nouvelles stèles dédiées à Oupouaout," *Bulletin de l'Institut Français d'Archéologie Orientale* 93 (1993), 220. DuQuesne lays great importance upon the stelae from the Salakhana tomb at Assiut, and indicates (in a personal communication) Assiut being the last town on the way to the oases. From the middle of the First Intermediate Period (ca. 2100 BC) this area was an important buffer zone between the kingdom of Thebes in the south (Dynasty XI) and that of Herakleopolis in the north (Dynasties IX–X). Hence, at an earlier time it had also been a center of military activity.

NOTES

1 The following remarks depend upon Barry Kemp, *Ancient Egypt. Anatomy of a Civilization*, 310–13. See as well David O'Connor, "The geography of settlement in ancient Egypt," in Peter J. Ucko, Ruth Tringham, and G. W. Dimbleby, eds., *Man, Settlement and Urbanism*, Duckworth, London (1972), 681–98. P. Wilbour was published and edited by Sir Alan Gardiner, *Papyrus Wilbour*, I–III, Brooklyn Museum, Oxford (1948).

2 Janssen, "Prolegemena to the study of Egypt's economic history during the New Kingdom," *Studien zur altägtyptischen Kultur* 3 (1975), 127–85. His magisterial work, *Commodity Prices in the Ramesside Period*, is an excellent source for the economics of ancient Egypt.

3 The edition of Caminos, *Late Egyptian Miscellanies*, has been cited frequently in this volume.

4 The following analysis is taken from my forthcoming analysis, "The Paradise of Scribes and the Tartarus of Soldiers." P. Anastasi III is covered on pages 69–113 of Caminos' edition. There is a very useful analysis of Oleg Berlev that deserves re-attention: "The Oldest Description of the Social Organization of Egypt," in *Problemy social'nych otnoßenij I form zavisimosti na drevnem vostoke*, Nauka, Moscow (1984), 26–34.

5 Caminos, *Late Egyptian Miscellanies*, 16–17.

6 Ibid., 373–428.

7 See note 32 to chapter 14.

8 Caminos, *Late Egyptian Miscellanies*, 431–46; add Serge Sauneron, "Les désillusions de la guerre asiatique (Pap. Deir el Médineh 35)," *Kemi* 18 (1968), 17–27.

9 Fischer-Elfert, *Die satirische Streitschrift des Papyrus Anastasi I*. See our comments in note 29 to chapter 13.

10 See excursus 2 to chapter 7.

11 This discussion is dependent upon Gnirs, *Militär und Gesellschaft*, 192–211.

12 Grandet, *Le Papyrus Harris I (BM 9999)* II, 243 n. 919. These "strongholds" are also present in the fragmentary papyrus referred to by Spalinger, *The Transformation of an Ancient Egyptian Literary Text*, chapter XI.

13 Butzer, *Early Hydraulic Civilization in Egypt*, 83.

14 Gnirs, *Militär und Gesellschaft*, 201–11. Her analysis is dependent upon the work of Karl Janssen-Winkeln: "Zum militarischen Befehlsbereich der Hohenpriester des Amun," *Göttinger Miszellen* 99 (1987), 19–22, "Das Ende des Neuen Reiches," *Zeitschrift für ägyptische Sprache* 119 (1992), 22–37, and "Der Begin der libyschen Herrschaft in Ägypten," *Biblische Notizen* 71 (1994), 78–97. To these studies add Andrzej Niwinski, "Bürgerkrieg, militärischer Staatsreich und Ausnahmezustand in Ägypten unter Ramses XI. Ein Versuch neuer Interpretation der alten Quellen," in Ingrid Gamer-Wallert and Wolfgang Helck, eds., *Gegengabe: Festschrift für Emma Brunner-Traut*. Tübingen: Attempto Verlag, Tübingen, (1992), 235–62.

15 "The fundamental modern political question is the relationship of military to civil society – a problem which did not have much meaning until the seventeenth

century AD when responsibilities for the two spheres were vested in different hands": David C. Rapoport, "Military and Civil Societies: The Contemporary Significance of a Traditional Subject in Political Theory," *Political Studies* 12 (1964), 198 n. 3. This passage should be kept in mind by any historian of the ancient Egyptian military.

GENERAL BIBLIOGRAPHY

The following works concentrate upon the military and related war matters of the Egyptian New Kingdom. Hence, this list does not include all of the studies referred to in the excurses or the footnotes.

Andreski, Stanislav. *Military Organization and Society*[2]. Routledge and Kegan Paul, London, 1968.

Avdiev, Vsevolod Igorevitch. *Military History of Ancient Egypt* II. Sovetskaya Nauka, Moscow, 1959.

Berlev, Oleg. "The Egyptian Navy in the Middle Kingdom." *Palestinskij Sbornik* 80 (1967), 6–20.

——. "Les prétendus 'citadins' au Moyen Empire." *Revue d'Égyptolgie* 23 (1971), 31–7.

Cifola, Barbara. "Ramses III and the Sea Peoples: A Structural Analysis of the Medinet Habu Inscriptions." *Orientalia* 57 (1988), 275–306.

—— "The Terminology of Ramesses III's Historical Records with a Formal Analysis of the War Scenes." *Orientalia* 60 (1991), 9–5.

Dothan, Trude (1982). *The Philistines and their Material Culture*. New Haven Yale University Press, London and Jerusalem, 1982.

Dothan, Trude and Dothan, Moshe. *People of the Sea. The Search for the Philistines*. Macmillan, New York and Toronto, 1992.

Edel, Elmar. "Die Seevölkerbericht aus dem 8. Jahre Ramses' III. (*MH* II, pl. 46, 15–18)," in Posener-Kriéger, Paule, ed., *Mélanges Gamal Eddin Mokhtar* I. Institut Français d'Archéologie Orientale, Cairo, 1985, 223–37.

Gardiner, Alan Henderson. "The Defeat of the Hyksos by Kamose: The Carnarvon Tablet, No. 1." *Journal of Egyptian Archaeology* 3 (1916), 95–110.

Gnirs, Andrea M. *Militär und Gesellschaft. Ein Beitrag zur Sozialgeschichte des Neuen Reiches*. Heidelberger Orientverlag, Heidelberg, 1996.

——. "Ancient Egypt," in Raaflaub, Kurt and Rosenstein, Nathan eds., *War and Society in the Ancient and Medieval Worlds*. Harvard University Press, Cambridge, MA, 1999.

Goedicke, Hans, ed. *Perspectives on the Battle of Kadesh*. Halgo, Baltimore, 1985.

Grandet, Pierre. *Le Papyrus Harris I (BM 9999)*. Institut Français d'Archéologie Orientale, Cairo, 1994.

Habachi, Labib. *The Second Stela of Kamose, and his Struggle against the Hyksos Ruler and his Capital*. J. J. Augustin, Glückstadt, 1972.

Harvey, Stephen. *The Cults of King Ahmose at Abydos.* University of Pennsylvania Dissertation, Philadelphia, 1998.

Heinz, Susanna Contanze. *Die Feldzugsdarstellungen des Neuen Reiches. Eine Bildanalyse.* Akademie der Wissenschaften, Vienna, 2001.

Helck, Wolfgang. *Der Einfluß der Militärführer in der 18. ägyptischen Dynastie.* Leipzig, J. C. Hinrichs, 1939.

Herold, Anja. *Streitwagentechnologie in der Ramses-Stadt.* Philipp Von Zabern, Mainz, 1999.

Johnson, W. Raymond. *An Asiatic Battle Scene of Tutankhamun from Thebes: A Late Amarna Antecedent of the Ramesside Battle-Narrative Tradition,* University of Chicago Dissertation, Chicago, 1992.

Jones, Dilwyn. *Glossary of Ancient Egyptian Nautical Titles and Terms.* Kegan Paul International, London and New York, 1988.

——. *Boats.* British Museum Press, London, 1995.

Keegan, John. *A History of Warfare.* Random House, London, 1994.

Kemp, Barry J. "Imperialism and Empire in New Kingdom Egypt (c. 1575–1087 BC)," in Garnsey, P. D. A. and Whittaker, C. R., eds., *Imperialism in the Ancient World.* Cambridge University Press, Cambridge and New York, 1978, 7–57.

——. "Large Middle Kingdom Granary Buildings (and the archaeology of administration)." *Zeitschrift für ägyptische Sprache* 113 (1986), 120–36.

——. *Ancient Egypt, Anatomy of a Civilization.* Routledge, London and New York, 1989.

Kitchen, K. A. "Historical Observations on Ramesside Nubia," in Endesfelder, Erika, et al., *Ägypten und Kusch.* Akademie Verlag, Berlin, 1977, 213–25.

——. "The Arrival of the Libyans in Late New Kingdom Egypt," in Leahy, Anthony, ed., *Libya and Egypt c. 1300–750 BC.* School of Oriental and African Studies, London, 1990, 15–27.

——. "Ramesside Egypt's Delta defense routes – the SE sector." *Studi di egittologia e di antichità puniche* 18 (1998) 33–8.

Lichtheim, Miriam. *Ancient Egyptian Literature* I–II. University of California Press, Berkeley, Los Angeles and London, 1975–6.

Liverani, Mario. *Prestige and Interest: International Relations in the Near East, ca. 1600–1100 BC.* Sargon, Padova, 1990.

Lundh, Patrik. *Actor and Event. Military Activity in Ancient Egyptian Narrative Texts from Thutmosis II to Merenptah.* Akademitryck, Uppsala, 2002.

Manassa, Colleen. *The Great Karnak Inscription of Merneptah: Grand Strategy in the 13th Century BC.* Yale Egyptological Seminar, New Haven, 2003.

Martin, Geoffrey Thorndike. *The Memphite Tomb of Horemheb, Commander in-Chief of Tut'ankhamn.* Egypt Exploration Society, London, 1989–96.

Müller, Marcus. *Die Thematik der Schlachtenreliefs.* Tübingen MA Thesis, Tübingen, 1995.

——. *Der König als Feldherr. Schlachtenreliefs, Kriegsberichte und Kriegsführung im Mittleren und Neuen Reich.* Tübingen PhD Dissertation, Tübingen, 2001.

O'Connor, David. "The geography of settlement in ancient Egypt," in Ucko, Peter J., Tringham, Ruth, and Dimbleby, G. W., eds., *Man, Settlement and Urbanism.* Duckworth, London, 1972, 681–98.

——. The Nature of Tjemhu (Libyan) Society in the Late New Kingdom," in Leahy, Anthony, ed., *Libya and Egypt c. 1300–750 BC*. School of Oriental and African Studies, London, 1990, 29–113.

——. *Ancient Nubia: Egypt's Rival in Africa*. University of Pennsylvania, Philadelphia, 1993.

——. "The Sea Peoples and the Egyptian Sources," in Oren, Eliezer D., ed., *The Sea Peoples and Their World: A Reassessment*. University Museum, Philadelphia, 2000, 85–102.

Oren, Eliezer, D., ed., *The Hyksos: New Historical and Archaeological Perspectives*. University Museum, Philadelphia, 1997.

——, ed. *The Sea Peoples and their World: A Reassessment*. University Museum, Philadelphia, 2000.

Partridge, Robert B. *Fighting Pharaohs. Weapons and Warfare in Ancient Egypt*. Peartree Publishing, Manchester, 2002.

Pusch, Edgar B. "Headquarters of thy Chariotry," in *Pelizaeus Museum Hildesheim. The Egyptian Collection*. Mainz, Philipp von Zabern, 1996, 126–45.

Raban, Avner. "The Medinet Habu Ships: Another Interpretation." *The International Journal of Nautical Archaeology and Underworld Exploration* 18 (1989), 163–71.

Redford, Donald. *History and Chronology of the Eighteenth Dynasty of Egypt: Seven Studies*. University of Toronto Press, Toronto, 1967.

——. "Egypt and Western Asia in the Late New Kingdom: An Overview," in Oren, Eliezer D., ed., *The Sea Peoples and Their World: A Reassessment*. University Museum, Philadelphia, 2000, 1–20.

——. *The Wars in Syria and Palestine of Thutmose III*. Brill, Leiden and Boston, 2003.

Rommelaere, Catherine. *Les chevaux du Nouvel Empire égyptien: origines, races, harnachement*. Connaissance de l'Égypte ancienne, Brussels, 1991.

Ryholt, Kim. *The Political Situation in Egypt during the Second Intermediate Period, c. 1800–1550 BC*. Museum Tusculanum Press, Copenhagen, 1997.

Sauneron, Serge (1954). "La manufacture d'armes de Memphis." *Bulletin de l'Institut Français d'Archéologie Orientale* 54 (1954), 7–12.

Säve-Söderbergh, Torgny. *The Navy of the Eighteenth Egyptian Dynasty*. Lundequistska Bokhandeln and Otto Harrassowitz, Uppsala and Leipzig, 1946.

Schulman, Alan R. *Military Rank, Title and Organization in the Egyptian New Kingdom*. B. Hessling, Berlin, 1964.

——. "Chariots, Chariotry and the Hyksos." *Journal of the Society for the Study of Egyptian Antiquities* 12 (1979), 105–53.

Shaw, Ian. *Egyptian Warfare and Weapons*. Shire Egyptology, Haverfordwest, 1991.

——. "Battle in Ancient Egypt: The Triumph of Horus or the Cutting Edge of the Temple Economy," in Lloyd, Alan B., ed, *Battle in Antiquity*. London, 1996, 239–69.

Smith, H. S. and Smith, Alexandrina. "A Reconsideration of the Kamose Texts." *Zeitschrift für ägyptische Sprache* 103 (1976), 48–76.

Spalinger, Anthony J. *Aspects of the Military Documents of the Ancient Egyptians*. New Haven: Yale University Press, 1982.

——. *The Transformation of an Ancient Egyptian Narrative: P. Sallier III and the Battle of Kadesh*. Wiesbaden: Harrassowitz, 2002.

Trigger, Bruce. *Nubia under the Pharaohs*. Thames and Hudson, London, 1976.

Turney-High, Harry Holbert. *Primitive War, its Practices and Concepts*. University of South Carolina Press, Columbia, 1949.

——. *The Military: The Theory of Land Warfare as Behavioral Science*. The Christopher Publishing House, West Hanover, 1981.

Vercoutter, Jean. "Le pays Irem et la penetration égyptienne en Afrique (Stéle de Saï S. 579)," in *Livre du Centenaire de l'IFAO (1880–1980)*. Institut Français d'Archéologie Orientale, Cairo, 1980, 157–78.

Vinson, Steve. *Egyptian Boats and Ships*. Shire, Princes Risborough, 1994.

Von der Way, Thomas. *Die Textüberlieferung Ramses' II zur Qadeš-Schlacht. Analyse und Struktur*. Gerstenberg, Hildesheim, 1984.

Widmer, Werner. "Zur Darstellung der Seevölker am Großen Tempel von Medinet Habu." *Zeitschrift für ägyptische Sprache* 102 (1975), 67–78.

Yoyotte, Jean and López, Jesús. "L'organisation de l'armée au Nouvel Empire égyptien." *Bibliotheca Orientalis* 26 (1969), 3–19.

Yurco, Frank J. "Merenptah's Canaanite Campaign." *Journal of the American Research Center in Egypt* 23 (1986), 189–215.

——. "Merenptah's Canaanite Campaign and Israel's Origins," in Frerichs, Ernest S. and Lesko, Leonard H., eds., *Exodus. The Egyptian Evidence*. Eisenbrauns, Winowa Lake, 1997, 27–55.

INDEX

General terms such as Syria and Palestine are omitted as well as the references in the footnotes and localities on maps 1–3.

Aata 5
Abdi-Ashirta 162–3
Abdi-Kheba 169
Abu Simbel 105–6, 209, 221
Abydos 19, 20–2, 193, 209, 217–21
Acco 160
Achaens 235
Aduruna 268
Aegean(s) 48, 255, 259
Aharoni, Yohanan 125
Ahmose (Pharaoh) xii, 4–6, 10, 13, 15, 17, 19–24, 46–7, 74, 76, 102, 107, 113, 121, 123, 146, 176, 184, 187, 273
Ahmose Pen-Nechbet 23, 170
Ahmose Son of Ebana 4–6, 17, 22–3, 26, 47–8, 51, 150, 172
Akhenaton *see* Amunhotep IV
Akhkhiyawa 235
Akkadian 169
Akko 259
Akyawash 235
Alalakh 114, 117
Alamo 235
Alashiya (Cyprus) 250
Aleppo 114–15, 117, 124, 125, 130, 195, 197, 210–11, 221
Alexander the Great 33
Alexandria 179
Amada stela 78
Amarna Letters (archive) 37, 132, 134–5, 137, 151, 160–4, 169, 171, 181

Amarna Period 10, 79, 149, 160, 162, 169, 171, 177–9
Amka 180
Ammiya 134
Amun 1, 24, 39, 59, 75–8, 111, 116, 135, 181, 187, 189, 195, 226 (division), 230 (division), 270–1, 273
Amunemheb 114–15, 170, 172
Amunemint 269
Amunemope 150
Amunherkhepeshef 178
Amunhotep I 5, 46–9, 175, 183
Amunhotep II 9, 13, 55, 71, 76, 78, 87, 97, 107, 118, 121, 124, 126, 136, 137, 140–1, 144–5, 148–9, 152, 170, 179, 187, 269
Amunhotep III 71, 126, 132, 134, 142, 160, 163, 172, 181, 197, 269
Amunhotep IV, Akhenaton 132, 134, 145, 160–1, 163, 165, 169–72, 174–5, 177–80, 182, 184
Amunhotep/Huy 178
Amurru 57, 134–5, 160–5, 171, 176, 180, 193, 195, 197, 210, 250
Anchef 178
Andreski, Stanislav 24, 244
"Annals" (of Thutmose III) 96, 115, 123, 131, 140, 171
Ansariyeh 125
anthropoid coffins 259
Antioch 114
Aphek 241